HATREDS WE LOVE

For my great aunts and uncles who never made it to American shores—
forever erased by the malignant tribalism of the last century.

HATREDS WE LOVE

The Psychology of Political Tribalism in Post-Truth America

Stephen J. Ducat

Skyhorse Publishing

Skyhorse Publishing books may be purchased in bulk at special discounts for sales promotion, corporate gifts, fund-raising, or educational purposes. Special editions can also be created to specifications. For details, contact the Special Sales Department, Skyhorse Publishing, 307 West 36th Street, 11th Floor, New York, NY 10018 or info@skyhorsepublishing.com.

Skyhorse® and Skyhorse Publishing® are registered trademarks of Skyhorse Publishing, Inc.,®, a Delaware corporation.

Visit our website at www.skyhorsepublishing.com.
Please follow our publisher Tony Lyons on Instagram @tonylyonsisuncertain

10 9 8 7 6 5 4 3 2 1

Library of Congress Cataloging-in-Publication Data is available on file.

Cover design by David Ter-Avanesyan
Cover image from Getty Images

Print ISBN: 978-1-5107-8080-4
Ebook ISBN: 978-1-5107-8091-0

Printed in the United States of America

Contents

Acknowledgments

Acknowledgment seems like a paltry understatement when crediting those whose contributions have made this book possible. Nevertheless, at the top of the list, I'd have to place my wife, partner, fellow psychoanalytic clinician, and most discerning reader, Susan Clifford. She had a remarkably nuanced understanding of the nature of my thesis, the shrewd intelligence to know when my language failed to convey it, and the grace to impart her criticisms in a way that neutralized my defensiveness. Of course, any lapses in coherence or infelicitous phrases that may have passed under her radar are entirely my responsibility.

Thanks to the publisher, Skyhorse, its senior acquisitions editor, Mark Gompertz, and editor Caroline Russomanno, who saw in my proposal a project worth bringing to life and one that bore relevance to the autocratic and tribal perils all citizens of nominally democratic nations face.

I'm grateful to Patrick Davies and Jeff Baird for their scrupulous attention to the endnotes section of this book. It was a task that I lacked the technical skill and patience to execute with any precision. But it was essential it be done right. Otherwise, this evidence-based polemic would be just another polemic.

I also owe profound gratitude to Illana Burk, a rich and generous font of PR wisdom. One hard and paradoxical lesson she taught me is that when it comes to publishing, one can only exist in reality if one exists virtually. To that end, I also have to thank Jeff again for his skill at putting together my author website, stephenjducat.com, and his patience with my paralyzing technophobic dread.

It would be an absurdly impossible task to give a complete list of the intellectual forebears and contemporaries whose work has made mine possible. But a short list would have to include the interdisciplinary scholarship of the Frankfurt School; the known and unknown theorists of the Situationist International and descendants; the long tradition of politically engaged psychoanalysts, including but not limited to Otto Fenichel, Wilhelm Reich, Erich Fromm, Vamik Volkan, Christopher Bollas, Steven Reisner, Jessica Benjamin, Neil Altman, Justin Frank, Sue Grand, and Nancy Hollander, and the many socially committed clinicians of APA's division 39; the sagacious and vital masters of political messaging George Lakoff, Drew Westen, and Anat Shenker-Osorio; Peter Pomerantsev's disturbing and enlightening work on contemporary Russia's apparatus of post-truth; and the empirical work of many eminent social scientists, especially Jim Sidanius, John R. Hibbing, Joshua Greene, Sam McFarland, and Lilliana Mason. I am also deeply indebted to the many fruitful conversations with my friend and comrade, Iain Boal. His insights and moral support have been invaluable. My writing and thinking have been sharpened enormously as a result of our years of collaboration and debates.

In addition, my examination of present-day events and developments is predicated on understanding their historical precursors. Because I am not a historian, my work draws on the scholarship of those who have devoted their lives to excavating vital truths about the past. In particular, I am grateful to the historical studies done by Timothy Snyder, Ruth Ben Ghiat, Richard Steigmann-Gall, Joanne B. Freeman, Jefferson Cowie, David Wengrow, and David Graeber. The latter two technically hail from other disciplines, respectively, archeology and anthropology. The in-depth research of each of these scholars has been indispensable to formulating an analysis of contemporary political tribalism. The most useful history is that which makes an evidence-based effort to illuminate the *motivations* of historical actors. These accounts go beyond dates, names, and achievements and bring to life the thoughts, emotions, and intentions of individuals and groups about which we have only incomplete data. All the historians I've listed meet this important criterion.

I fully recognize that the scholars whose work has been so vital to mine may take issue with my reading and application of their research and insights. And, of course, they bear no responsibility for my conclusions or the extent to which their findings have been incorporated into my own unconscious confirmation bias. Nevertheless, I am grateful for their contributions and have made a good-faith effort to apply their scholarship where it seemed intellectually justified.

Introduction: Paleo-Psychology and Modern Politics

On a bucolic hillside, the sheep are placidly grazing. Looming over them is a campaign billboard featuring a nattily dressed wolf politician whose lapel is accessorized with the de rigueur American flag pin. Next to his image is the caption, "I am going to eat you." Two sheep look up admiringly at the ad while one says to the other, "He tells it like it is."

That Paul Noth *New Yorker* cartoon appeared in the first year of Donald Trump's presidency and succinctly captured the tragic psychology of contemporary political tribalism.

Ordinary Republican voters are becoming MAGA mutton in the slavering maws of their own leaders and the wealthy predators that fund them. The GOP elite's voracious appetite for power and wealth spares no one, least of all their base. In other words, conservative politics is killing conservatives. The politicians empowered by the Republican electorate with each election pass laws and enact policies that sicken and shorten the lives of their loyal constituents. GOP lawmakers reject Medicaid expansion, oppose a variety of public health measures, stop attempts to lower prescription drug prices, ban medically safe abortions, vote against even the mildest constraints on the purchase of assault weapons, fight increases in the minimum wage, spread vaccine misinformation, and work assiduously to facilitate the ability of corporations to use the air,[1] water,[2] and land[3] we all share—and increasingly, our bodies[4]—as a privatized toilet.

Like Mr. Wolf's matter-of-fact campaign pledge, none of those actions have been hidden from public view. (Indeed, this has become the era of "saying the quiet part out loud"—one of the most frequently uttered clichés of the MAGA epoch.) The consequences for the voters who put those legislators in power have been dire. GOP constituents have a markedly reduced duration and quality of life. That is the conclusion of an eighteen-year longitudinal study published in the *British Medical Journal* in 2022.[5] Analyzing US mortality and election data, the researchers found that those who lived in counties that elected Republicans were much more likely to die prematurely from the top ten causes of death than those who resided in counties that put Democrats in office.[6] And the gap between red and blue areas grew 600 percent over the study period. The COVID pandemic and the GOP response have only exacerbated that discrepancy.[7]

In 2023, the Pell Center for International Relations and Public Policy conducted a massive and rigorous study[8] on partisan differences in life expectancy. It was even more pointed than previous research because its methodology enabled conclusions beyond correlation, which permitted the authors to identify the primary *causal* factor. Controlling for race, income, education level, urbanization, and the availability of good medical care, the singular variable that determined life span was whether citizens lived in counties that spent tax dollars on public goods and services, including health programs.

As mentioned, Republican politicians are notoriously loath to invest in caring for their working- and middle-class constituents. Subsidizing and deregulating corporations and reducing taxes on the wealthy are long-standing features of the conservative governing ethos. The well-being of ordinary residents is a secondary concern. It is no surprise red regions have significantly reduced life expectancy—by four and a half to six years.

Commenting on those findings, a public health expert, Jeanne Ayers, emphasized, "We don't have these differences in health outcomes because of individual behaviors; it's related to the policy environments people are living in."[9] Those regional differences are not trivial. The study authors note that Americans with the misfortune of residing in Republican counties experience foreshortened lives on par with the people of El Salvador, Belarus, and Libya.

One question not addressed by that research is why the citizens most harmed by GOP policies keep returning the architects of those policies to power. That requires an analysis that goes much deeper than demography, one that can illuminate the *psychological* differences between the red and blue subsets of the electorate. That of course is the focus of this book, and it will be addressed from multiple angles.

Perhaps even more notable are those who have volunteered to sacrifice themselves as pro-Trump kamikazes.[10] Willing to die to vanquish their leader's enemy du jour, some of the former president's ardent fans have chosen MAGA martyrdom as the ultimate expression of their devotion. If we shift the carnivorous metaphor I opened with to a carceral one, Voltaire's famous aphorism comes to mind: "It is difficult to free people from the chains they revere."[11] Echoing their cult leader and aspiring monarch, many of his zealous admirers seem to believe that all attempts to hold Trump to account for possible crimes are witch hunts; all unflattering news about him is fake; all incriminating evidence is false; all acts of violence committed by his followers are false flag operations; all elections he loses are rigged, and all his critics are traitors. For an increasing number of his avid adherents, those critics and their families deserve death, as do members of law enforcement, prosecutors, and judges who challenge Trump's claims of impunity.[12] And if delivering that sentence means you perish as well, that is a cost worth bearing.

As a psychoanalyst and lifelong observer of politics, I have been consistently puzzled by how citizens can be so easily persuaded to vote and otherwise act against their self-interest. I'm not alone. It is a question that has haunted scholars, political activists, and psychologists for centuries. It took the 2016 election of Donald Trump and the gushing displays of idolatry on the part of those most hurt by his actions for me to realize just how naïve and profoundly limited my understanding of self-interest was. There is an interest that can sometimes and often does supersede life itself—maintaining one's good standing in the tribe.

Humans privilege the experience of belonging to and being recognized by a group over nearly every other consideration. From prenatal life to our final moments of sentience, we are part of a network of relationships upon which we depend for physical and psychic survival. There is no point in life where we can escape from a fundamental truth: without others, we cannot be a self. That applies to our entire developmental journey, from the earliest dyadic matrix of infancy to the complexities of community life in adulthood.

The centrality of our group identity does not diminish, regardless of how tribal boundaries are defined or what traits confer membership. It is a need built into our species' nature. Modern humans result from a process of natural selection that has conferred a reproductive advantage to those with more highly developed capacities to accurately read, cooperate with, and care about others in their group. Those who failed to do so were not only subject to lethal exile but finished their days as evolutionary dead ends.

Of course, this has not led humans to become creatures expressing only peace, love, and understanding. That is because the considerable rewards of one's community have also redounded to those members capable of hating, plundering, and annihilating enemy or competing tribes. *Intra*tribal cooperation evolved, in part, as an effective weapon of *inter*tribal competition. That was one path to creating our dual nature as compassionate cooperators *and* ruthless predators toward other humans. Those conflicting qualities of the human psyche have enabled multiple and varied forms of social organization to emerge.

What Is a Tribe?

My use of the term *tribe* is colloquial. It does not refer to a specific category of social organization. In strictly scholarly work, there might be a distinction between family, clan, tribe, band, chiefdom, and modern state. Although, even those labels are problematic, especially when used to buttress a linear progress narrative of human history. The archeological evidence does not support the idea that those different forms of social cooperation represent ever-increasing stages of maturity and sophistication of our species' development.[13] I've chosen to use *tribe* as a term of art because it is already a part of everyday political discourse that enjoys some degree of shared meaning. For this book, a tribe is a group based on interdependence, shared values, a political worldview, partisan affiliations, and interests that give its members a sense of belonging, commonality, and identity.

Tribal identity can derive from membership in a formal institution like a political party, a local group of activists, or a mass movement comprised of people we've never met but who seem to share our beliefs and understandings of the world. The latter experience of a tribe may be similar to how anthropologist David Graeber and archeologist David Wengrow talk about cities.[14] They see them as imagined communities to which we nevertheless feel we belong. We may not know most people in a town, but we can still experience a social and psychological kinship with them. We might have little in common with most residents besides occupying the same geographical space. Similarly, tribal bonds can exist without necessitating real-world contact with tribal others, to which the plethora of online virtual communities can attest. Those digital tribal spaces can confer deep bonds of connection, help us find a life partner, drive people to suicide, inspire murder and genocide, or provide forums for planning a coup.

That, nowadays, a tribe may not have an empirically defined territory does not make membership any less compelling. In many ways, political victory in the current era goes to those who can successfully encase their cause or actions within a membrane of tribal identity, something those on the Right intuitively understand far more than liberals. For conservatives, there are identities such as a "family-values Christian," "second amendment advocate," "warrior for medical freedom," "protector of the unborn," or "defender of Western civilization" that eclipse class as a driver of political affiliation and behavior. Communities of the like-minded will welcome you. Membership in such groups can sometimes make voting against one's material self-interest seem rational. Low wages, lousy health insurance, deadly pandemics, killer heat waves, apocalyptic floods, cancer clusters, and mass gun murders of children may be troubling. However, they pale next to the apparent dangers of the War on Christmas, microchipped vaccines, George Soros–funded globalists, critical race theory, wokeness, child-corrupting drag queens, the End of Men, and the threat that swarthy hordes from shithole countries are replacing white people. (To avoid visual clutter, I'm leaving the scare quotes off these imagined perils.) To mobilize their voter base, Republican politicians have been quite effective at crafting group identity–linked issues, conjuring fictitious crises, and whipping up groundless moral panics.

Climate change denier and fossil fuel mercenary James Inhofe hit the rhetorical trifecta with his 1994 campaign slogan, "Guns, God, and Gays," when it moved working-class Oklahomans to send him to the Senate.[15] Even the tremors from fracking-boom-induced earthquakes in the state did not shake their support for him and his petro-boosterism.[16] Of course, that is only one example of the triumph of tribal identity over objective (not just perceived) well-being.

Most political group- and issue-based identities tend to fall under the partisan labels of Democrat or Republican, now the overarching tribal identities in the United States, and even correspond to politically homogeneous zip codes. That political self-segregation and its consequences will be the focus of chapter 8.

In experimental settings, those tribal identities remain firmly intact even when the parties that study subjects belong to, or the leaders they venerate, seem to reverse policy positions. Tribal members come to endorse those new positions *because* their party or leader seems to have done so.

As central as tribalism is to politics, it is not the singular cause of destructive irrationality in public life. It is but one predisposition in our species-nature that interacts with others, along with a multiplicity of environmental factors. The combination of these influences has led to the crisis of intergroup enmity in which we find ourselves. But in talking about a trait being an evolved aspect of human psychology, we have to speak with some precision. Evolution has not selected for specific psychological traits—being loving or hateful, generous or withholding, violent or peaceful, compassionate or sadistically cruel, cooperative or competitive. Instead, evolution has produced a capacity to *adapt* to a wide range of ever-shifting contexts—to be what our surroundings and communities require. This general truth applies to tribalism specifically. Intra-tribal affiliation and intertribal hostility (or at least suspicion) are fundamental to our species-nature. They even precede our branch on the hominid tree. Although, how that predisposition gets expressed (e.g., who gets counted as an "us" or a "them," and whether we want to kill or marry them) is radically context-dependent.

As I will discuss in much greater depth in later chapters, there is not one homogenous psychology of tribes. There are very different forms of political tribalism, especially regarding how outsiders are viewed. Some partisan groups and identities are *xenophobic*. They view out-group members as a threat, especially if they look and speak differently. The perceived danger is often managed by building literal or policy walls. In extreme cases, interlopers might be subject to incarceration, torture, or murder. Xenophobic tribalists prefer to stay with their "kind" and are more likely to live in rural areas where they can distance themselves from others. Unsurprisingly, such traits comprise conservative tribalism.

That is not an intellectual abstraction for me. Living in a rural Oregon mountain town in a 60-40 Republican-dominated part of the state, I'm surrounded by avid secessionists who long to join Idaho. They imagine our neighboring state to be a homogenous white Christian homeland where they can live unperturbed by Black Lives Matter protesters, environmental regulations, feminists, and history books that make them uncomfortable.

On the other hand, there are *xenophilic* tribalists. They are part of groups with more permeable boundaries and tend to be curious about and welcome tribal outsiders. Members of those tribes are attracted to differences. They want to interact with those whose foreign ways might include a strange language, unfamiliar dress, or novel cuisine. These tribalists tend to be drawn to big cosmopolitan cities, especially on the coasts, where those from distant lands are more likely to concentrate. We could call people with those traits liberal tribalists.

Since both seemingly opposite forms of tribalism exist worldwide, there must be something adaptive about each. And it could be that a society functions better or is more resilient in the face of changing environmental conditions when it contains individuals and groups that embody each of those very different orientations. Later chapters will dig into that possibility further.

And before leaving the topic of natural selection, it is vital to challenge the "fruit-of-a-poisonous-tree" argument that some progressive critics sometimes use to dismiss arguments based on evolutionary theory. The idea proffered by a few on the Left is that because evolutionary arguments have occasionally been deployed to buttress justifications for racism, misogyny, and other forms of domination, evolutionary theory itself is necessarily corrupt, reductionist, and an ideological handmaiden of various forms of oppression. Accepting this would be akin to repudiating physics because it was a discipline central to developing nuclear weapons. Therefore, all progressives should view it as a reactionary and dangerous discourse that must be banished. That is a logic ludicrous on its face.

The Politics of Truth and the End of Consensual Reality

This book will also address something central to political tribalism, which many scholars and journalists call "tribal epistemology" or "post-truth." That refers to the different informational universes in which partisans reside—comprised of their news consumption, primarily channeled through social media and their perception of the community's acceptable beliefs. These epistemological lenses determine how group members see themselves individually and collectively and guide their understanding of the world.

What might constitute evidence for most liberals would be the weight of expert opinion, which is subject to change as conditions and the consensus of experts shifts. Nevertheless, it would be safe to say that experts, at minimum, are individuals trained in the topics they speak about, utilize the scientific method, form logical hypotheses, test them using valid empirical methods, and submit their data, interpretations, and conclusions for peer review. The widespread and sometimes self-serving joke on the Left that facts have a liberal bias has more than a bit of truth. Of course, glaring exceptions to this can indeed be found. They would include vulgar post-modernists who argue that there is no truth or at least that it is unknowable, September 11 "truthers," some apostles of identity politics, and New Age anti-vaxxers—all of which are indifferent to evidence. Nevertheless, liberals tend to accept, for example, the scientific consensus on climate change, which is reinforced by tribal pressure to embrace such a notion, not to mention readily observable facts about the changing world. While liberals certainly do not have a monopoly on the truth, their tribal means of assessing it tend to require engaging with factuality and tolerating the ambiguities that can often entail.

For post–Tea Party and Trumpworld conservatives, evidence consists of what the former president, his surrogates on Fox News, and their favorite YouTube "authorities" say it is, even if those "experts" capriciously reverse themselves the next day. Authoritative persons outside this universe, especially those who contradict Trump or revered right-wing pundits, are regarded with suspicion. And sometimes, as noted earlier, they are subjected to homicidal threats, which are occasionally carried out. Climate change is a hoax because conservative tribal leaders and fellow members say so and because disbelief in it is fundamental to maintaining tribal membership. What makes most right-wing politicians dismiss the consensus of climate experts is that they are paid to do so, although there are undoubtedly some sincere, true disbelievers. Fossil fuel campaign funding is a not-so-hidden motivator for science denial.

For many on the Right, empirical evidence, such as record heatwaves, devastating firestorms, and hurricanes' increased frequency and magnitude, carry no weight. Trusted sources of tribal epistemology will offer up more comforting "truths" that help explain away such signs so that group members can retain tribal beliefs with a minimum of cognitive dissonance—even if it's their neighborhood that burns down or their low-lying community that gets inundated by record sea-level rise. They "know" (at least at an inchoate paleo-psychological level) that tribal exile would be a kind of death more fearsome than any real-world disaster.

The Nonsensical Nomenclature of Our Political Spectrum

I must apologize to the reader in advance for using partisan labels—Left and Right—based on an inherently contradictory and confusing spectrum. However, because it is the language in which people speak about political beliefs and identities, it is necessary to use those terms. Alas, I cannot declare these incoherent labels null and void through authorial fiat. But it would still be helpful to understand what makes our everyday political continuum so absurd and why we need a new one. Instead of a spectrum with greater democracy at one end and greater autocracy at the other, we have one in which both ends are autocratic.

Let's look at some of the features of societies at the allegedly opposite polls of the spectrum. We see rigid hierarchies of power, dictatorships, leader cults, myths that substitute for history, propaganda that masquerades as news, and paranoid fantasies of victimization by outside groups whom regimes blame for all social problems. In addition, these governments feature state-sponsored persecution, massive surveillance, incarceration and murder of dissidents and political opponents, devaluation and scapegoating of ethnic minorities, suppression of civil liberties, the criminalization of independent journalism, and the militarization of civil society.

By what twist of logic could Joseph Stalin and Adolf Hitler, Louis Farrakhan and David Duke, Osama bin Laden and Timothy McVeigh, ISIS and the KKK, Kim Jong Un and Benito Mussolini, or the Mao-inspired Red Guards and the Trump-inspired Proud Boys be construed as opposites? While they have distinctive personalities and different styles of rule, and proclaim fealty to contrasting ideologies and authoritarian leaders, the worlds they create or hope to are profoundly similar. There have only been a few moments in history, like the 1939 Molotov-Ribbentrop Pact between Stalin and Hitler, when the two primary models of totalitarian state power revealed their fundamental kinship. But, in many instances, the family resemblance has been discernible for those willing to look closely enough.

Vladimir Putin, an astute Machiavellian who understands the fundamental unity between these imagined polarities, has embraced autocracy regardless of the ideological costume he wore. At one time a loyal "communist," he now endorses fascism.[17] An apostle of official state atheism in the Soviet era, Putin is now a reborn Russian Orthodox Christian. As an ideological chameleon, it is only his skin that changes. That is one of the reasons that Donald Trump—a man also devoid of any principle or motive beyond power, vengeance, and self-enrichment—so admired and sought to emulate Putin.

One expression of that enduringly corrupt political nomenclature was the very name of the former "Soviet" Union. In contrast to Marx's vision, Leninism could be considered one of the earliest forms of pseudo-populism—a politics of gaslighting that fights for the power of elites in the name of ordinary folks. After the Russian Revolution in 1917, the regime helmed by Lenin, Trotsky, and the Bolshevik Party was a government in which the voice of workers was quickly displaced by autocrats acting *in the name of* workers. Assuming their leaders' good faith, revolutionaries fought valiantly to depose the old tyranny, only to find themselves under the thumb of a new one. This pattern of fake populism fits all the iterations of Bolshevism—the Soviet Union, post-1949 China, Castro's Cuba, Communist Vietnam, etc. But it also characterizes mid-twentieth century German, Spanish, and Italian fascism, Putin's Russia, contemporary European neofascist movements, and Trumpism.

Those movements claim to represent the popular will while simultaneously engaging in a scorched-earth effort to burn democracy to the ground and establish dictatorships. Understanding this, we can see why manic MAGA warrior Steve Bannon would call himself a "Leninist" who wants to "destroy the state."[18] And as he has made quite clear, smashing the state actually means anointing Trump as its permanent head. Again, the absurdity of the conventional political spectrum comes into sharp relief. A very abbreviated look at the history of early Soviet Russia's efforts to strangle nascent democratic movements may be illuminating.

From its inception, the Soviet Union was a case study in Orwellian pseudo-populism, beginning with its name. The original soviets were workers' and community councils run primarily by consensus that coordinated their activities through a non-hierarchical federation. Decisions were made by democratically elected delegates who did not have power over their base but merely conveyed the collective will in negotiations. And they were a significant force in the effort to overthrow the autocratic rule of the Czar. Immediately after the revolution, the soviets were enticed to share power with the Bolshevik regime. The government insisted they would "represent" the interests of the councils. Through incremental legislative and bureaucratic castration, the soviets were transformed from decision-making bodies into advisory groups.[19]

By 1921, the workers' and sailors' councils of the port city of Kronstadt, fed up with their eroding political agency, rebelled against the Bolshevik government, their usurpation of the democratic power of the soviets, and the suppression of civil liberties.[20] Leon Trotsky, head of the Red Army and member of the elite Politburo, responded by ordering the military to put down the resistance with lethal force, slaughtering those who had taken the promises of the revolution too seriously.

Trotsky explained at the Tenth Party Congress that those obstreperous workers had "made a fetish of democratic principles. They have placed the worker's right to elect representatives above the Party. As if the Party were not entitled to assert its dictatorship even if that dictatorship temporarily clashed with the passing moods of the worker's democracy!"[21]

Once the actual soviets were eliminated as an institution of real power, the name was then appropriated and applied to the government run by the Bolsheviks that had crippled them. From that point forward, the word *Soviet*, shorn of its original meaning, came to embody a very non-Marxist irony— not the "dictatorship of the proletariat" but a dictatorship *over* the proletariat. (This stunning act of appropriation may bring to mind a similar colonial process with which Americans are familiar—the tendency of many US cities and counties to take on the names of the native inhabitants who earlier had been expelled or annihilated.) That brutal crushing of the Kronstadt rebellion was a decisive early loss in the war waged by the Soviet Union against the united soviets. In Bolshevik Russia and across its new empire, "communism" would triumph over communism.

Given all that history, the only political spectrum that makes sense is one with egalitarian policies and economic, social, and political democracy on one end and autocracy, police state infrastructure, government media monopoly, corporate impunity, xenophobia, and inequity on the other. Between those polarities, the continuum would feature forms of government or political beliefs closer to one or the other end.

There are indications that many political pundits and scholars already intuitively use the framework I am suggesting here. Particular leaders and parties across many countries—the United States, Russia, China, Pakistan, Israel, and Iran—tend to be called "conservative" or "right wing." Those described that way generally support rigid moral frameworks, traditional sexual or religious proscriptions, patriarchal values, the interests of the economic elite over ordinary citizens, authoritarian policies, the repression of ethnic minorities, limiting or crushing political opposition, impediments on free speech and the press, coercive violence, relationships of domination, and xenophobic tribalism. In contrast, some parties, social movements, and leaders push for greater democracy, civil liberties, egalitarian policies, mutuality over domination, and religious, gender, and ethnic plurality. They tend to be described as "liberal."

The Value and Perils of Partisan Labels in the American Context

First, I must acknowledge that authoritarian rule, fascist movements, and right-wing xenophobic tribalism are multi-national problems. Even those expressions that seem limited to the United States are linked with similar others in a global network of support and mutual influence.[22] Notably, Vladimir Putin has helped to generate and sustain that neofascist network by hosting international gatherings of right-wing militia groups, training them, and providing financial backing for their efforts.[23] One particularly disturbing example of the globally integrated nature of that threat is the choice of the American Conservative Political Action Committee (CPAC) to feature Hungarian white supremacist Viktor Orbán at its annual conference. But given time and space constraints, my focus will be limited mainly to the American expressions of this multinational tendency. Also, it is the setting I know best because it is where I've spent my life.

While I use labels like liberal, conservative, libertarian, Democrat, and Republican, they can be misleading. Relying on the useful shorthand of these political identity categories and describing the psychological variables with which they are associated can give a false impression that I'm discussing pure types. The reality is that there is a spectrum. The majority of studies I draw on reflect the fact that most variables exist on a continuum. Political identity and beliefs are generally assessed with measures that allow for degrees of agreement or disagreement. The same is true of the psychological traits researchers hypothesize might correlate with a partisan identity or stance on an issue. They are evaluated on a scale that reflects the intensity or magnitude with which someone might possess a trait. The only assessment that would be an all-or-nothing measure would be voting behavior, which usually involves binary choices.

Some people wear their identity labels lightly. Occasionally, they might even vote for candidates in the other party, although that is becoming increasingly uncommon. Those voters are often called "independent," but politically and psychologically, they're better described as pale partisans. As of 2018, about 17 percent of the public are Democratic-leaning independents (who overwhelmingly disapprove of Trump), 13 percent are Republican-leaning independents (most of whom support Trump), and only 7 percent are genuinely unaligned.[24] The latter group is the most politically disengaged and less likely to vote.

For others, partisan identity is a deeply etched and defining aspect of who they are. Some are so embedded in their political worldview that they will readily join a lynch mob, such as the January 6 MAGA terrorists who erected gallows outside the Capitol to hang Vice President Mike Pence and Speaker of the House Nancy Pelosi. Before and since the 2021 Trump coup attempt, there has been renewed attention to right-wing terrorism as a threat to domestic national security and the resilience of democracy.

The term *violent domestic extremism* has become a common term of art, at least outside the MAGA faction.[25] While it names a real threat, the problem is that it elides the continuity between the current Trumpian GOP in the US Congress and its military wing (the Proud Boys, Oath Keepers, and other anti-democratic terrorist groups). If describing one of America's two mainstream parties as having a military wing seems hyperbolic, consider one study that found that twenty percent of GOP officials and officeholders are members of right-wing paramilitary groups like the Oath Keepers.[26] Even in my famously deep-blue state of Oregon, the local Republican Party employed fascist militias to run security operations at MAGA rallies.[27] Anti-democratic Brown Shirts provided similar services in Colorado, Minnesota, and other states.[28]

Then there are the "lone-wolf" freelancers who arrogate to themselves the responsibility to hunt down enemies of Trumpism.[29] As we all witnessed, that component of the MAGA army was brought into sharp relief by the insurrection at the Capitol. This book will show that contemporary "mainstream" conservatism and their gun-toting "extremist" allies share a common psychology, the same set of moral intuitions, and political end goals.

What Are Liberals, Conservatives, and Libertarians?

I realize that my use of those labels may not fit with how they are defined by many readers. So, it is vital to unpack how I'm deploying them at the outset. While the terms *liberal* and *conservative* tend to overlap with the party identities of Democratic and Republican, respectively, they are not always equivalent. Liberals and conservatives exhibit enormous heterogeneity. For example, some under the liberal umbrella would be content to see large corporations subject to more regulations, especially regarding employee and CEO pay disparities. Others would like to see big companies broken up into worker-run collectives in which profits are shared and production coordinated with other cooperatives. (I can already hear my anarchist and socialist readers slamming this book shut over the insult of being lumped in with what they understand liberals to be. But hear me out.) Some conservatives, on the other hand, would feel a sense of accomplishment if minimum wage laws were weakened. Others will not be satisfied until child labor laws, workplace safety regulations, and legal limits on pollution are overturned.

Some readers may be puzzled, if not horrified, to see that my political taxonomy does not draw a sharp line between *liberal* and *left*. The liberal rubric is often used dismissively by some on the Left to describe those who seek only reformist Band-Aids for the deep wounds inflicted by predatory capitalism and thus leave the deep structures of oppression unaffected. Then there is the term *neo-liberalism*, which denotes the project of ensuring untrammeled free markets, deregulated resource extraction, and austerity for those who can least afford it. Left, by contrast, can refer to a movement that seeks to challenge both approaches deeply. The problem is that there is no consensus on those meanings. Many see a continuum from lesser to greater radicalism as one moves from liberal to Left. Others argue there can be no meaningful distinction because so many people use them interchangeably.

Moreover, some on the Left think critically about ideas and leaders, hold identities flexibly, thrive on free speech, and welcome debate. In contrast, some are authoritarian, attached to black-and-white categories, rigid, and censorious. I would describe the former as liberal and the latter as illiberal. That highlights another layer of complexity in attempting to nail down these terms: they name more than just political positions but ways of thinking and feeling about politics. In that sense, *liberal* may be a richer and deeper term of art because it can capture the psychological register of political life. *Left*, on the other hand, is an attempt to place an individual or group on a fictional and contradictory continuum that paradoxically features nearly identical poles. While both terms are fraught with ambiguity, neither can be dispensed with.

Liberals and conservatives cannot be automatically assumed to belong to particular parties or predictably adopt specific policies. The research summarized in this book shows that their *psychology* and *implicit moral values* most reliably differentiate those two groups and predict their behavior in different social and political situations. So, if you are driven by concerns for fairness and equity, are attracted to diverse ideas and people, identify with humanity as a whole, and have a high tolerance for ambiguity, you are more likely to be a liberal. If your overarching concerns are purity, loyalty to your community and its leaders, the danger of outsiders, establishing dominance of your group over others, and achieving certainty, chances are you are a conservative. If you don't care much about fairness or purity but covet the freedom to do what you want regardless of its impact on others, you are probably a libertarian. (Many conservatives obviously share that last quality.) The research from which these conclusions are drawn will be described in greater detail in later chapters.

But it is important to reiterate that even though those traits tend to cluster under the headings of liberal, conservative, and libertarian, like psycho-diagnostic categories, they exist on a continuum and pure types don't occur—although many individuals can come close. In addition, while relatively stable, the expression of those different partisan frames of mind can be context-dependent. As the social forces that impinge on people change, so might their political psychology. What is essential to understand is that those qualities, to whatever extent they operate in particular people, are the upstream drivers of the policies, parties, and politicians that citizens endorse.

What Conservatives Seek to Conserve

Regardless of faction, the fundamental affinity among all iterations of contemporary conservatism is revealed by what they seek to *conserve* or restore: traditional status hierarchies. That includes those of class, wealth, gender, sex, race, and religion. They complain about government power primarily on those occasions when elected representatives seek to use the power of the state to level the playing field by ensuring equality of opportunity. When liberal lawmakers attempt to challenge those hierarchies, right-wing "populists," without any apparent sense of irony, denounce them as elites.

But don't take my word on what comprises the essence of conservatism. Friedrich Hayek, widely celebrated on the Right as the high priest of free-market fundamentalism, was far more nuanced in his thinking than his contemporary apostles. He even repudiated the label of conservative. In his book *The Road to Serfdom*, originally published in 1944, he said, "A conservative movement, by its very nature, is bound to be a defender of established privilege and to lean on the power of government for the protection of privilege."[30] That is not only a clear, succinct, and accurate description; but it also challenges the myth that conservatives aim for "small government." As Hayek notes, the defining conservative approach to the power of the state is to wield it to defend the interests of actual elites. That is in sharp contrast with the ideological sleight-of-hand finessed by MAGA Republicans, which is to redefine "privilege" as no longer a property of the political and economic ruling class but that of liberals, intellectuals, journalists, and artists.

The term "free market" continues to be one of the common tropes deployed by conservatives. The connotation is that the unimpeded ability to exchange goods and services and extract profit is the essence of freedom. That rubric ignores the many hazards and malignant consequences that flow from governments abdicating their regulatory functions—exploitation, environmental degradation, price gouging, and dangerous products. There is another effect that explodes the myth that unbridled capitalism is necessarily an emancipatory force—market authoritarianism.[31]

That is a term used by scholars to describe those countries where a deregulated economy is combined with political repression. That manifested most vividly in Pinochet's Chile and continues in post-Mao China, post-Soviet Russia, and the developing world. The deregulated marketplace was often a cover for deregulated corruption. For multinational corporations, democracy can seriously impede seizing the global commons for resource extraction and other profiteering. Much better to finance the campaigns and rule of mercenary autocrats who can be bribed and counted on to pimp out natural resources, crush unions, and minimize worker protections.

The Republican Party has undergone a profound transformation, most dramatically expressed in the Trump era. It has metamorphosed from an institution motivated by conservative *policies* to one driven by conservative *psychology*. The GOP used to at least pay lip service to deficit reduction, the size of government, a strong national defense, ardent patriotism, and economic prosperity. What animates the party now is only servile deference to an authoritarian leader. That was exemplified by their 2020 "platform," which consisted of no issues beyond unquestioning fealty to Trump.[32]

I Say Democracy; You Say Republic. Let's Call the Whole Thing Off

Any discussion of political labels would be incomplete without weighing in on the contentious debate about what we Americans should call our form of governance. Among the mythic rewritings of US history by the MAGA Right is the assertion that America is not a democracy but a republic. That story is being told by Republicans in their efforts to legitimize and conjure up an historic rationalization for their multiple moves to take this country in the direction of autocracy. A short list of the most widely known of those moves would have to include voter suppression, their promotion of fake electors, false claims of voter fraud to disenfranchise citizens across the nation, partisan gerrymandering, the ousting of Democratic representatives from Tennessee to Montana, and their ultimate assault on democracy—the January 6 coup attempt. Even after that treasonous attack, the GOP made strenuous efforts to recast the terrorists as heroic patriots. And Trump promised to pardon them, should he regain the White House in 2024. All of that was and continues to be justified as a bulwark against the "tyranny of the majority." While most Americans oppose their efforts, conservative leaders are less troubled by minoritarian tyranny.

At the current moment, the Conservative Political Action Committee (CPAC) remains the most passionate group of MAGA conservatives. If giving top billing to the fascism-adjacent Viktor Orbán was too subtle a marker of the American Right's love affair with autocracy, Jack Posobiec stepped up in 2024 to clarify the matter: "Welcome to the end of democracy. We're here to overthrow it completely."[33] His promise was greeted with thundering applause by the MAGA audience.

When it comes to actual policy, many Republican anti-democratic initiatives have been a bit more under the radar, such as efforts by red state governments to nullify or override public health and safety measures passed by voters in blue cities.[34] This national strategy includes the move by the Tennessee GOP state legislators to end Nashville's popular police oversight board designed to monitor and mitigate racially motivated shootings by local law enforcement. In

Texas, Republican legislators blocked measures passed in Austin and Dallas that would mandate water breaks for construction workers. Mississippi Republicans imposed on Jackson, which has a large plurality of Black residents, a separate police and court system for white people. And in Missouri, GOP legislators are trying to wrest control of police oversight from the city government of St. Louis.

As Constitutional scholar Akhil Reed Amar writes in his myth-exploding essay on the *Federalist Papers*, most of the founders did not differentiate between "democracy" and "republic."[35] There was a lot of overlap between those two terms. Democracy could be direct and indirect. Authors that preceded Madison in the Federalist anthology praised the direct democracy of New England town meetings and referred to them as "republics." Many were advocates and practitioners of popular rule.

Madison was the one who made a sharp distinction between a democracy and republic, which is why he is the only writer in the *Federalist* volume cited by contemporary right-wing anti-democracy ideologues. His conception was not widely embraced at the time. And Madison himself was clear that he was an outlier on this matter.[36] Amar notes that at the founding of the nation, "democracy" was an edgier and more inspiring term of art; it marked one as a more radical and passionate opponent of aristocracy.

There are other political labels left behind by the realities they originally intended to describe, such as "mainstream" and "extremist." That is especially true when trying to understand the identities of contemporary white supremacist and neofascist groups. Pundits still describe them as "fringe," even while they are being invited into the welcoming embrace of the GOP with the former president telling them, "We love you; you're very special."[37]

Neo-Nazi Normcore and Fascist Normalization

Normcore began as an aesthetic in fashion and culture that rejected niche-market particularism by adopting bland, suburban, non-individuating styles. They might include washed-out jeans, hoodies, corporate logo T-shirts, ball caps, white sneakers, and cargo shorts—outfits suitable for mall-cruising and mundane practices like watching football and reality TV and going bowling. As an anti-identity identity, it marked one as part of an imagined global mainstream. A portmanteau of "normal" and "hardcore," normcore was conceived as an antidote to the ironic pseudo-bohemian affectations of hipster style (handlebar mustaches, neo-primitivistic tattoos, beer yoga, and artisanal cupcake emporiums). Ultimately, however, normcore could not evade irony as a self-conscious style of non-self-consciousness. More troubling has been its ironic appropriation by right-wing tribalists.

Like all fashion, normcore was subverted and coopted in unexpected ways. At the Charlottesville, Virginia, Unite the Right march, preppy-looking fascist young men discarded their white robes and swastikas for white polo shirts and beige chino pants. They adopted a bland Universalist style to camouflage their very particularistic tribalism. The shift from Klan couture to J. Crew had been years in the making. And yet, their efforts to hide one aspect of themselves revealed another—their paradoxical role as conformist rebels. They are warriors against difference, heterodox crusaders for homogeneity, and revolutionaries who long to restore the Ancien Régime. Whether causal or just coincidental, the sartorial mainstreaming of the radical Right has been accompanied by their political normalization. White replacement theory is now a delusion central to the identity and unquestionable catechism of one of America's two major parties.

Initially, I'd planned to devote an entire chapter to right-wing extremist and fascist tribalism. However, that no longer makes sense. "Extreme" has become an incoherent modifier in a world where those on the fringe have ceased to be outliers. At the end of 2022, Donald Trump had just finished extending his Thanksgiving hospitality to an undisguised neo-Nazi, Nick Fuentes. Only a handful of GOP representatives expressed any disapproval. It is clear that white supremacists have not only found a place in the Republican Party; they *are* the party. Moreover, as I argue throughout this book, there has long been a psychological and political continuity between openly racist and xenophobic conservatives and those on the Right who express the same worldview in more "moderate" and measured tones.

In other words, the neo-Nazi Right and more mainstream conservatives are linked in how they seem to share the same moral intuitions. Undisguised white supremacists have not been studied as a separate group by "moral foundations" researchers.[38] (I will be discussing that body of research in later chapters.) Nevertheless, they speak in a language that is explicit about their deeply held and typically conservative moral orientations, especially regarding purity and in-group loyalty. Both of those values are expressed through race. Purity is understood in racial and bodily terms. For example, avoiding contamination from outside racial groups through miscegenation is vital. They also seem to understand in-group loyalty as fidelity to one's racial group, hence the term *race traitor* for those who fail to live up to that value.

Where I Stand

Some readers might wonder where I place myself, although I've not been particularly coy up to this point. I am not a disinterested observer of political tribalism writing atop the Olympian vertex of academic neutrality. As someone embedded in partisan identity—its emotions, beliefs, values, and complicated alliances, I am an *interested* observer and try to be a mindful participant. The challenge is holding the tension between feeling tribal passions *and* the intellectual and moral need to reflect on and question them. Since the book is animated by what matters to me, it could be called an evidence-based polemic. It is founded on many examined assumptions, some that doubtless remain unexamined, and deeply held biases. In some ways, my approach parallels the changes in news reporting that the contemporary GOP has necessitated.

In particular, Donald Trump's easy but malignant mendacity has forced news organizations to choose between two forms of "bias." They could call out official lies and become a partisan of truth that nowadays tends to favor one side in political debate or follow the traditional journalistic tendency to be stenographers of the powerful. "Neutrality" in journalism and scholarship has led to the moral hazard of affirming the "both sides" fiction—the idea that adherents of all political persuasions are equally corrupt, self-serving, or dishonest. While there are no angels or devils in contemporary politics, Republican members of Congress have been open about their Faustian bargain with Trumpism. No longer burdened by the weight of an ethical soul, their political careers have gained considerable lift.

Similarly, the dangers of political tribalism are not symmetrical. While left-wing tribalism can be problematic in numerous ways and even operate as a profoundly repressive force, in the United States it is primarily right-wing tribalists who seek to disenfranchise, coerce, and, if necessary, kill others to achieve political and social dominance. MAGA Republicans loudly proclaim their love for "America" but hate Americans—at least the majority of them who are not members of the GOP tribe. Currently, domestic terrorism is a threat that emanates almost entirely from the Right.[39] As will be described in later chapters, domination is fundamental to conservatives' psychology and political aims. And, since domination is a relationship, their ends mandate the subordination of others.

My Assumptions

I have not written this book to persuade the reader that coercive domination is undesirable, that the right to purchase and shoot an assault weapon should not eclipse the right of others not to be shot by one, or that lying should not be a fundamental tool of statecraft. I am not seeking to convince anyone that destroying the biosphere is not worth the short-term profit it yields for a few. Likewise, I see no point in arguing that the demise of what remains of American democracy and its devolution into civil war and autocratic rule would be a tragic and bloody outcome. Instead, this book is for those who already share those assumptions and values but struggle to understand the psychology of those who don't. The final chapter will consider possible bridges between partisans who see one another as threatening enemies.

We who cherish democracy, justice, and the environmental commons may be most of the population. But because of the structural bias built into the electoral system (a factor at play in multiple issues discussed in this book), we do not have representation commensurate with our numbers. If we don't want to resign ourselves to impotent screaming in the rapidly diminishing wilderness, our numbers will have to increase even further. That requires gaining a window into the inner worlds of the plurality of Americans who oppose or are indifferent to what we care about. We must understand what matters to them, how they think and feel, and how their world is constructed. I hope those who find the ideas in this book helpful can take the next step and transmute them into impactful political interventions.

It is a sobering paradox to consider that fascism, in many places it emerged, has been an outcome of democracy, whether from its collapse through coups or its degeneration through elections.[40] When citizens live in a media ecosphere where truth no longer matters and are driven by xenophobic anxieties, a free election can paradoxically lead to the end of elections. The tragic Hegelian joke has been played out too often; democracy can be a path to autocracy. In other words, once liberal values are shorn from democracy, fascism may be the consequence. I fear that with the rise of the MAGA faction, even if Trump's fortunes fade, we may witness the twilight of liberal democracy.

Why Bother with Electoral Politics?

I came of age politically in 1970s Berkeley, California. My partners-in-thought-crime and I were steeped in and inspired by the writing and notorious actions of the Situationists[41] and other groups opposed to domination in all forms, whether capitalist or Stalinist. Our vision of a new world and how to get there was informed by the history of radical democratic revolt and the non-hierarchical forms of political self-organization they engendered, like the workers' councils of Kronstadt mentioned previously.

Moreover, the issues that animated us were far more than society's oppressive economic and political macro structures. We were most moved by the ordinary experience of daily life in late capitalism—how everything and everybody tend to be reduced to things and their prices. We also refused to normalize the quotidian humiliations that flow from working in settings where survival is predicated on following orders in command-and-control hierarchies. Democracy, we insisted, should not be limited to the ballot box.

One of our guiding assumptions, not entirely wrong, was that electoral politics often changed very little. Choosing between representatives of the ruling elite was scarcely a choice. Electoral battles between Tweedle Dee and Tweedle Dum were hardly meaningful contests. Arguing for one and not the other seemed like battling over distinctions without a difference.

Back then, that dismissive perspective was easier to hold. Republicans were, like they are now, generally unambivalent defenders of America's oligarchy of wealth. And Democrats were often mercenary collaborators with corporate power or weak and capitulating critics of it. Those on the Left who participated in that charade were seen as either fools or corrupt. Then Reagan, the Bushes, and Trump were elected, each Republican administration more malignant and anti-democratic than the one that preceded it. At this moment, we are only one election away from the disappearance of even the hobbled form of democratic rule that now prevails.

Those who scoff at the importance of voting as one among many ways of exercising political agency tend to forget or minimize the fact that German and Italian fascists came to power through elections. Likewise, Putin's path to becoming a fascist dictator began with the ballot in 2000. So did fascism-adjacent leaders like Orbán and Bolsonaro. All too often ordinary people actually vote for those who would later crush their freedom.[42]

Although a few on the Left might still believe voting doesn't matter, the Right understands that elections have consequences and electorates enable them. That is why Republicans work so hard to prevent Democratic constituencies from voting and are so terrified of their own supporters. The GOP and its broadcast division, Fox News, have turned their followers into a kind of fascist Frankenstein. Like Shelley's creature, the monster now threatens its creators.

Nurtured on a steady diet of conspiracy theories, science hatred, displaced grievance, sadism, racial resentment, and xenophobia, the base may be loyal for now, but if not fed what has sustained them, their progenitors could be the next meal. Republican politicians deemed insufficiently MAGA by colleagues are often threatened with being "primaried" by that snarling and hungry beast. Even though so many of the former president's endorsees have lost in general elections, party members tremble with fear that if Trump gives the word, his ballot box of deplorables will be unleashed to destroy them in the primaries.

It is more apparent than ever that boycotting electoral politics is a default surrender to those seeking to destroy any form of multiethnic democracy and the civil liberties that enable it. Voting is a crude, flawed, and insufficient means of changing life and the oligarchic forces that shape it. But not doing so hands over power to those who long for a king. For my friends who might still insist that elections are meaningless political theater, I would offer a slightly modified version of Pericles's ancient admonition: You may not be interested in elections, but elections are interested in you.

Hatreds We Love?

The title of this book aims to do more than grab your attention with a counter-intuitive conjunction of opposites. My intention is to convey something about the paradoxical nature of hatred, the central emotion animating political tribalism. It has been said that hate is like drinking poison and hoping someone else dies. In other words, those who carry it are often the ones who suffer from its toxicity. But hatred is far more than a consuming revulsion felt toward another. It creates clarity out of ambiguity and defines our friends in addition to our enemies. Despising outsiders can facilitate loving insiders. It is a frequently observed phenomenon among combat veterans that even though their military experience may have been a traumatizing horror show of cruelty and suffering, they long for the camaraderie of their fellow soldiers.[43] For some, no peacetime love can compare to that bond.

The relatively benign experience of team sports, a form of ritual combat, is the variety of tribalism familiar to more people. For fans, the competitive hostility they might feel toward the opposing team is of a piece with the kinship, love, and pride felt for the home team.

In warfare, politics, and everyday bigotry, hatred can aid in disavowing and projecting ugly aspects of ourselves. In this process, reviled antagonists become vitally necessary as psychological waste bins. Thus, enemies are sometimes crucial for our psychic equilibrium and self-acceptance. We need our nemeses however much we might seek their annihilation. Hating *them* for seeming to embody what we don't want to perceive in *us* can make it easier to love one another.

My Hatred

The purpose of this book is not to analyze my own tribal passions, but it would be profoundly dishonest to deny them. I, too, can hate. During those dread-filled pandemic grocery shopping excursions in 2020, it wasn't uncommon to read accounts of MAGA anti-maskers coughing and laughing in the faces of clerks and other customers, defiantly proclaiming that their freedom to infect, sicken, and kill others would not be abridged. In those moments, it was easy to fall down zero-sum rabbit holes—to wish for the death of those happy to annihilate the rest of us.

Of course, fantasizing about another's destruction is not the same as acting to bring it about. Only my sometimes-flagging capacity for self-reflection keeps me from becoming a version of those I might despise. I do not want to turn into a sadistic and violent dehumanizer of my political opponents. One way to not become a perpetrator, to keep my hatred from being enacted, is to harbor no illusions about my virtuous heart. Befriending my murderousness keeps me from becoming a murderer.

It is essential to remember that we are all capable of being perpetrators, victims, protectors, and rescuers. That truth is regularly forgotten by those who commit genocide and mass murder and torture their enemies. From the Inquisition to the witch hunts, to the Holocaust, to the October 7, 2023 butchery by Hamas, to the collective punishment visited upon the innocent civilians of Gaza, persecutors have often imagined themselves as agents of the divine or unflinching saviors of their victimized people. And so, their violence is always experienced as defensive and ennobling. War crimes are often committed as vengeance against war crimes.

"Ethnic cleansing" is not a random metaphor for deporting or obliterating an unwanted group. It speaks to a fantasy of purity, whether spiritual for the holy warrior or racial for the ethno-nationalist. We can only stay clean by eradicating the dirty "other." If the very existence of the enemy group is a moral stain, nothing could be more righteous than removing it. Thus is born the profound entitlement to act on our hatred and torment and annihilate others.

The challenge for me as a psychoanalyst of politics is to enter and understand the inner worlds of my xenophobic and exterminationist adversaries without becoming them. This book is, in part, an effort to transmute my own hatred into generative anger. Audre Lorde noted that the aim of hatred is "death and destruction," whereas the goal of political anger is "change."[44] Nevertheless, despair, trauma, and thoughtlessness can easily lead the latter to collapse back into the former. In the next chapter, we will plunge deeper into the psychological complexities of tribal enmity and the hatred that animates it.

CHAPTER 1

Tribal Mind/Tribal Brain—
Xenophobia, Disgust,
Hatred, and Fear

"Get your guns and shoot them!" "Kick their knees in!" "Stomp them to death!" There was nothing subtle about the chilling calls for mass murder. You might assume these were issued in one of many global hotspots of ethnic conflict or civil war—Bosnia in 1992, Rwanda in 1994, or Myanmar in 2017. Actually, they appeared on a public Facebook page serving a tiny town in a remote rural Oregon county.[1]

Folks here pride themselves on not being on the way to anyplace else. They are also fond of proclaiming the love and concern everyone feels for others in this mountain community, where people really do wave at strangers passing on traffic-free country roads. And yet, despite the area's seven-hour drive from any major Oregon city and the sincerity of fellow feeling, the sense of threat was quite palpable—so much so that seventy armed townsfolk showed up on a day in June 2020 with assault weapons at the ready.[2] One of these self-appointed guardians of public safety even assumed a sniper position atop a building near city hall.

The call to arms was prompted by social media rumors of a bus caravan of Antifa and Black Lives Matter warriors who were on their way to trash town businesses and attack residents. The feared marauders, needless to say, never showed up. The catalyst for the imagined invasion was a planned vigil by a handful of local activists, primarily elderly, to honor the memory of George Floyd, the victim of police murder in Minnesota. Even more disturbing, this story was repeated throughout other deep-red areas of the state, in at least a half dozen small rural towns.[3]

Years after that episode, country singer Jason Aldean would pen the perfect anthem to accompany those and future eruptions of armed xenophobic paranoia, "Try That in a Small Town." In his music video[4] and lyrics,[5] this Trump-revering crooner conflates robbers, rioters, carjackers, and demonstrators against police violence in what has been a meme of fascist propaganda for many generations: political protesters are criminals, and they need to be stopped with vigilante violence. Aldean calls upon his "good ol' boys raised up right" to get out their guns and beat back the invading cosmopolitan hordes. His video was filmed in front of the infamous Tennessee courthouse that in 1927 was the backdrop for the lynching of a Black man. Just a coincidence, Aldean insisted. (What does not seem like a coincidence is that after his music video was condemned for its racist subtext, the song rose to number one. That appears to be one of the more glaring examples of racism being used as a marketing tool in country music more broadly.[6])

What could lead people to so easily believe they might be overrun by an army of swarthy barbarians from the country's urban multicultural Gomorrahs? How could they be so credulous that they were ready to slaughter this unseen enemy? What would cause people so removed from any big-city strife to feel such vulnerability? These are questions that this chapter will attempt to answer.

The Big Picture: Tribalism and Our Species-Nature

While humans are not unique among animals in their tendency to form tribal bands, we are the only creatures who dress up our alliances in the justifying cloak of religion or ideology. Like all other animals, we seek to protect ourselves against perceived threats. But unlike other animals, we imagine that ideas, symbols, belief systems, and religions can protect us against threats or are threats themselves. Unlike other animals, humans are willing to kill themselves and others in the name of such mental abstractions. In other words, we imagine ideas as both peril and salvation. And, of course, the ideas we will die or kill for are those intrinsic to our tribal identity and membership. Yet tribalism is about more than these intangible constructs.

For humans, tribal bonds are fundamental to life, as essential as air, water, and food. Why would this be? One way to answer that question would be to view life as a temporary resistance to the unraveling forces of entropy. Energy must be taken from the environment to maintain the organization that characterizes life. We could think about the social organization enabled by tribal bonds as a means of drawing on collective forces, thus exponentially increasing our limited capacities as separate individuals. These connections with others expand our ability to forestall entropic disorganization, the ultimate expressions of which are death and decomposition. Put more simply: we hold it together by working together.

The vital power of the group may help us further understand the paradoxical willingness of people to die for the tribe. We often consider ourselves superior to seemingly mindless ants that appear to prize the welfare of the colony superorganism over individual lives. Yet, the history of humanity is riven with the theme of individuals forsaking their solitary identities for a collective one. Whether one is donning a military uniform and marching eagerly into the meat grinder of war or, in the peak pandemic years, sporting a MAGA hat unmasked and unvaxxed at a COVID-saturated indoor Trump rally, our group identity can supersede all other considerations. Here we come to the heart of a head-scratching irony that has perplexed many: tribal membership is so central to human life that we can be indifferent to our mortal peril. That is one of many paradoxes and contradictions we have evolved to bear.

The chapter ahead will attempt to shed light on many of them. As we proceed, it is essential to acknowledge that evolution has no intention, no final aim, or what philosophers have called "teleology." The evolution of life is not an uplifting progress narrative. It has started over at various points and may do so again for many reasons.

There is another caveat regarding the evolution of human psychology: just because a current trait of the human mind was once adaptive does not mean it remains advantageous or desirable. Nor does it mean that its expression is inevitable. Moreover, many evolved traits coexist with others that predispose us to opposite behaviors.[7]

A formerly adaptive trait can be retained but be a significant fetter on human development and well-being. Such is the case with our predisposition to fear and hate outsider groups. At play is a set of impulses and instinctive behaviors that were once essential to survival and the opportunity to pass on one's genes. At a later point, they can become the biggest upstream threat to the continued existence of humanity and the biosphere upon which we depend.

Human history also lacks teleology. It exhibits no evidence of inevitable progress or a preordained outcome or goal. On the one hand, there appears to be an evolving trend toward greater democracy and diminished suffering. On the other hand, this is counterbalanced by the growth of autocracy worldwide, the rapid eclipse of democratic institutions in the United States, and the global extinction of many life forms that humans are rapidly engendering. We can direct our tribal energies toward either outcome.

As central as group identity has been to humanity's survival, there is nothing inevitable about cooperation, like so many other evolved traits. Historian and environmental philosopher Melanie Challenger points out that people are *conditionally* cooperative. We could view being social as one among many coexisting and sometimes contradictory schemas that can be activated under certain conditions and not others. In some circumstances, people will care and sacrifice for unrelated tribal outsiders. Occasionally, we will risk our lives to join the pillage and plunder that our group perpetrates on out-groups. Yet, certain other conditions can lead us to exploit or prey upon members of our tribe in the pursuit of individual benefit. We tend to view people who commit brutal crimes against fellow tribe members as psychopaths. But when they perpetrate the same abuses against those in out-groups, they are sometimes lauded as heroes.

In the case of tribal war, tender affection and hostile aggression can coexist in the same people. In this regard, what comes to mind are the bizarre photos brought to light following World War II of Nazi death camp staff on their day off at an SS holiday retreat adjacent to Auschwitz.[8] They are pictured posing relaxedly with one another. Their warm and playful expressions tell us it was a welcome day off from the daily grind of implementing mass extermination. Brutal violence toward the out-group is perfectly compatible with loving-kindness toward and congeniality with members of your group.

Perhaps the Nazi example is too culturally distant for some. More readers may have seen images of the postcards that circulated in certain parts of the Jim Crow South in the 1920s.[9] They depicted white families in their Sunday finery, fresh from soul-cleansing church services, enjoying the warmth, good cheer, and tasty refreshments offered by their fellows while a Black lynching victim swung from a rope in the distance. The conjoining of sanguinary depravity with genteel civility illustrates the kind of moral dissociation that malignant tribalism can make possible.

Should the reader find comfort in the belief that the moral dissociation of the Jim Crow South is just a relic of the last century, let me make you a bit uncomfortable. For years, hosts on Airbnb have been offering former slave quarters to those seeking a romantic getaway.[10] Similarly, one reviewer on Trip Advisor who stayed at Virginia's Prospect Inn waxed rhapsodic over "the charm of the plantation."[11] "Plantation" does sound a lot more enchanting than slave labor camp. Those who market them for weddings and other celebrations[12] seem to know how to put a soft-focus lens on the historical reality of their real estate.[13] We Americans have always had a talent for sanitizing our past, as if that were more patriotic than sober reflection. On the other hand, Germans are far more willing to face the atrocities of Nazi tribalism and are highly unlikely to repackage Dachau and Buchenwald into wellness retreats. They seem to prefer the burden of understanding and learning from the past over the cheerful amnesia of Americans.

How Our Conflictual Psychologies Contribute to Partisan Tribalism

Certain conditions, like a shared natural disaster or an attack by a foreign enemy, can predictably activate our capacity for cooperation. In contrast, other situations, such as an actual or perceived scarcity of resources, can mobilize our ability to pursue narrow self-interest at the cost of our ties to others. It would be clearly folly to declare that one of these conflicting tendencies is our "true" essence. Social psychologists have created a discipline devoted to manipulating environmental conditions to evoke disparate aspects of our contradictory nature. Some of that work will be highlighted later in this chapter. Nevertheless, people differ in the endowments they bring to changing situations. One of those variable predispositions concerns our intuitive sense of tribal borders and how they should function.

Group membership is vital to all of us. But there are stark partisan differences in what it means to belong to a tribe. That partly concerns the very different ideological notions of a group boundary. For conservatives, that membrane or boundary should be relatively impermeable; those of other religions, ethnicities, or races don't belong inside. For example, that can help us understand the increasingly emotional investment Republicans have in limiting or stopping immigration, especially those whose color marks them as outsiders, and for constructing barriers at the border that are imbued with the fantasy of impermeability.

For liberals, the tribal boundary should be semi-permeable, which selectively allows some people to enter but not others. There is a recognition that certain outsiders could enrich the group. They may look, speak, or worship differently than those already insiders but embrace the fundamental values held by longtime residents, such as civil liberties and democratic governance. There is also the awareness that some strangers might not be a good fit and should be excluded. When liberals err in their construction of boundaries, it is most often in the direction of excessive permeability.

So, in many ways, the different partisan approaches to tribal identity concern how they view the membranes that enclose them—rigid or flexible, hermetically sealed or partially porous. While a later chapter will address some of the limitations of liberal political psychology, I am far more worried about the consequences of present-day right-wing tribalism. And I have good company in this anxiety. According to FBI Director Christopher Wray, white supremacists and far-right militias constitute the most significant domestic terrorism threat we face.[14]

The overriding concern of these groups is boundary permeability—the borders of race, culture, sexuality, and gender.[15] And they have shown themselves quite willing to kill and die to shore up those barriers. Because Donald Trump has identified himself as the principal avatar of their xenophobia, they have gleefully volunteered to function as his private army. Trump, in turn, has reciprocated their love, suggesting that he would pardon the January 6 coup plotters should he return to office in 2025.[16]

All that is required of his armed followers is that they back his efforts to end any democratic impediments to autocratic rule. Trump has made no effort to disguise that intention. In what has become an all-too-familiar pattern of normalizing the aberrant, he casually admitted that the aim of his multi-front assault on democracy was to get Mike Pence to "change the outcome" and that his vice president should have "overturned the election."[17] Once on the throne, he can finally complete his "big, beautiful wall," the organizing metaphor of his reign.[18] Only if he can attain unaccountable power can the dangerous, polluting racial outsiders be kept from sullying white America. And most Republican members of Congress are aligned with those goals.

In case anyone doubted that the GOP is now the Trump party, the Republican National Committee, by a unanimous vote, censured the two singular dissenters in their caucus, Liz Cheney and Adam Kinzinger. Their transgression? They sought to hold the Capitol rioters and the former president accountable for their actions. In the same document announcing the censure, Republicans declared that the January 6 terrorists—who assaulted cops using metal poles festooned with Trump and Confederate flags, attempted to lynch the vice president, defecated in the Capitol Building, and tried to stop the certification of Biden's victory—were engaged in "legitimate political discourse."[19]

It isn't just the MAGA faction's militant opposition to democracy that is troublesome. It is also what they want to do with the autocratic power they seek, even beyond instituting xenophobic policies. We are getting a window into that agenda at the state level. Extending their decades-long culture war Jihad into primary and secondary schools, Republicans at the local level have embarked on a frenzy of book banning and curricular censorship.[20] Their target is the teaching of facts, historical and scientific, that make white Christians feel "discomfort."[21] There are proposals to monitor what teachers say with microphones and cameras.[22] In many respects, those culture war skirmishes are iterations of a large xenophobic crusade—the right-wing effort to banish the foreign, the unfamiliar, and the perspectives that challenge unexamined assumptions. Those threats require different walls—laws and policies that keep out the strange in all its forms.

One of those assumptions is the conservative creed of dominion over the entire natural world in the form of unrestrained resource extraction. That belief has placed much of the planet's flora and fauna in unprecedented peril— whether cloaked in Biblical mandates, Randian libertarian entitlement, or corporate defenses of "property rights."[23] That notion has combined with right-wing denial or indifference to climate change, resulting in the loss of plant and animal species at a dizzying pace. In other words, under the contemporary rubric of "conservatism," they seek to conserve very little, especially what we most need to live.

We will all lose if this right-wing tribal vision of winning is realized. Because the stakes are so high, it is imperative to understand the psychology of tribalism, especially forms that may be ultimately inimical to life. We are facing the grim irony that this essential feature of human nature, our often-blind loyalty to groups, may lead to the disappearance of humans from nature.

Xenophobic Tribalism and the "Securitarian" Personality

Following Donald Trump's electoral victory in 2016, *Forbes magazine* interviewed the new president's son-in-law Jared Kushner about their campaign strategy.[24] Kushner noted that he wanted to make optimal use of their resources. So, the GOP team was highly selective about where they spent television ad dollars. Campaign researchers were not only able to identify which TV shows were favored by Republicans but also which political issue was associated with each program. They learned that avid viewers of *The Walking Dead* were particularly concerned about immigration. The show depicted caravans of filthy, depersonalized, and soulless wanderers who offer nothing and want to eat your brains. That sounds a lot like the immigrant monsters Trump had been conjuring throughout his campaign. As you learn more about the "securitarian personality," it will be clear why that ad buy was a laser-guided strike directly into the MAGA amygdala.

Psychologist John Hibbing wrote *The Securitarian Personality* in 2018.[25] At that time, Trump had been in office for two years. Many social scientists and non-MAGA members of the public struggled to understand the psychological foundations of Trump's base. Using focus groups, interviews, and extensive surveys, Hibbing's research was aimed at the most ardent supporters of the president—not just his voters but those who deeply venerated him.

However, since then, Trump veneration quickly became the only acceptable public stance if one wanted to remain in good standing with the GOP. Party members who failed to exalt their spiritual leader and join the Trump cult of personality were labeled RINOs (Republicans in Name Only), censured, deprived of committee assignments, threatened with MAGA primary challengers, or forced into retirement. Republican members of Congress who took positions contrary to the MAGA party mainstream received death threats.[26]

To be viewed as a tribal loyalist, it was not enough to simply sing the leader's praises. One also had to sign on to the new GOP catechism—that the 2020 election was stolen from Trump, the violent coup plotters of January 6 were actually freedom-fighting patriots, and laws had to be passed to ensure that handpicked partisan functionaries, not a majority of voters, would determine future election outcomes. Across the country, GOP state legislators passed voter suppression and election nullification laws.

In light of these developments, it seems highly likely that the percentage of conservatives who constitute what Hibbing calls "Trump venerators" has become the only politically viable force within the Republican Party, Congress, and the base. If the MAGA faction has become virtually the only faction on the Right, Hibbing's studies have even broader applications for American conservatives. With that in mind, unless stated otherwise, I will use "MAGA faction," "GOP base," "Republican," "right-wing," and "conservative" interchangeably.

Before the Trump era, distinctions between those terms might have been meaningful. There may very well be Republican politicians who quietly dissent from MAGA orthodoxy in their minds. However, those who aren't Liz Cheney or Adam Kinzinger are either silent, on the verge of retirement, or simply unwilling to endure another campaign suffering the abuse of their Trumpian colleagues and so refuse to run again. As far as the base is concerned, 76 percent of voters who cast ballots for Trump in 2020 venerate him enough (as of January 2022) to want him to run in 2024.[27] It is safe to assume that they've made peace with the Big Lie (they either believe it or don't care) and are untroubled by his efforts to overthrow the election results and install himself as a virtual king. And many appear to long for him to be an autocratic leader.

As Hibbing's research shows, the overarching imperative of this faction is to protect the tribe from threatening outsiders and combat those on the inside who are either collaborators with the external enemy or don't recognize the danger they pose. This preoccupation with outsider groups is driven by a deep sense of collective vulnerability or insecurity, hence the name "securitarian" that Hibbing gives to this tendency, which he sees as both an enduring trait of personality and a political worldview. He notes that this phenotype can be found in many nations and throughout human history.[28] Trump has become the role model for xenophobic democracy-hating autocrats across the globe, from Brazil to the Philippines to Hungary. Even in liberal Germany and New Zealand, neofascists and anti-vaxxers, who have often marched together, could be seen wearing red MAGA hats. When xenophobic leaders are voted into office, their ascension to power likely reflects the securitarian concerns of most of the population, at least those engaged enough to show up at the polls. As noted in the introduction, nearly all fascist regimes were brought to power through democratic elections.

The Many Fronts in the War on Outsiders

In the United States, anxiety about the corrupting, polluting effects of immigration can be traced to its founding. However, the specific ethnic or racial group that constituted the alien threat was ever-changing. Benjamin Franklin warned about what he saw as an impending German immigrant invasion. In his colorized xenophobic nightmare, he described them as a "swarthy" peril that constituted a "herd." So, unlike English-speaking settlers, they would likely "be so numerous as to Germanize us instead of our Anglifying them."[29] Thus was born an early Great Replacement theory.

Fast forward to the present; two-thirds of Republicans surveyed in a University of Massachusetts-Amherst study agreed with the following statements: "The growth of the number of immigrants to the US means that America is in danger of losing its culture and identity" and "The Democratic Party is trying to replace the current electorate with voters from poorer countries around the world."[30] The endorsement of these notions was highly associated with the belief that Trump won the 2020 election.

An NPR/Ipsos survey conducted in July 2022 showed that securitarian anxieties on the Right have become profound. Seventy-six percent of Republicans believed there was an immigrant "invasion" at the southern border of the United States. However, 91 percent of those who watched Fox News and other conservative news outlets believe that.[31] But even Democrats were not immune to that disinformation. Forty percent of them accepted the false narrative. However, unlike Democrats, most Republicans endorsed many other factually incorrect ideas about immigrants. Specifically, they believed that, compared to US citizens, immigrants were likelier to commit crimes, carry fentanyl into the United States, and go on public assistance.

Given the steady xenophobic drumbeat from the likes of Tucker Carlson and other prominent white supremacist public figures, it is not surprising that even with Trump out of office, Trump*ism* has become increasingly hegemonic. While not broken out by party affiliation, researchers in 2018 found that most Americans opposed building a border wall. Four years later, more approved than disapproved of such a barrier. Support for granting a path to citizenship for immigrants brought to the United States illegally as children has declined from 65 percent back then to 51 percent now. Even the sense of America's defining character has shifted in a securitarian direction. In 2018, 75 percent of US citizens saw immigration as foundational to our national identity. By 2022, that number went down to 56 percent.[32]

Xenophobic concerns are linked to a variety of seemingly unrelated attitudes. In one study, researchers found that the vast majority of subjects who professed a disbelief in the notion of systemic racism—that white skin conferred social and economic advantages—did not accept the idea that the January 6 Capitol attack was an insurrection.[33] They also did not believe that Biden had legitimately won the 2020 election. Given the MAGA faction's perception that elections are a means to replace and disempower them using "poor" (read non-white) immigrants, the link between their xenophobia and belief in the Big Lie seems like a causal one—with the former being the catalyst for the latter.

The Role of "Big Government" in Right-Wing Demonology

Nearly every apparently separate issue of concern to conservative voters appears to derive from xenophobic anxiety. For example, the need to hamper government and its ability to regulate is driven by the sense that the state, especially at the federal level, is a force that prevents us from protecting ourselves from outsider threats.

Those who run corporations may push xenophobic narratives, but their hatred for the regulatory functions of government is more pragmatic. They oppose anything that impedes profit-taking or hampers the impunity many businesses enjoy for the harm their "cost externalization" might cause.

But in the view of the GOP base, the government wants to disarm us and prevent us from protecting our families from criminals. It tries to weaken us and crush our freedom by telling parents, who know what's best for their children, what has to be taught in schools, and whether they should wear masks or get vaccinated. It determines what chemicals we can put on our crops, how to care for our health, what to put in our gasoline, which animals we can kill, and which must be protected.

Regulation, even though it might protect citizens from harm and ensure a greater degree of actual security, is despised by the conservative electorate because it is viewed as a kind of castration. This sort of government is seen as an outsider threat that wants to put its citizens in chains, cripple their initiative, and deprive them of agency. Government policy directed at the common good, especially the tax-funded social safety net, is seen as a theft from those who work hard that is then handed over to those who refuse to work. And, as the sociologist Arlie Hochschild has observed, the conservative working poor resent the unemployed or underemployed poor (often assumed to be non-white) because the latter are seen as cutting in line ahead of those more deserving of perceived scarce resources.[34] Many on the Right imagine aid to those in need as a kind of carceral coddling, a form of caretaking that enfeebles its recipients in a prison of dependency.

Furthermore, those the state seeks to protect and subsidize aren't seen as *real* Americans. Immigrants, the homeless, racial minorities seeking "special rights," union members, criminals, environmentalists, Muslims, and welfare recipients are perceived as undeserving outsiders within our borders, especially since they are regarded as Democratic constituencies.

Ronald Reagan best captured the sense of the government as a menacing interloper whose offerings are a poison chalice when he said, "The nine most terrifying words in the English language are, 'I'm from the government, and I'm here to help.'" That much-repeated folksy Reaganism turned out to be a very effective way to disseminate and make palatable the libertarian inversion of social assistance so that it connoted harm. It helped to render intuitive to those on the Right the belief that efforts of citizens to aid one another through governmental pooling of shared resources would just make everything worse.

The notion of 'government' is often deployed as a *fantasy*, an imagined entity onto which noble or malevolent intentions can be projected. For the Left, it can be seen as an idealized protector of the common good. For the Right, especially when out of power, it is generally viewed as a malignant tool of those seeking to dominate, intrude, and restrict—an enemy of everyone's freedom.

Of course, actual governments can be malevolent or benign. They are capable of extraordinary violence and oppression. Or they can function as institutions for coordinating and implementing the care and generosity of citizens. Governments are often captured by corporate interests to ensure they are not liable for any damage caused by ruthless profiteering. Sometimes, they can be a powerful brake on the harm, pain, and ruin resulting from unrestricted capitalist pillage and plunder. Of course, real-world governments generally embody all those functions at different times and in different contexts, depending in part on whose philosophy and values are driving policy and practice.

In addition, how governments function depends on their structure, the laws that determine their powers, whom they are designed to serve, and the degree to which those who work in them can be held accountable through elections and other legal mechanisms. But these factors are also driven by what citizens *imagine* governments to be. That is where the fantasies I've described play a role in what is possible. The tropes we use in our conversations about government shape the structures and laws we create. So, in many respects, our fantasies aren't simply distortions of reality but play a vital part in the reality we create for ourselves.

Hatred and fear of government are not evolved features of human psychology. But a vigilant attunement to outsider threats is. The genius of libertarian think tanks and corporate PR consultants is their intuitive ability to harness this enduring feature of our paleo-psychology to their economic and political aims. For example, to get a plurality of citizens to reject the personal and community benefits resulting from a meaningful progressive tax system, corporate and wealth taxes must be seen as a form of robbery threatening everyone. Robin Hood has to be depicted as Joseph Stalin. From this perspective, it is a short step from legal mandates that require the wealthy to pay their fair share to forced collectivization and the gulag.

Similarly, after the August 8, 2022 FBI search of his Mar-a-Lago estate for the top-secret documents he had stolen, Donald Trump, never missing a grifting opportunity, found a way to raise money off of it. The email pitch to his marks depicted the search as an invasion by predatory outsiders.[35] Those government thugs were not just a danger to him but to the base as well. The message screamed with the typical Trumpian all-caps alarm, "THEY BROKE INTO MY HOME!" And, "They're coming after YOU." That was followed by a "poll" question: "Do you agree President Trump is being persecuted?" Deploying the reliable right-wing villain, Big Government, he could once again portray himself and, by extension, his base as victims of that malevolent alien force. And his con worked, enabling him to rake in millions within a few days.[36]

Of course, Trump is not the first right-wing politician to blur any distinction between the wealthy elite and ordinary citizens. The aim has always been to encourage the latter to identify with the former. For many decades it has been common practice for conservatives to conjure a demonic vision of government and portray it as such a grave outsider threat that it should be "drowned in the bathtub," as libertarian anti-tax zealot Grover Norquist once famously proclaimed.[37]

The Enemy Within and the MAGA War on Democracy

One way that conservatives have found to disparage liberal foes who see government as a potential force for the benefit of all is to imply directly or indirectly that they are not "real" Americans. This rhetorical move to "foreignize" Democratic voters and their representatives has been an effective way to represent to the MAGA base the threatening nature of political opponents, i.e., to depict them as tribal outsiders. One of the first such campaigns, effective among Republicans, was Donald Trump's promotion of the "birther" lie.[38] That was the fictional claim that Barack Obama was born in Kenya and was a secret practitioner of Islam. The narrative brought together a triad of qualities that rendered him dangerously alien to the GOP base. He was not only Black but also African and Muslim—definitely not one of "us."

That brings us closer to understanding the growing Republican consensus that democracy is a serious problem and why they explicitly desire to end it.[39] From their perspective, universal adult suffrage is not just an impediment to conservatives' return to power. It also makes it harder to create the ethnically and culturally homogenous world they want to live in. In other words, the threat posed by equal access to the ballot is that the wrong people can vote.

Former Arizona state house candidate and MAGA activist Selina Bliss said, "When I hear the word 'democracy,' I think of the democracy of the Democratic Republic of the Congo. That's not us."[40] The problem, according to this racialized depiction of democracy, is that it allows "them" to vote. Perhaps, had Bliss known more about the Congo's history of brutal authoritarian rule and corruption and that it was democratic in name only, she might have felt more of a kinship with that nation.

Republicans fear that non-white, non-Christian, and Democratic voters want to take the United States into a disturbingly cosmopolitan and multicultural future, which the GOP base views as a dystopian nightmare. Though not "communists," they are what Trump's role model Senator Joseph McCarthy called "the enemies within."[41] To save the country, those people must be stopped. And the only way to do that is to destroy democracy. Nearly every red state legislature has passed or proposed voter suppression and election nullification laws.

That is how autocracy—whether helmed by Donald Trump, Ron DeSantis, or another MAGA Republican—is linked to securitarian anxieties. For the GOP political elite, xenophobic narratives are the bait dangled before the base to engender approval for authoritarian rule. And for the base, supporting authoritarian rule is the means of protecting themselves from the outsiders the base believes are plotting to replace them. As Hibbing documented, those who revere Trump are willing to endorse autocracy if it furthers their sense of tribal security.[42]

The Party of Barbed Wire vs. the Party of the Welcome Mat

While xenophobic appeals are compelling to securitarians, they don't reach the other enduring personality and political type Hibbing calls "unitarians."[43] While this term does not refer to the religious institution of the same name, there are similarities. Both are ecumenical rather than sectarian. Like members of the church, Hibbing's unitarians are citizens whose tribal identity encompasses humanity as a whole. Hence, their group boundaries are more porous and mutable. They are more concerned about tyranny within their groups than threats from the outside. The greatest danger is insider villainy, such as the corrupt, unjust, and cruel exercise of power, the mistreatment of minorities, and the theft and hoarding of community resources. Unitarians tend to welcome outsiders and seek to create pathways to be granted insider status.

One way to think about these two conflicting predispositions is that they reflect different adaptions to a conflict at the core of our species' nature. On the one hand, we are utterly dependent on relationships with others, especially early in life—for protection, physical and emotional care, comfort, recognition, and material needs. As we grow, this develops into an interdependence that extends well beyond our kin group and community to include neighboring communities and, ultimately, the world. Outsiders bring ideas, innovations, resources, trade, exciting novelty, and genetic diversity. They can ally with us to better our ability to manage a wide range of threats, whether military or the caprices of nature. Intertribal relations have been crucial to our evolution as a species.

On the other hand, relationships with other groups were sometimes uninvited and occasionally resulted in brutal conquest by tribal outsiders. Failure to be wary of foreign threats could place communities and individuals at risk of theft, infection from unknown pathogens, torture, rape, enslavement, or even extermination. To be indifferent to this possibility and forsake a vigilant posture toward the intentions of outsiders could lead one's group, in the case of genocide, toward extinction.

The tension between these two predispositions has been an evolutionary selection pressure for *both* human phenotypes, which in some ways can map onto our current left-right partisan divide. Liberal unitarians are the modern xenophiles who perpetually conflict with the conservative securitarian xenophobes of the present day. At some times and in some places, this tension can escalate to civil war.

Those on the unitarian Left keep their eagle eye on the possible corruption and autocratic tendencies of our leaders and the way those deemed outsiders are often mistreated. Extreme income inequality is seen as a threat. This is not just because the privileged few can monopolize resources but also because their disproportionate wealth allows them undue and corrupt influence under our current system. Therefore, unitarians believe that measures must be taken to alleviate these disparities. In addition, unitarians make the intuitive assumption that people of all nations are connected through a global network of mutual influences. Collaboration—not conflict, isolation, or conquest—is the guiding ethos of this worldview.

The Tribe of Humanity

Another body of compelling research taps into a cluster of traits similar to what Hibbing has found in unitarians. For decades, Sam McFarland has been studying people who identify with humanity as a whole—not just a political party, religion, locality, or nation-state. He even developed a way to measure that trait, the Identify with All of Humanity (IWAH) scale.[44] That enabled him to look at other psychological characteristics associated with high or low scores on that measure. McFarland has shown that those who view themselves as belonging to the broad tribe of all humanity also tend to be more empathic, caring for others, and open to new experiences. In addition, they are more likely to embrace transnational notions of universal justice, attribute a full range of human emotions to ethnic out-groups, see themselves as liberal, and align with the Democratic Party.[45]

Those who score low on that scale tend to be ethnocentric, authoritarian, prefer relationships of domination, identify as Christian fundamentalists, and privilege in-group loyalty above other moral values. The IWAH scale predicts more than attitudes and other psychological traits. Those who score high on that measure *behave* differently in the world. They educate themselves about global humanitarian concerns, donate to international charities, and make practical commitments to global human rights. For example, a study compared human rights organization Amnesty International members with executives at the helm of various chambers of commerce. While the scores of business leaders did not appreciably differ from those in the general population sample, Amnesty activists scored above the 75th percentile, with 42 percent showing results in the 99th percentile.[46] While the findings of that research may not be surprising, they remind us that an *inclusive* form of tribal identity exists, and probably always has, alongside the more exclusionary xenophobic variety. In the early history of the United States, that outlook was best articulated by one of the handful of founding fathers who opposed slavery in deed and words,[47] Thomas Paine. He said, "The world is my country, all mankind are my brethren, and to do good is my religion."[48] It would be hard to find a more succinct expression of a liberal worldview.

When Insiders Look Like Outsiders

Those on the securitarian right not only suspect that outsiders can't be trusted, but there are always possible tribal traitors on the inside who might be in league with those who would seek to do us harm—a proverbial "fifth column." The only way to stay safe is to separate ourselves geographically and socially from those who are different and remain well-armed. We must not only support the police without question (unless they are trying to keep armed "patriots" out of government buildings) but also militarize them to combat the criminal gangs in our midst adequately.

From the securitarian perspective, lawbreakers must be punished harshly with long sentences. Because criminals are fundamentally bad people, they cannot be rehabilitated and will always pose an outsider threat. Non-white people have to be viewed with suspicion because they live in communities where crime is an acceptable way of life. As the daily Fox News stories tell us, they always look for ways to break into our homes, shoot us in our beds, and take our stuff. While they might not be as bright as white people, they are more aggressive.

In their view, liberals must be defeated by any means necessary because they want to let felons loose, disarm the police, confiscate the guns of good citizens, and allow non-white people to take over the country and ultimately replace us. That's why Jews and other white liberals constantly fight for the interests of Mexicans and Blacks. Those same left-wing forces are always wanting to cut the national defense budget. They hate white Christian Americans and want to weaken us. They side with our enemies and want to surrender our sovereignty to outsider countries like China. Liberals even want to brainwash our children through public education. The Left pushes a hate-America and anti-God curriculum—teaching about the history of slavery, promoting homosexuality by telling kids that it is okay to be gay, and using science to undermine our children's faith in biblical truth.

Increasingly, those on the Right define the enemy as fellow citizens who support dangerous outsiders, which seems to be propelling us toward some iteration of civil war. As Hibbing's research shows, it is not just that 75 percent of the MAGA faction feel threatened by immigrants, but that 74 percent also view liberals as a threat. Those on the Left, the "unitarians," are not dangerous because of any direct violent threat they might pose. Instead, securitarians see them as permitting our country to be "invaded" by dark-skinned immigrants who want to rape "our" women, impose their religions, steal our jobs, and go on welfare. (Conservatives seem not to have pondered the contradiction in the latter two points.) Liberals are also a threat because they support government intrusion into "private" life, such as pandemic mask requirements and vaccine mandates.[49] Yet, somehow the Supreme Court mandate that unwanted pregnancies must be carried to term is not regarded by those on the Right as an infringement on personal autonomy.

Because 69 percent of Hibbing's liberal subjects feel threatened by conservatives,[50] some might argue that these two phenotypes are symmetrical. However, this is another area where the "both sides" argument falls apart on closer examination. It seems self-evident that the danger is coming mainly from the Right, at least in terms of physical peril. They have been much more likely to be unvaccinated, unmasked, and COVID-infected than liberals. Moreover, they believe that any requirement to do anything to protect others is an intolerable violation of their fundamental rights.[51]

It is in the area of deliberate and targeted violence where any claim of equivalence reveals its falsity. Those on the Right possess a vast and growing number of military-style weapons. They also have a well-documented history of using and threatening to use them against unarmed citizens, Congressional representatives, and ethnic minorities deemed internal outsiders.[52] When their leader, Donald Trump, issues a MAGA fatwa, his obedient followers respond. So far, there appear to be no liberal militias, death threats against right-wing school board members or nonpartisan election officials, or attempted kidnappings of Republican governors. Unlike the fear experienced by the Right, liberal fear of the tribal other—conservatives—has not manifested itself as armed violence. Instead, liberal fear seems to be organized around the realistic possibility that freelance MAGA terrorists will act on their threats.

That brings to mind a warning from Alexander Hamilton and James Madison that still echoes across the centuries about the greatest threat facing the United States. They anticipated that it would not come from an outsider threat but from an internal faction in pursuit of domination and unmitigated self-interest. They would be a militant force "adverse to the rights of other citizens or the permanent and aggregate interests of the community."[53] That bears a striking similarity to the concerns of Hibbing's unitarians. And the threat depicted seems like a pretty good description of the MAGA faction's current political ambitions.

One of the many insights we can glean from the January 6 insurrection against the presidential vote count is the extent to which securitarians view untrustworthy members of their tribe as dangerous. No one in Trump's circle came close to Pence's fawning servility, but that did not protect him. The effort to lynch the vice president for refusing to overturn the election shows that, in Trumpworld, no matter how sycophantic one might be to the boss, even the slightest failure to align with him could have lethal consequences.

The Psychology Behind Our Political Passions

One of the strengths of Hibbing's framework and the survey items that formed the basis of his theory is that he is looking at attitudes and traits that are not explicitly linked to hot-button political issues, like abortion, prayer in schools, or welfare policy. Unlike some measures of authoritarianism, he avoids those questions because they would make the questionnaire simply a tautological index of conservative beliefs and not necessarily reveal the upstream psychological predispositions that *result* in particular political stances and opinions.[54]

Along those lines, one of the most repeated findings of research looking at the many psychological differences between liberals and conservatives is the tendency of those on the Right to be less open to new experiences.[55] This well-established conservative aversion to the novel or strange seems to extend to unfamiliar or different-looking humans in the form of xenophobia. Causality could also operate in the other direction. In other words, it is possible that the evolutionary selection for outsider suspicion became generalized to strangeness more broadly. In any case, based on the knowledge of the presence or absence of this trait—openness to new experiences in general or new (outsider) humans more specifically—it seems likely that it would predict someone's stance on a variety of political issues, like immigration, voting rights laws, and defense spending. Were there further research to confirm that speculation, it would tell us that the tendency to welcome outsiders or build a wall against them is more foundational to partisan identity than anything on the ballot at a given moment.

The Politics of Disgust and Purity

Disgust is a primary human emotion that has kept us safe from toxic substances and pathogens throughout history. The sensory pathways of Homo sapiens have evolved to be highly attuned to markers of decay, rot, infection, and contamination of all sorts. Unfortunately, this well-developed capacity for revulsion has long been recruited by propagandists and directed at out-groups, often comparing tribal others to vermin, insects, pollution, and disease. And in many places, such as Nazi Germany, Rwanda, the Balkans, and Myanmar, these attributions have paved the way to genocide by making minorities or other out-groups seem not quite human.

Conservatives tend to equate being "dirty" with being "bad." Humans cross-culturally are inclined to associate cleanliness with orderliness. And both tend to be linked with moral virtue. That is especially characteristic of those on the Right. The assertion of absolute purity, goodness, and righteousness is often facilitated by disowning and projecting one's own moral, sexual, and literal dirt onto tribal others. And sometimes, those tribal others are forced to embody those projections of filth, such as in the Warsaw ghetto and Nazi death camps where inmates were prevented from maintaining physical hygiene and positioned to be literal vectors of disease. A few years ago, we witnessed a similar process in Trump's immigrant detention facilities along the southern border. Reporters described the asphyxiating stench due to deliberate overcrowding and lack of hygiene facilities.[56] Those put in such a position are forced to function as the psychic toilets of their captors.

The research on personality differences between liberals and conservatives has repeatedly shown greater disgust sensitivity of those on the Right.[57] Conservatives tend to be particularly concerned with *racial* purity. Going back to America's "one-drop rule" that guided the determination of race in the nineteenth century, it was clear that "negritude" was perceived by many as a contaminant that rendered an offspring not "purely" white. In the Jim Crow South, the imperative to separate races extended to water fountains, swimming pools, and bathrooms, as if Blackness were contagious.

Former slave states were so preoccupied with codifying racial purity in law and protecting whiteness from imagined threats that Nazi lawyers traveled to the United States to study American racial jurisprudence more closely. They used our statutes as templates for their race laws.[58] Ironically, among Nazi legal scholars, there was a lively debate (while debates were still possible) about whether American race laws were perhaps too harsh to be adopted by Hitler's regime.

There have been multiple expressions of right-wing disgust at the political enemies du jour in the present era. Sometimes it was powerful women who were depicted as repellent outsiders. Trump famously voiced his revulsion at female emanations, whether it was Megyn Kelly's "bleeding from wherever" or Hillary Clinton's debate bathroom break, which he found "disgusting." For the most part, however, his most frequent expressions of disgust were reserved for immigrants, brown ones in particular.

In *Mein Kampf*, Adolf Hitler warned of the non-Aryan "contamination of the blood," which he regarded as a "poison invading the national body." In an echo of the leader who promised to "make Germany great again,"[59] Donald Trump also seemed to fulminate against racial pollution. In a 2023 interview with a right-wing website, he said immigrants were "poisoning the blood of our country." He went on, "It's so bad, and people are coming in with disease. People are coming in with every possible thing you could have."[60] In addition, he claimed that non-white immigrants were being disgorged by foreign "insane asylums," an assertion that, like his other attributions to immigrants, was wholly without foundation.[61]

The former Fox News white nationalist and Trump acolyte, Tucker Carlson, echoed those sentiments. He said foreigners seeking to enter this country would "make the US dirtier."[62] That brings to mind the famously pithy definition of dirt proffered by anthropologist Mary Douglas as "matter out of place." And that appears to be precisely how conservatives, especially the MAGA faction, view immigrant outsiders.

One way to understand what makes some people vulnerable to anti-immigrant appeals is to consider the role of what evolutionary scientists refer to as "the behavioral immune system."[63] That is an intuitive psychological mechanism that has evolved throughout human history, leading people to avoid potential sources of pathogens based on specific sensory cues. They might be a foul smell, a bad taste, and an abnormal appearance, or all three that evoke disgust. Certain substances with a high risk of microbial contagion are especially potent in activating that response, such as feces, vomit, and other bodily fluids. Sometimes, specific physical differences that might suggest illness or even subtle variations in expected physiognomy can induce fear and avoidance. Despite the high rate of false alarms, evolution readily selected it because of the trait's survival advantage. At some times and places, this mechanism extended to certain social groups, especially unfamiliar outsiders or members of one's group that displayed strange or unusual qualities.

There are notable parallels between our physiological immune system and the behavioral one described here. To avoid an overreaction of our immune cells, they must develop tolerance. In other words, they have to learn not to react (most of the time) to things like foods and our own bodies. Achieving that tolerance requires recognizing the molecular markers of genuinely harmful pathogens and differentiating them from those on our organs and other tissues.

Sometimes, our immune cells encounter a bacterial or viral pathogen that might bear a superficial resemblance to parts of our own body. While our immune system can remember the threatening microorganism, it may get paranoid and attack anything resembling it. That is one way we can develop an autoimmune disease. Ironically, these efforts at self-protection can result in severe and sometimes life-threatening harm.

Similarly, our behavioral immune system often produces false positives, especially when directed at people. "Why do we want all these people from shithole countries coming here?" former president Donald Trump asked in a 2018 White House meeting.[64] A mechanism that evolved to avoid danger can, out of ignorance or political utility, identify unfamiliar people, such as members of other racial or ethnic groups or immigrants, as threats that must be avoided or attacked.[65] We intuitively misinterpret markers of difference as markers of danger, an error that can be harmful, even lethal, to both them and us.

No provocation is required for those predisposed to respond this way, like today's MAGA faction members. For others, a trigger might be needed to activate this behavioral immune response. The activation could be the drumbeat of xenophobic pre-war propaganda or the regular infusions of Fox News stories about dusky home invaders or immigrant caravans.

This psychological "immune" response manifesting in disgust toward outsiders also can be elicited by a preexisting concern about pathogens and disease.[66] Interestingly, high pathogen infection rates in some areas of the United

States are highly associated with anti-immigrant attitudes.[67] Of course, there could be other variables upstream from those effects. For example, we would expect Republican-dominated state governments to have poor public health outcomes (as described in the introduction) and feature more anti-immigrant rhetoric in its public discourse.

Those on the Right may have a literal distaste for strangers. Perhaps related to their lower threshold for disgust, conservatives possess more bitter taste receptors and a greater sensitivity to bitterness. The density of tongue papillae (one way of assessing taste sensitivity) predicts the likelihood of holding conservative beliefs. The study's authors note that disgust sensitivity partially mediates this relationship.[68] In other words, the more easily you feel disgust, the more likely that having more bitter taste receptors will predict conservatism. Interestingly, partisans who tend to taste bitterness more readily also seem to exhibit more emotional bitterness and grievance. However, there is no evidence that I'm aware of that would show a causal relationship.

Here I must include an important caveat. The association between disgust sensitivity and conservatism cannot justify a conclusion that being a Republican is somehow pathological. A conservative could easily argue that the research shows that liberals are clueless regarding the dangers of both pathogens and foreigners. They might point to the mass death through infectious diseases inflicted upon native peoples by infected European colonizers throughout the Americas over the last half dozen centuries. Unwanted immigration (i.e., invasion), they might hasten to add, has a well-documented history of lethality—whether from pathogens or armed marauders.

Conservative Pandemic Denial and the Failure of Disgust

That caveat aside, the biggest problem with current conservative disgust-mediated xenophobia is the Right's failure to act on their instinct for pathogen avoidance in any rational way. The Republican's paradoxical response to the COVID-19 pandemic starkly illustrates this failure. Given their proclivities, we might have expected them to apply their greater capacity for disgust and microbial threat salience to the goal of protecting themselves and their loved ones from a devastating and often lethal pathogen. Instead, for multiple reasons examined later in this book, public health measures—vaccinations, masking, and social distancing—were viewed as the actual threats. And those who advocated for them—doctors, nurses, and scientists—were often verbally and physically attacked as the disgusting, invasive outsiders. In fact, as of this writing, GOP members of Congress are vowing to investigate and perhaps prosecute

Dr. Anthony Fauci, purportedly for his role in various baroque conspiracies.[69] His real "crimes" seem to have been treating COVID-19 as an actual threat, advocating for public health measures to address it, and generally refuting MAGA disinformation, including bogus treatments.

Republican politicians from the former president on down alternately insisted the pandemic was unreal, benign, or the consequence of various global conspiracies. When it was acknowledged, the pandemic was blamed on various tribal outsiders like China. GOP mayors and governors pursued policies and enacted laws that actively sought to increase the spread of COVID, even at the cost of killing their constituents. Quack cure recommendations and anti-vax hysteria resounded throughout the right-wing media ecosystem, leading to a profoundly partisan asymmetry in the death toll. Those who refused vaccines and died in ICUs were disproportionately Trump voters.[70] As a political strategy, however, this approach worked. Biden, who did what he could to counter Republican disinformation, was nevertheless blamed by a majority of the country for the failure of the pandemic to resolve.[71]

The Road from Xenophobic Disgust to Voter Suppression

By December 2021, the Brennan Center for Justice counted thirty-four voting restriction laws that GOP-dominated state legislatures passed in nineteen states.[72] And 440 more were introduced in forty-nine states in 2021 alone. In addition, nonpartisan election officials are being replaced by Republican appointees to enable the nullification of election results that don't lead to GOP victories. These laws will provide a legal route to a GOP seizure of power locally and nationally. That will enable them to achieve what the January 6 coup attempt, a slate of fake electors,[73] MAGA death threats against poll workers, and Trump's efforts to intimidate election officials from his own party could not.[74] And unsurprisingly, Senate Republicans in January 2022 voted unanimously against voting rights legislation that might have mitigated some of the worst effects of these laws.

After spearheading that vote, Senate Minority Leader Mitch McConnell uttered a breathtaking slip of the tongue. Explaining why national voting rights legislation was unnecessary, he said, "Well, the concern is misplaced because if you look at the statistics, African American voters are voting in just as high a percentage as Americans."[75] While he likely did not intend to phrase his views this way, it was consistent with his colleagues' worldview and the MAGA base: Non-white voters are tribal outsiders. Therefore, their unrestricted enfranchisement must be held in check if "we" are to remain in power.

This interpretation might be an unjustified overreach had McConnell not made this "misstatement" in the context of his party's actions over the past decades. But that is not the case. From Nixon's quaintly subtle "Southern Strategy" to Reagan's not-so-subtle dog whistle about "welfare queens" to Trump's bull-horn appeals to white nationalism, the GOP has long made it quite clear who are "we" and who are "they."

Moreover, the red-state anti-democracy laws disproportionately impact communities of color.[76] And, of course, that is the point. As much as Republican officials across the country deny the existence of systemic racism and are rushing to ban the teaching of this concept in schools, they are work-ing feverishly to inscribe it into the voting system. White Republicans are becoming demographic dinosaurs: xenophobes whose numbers are steadily shrinking.[77]

Key features of the current American political system—the Electoral College, the Senate, and the filibuster—are already skewed toward the over-representation of a rural conservative minority. However, the percentage of the population that embraces the GOP worldview is diminishing so fast that the bias built into the present system may be insufficient to nullify the will of the pro-democracy and multiracial majority.

Preempting the political consequences of that "problem" requires a three-pronged strategy. First, through partisan demagogues like Tucker Carlson, the media wing of the GOP needs to ramp up efforts to activate xenophobic anx-ieties in the base and link those fears to the voter-fraud fiction and Trump's stolen election lie.

Second, racial bias has to be embedded into the legal infrastructure of voting. While the language of anti-voting laws will always appear race-neutral, other actions make the racial logic obvious. It is revealed by the districts they target with gerrymandering, the banning or restriction of voting by mail, the elimination of Sunday voting, the removal of drop boxes, and the radical reduction of polling locations in specific neighborhoods.

Third, Republican functionaries at both a local and national level must engage in a multifront campaign to deny the history and present reality of sys-temic racism. As members of the MAGA faction utilize voter apathy to place themselves on local school boards, they seek to incorporate this denial into history curricula, in which unpleasant facts about the history of race relations in the United States are disallowed. The notion that racial bias is structured into the political and economic system independently of individual prejudice is readily dismissed as the whining bleats of liberals and minorities seeking special privileges. If those efforts succeed, they will help to blunt the possibility of white voters empathizing and aligning with voters of color.

The Limits of "Authoritarianism" as an Explanation for the GOP War on Democracy

The MAGA faction is determined to rig elections (the disavowed reality behind the projection discernible in their "stop the steal" meme) and support autocracy at home and abroad. As a result, many observers and social scientists have described the current GOP leaders as authoritarian and their base as authoritarian personalities. Hibbing has criticized the use of this label to explain MAGA voters. He claims that the base's autocratic sensibility is not a character trait but a "situational" tactic. Were there democratic means for their revered leaders to ascend to and hold power, they would be situational democrats. He argues that what matters to them is how their xenophobic program can be implemented.[78]

However, Hibbing's counterfactual hypothesis is unlikely ever to be tested. As described above, the GOP white base is a shrinking minority and would lose a genuinely democratic election. And they seem to understand that, hence their apparent support for the slash-and-burn campaign against voting rights their representatives are pushing.

Nevertheless, Hibbing's critique of the authoritarian personality construct has a lot of merits. He identifies the main weakness of that framework, which is attributing a context-independent set of traits to those who love and obey dictators. Qualities such as submissiveness, conformity, aggression, and reverence for conventional norms and religion are primary characteristics that comprise what some call the authoritarian personality. Hibbing's work shows that these traits don't apply to all base members across the board. And more importantly, they are expressed in some situations, but not all, toward some authorities and not others, and primarily to achieve particular aims.[79]

As anyone who has witnessed the most ardent Trumpers at rallies knows, they are hardly docile. They rigidly conform to the expectations of *their* group but not those of the larger society. They can be pretty violent and function as a national lynch mob. The victims of their violence are not selected randomly but are determined by the political needs of their leader. Also, those in the Trump base have contempt for many social norms. Authoritarian behaviors are expressed but primarily to serve their overarching goal—protecting the tribe from outsiders perceived as a threat. Like their leader, members of the MAGA faction will break any law, defy any convention, assault any opponent, defy any legitimate authority, and pervert any religious ethic—as long as they believe such actions will serve tribal security.

The embrace of traditional religiosity, especially fundamentalist creeds, is often associated with authoritarianism. And indeed, the GOP base can sound like one of their aims is a Christian theocracy. Some can appear profoundly religious and might view *The Handmaid's Tale* as a utopian fantasy, like so many "people of faith." However, they are very selective in their reverence for scripture. They love the vengeance in extracting "an eye for an eye." However, they recoil at the injunction to "turn the other cheek."[80]

More to the point, what they love about Christianity is not any homily attributed to Jesus but the crucifixion itself. That is the part of the story they identify with the most. Hibbing says, "Securitarians are in their element when they believe they are under siege."[81] Their favorite narratives are those that involve fantasies of their persecution. In the face of perceived out-group threats, they know what to do: build walls and, if necessary, go to war. Every December, we can count on Fox News to dust off one of their most coveted holiday fables, the War on Christmas.[82] Nothing activates their audience more than imagining that Jews, Muslims, atheists, and other spiritual outsiders want to attack white Christians by wishing them a "happy holiday." So, ardent religiosity, like so many authoritarian traits, is manifested by the MAGA faction. However, it is an epiphenomenal quality brought into being by the imperatives of securitarian tribalism.

Of Mice and MAGA

One of the most intriguing suggestions in Hibbing's work concerns the possible genetic links to the securitarian phenotype. He describes the work of Hopi Hoekstra, a Harvard biologist. She was fascinated by a particular difference between two otherwise similar species of mice. Oldfield mice create burrows that feature escape tunnels. Should a predator such as a snake show up at the entrance to their burrow, they can flee out the back. Deer mice, on the other hand, while closely resembling their Oldfield cousins, don't seem to concern themselves with such contingencies, as they never build escape tunnels.

Hoekstra and her colleagues discovered that Oldfield mice, raised in cages where digging was not possible, nevertheless, when placed in environments where their instincts could be expressed, began to create burrows with tunnels. When crossbred with deer mice, the offspring made burrows featuring bugout passageways. The implication is that this behavior is genetically driven and controlled by dominant genes over those of the less industrious deer mice. A mix of offspring was produced once the heterozygous prepper mice (those with only one copy of the Oldfield mouse genes) were further bred with deer mice. Some were tunnel builders, and others were not. That enabled Hoekstra and her team to analyze the genetic differences between the mice that intuitively prepared for outsider threats and those that did not. She discovered that a tiny portion of DNA on Chromosome 5 programmed this behavior.

What is remarkable is that the Oldfield mice were not more anxious and did not have any prior experience with predators. Instead, they arrive in the world with a genetic predisposition to ward off the dangers of intruders.

While humans are far more complex creatures than mice, we are also animals subject to genetic influences that increase or decrease the probability of certain behaviors. And we know that humans display a similar set of binary phenotypes. One, the securitarians, are instinctively focused on the possible threats that outsiders pose. The other, unitarians, are welcoming to outsiders and more worried about corruption and injustice within their groups. Furthermore, Hibbing's research suggests that securitarian and unitarian personality traits are stable over the life course of individuals.[83]

While specific genes that are responsible for the expression of these personality phenotypes have not been identified, there is some evidence for the heritability of prejudice against out-groups.[84] And there is good evidence that the variance in political ideology generally has a substantial genetic component.[85] In another study of over twelve thousand pairs of twins, assessed over forty years, and in five different democratic nations, heritability accounted for 30–60 percent of the variation in how subjects positioned themselves on a "Left-Right" continuum, regardless of how it was defined.[86] Nevertheless, outsider fear and hostility are among the most consistent and defining features of right-wing identity. It is readily observable across multiple nations.[87] So it is not such a great leap to infer from the genetic links to conservatism and liberalism more generally a significant heritable factor involved in the unitarian and securitarian personalities

The fact that eugenic, reductionist, and deterministic models of heredity have been rightly tossed in the dustbin of intellectual dead ends is no reason to avoid examining its role in human social life. Current partisan identities are too recent to be products of evolution. And political cognition and behavior are much too complex to be driven by a few genes. Genome-wide association studies, which look at the possible associations between particular traits and genetic variations, have found that genetic influences on political behavior result from many genes with minor effects.[88] That is similar to the role of genes in other complex behaviors.

While an oversimplification, a gene could be thought of as a blueprint for manufacturing certain biochemicals, such as neurotransmitters or hormones. When it is activated, a gene initiates a process of synthesis that eventually leads to a specific chemical. That substance, in turn, induces various physiological events, including attitudes and behaviors toward others. Those two personality phenotypes, securitarian and unitarian, seem to result from evolutionary selection pressures and are thus partially driven by genetic predispositions. If so, we might see biochemical differences between those who fear and hate outsiders and those who feel a kinship with them. The hormone oxytocin might be a gene product that helps make sense of these radically different forms of human tribalism.

When Love Becomes Hatred: The Oxytocin Story

Many refer to it as the "love drug." Oxytocin is a hormone produced in the hypothalamus, a forebrain region, and released into the bloodstream by the posterior pituitary gland. It affects many organs and impacts multiple functions. By stimulating uterine contractions, oxytocin accelerates labor and thus speeds up childbirth. It plays a role in infant-mother attachment and the production of milk. And it is a significant catalyst in forming bonds between people more generally. Even between dogs and humans, physical affection increases and is increased by oxytocin in both parties.[89] Understandably, it has been called the "cuddle chemical." But there is a less sanguine side to this neurochemical.

In double-blind and placebo-controlled trials, subjects were randomly assigned to different groups.[90] Subjects who were administered oxytocin increased their expression of bias toward their group and increased the propensity to derogate members of other groups—two qualities that make up ethnocentrism and potentially intergroup violence. The effect of increased in-group favoritism was more robust than out-group hostility, which the researchers interpreted as indicating the latter was secondary to the former. In other words, the main effects were to increase identification with, loyalty toward, empathy with, and trust in one's tribe. The sense that there is something to protect and wall off from outsiders would thus increase. That is how a pro-social attitude toward "us" could translate into an anti-social stance toward "them."

Not surprisingly, oxytocin can also increase conformity to one's group.[91] In another double-blind, placebo-controlled study, this neurohormone facilitated cooperation among in-group members, enabling them to attack out-groups more efficiently.[92] Researchers have made sense of the seemingly paradoxical effects of oxytocin through the social salience hypothesis.[93] Because oxytocin increases the salience of one's social relationships, one is both attuned to its many rewards as well as threats to it. For example, in nonhuman animal mothers, oxytocin increases the bond with her offspring and the ferocity with which she protects those infants from outsider threats. So, when it comes to tribal bonds that are exclusive rather than inclusive, hatred becomes the paradoxical consequence of love. This observation is consistent with Hibbing's thesis that, for securitarians, the problem with "them" is that they are not "us."[94]

In a third double-blind and placebo-controlled experiment, oxytocin increased the likelihood that group members would lie if it seemed to benefit their group, even when the dishonesty did not serve the individuals them-selves.[95] These findings are especially intriguing given how lying, conspiracy theories, and the repudiation of historical and scientific factuality seem so intrinsic to MAGA faction political tribalism.

I hasten to point out that this detour into the fascinating social and polit-ical implications of oxytocin levels is not intended as a singular explanation of xenophobia. Instead, I offer it as a speculative model for how genetic differences in neurohormone levels or function could conceivably lead to distinctive per-sonality phenotypes. Further research will be needed to demonstrate whether or which hormones mediate the hereditable differences in attitudes toward out-siders identified in studies.

Be Afraid, Very Afraid

Fear is another primal emotion that animates political passion and is often upstream from many policies and candidate preferences. The George W. Bush administration made the felicitous discovery that the president's approval rat-ing went up every time they raised the color-coded terrorist threat level. That led to pressure on then Homeland Security Secretary Tom Ridge to increase the level just before the 2004 presidential election.[96] We will likely never know how many times they jerked that chain gratuitously. Nevertheless, it does illus-trate the political utility of frightening citizens, especially when the threat the government conjures can be located in outsiders. It is no wonder that Trump's initial rhetorical move in his first presidential campaign was a jeremiad against Mexican "rapists" and the magic wall he would build to protect us from them.

In the past, conservative threat salience had translated into intuitive sup-port for the military, police, and spy agencies. In the Trump era, a very counter-intuitive development emerged. Right-wing threat sensitivity translated into opposition to those same forces of law and order when they challenged the former president's and his allies' impunity. This shift highlights how fungible the object of fear can be. In this case, the forces that conservatives once viewed as protective are now seen as the danger from which they needed protection. As the MAGA GOP now openly endorses autocracy, their members of Congress increasingly take the position that the law of the ruler should eclipse the rule of law.

We have witnessed a move in the opposite direction for liberals. They viewed the FBI and CIA as suspicious, if not malevolent entities, until the Trump era. One reason for this reversal, which I discuss in greater detail in later chapters, is that these institutions of law and order came up against Trump's open cor-ruption, treasonous alliance with foreign dictators, and brazen assertions of impunity. Consequently, many on the Left even surprised themselves by valorizing those law enforcement agencies and seeing them as potential instruments of justice.

Many scholars have described the greater threat salience of conservatives. But as Hibbing notes, the concerns that drive the MAGA faction are pretty specific—tribal outsiders, especially non-white immigrants, and the American liberals who seem to welcome them. In his research, "Trump venerators" (his term for subjects who believed that Trump was "one of the very best presidents in the entire history of our country") listed immigration as their top concern by a wide margin over eighteen other issues. National defense and security (arguably, another issue saturated with outsider anxiety) came in second.[97] Notably, the only difference between them and "non–Trump-venerating conservatives" was the magnitude of their anti-immigrant concerns.

The brains of conservatives get more activated in response to negative imagery (fear or disgust-inducing).[98] Those of liberals respond more to positive images. Interestingly, the negative images that disproportionately activated liberal brains were pictures of others suffering—suggesting the possibility of greater empathy by liberals. The area that lights up in this condition is called somatosensory 2. That result is consistent with findings discussed in this chapter regarding conservatives' relatively diminished empathy and compassion and, thus, greater proneness to sadism. Researchers blinded to the political orientation of subjects could successfully predict it based just on the patterns of brain activation seen on neuroimaging.

Hibbing argues that threat salience is not necessarily fear.[99] In his view, conservatives focus more on the negative, not because of fear but because they give potential threats more attention. However, fear and attention may not be mutually exclusive states. We know that people can respond in variable ways to fear. Some might flee. Some might fight. Others might freeze (a response seen in prey animals). Still, others might pay vigilant attention, like the conservative subjects in these studies. So, it seems quite possible that fear might activate attention circuits for some people.

Neuroscientist Robert Sapolsky has noted that conservatives aren't alone in having elevated threat sensitivity.[100] It is possible to induce a transient conservative worldview in liberals under experimental conditions by evoking fear. Others have replicated this fascinating finding. Consistent with these studies is the hoary aphorism that defines a conservative as a liberal who's been mugged.[101]

It is not just fear that can pull liberals in a conservative direction. Other researchers have found that liberal thinking is characterized by a greater tolerance for ambiguity and an increased capacity for context-dependent cognition and complexity in general.[102] That imposes a significant demand on the brain, enhancing what psychologists call the "cognitive load." Many things can compromise one's ability to manage this increased cognitive load, like stress, threats to one's safety, multiple demands, and even alcohol. That can lead to a shift to conservative modes of thinking, as if the brain is switching to a weaker reserve battery once its main power supply is exhausted.

However, if you're good at something, that task is easier. Since conservatives are well-practiced at threat detection, it's less of a cognitive load for them than for liberals. The amygdala is the area of the brain that specializes in threat salience. Neuroanatomical studies have shown that the brains of conservative subjects are blessed with larger amygdalae.[103] While no one has confirmed the direction of causality, I suspect it may be bidirectional. In other words, as conservatives practice threat monitoring, they may induce a neuroplastic hypertrophic change in their amygdalae. And, the more "muscular" that part of their brains becomes, the more effective they could get at attending to potential threats.

In fact, for those on the Right, threats may be coveted as much as they are feared. The need to attend to dangerous outsiders is such a powerful *raison d'être* for conservatives that dealing with threatening others seems to be a deeply rewarding enterprise. Tasha Adams, the ex-wife of Stewart Rhodes, who founded the Oath Keepers right-wing militia group and has been convicted of seditious conspiracy for the January 6 coup attempt, captured this sensibility well. She recalled her life among these MAGA militants: "They hear civil war. To them, this is the civil war they've been waiting for. A lot of these guys live for this … They spend their lives preparing for it. They look forward to it."[104]

That possibility is suggested by the findings of a large multinational study that included non-Western and Western nations.[105] Right-wing subjects from countries experiencing high threat levels (operationalized as a combination of economic peril, lower life expectancy, and increased homicide rate) had far greater happiness and well-being than left-wing subjects. The differences were negligible in nations with low levels of threat. We can only speculate about the reasons for this association. One possibility is that it can be very satisfying when one's concerns match reality. If one expects danger and it shows up, it reduces ambiguity, and the world makes sense.

CHAPTER 2

Tribal Mind/Tribal Brain—
Dominance, Guilt, Shame,
and Empathy

"Feminazi." The infamous anti-feminist term of derision was first coined by Rush Limbaugh, the talk radio ur-troll who has offered inspiration to generations of embittered restraining-ordered ex-husbands, right-wing misogynists, and neofascist incels. It was a slur directed at women who lobbied for equal rights in politics and public life, one that revealed far more than his bemused contempt for "uppity" women. The ease with which advocates for equality could so easily get imagined as jack-booted dominatrices highlights a core feature of conservative psychology.

For the past seven years, soldiers of the MAGA culture war have agreed on one thing; the most satisfying among the spoils of victory is the feeling of "owning the libs." It is a phrase that evokes a fantasy of conquest but in a more Sisyphean crusade, i.e., one that never ends. It is the titillating frisson that Trumpworld trolls enjoy after believing that they have humiliated, offended, or traumatized liberals. While that phrase may evoke multiple associations, *ownership* readily brings to mind slavery—the most primal expression of the ownership of other humans. It is also the ultimate expression of domination, an aim that drives and even defines conservatism—from the Confederacy to the present moment, from Rush Limbaugh to Donald Trump.

Power as a Zero-Sum Game

Conservatives are known to be quite comfortable with hierarchical relationships between groups as long as they are on top.[1] And perhaps, as a result, their well-being tends to be unperturbed by conditions of social inequality.[2]

As we might expect, that is much less the case for liberals. Researchers refer to this preference for group-based inequality as "social dominance orientation" (SDO).[3] SDO is a personality trait found in multiple cultures and is characterized by approval of oppression and aggressive behavior directed at out-groups. Unsurprisingly, Hibbing's securitarian Trump venerators scored relatively high on a measure designed to assess this quality. The anti-egalitarianism of such individuals translates into support for a wide range of "hierarchy-enhancing" social policies and candidates. Those with a high SDO are predictably more bigoted toward many out-groups—the poor, ethnic and racial minorities, immigrants, refugees, and non-heterosexuals.

That derogation and subordination of tribal outsiders seem to be the organizing core of a surprisingly coherent worldview. As the developers of this concept and associated measure point out, SDO predicts:

> ...the endorsement of a range of group-relevant social *ideologies*, including political conservatism, noblesse oblige, just world beliefs, nationalism, patriotism, militarism, internal attributions for poverty, sexism, rape myths, endorsement of karma, the Protestant Work Ethic, and other consequential hierarchy-enhancing legitimizing beliefs, across a variety of cultures, [as well as] support for wars of aggression, punitive criminal justice policies, the death penalty and torture, and opposition to humanitarian practices, social welfare, and affirmative action.[4]

The authors of that SDO study point out that all those ideologies and policy positions are outgrowths of a social dominance orientation. That is why people who hold some of these beliefs often adhere to all the others. In other words, they are correlated in the minds of conservatives because they derive from a common personality trait. It is a characteristic that also seems to have a significant genetic component[5] based on studies comparing identical and fraternal twins.

It is important to note that people can support the same policy for radically different reasons. For example, liberals tend to oppose wars of aggression, while conservatives are more likely to support them. However, at the beginning of the Iraq War, some liberals favored it, even enthusiastically. That was because the initial propaganda for that intervention framed it as a rescue mission to save oppressed Iraqis, which tapped into the liberal sense of out-group altruism—a central part of their unitarian personality orientation. So, they would be highly unlikely to endorse other beliefs often associated with supporting wars of aggression.

Conservatives supported the war but for reasons more consistent with their social dominance orientation—to punish Saddam Hussein for challenging and threatening the United States, as an expression of national entitlement to police the world, and out of a conviction that dangerous outsiders imperil us and so we must strike first. We would expect them also to endorse the other beliefs associated with an SDO, such as the notion that poverty results primarily from character flaws in the poor.

For those with a high SDO, membership in and loyalty to their tribe seems to take precedence over everything else, including policies and issue stances. In other words, conservative identity appears to be more important than conservative positions. If true, the latter would be sacrificed to preserve the former. That speculation has been affirmed in fascinating research conducted by political psychologist Lilliana Mason.[6] In experimental settings, she found that when liberal policy positions are attributed to conservative politicians, subjects who identify as Republicans tend to support them. And when those same positions are labeled in a way that suggests they originate from liberal policymakers, they are opposed. Likewise, the same Republican subjects can be persuaded to oppose conservative ideas when researchers attribute those ideas to liberal politicians.

Lest liberals feel above such tribal influences, similar findings have resulted from studies with subjects who identify as Democrats. However, Mason's work showed an *asymmetry* between Republicans and Democrats in the magnitude of tribal identity effects. She describes a 2016 Gallup poll: "In the week before the 2016 election, 16 percent of Republicans and 61 percent of Democrats believed the US economy was getting better. The week after the election, 49 percent of Republicans and 46 percent of Democrats believed the economy was improving." In other words, after only two weeks, 15 percent of Democratic voters reduced their positive assessment of the economy. Whereas 33 percent of Republicans suddenly saw the economy as better.[7] It seems likely that the greater effect of tribal identity among conservatives is attributable to their high social dominance orientation, leading them to privilege their group identity more than we see among liberals.

We can conclude that group identity eclipses reality whenever they conflict. In other words, our tribal affiliation unconsciously influences the story we tell about the facts of the world. That is particularly so when the group comprises individuals with high social dominance orientation, which is the case with the MAGA faction—now the vast majority of Republican voters.[8]

The fact that tribal identity also has primacy over issues helps us understand a few paradoxes that have baffled many. We have seen the willingness of GOP "deficit hawks" to embrace the national debt incurred by their leaders. We have also seen the sanctimonious moralizers of the Republican evangelical coalition show profound indifference to Trump's amorality, infidelity, admitted sexual predation, and blatant ignorance of anything biblical. The justifying story they tell themselves is that, like King Cyrus of ancient Persia, Trump has been chosen as a flawed vessel for God's will.[9]

Then there is the Republican reversal of the party's enmity toward Russian dictators. They were hated during the Cold War but are loved now. Putin attacked American democracy in the 2016 presidential campaign following Trump's invitation to do so, which made him a tribal ally to the GOP. At one time, any American leader who openly expressed trust in the word of a foreign autocrat over American intelligence agencies, which the former president did in his 2018 Helsinki meeting with Putin, would have been denounced by Republicans as a traitor.[10] But after he expressed it, there was no audible outrage among the MAGA faction in Washington.

Last but not least, in this catalog of identity-driven policy inversions, there is what occurred on January 6. Anyone watching the attempted coup on television could see supposedly cop-loving conservative activists using the poles attached to their Blue Lives Matter flags to bludgeon the skulls of police. As the crowd smashed its way into the Capitol Building, they chanted, "Fuck the blue!" [11] And, as mentioned earlier, erstwhile law and order zealots condemned, issued death threats, and carried out actual assaults on the FBI for daring to search Trump's estate for stolen government documents. Those actions by militant conservatives seemed to reflect another evident trait of those on the Right—a diminished capacity to appreciate irony.[12]

Mason notes that most Americans tend to *think* along liberal lines but are more likely to *identify* as conservative. So, when a party successfully appeals to that conservative identity, it will supersede those voters' beliefs or positions. Furthermore, voters tend to adopt the policy positions of the party with which they identify rather than picking a party that matches their issue stances.[13]

To a considerable extent, issues are post-hoc justifications for tribal identity.[14] So, when a tribal leader, like Trump, reverses a position held earlier, it has no impact on the approval of that leader or the loyalty of followers. Moreover, partisans, especially Republicans, would prefer to change their positions on issues if they could maintain their tribal membership.[15]

That is one crucial reason Democrats' focus on policy has become such a losing strategy. Republicans, on the other hand, seem to understand that, at the present moment, having issue positions is politically pointless. In 2020, the GOP dispensed with a platform altogether.[16] The campaign was all about tribal identity expressed through the personality cult of Donald Trump.

Given that Trump seems to have no beliefs or political principles, some might wonder why he became a Republican and, in fact, the political and spiritual leader of that party. But in light of the above, it is clear that the GOP was not an arbitrary choice. Trump's foundational psychology, his social dominance orientation, and related autocratic instincts are perfectly aligned with the mindset of conservatives, whether those in Congress or those who comprise his base. When he and his party do seem to advocate for particular issues, their SDO is the upstream driver.

While there are two types of polarization, tribal (social) and issue-based, sometimes they are fused. In other words, issues can *become* part of tribal identity. For example, Mason's research has shown that "pro-choice" and "pro-life" are stronger identities than party affiliation.[17] The strength of *identification* with an issue is more predictive of activism than is the extremity of one's issue position.[18] The power of issue identity is that it is a way of being connected to others with the same belief. So, the content is less important than the group bond being affirmed.[19] So much of politics is identity politics. The beliefs we must espouse mark us as tribal members in good standing. Issues are ideological MAGA hats or Black Lives Matter T-shirts.

Skin pigment is another one of those markers. By 2013, racial and partisan identity had become so aligned that race alone, not racial policy, strongly predicted party affiliation.[20] When partisan identities align with other social identity components (e.g., race, ideology, religion, culture), tribal boundaries become less porous, more rigid, and more emotionally compelling. And political opponents are more likely to be viewed as enemies that constitute an existential threat. As a consequence, coexistence is no longer possible. Survival mandates the defeat or destruction of those out-groups.[21]

One of the impressive cultural features of the MAGA faction is the extent to which it offers its members a profoundly aligned tribal identity. Membership weaves together many strands of identity. Even as separate threads, they constitute deeply held components of collective selfhood—whiteness, Christian belief, exurban/rural geographical residence, love of guns, and hatred of abortion. Race, religion, place, and identity-saturated issues comprise so much of what people understand themselves to be that it is easy to see why they might cling tenaciously to a tribe that can align all these vital aspects.

If certain beliefs become fused with our sense of self and membership in identity-defining groups, we might find them refractory to change in the face of disconfirming evidence. People might even double down in response to facts contradicting their deeply held notions. Indeed, this is what numerous studies using a variety of methodologies have demonstrated.

One such study examined the political echo chambers so common on social media platforms.[22] These are forums where viewers are not only exposed to a narrow slice of partisan opinion but, by responding to some posts, are flagged by platform algorithms and presented with posts even more extreme than the ones they liked. The conventional wisdom on the remedy for this sort of balkanized information process is to find a way to expose partisans to opposing points of view.

Unfortunately, when researchers ran that experiment—enabling participants to encounter views contrary to their own—subjects adhered more strongly to their prior beliefs and embraced more fringe versions of them. The researchers describe one of their subjects, an ambivalent Trump voter who held some counterintuitive liberal positions. However, after exposure to posts from prominent Democratic politicians and op-ed columnists, he went from being a center-right libertarian to an all-in, Trump-worshiping MAGA devotee. He also limited his information sources even further.

One path that can lead an issue to become bound up with identity is a threat to one's status. There are two types of status threats, those that concern outsiders and those that involve fellow tribe members. As revealed in Hibbing's research, immigrants seem to constitute the greatest outsider status threat for conservatives. They are imagined as soldiers in a swarthy army seeking to take over and replace white Christians—the relentless "caravans" of Fox-fueled nightmares. And they are seen as being welcomed by the internal outsiders among us, such as naturalized citizens, Jews, Muslims, African Americans, and Democrats.[23]

As revealed in a fascinating 2016 study of Obama-to-Trump voters, that shocking and counterintuitive shift was *not* due to a decline in the economic status of these citizens, as some pundits have speculated.[24] Instead, their attraction to Trump resulted from a fear of declining social status, a fear catalyzed by GOP and Putin-assisted campaign rhetoric. An identity as white that might have been lightly held became much more salient when galvanized by right-wing threat appeals. Those voters came to believe that as white Christians, especially males, they were about to sink to the bottom in the racial and gender privilege hierarchy—to be "replaced," as neo-Nazis would phrase it, by domestic outsiders. However, as powerful as this kind of status anxiety can be, the threat to our status *within* the tribe and rejection by "our own kind" can be even more troubling.

The Power and Pain of Tribal Exile

The most significant risk of going against the perceived interests or beliefs of the tribe is that it could lower our status with fellow members or, even worse, result in exile. Here, we get closer to the real power of tribal bonds—why people would forsake their health, financial well-being, and even their families to remain in good standing with the group.

The imperative to uphold one's status with others is the self-interest that supersedes all others. For most of human history, exile carried the risk of starvation, succumbing to human or other predators, and early death. Short of expulsion, earning the disfavor of fellow tribe members could mean reduced respect, being relegated to low-status work, a reduced share of collective resources, and foreclosed mating choices. In all probability, these potential consequences created selection pressure for individuals who privileged their standing among peers above most other considerations.

While the effects of earning the anger or rejection of one's group members may no longer be as dire (although nearly lynched Mike Pence might disagree), human minds come bundled with evolved genetic software that makes the experience a pretty aversive one. Neuroimaging studies show a striking overlap between the brain areas activated when subjects experience social pain or rejection and those regions involved in the experience of physical pain—although some of the specific neurocircuits can vary.[25] In one fascinating placebo-controlled experiment, acetaminophen, a CNS pain suppressant, reduced the subjective feeling of emotional hurt in a laboratory-generated experience of social rejection.[26] In addition, functional MRI images showed that the drug blunted the social pain regions of the brain. Subjects who received the placebo demonstrated neither of these effects.

Given our radical dependence on others, both in our prolonged infancy and throughout life, it makes evolutionary sense that there would be a reproductive advantage for those in whom social separation, especially rejection, induces profound psychic suffering. The late psychobiologist Jaak Panksepp, whose research focused on animal emotions, had postulated that the neural networks associated with attachment to others became linked to the physical pain system to ensure that emotional alarms would go off when our social bonds were at risk.[27]

So, given the anguish that ostracism by our group can induce, it is a built-in imperative to do and be whatever is necessary to retain our status as a tribal member. As we've seen in recent years, that can mean believing or appearing to believe pathological liars and utterly implausible conspiracy narratives. It can mean overthrowing democracy in the name of "patriotism." It can mean murdering or threatening to murder any individual or group whom our tribe or its leader has designated an enemy.

It can mean taking no precautions to protect ourselves or our loved ones from a potentially debilitating or fatal disease because such precautions have been tainted with the imagined evil intent of our tribal foes. In many conservative communities, wearing a mask was equivalent to wearing the enemy's uniform. The COVID pandemic became so saturated with tribal identity that cross-country plane flights began to look like the early skirmishes of a civil war. Nevertheless, it is noteworthy that while many members of the MAGA faction have proclaimed their opposition to vaccines, some have discretely entered the back doors of pharmacies to get the jab.[28] In other words, they wanted to live but without the risk of social death.

Liberal Guilt vs. Conservative Shame: The Impact of Tribal Emotions in Public Life

Guilt and shame are emotions that sometimes break down along partisan lines. They are also powerful drivers of political behavior. Guilt is about a relationship—how one has harmed others, let them down, or failed to contribute to their welfare. It is the emotional experience that accompanies the belief that we have done something "bad." One is still part of the group but must make reparation for the harm done. People of all classes, partisan identities, and ethnicities can experience guilt. It can be a powerful motive felt by the relatively privileged who are capable of empathy and compassion, leading to support for policies and candidates that promise to alleviate the suffering of those less privileged. Guilt (along with self-interested motives like tax deductions) can drive philanthropy among the very wealthy.

Shame, by contrast, is about oneself as a whole, about *being* something bad. It is also a relational emotion but one associated with the prospect of exile from the group. The feeling can be that one is so thoroughly bad no repair is possible. One has not just done something shitty; one *is* shit and is at risk of being eliminated from the group. As we might intuit, shame, more than guilt, is associated with psychopathology, especially depression.[29]

In general, conservatives tend to be more shame-oriented. They may not necessarily *feel* shame but tend to advocate it as a tool to maintain the individual's and the group's moral virtue.[30] Many on the Right see it as a bulwark against failure to defer to worldly or spiritual authorities, acts of impurity, or showing moral weakness. To a great extent, shame and pride are the animating emotions of right-wing political tribalism. They are feelings associated with one's status in the group—whether dishonored or honored, mocked or admired, devalued or revered. Avoiding other group members' disrespect, contempt, and rejection and earning their recognition, love, and acceptance takes precedence over any other self-interest, including life itself—as demonstrated by suicide bombers, COVID-denying indoor MAGA rally attendees during the height of the pandemic, and the eager cannon fodder of innumerable wars.

As David Keen, a professor of conflict studies at the London School of Economics, has noted throughout his research on the politics of shame, conservative shame is almost always about real or imagined status loss—appearing weak, subordinate, or defeated.[31] For many on the Right, harming others, especially those in devalued or enemy groups, rarely evokes shame and can be a source of pride that earns them the esteem of their tribal fellows.

To be *seen* hurting tribal enemies is a form of right-wing virtue signaling. In other words, sadistic trolling and even violence can be driven by more than pleasure in another's suffering. That behavior may also be a show for others—a performance of shamelessness. In addition, it can serve as a defense against guilt, an emotion that, for some with a fascist orientation, may carry the taint of weakness. Compassion for the pain endured by those who are viewed as ethnic, gendered, or political outsiders suggests to perpetrators on the Right a certain feminizing softness. Regarding tribal enemies, caring is equivalent to cowardice and submission. To put it another way, shamelessness is deployed as a defense against guilt because guilt, for the fascistic sadist, is shameful.

While my focus here is on the US context, it must be mentioned, at least in passing, that the American Right does not have a monopoly on performative shamelessness. In this country, MAGA Republicans have denied or minimized slavery as the cause of the Civil War (or even reframed the abduction and bondage of Africans as a jobs program),[32] waxed nostalgic about the "Lost Cause," and protested over moving the statues of Confederate "heroes" into museums. Similarly, as Keen has observed, some on the British Right have recast the brutal history of their empire through the wistful, sepia-tinted lens of colonial romance.[33] Tory and neofascist apologists for the depredations of *fin de siècle* corporate pirate Cecil Rhodes, the infamously murderous and enslaving thief of African land, labor, and sovereignty, were outraged when protesters at Oxford University sought to have a statue honoring Rhodes removed. English conservatives issued their familiar wail against liberal "wokeness" and exclaimed their pride in traditional British values and the noble civilizing aims of empire.[34]

It turns out that simple psychopathy may not be so simple after all. For some, it may not be driven by just an absence of conscience but by a *motivated* absence of conscience. Behavior that seems shameful to the rest of us—the violent mistreatment of others—may be proof to some perpetrators and their tribal comrades that they have nothing to be ashamed of.

Keen found precisely that dynamic at play when he interviewed preteen former child soldiers in Sierra Leone for his analysis of the role of shame in politics and war.[35] At the residential facility where these children were enrolled in a rehabilitation program, Keen inquired about their experience and emotions after they spent years committing horrific atrocities on innocent civilians in that country's civil war. He was initially shocked that so many would express indifference and laugh about their actions.

Keen eventually understood that he was witnessing expressions of defensive shamelessness. Their callous bemusement was a necessary psychic shield that the treating staff was careful not to shatter abruptly. They aimed to only *gradually* facilitate the children's awareness of the trauma they caused others so as not to flood the boys with shame and self-contempt. Their caretakers understood the young former perpetrators' strenuously proclaimed comfort with the butchery they perpetrated to be a brittle carapace that protected a fragile and traumatized inner core. Before being conscripted, many had watched their own families be mutilated and murdered. One central therapeutic goal was to make these children resilient enough to tolerate appropriate guilt over their terrible actions.

Forensic psychiatrist James Gilligan worked with a very different set of perpetrators, highly violent criminals, who nevertheless appear motivated by a similar psychology.[36] He found that the early histories of these men were replete with severe psychological and physical abuse and neglect. They were all shamed and humiliated. Many described the experience of terrorizing their victims as the only way they could feel respected. Putting a gun in someone's face conferred a sense of recognition and pride they could not achieve in any other way. Correspondingly, criminal predators seem to read the fear in the eyes of those they tormented as a sign that they, the perpetrators, had somehow transfused shame and powerlessness into others. For Gilligan's subjects, victims functioned a bit like the sin-eaters of old who, by absorbing the spiritual stains of others, allowed the souls of the donors to enter heaven unsullied. Because the relief provided by that psychic purging was a fantasy and thus fleeting, those violent criminals had to find other scapegoats.

Perhaps unsurprisingly, when the prisoners Gilligan studied could experience guilt, the likelihood of committing further violence was decreased. In contrast, inducing shame and humiliation, the apparent emotional aim of so much of America's carceral policy, leads to a higher propensity to commit violent crimes.[37]

There are different pathways by which shame results in the victimization of others. Not every violent perpetrator has an early history of humiliation or abuse. For some, the preoccupation with warding off shame comes from other social contexts in which the respect of one's peers is predicated on suppressing empathy and performing monstrous atrocities, such as the "ordinary men" of the paramilitary death squads, the Einsatzgruppen, of Nazi-occupied Europe.[38] Shame in that setting consisted of the "unmanly" refusal to carry out one's duty. Compassion for victims was understood as a humiliating weakness.

Keen's study of Adolf Eichmann's career as a genocidal mass murderer draws on numerous documents and interviews that offer a window into the inner world of one of the Holocaust's more notorious functionaries.[39] While the transcripts of his war crimes trial in Jerusalem paint a picture of an affectless bureaucrat, the very embodiment of evil's banality, other more candid accounts show he was actually riven with anguish. Eichmann's torment was not about the suffering he caused but the fleeting squeamishness he felt at witnessing the consequences of his orders. The few occasions when he hesitated to act with maximum brutality filled him with shame.

Like many in the Einsatzgruppen, there is no evidence that Eichmann's childhood featured humiliating abuse. But also, like them, he was a grown man embedded in a culture of fascist masculinity that admired ruthless cruelty and reviled "soft" compassion. He did struggle with shame, but it was over not completing the job of exterminating all Jews. What filled him with pride was doing his duty, whatever that involved. He was not indifferent to the nature of that duty. Indeed, embracing cruelty and not shrinking from it was a mark of integrity. Chapters 6 and 7 will explore how MAGA males similarly see the willingness to inflict suffering on tribal enemies as an inoculation against the humiliating shame of "feminine weakness."

As we'll see in the next chapter, some corners of the identitarian Left also tend to wield shame against contrarian allies. In those cases, shaming can render heterodox fellow leftists "canceled," called out, or ostracized. When that becomes the threat of job loss, it can become a driver of self-censorship and compensatory virtue signaling.

Nevertheless, guilt over real or perceived harm to others seems to predominate among liberals. Indeed, "liberal guilt" is a political term of art with a long history, primarily as part of the conservative nomenclature of mockery directed at the Left for its putatively neurotic anguish over others' suffering. We might view that as an attempt by those on the Right to make liberals ashamed of their guilt. Conversely, some sing its praises as a mark of conscience,[40] a political emotion all should cultivate. Whether denounced as an emotion of hypersensitive fools or an admirable moral virtue, there is general agreement that guilt is a feeling associated with a liberal worldview.

Liberal guilt seems derivative of the two most robust moral foundations of those on the Left: fairness and avoidance of harm.[41] In a series of six studies[42] using a variety of sample populations, researchers found liberals far more than conservatives to be concerned about people in hypothetical scenarios who were falsely accused of crimes. In contrast, subjects on the Right were more troubled by actual perpetrators going unpunished. Neither group of partisans found either outcome acceptable; the difference was relative but significant. When the investigators dug deeper into what motivated these distinct concerns, liberal subjects cited the unfairness of false accusations.

By contrast, as we might expect, conservatives were most troubled by the threat that an un-incarcerated criminal might pose and the outlaw's disrespect for authority. Extrapolating that to partisan differences in criminal justice policy, it seems that conservative threat salience and deference to their own tribal authorities override much of the guilt they might feel over not protecting the rights of the accused, which may translate into a higher tolerance for unintentionally punishing the innocent. However, at the current MAGA moment, when tribal loyalty supersedes everything, what constitutes a threat and whose actions are deemed criminal are being radically reinterpreted. Orwellian inversions have become the norm, such as the ongoing efforts to recast attempts to overturn an election and lynch public officials as acts of patriotic heroism. And those who have been jailed for assaulting the police and vandalizing the Capitol, Trump semantically ennobled as "hostages."[43] On the Republican side of the looking glass, those who tried to protect democracy and certify the election were depicted as traitors. And those who sought democracy's demolition are perceived as persecuted saviors.

Shame is not just something *felt* by individuals. It is also wielded as a weapon by the group against those who violate tribal codes, especially those accused of disloyalty. As a violation of a core moral foundation for conservatives,[44] disloyalty is regarded as a virtual capital crime, one that can be punished by threatened or actual death.[45] Shame is the MAGA warrior's affective ordnance of choice and aims at social death. Whether deployed by Trump, his acolytes in Congress, or his lynch mob of trolls, the goal of shaming is not just to mark apostates and critics as tribal outsiders but to designate perceived or actual political enemies as outside of humanity and worthy of extermination. On countless occasions, we have seen just how short the path can be, from humiliating denunciations by the leader to physical violence by followers against Trump's targets. His devotees have so thoroughly internalized Trump's worldview and wishes that they no longer need an explicit call to action.

In January 2024, one Trump-worshipping zealot, Justin Mohn, decapitated his own father for the crime of working for the federal government during the Biden administration, which the murderer deemed treasonous. It would be too easy to dismiss this as the aberrant action of an isolated paranoid schizophrenic. As his former roommate noted, Mohn's psychotic fantasies about the putative deep state first emerged with Trump's rise to power in 2016. In the killer's YouTube video, in which he proudly displayed his father's severed head, Mohn echoed the former president and proclaimed, "America is rotting from the inside out as far left, woke mobs rampage our once prosperous cities." He viewed his actions as the opposite of shameful—something that his real or imagined cohorts and his spiritual leader, Trump, would regard with great admiration. Former FBI Deputy Director Andrew McCabe did not read this disturbing murder as simply the act of a lone schizophrenic but as part of a larger political movement. He said, "You can make some assumptions based on his claims in the video that he's been motivated by politics" and that

Mohn's language is "rhetoric that you hear from some politicians that we've heard recently in the primary season."[46]

Shame and Guilt in Donald Trump

In my clinical practice, I often encounter patients who grew up in families that conflated guilt and shame. These can be individuals raised in fundamentalist or emotionally abusive homes in which doing a bad thing makes you a bad person and where humiliation is the primary mode of "discipline." That means that no harm caused can ever be repaired. Life becomes an endless accumulation of reasons to feel shame. Some people collapse under the weight of their ever-growing "criminal record" and sink into a chronic depression.

Others whose early life was marked by mocking, belittling, and humiliating treatment might flip in the opposite direction—deny ever having made a mistake, lost a competition, failed to excel at something, or hurt another. To maintain this defense against falling into shame, they cannot apologize or take responsibility for any wrongdoing. They appear to others as insufferably arrogant and entitled. That is the narcissistic solution to shame. But that veneer is brittle and quickly shattered by the mildest criticism, to which they can respond with fury and humiliating insults. A particular former president may come to mind here.

One of the more common criticisms of Donald Trump is that he feels no shame. On the contrary, his compulsive and cartoonish braggadocio is best understood as a defense against shame. Trump's famously thin skin is the tell that reveals the shame he struggles to ward off. As we have all observed, his attention to the possibility of being a "loser" is ceaseless. And when threatened, that label is the first projective arrow he reaches for in his quiver of puerile insults. Trump's anxious preoccupation with losing has been made all the more salient since actually losing so many battles—the presidential election, the multiple electoral failures of his endorsees, and innumerable court cases.

In Trump's refusal to apologize for any wrongdoing, he personifies what has become, in the present era, a foundational difference between conservative and liberal notions of honor and shame. For those on the MAGA Right, apologizing is a shameful expression of weakness. In their view, regret and guilt are for losers. Remorse and contrition mark one as a bottom in the perennial sadomasochistic battle for dominance. When liberal politicians acknowledge the harm done by prior policies and military actions, conservatives accuse them of embarking on humiliating "apology tours."

In contrast, for most liberals, apologizing is an affirmation of honor. It is a show of compassion, responsibility, and integrity. It marks one as resilient and robust. Acknowledging mistakes demonstrates one's capacity to learn from experience instead of arrogantly doubling down on past errors. It allows for collaboration and mutuality with others rather than remaining locked into a framework of conquest and submission. Liberal leaders are more likely to apologize because they are not ashamed to be seen as flawed humans and don't insist on being worshipped as deities or feared as vengeful autocrats.

Nevertheless, it cannot be denied that performative shamelessness has been one of Trump's most politically effective defenses against shame. He has dined with Nazis, bragged about sexual assault, vowed to jail and execute opponents, and promised to reign as a dictator should he win a second term. His thumb in the eyes of decency, grace, and democratic values has been celebrated by his base and made him more beloved by them. Trump is their spokesmodel for psychic impunity. He presents himself and is taken in as the permissive superego of conscience-free predation. Every racist utterance and every degrading insult toward women only further burnishes his brand. Nothing could be more compelling to a predominantly white male working-class body of supporters whose economically unprivileged lives do not allow escape from a multitude of petty and profound humiliations, who can never talk back to the boss, and whose rage and resentment must always be displaced onto targets that can't retaliate.

Trump's lack of guilt, a hallmark of sociopathy, brings his pathology into sharper relief. He has never exhibited any concern for the harm his words and actions have had on others, at least in public life. Indeed, Trump seems to relish the suffering he can inflict on his growing list of perceived enemies, a cruel glee mirrored by the most ardent among his base. In later chapters, I will unpack his sadism and the amen chorus of cruelty his followers comprise.

Empathy and the Humanity of the Tribal Other

Not only are out-groups seen as less than human, but their suffering is also far less disturbing to in-group members. Counterintuitively, victims are viewed as less-than-human outsiders and regarded with less compassion due to their victimization.[47] That may be a psychological defense against one's own vulnerability to such misfortunes, enabling distancing through devaluation. For those who believe in a just world presided over by a fair-minded deity, the thought might be, "That could never happen to me. God lets them suffer because they are not as worthy as I am."

Functional MRI studies of different groups found that when subjects were shown various images of out-group members, the brain areas that govern the capacity to mentalize (imagine) the inner worlds of others shut down.[48] That was not the case when viewing members of their own group. Since subjects show impaired empathy for members of artificially created outsider groups, we might expect the same results in studies of those who belong to groups engaged in bitter real-world conflicts. That is just what researchers have found. In one study of Palestinian and Israeli teenagers, subjects had a similar diminished brain response to images of people suffering pain if the victims were members of the other group.[49]

Echoing those results was a study using images of people with easily observed phenotypic racial differences.[50] Chinese and Caucasian subjects viewed photos of same- and other-race individuals in pain. Using a functional MRI, they showed much greater activation of brain areas associated with empathy when looking at pictures of members of their own racial group. One interesting twist in this research was that the authors put their subjects in mixed-race groups and led them through activities that resulted in a strong in-group identity. And yet, this did not prevent an unconscious racial empathy difference from showing up.

We Dehumanize Others When We De-animalize Ourselves

Many social scientists view anthropomorphism as one of the greatest scholarly sins. Of course, the projective attribution of human qualities to animals is an intellectual error. However, humans' disidentification and imagined discontinuity with the rest of life is a greater problem—both in understanding ourselves as a species and making sense of the world more broadly. It can also have lethal consequences for humans.

"You wouldn't believe how bad these people are. These aren't people—these are animals," Trump declared about undocumented immigrants.[51] Melanie Challenger, whose work I described earlier, points out how humans' attitudes and responses to animals inform their aggression toward other humans. We generate neurochemical responses when we think about particular animals, especially animals we view as prey, predators, or disgusting. Then we use this capacity in our efforts to dehumanize those in out-groups. That enables us to diminish our empathy so that predation or persecution can be less conflictual.

She talks about Albert Bandura's work on moral disengagement. He and his coworkers asked subjects to deliver shocks to certain target people. Those targets who were spoken of as if they were not human received more shocks. We know from many studies, and most vividly from the war propaganda posters compiled in Sam Keen's *Faces of the Enemy*, that depicting the enemy as a certain kind of repellent or threatening animal is a standard trope of psychological warfare.[52] This tactic has accompanied many armed conflicts and preceded numerous genocides.

In his book *Less than Human*, David Livingstone Smith discusses a widely prevalent trait among humans, which is to attribute essences to different kinds of non-human animals and diverse groups of humans.[53] Psychoanalyst Erik Erikson's term for this is *pseudospeciation* which he suggests is a feature of every form of ethnic or racial bigotry.[54] It has roots in our evolution. The ability to generalize species traits from individual animals has had obvious survival advantages. The capacity to "stereotype" lions based on the experience of very few individual lions helped early humans avoid unpleasant surprises. The problem comes when we apply this cognitive shortcut to human out-groups who are not different species but are comprised of individuals whose behavioral repertoire is as varied as those in our group.

Lest we conclude this is a tendency limited to white colonial Westerners, Challenger details many examples in which certain indigenous groups view only themselves as fully human. She effectively dismantles the noble savage fantasy that indigenous peoples are somehow exempt from the more disturbing aspects of our species' nature, which liberals may be more prone to believing than conservatives. People on the Left sometimes exhibit a kind of "positive" dehumanization, whereby an oppressed or colonized out-group is idealized rather than devalued. However, neither devaluation nor idealization affords such groups full status as complex humans.

Nevertheless, some critical differences exist in the attitudes of some indigenous peoples and those of the modern/colonial West. Pre-industrial groups' psychological stances toward the animals hunted for food are among those differences. In the post-industrial West, killing animals is facilitated by mentally terminating their agency, capacity for emotion and attachment, the salience of their pain and suffering, and most importantly, their kinship with humans. That is not unlike how soldiers are trained to regard the people they are sent to kill in war. In both cases, denying the selfhood and inner life of that which you will destroy is a mental rehearsal that enables the actual murder.

In contrast, many indigenous cultures have ways to resolve or attempt to resolve the conflict they might feel over destroying another and managing the anguish and pain that might befall them as predators. Some cultures do this through rituals that express respect for those creatures one kills for food. Central to these practices is acknowledging the agency of these animals and the kinship that human hunters feel with them. Prey is regarded as a non-human person with whom one negotiates before ending its life.[55] Hunting is seen as part of a relationship of reciprocity and mutual responsibility with the hunted.

They understand that animals are persons and humans are animals. Homo sapiens may covet delusions of superiority and feel entitled to dominance in our waking lives. But in our nightmares, occasional reminders of our early history as prey exist. Even now, we are all part of a food chain in which every creature in that chain eats and gets eaten by something, either during its lifetime or after death.

Very different assumptions drive assembly-line animal killing in the West and have some unexpected consequences for people. Challenger discusses the trauma-induced lack of empathy for other humans experienced by slaughter-house workers where animals, imagined as things, are "processed" on an indus-trial scale. There is a correlation between child abuse and domestic violence and the proximity to a slaughterhouse. Of course, causality cannot be established here. Nevertheless, such associations have not been seen in other industries, and the findings have been replicated in multiple countries. Other studies have found slaughterhouse workers are more likely to engage in antisocial behavior and sexual assault specifically.[56]

The link from slaughterhouses to human killing fields is not as big a leap as it might first appear. Research by Kristof Dhont and his team has shown that animal devaluation is highly associated with prejudice against human out-groups.[57] And, perhaps unsurprisingly, scoring high on social dominance ori-entation accounts for the bulk of this association.

Don't Be Meat: Fear of Death, the Disowning of Our Animal Nature, and Tribal Bonds

Mortality salience is another factor that links tribalism and the denial of our continuity with non-human animals. That is a phenomenon studied in a vari-ety of social science research programs. It is just what it sounds like—the mental vividness of our mortality. Awareness of death moves in and out of the foreground of consciousness. Even when activated subliminally (below the threshold of conscious awareness), it can profoundly impact our attitudes and choices, including those related to political partisanship.

Terror Management Theory (TMT) is the broad rubric for that field of study.[58] Sheldon Solomon is one of the more prominent researchers in that area. In one of his controlled studies, subjects were either reminded of their mortality or something unpleasant but not fatal.[59] Only those for whom mor-tality was made more salient showed an increased attachment to their group. Love for their tribe, however defined, grew more intense, along with hatred for outsiders.

That brings to mind what may be an infantile precursor to this response. Researchers will place a mother and her toddler in a room to study attachment styles in very young children. Then a stranger will enter, which the child often experiences as a threat during this developmental period. Observers will then note whether the child exhibits "proximity-seeking" behavior, i.e., whether he or she goes to the mother for reassurance and finds comfort. Researchers also assess the extent to which the child feels free to explore the room in the mother's presence while at the same time keeping an eye on her. When observers notice these behaviors, they are interpreted as signs of secure attachment. On the other hand, evaluators view his or her attachment as insecure if the child appears anxious, inconsolable, unable to explore or play, or avoids or clings desperately to the caregiver.

This model for evaluating attachment is called the "stranger situation." We can think of it as evoking an early iteration of mortality salience. While young children rarely have a conscious understanding of death, which in this period is too abstract to grasp, they have powerful instincts honed by evolution to maintain a connection to caretakers at all costs. It has always been and remains a life-and-death matter. In addition, it may be that stranger anxiety, a phenomenon most parents have observed, is an infantile variation of outsider threat. Indeed, if we ponder the literal meaning of xenophobia—fear of the strange— it suggests that the worry at the heart of the securitarian imagination may be an adult iteration of that primordial childhood anxiety. In this terrifying but inchoate fantasy, immigrants can be reflexively experienced as scary outsiders who will take me away from my group/family and rupture the bonds that keep me safe and nurtured.

In adulthood, activating death fear seems to be a powerful catalyst for consolidating one's group identity. It can even move tribal identity in the direction of more securitarian politics. In another of Solomon's studies, when pro–Hillary Clinton voters were exposed to stimuli that raised mortality salience, they became more favorable toward Donald Trump.[60] We can understand this as a shift to the candidate who embodied greater in-group bias and devalued out-groups, i.e., the more xenophobic candidate. This raises the intriguing question of whether or to what extent insecure attachment makes people, even erstwhile liberals, more susceptible to endorsing securitarian politicians when mortality concerns are evoked.

Investigators directly looked at the association between mortality salience, attachment security, and political partisanship in a study conducted during the 2004 presidential campaign.[61] Using a measure of adult attachment security, the research team found that when mortality salience was experimentally induced, those insecurely attached tended to increase their support for George W. Bush. When mortality was rendered more salient in securely attached subjects, they were more likely to increase their support for John Kerry. Like many Republican politicians of the modern era, Bush was a candidate whose campaign and presidency were reliant on generating anxiety over outsider threats. When the inability to feel securely attached to intimate others persists into adulthood, people can be more vulnerable to such appeals.

The link between mortality salience and the repudiation of our animality is among the most intriguing findings in the large body of TMT research. A team of investigators conducted interrelated studies examining the relationship between mortality salience, disgust, and denial of humans' continuity with other animals[62]—all factors that can catalyze xenophobic political tribalism. They found that reminders of death evoked increased feelings of disgust toward bodily products and a distinct preference for essays that emphasized the value of differentiating humans from other animals.

Why would such links exist? I speculate that non-human animals are thought of primarily in terms of their flesh. We are accustomed to seeing their body parts at the store. In other words, they are the literal embodiment of death. If something reminds us of our mortality, it generates conscious or unconscious anxiety, which we manage in various ways. One response would be to distance ourselves from human creatureliness, resulting in greater disgust for bodily fluids and other somatic homologies with non-human animals. We project animality onto out-groups who are easier to hate, induce our disgust, and are sometimes considered suitable for killing.

These projections also include disavowed emotions. In a series of studies, researchers found that people tend to attribute emotions viewed as more primitive and animal-like (such as fear and happiness) to out-group members.[63] In contrast, subjects are more likely to believe that people within *their* group display more "sophisticated" and "human-like" emotions, such as guilt and shame. When we put this together with other research described previously, it becomes increasingly clear that the denial of our animality and its projection onto others plays a significant role in the ease with which we can lose sight of the humanity of outsiders.

Bleeding-Heart Liberals and Heartless Conservatives: The Stereotypes and Realties of Partisan Differences in Empathy and Compassion

Many assumptions about empathy, compassion, and political identity seem intuitive. Yet, much of the psychological reality of what we feel and for whom may strike us as counterintuitive. For example, it might seem obvious that if partisans could only increase their capacity for empathy, antagonism for the other side would diminish. However, according to one study, those predisposed to experiencing a high degree of empathy tend to feel it more intensely toward *their* political tribe. As a result, they are highly attuned to the possible harm that out-group partisans might inflict and thus increase feelings of hostility toward them. That echoes, in some ways, the paradox of oxytocin described earlier.

Readers may recall that this putative "cuddle hormone" increases bonding with one's group members and aggression toward outsiders.

While the term empathy is defined differently by different people, some social scientists and most clinical psychologists use it to describe a person's capacity to see the world through another's eyes. To use a less familiar psychological term of art, it refers to the ability to *mentalize* another—to represent the cognitive and emotional experience of others in one's mind. Psychoanalytic researchers Anthony W. Batemen and Peter Fonagy define mentalization as the ability to "see ourselves from the outside and others from the inside."[64]

Compassion, on the other hand, involves caring about and feeling for another. It is certainly possible to understand the minds of others (as all successful con artists do) but feel no concern about them. Even more confusing, empathy and compassion are often used interchangeably in some social science literature. Most psychologists would agree that *sympathy* is the experience of sharing the emotional state of another. Even in the face of all this definitional imprecision, some research findings are worth noting.

In a cross-national study, liberals not only claimed to experience more empathy than conservatives, confirming what some might expect, but were also more *motivated* to feel it.[65] That introduces another fascinating layer of complexity (something that liberals love but conservatives hate[66]). And that is the question of what emotions we want to acknowledge and which we want to disclaim.

In other words, partisans may be divided not only by the emotions they experience but also by which ones they want others to *think* they feel. "Social desirability" is a research term for what subjects in a study think looks good to others or what they want to believe about themselves. It is a variable that can make it hard to interpret the results of any self-report study. Questions on a survey have to be phrased in a neutral enough way not to activate this bias.

In the mentioned study, the researchers turned this problem on its head. The aim was to find out what subjects thought was desirable, what they believed was *good* to feel, not just what they did feel. The experimenters were able to uncover partisan differences in emotion-related value systems. The study's finding was consistent with what anyone attending to everyday political discourse in American culture can readily observe: if you're a liberal, empathy is generally an unalloyed virtue that should be displayed with great fanfare. It is an emotion consistent with the specific policy aims of the Left—political, social, and economic equality and using shared resources to help those in need (sometimes called an ethic of care). Liberals in this study were, on the whole, more willing than conservatives to help others.

For conservatives, empathy and compassion are not especially desirable emotions, a stance congruent with a view of inequality and inequity as acceptable and inevitable. They also see such disparities as a reflection of the deficient character of the poor or the innately superior ability of the wealthy. Power and dominance over others are necessary for survival, reflect strength and independence, and are, therefore, virtuous. Conservatives believe empathy and compassion for those at the bottom would be inappropriate, if not immoral, since their economic hardships result from personal failings, weakness, and bad behaviors. Helping them only rewards laziness and moral turpitude and promotes dependence.

Shifting to the issue of partisan differences in compassion specifically, perhaps the most revealing research in this area is a series of studies looking at whom we care about, what the investigators term as different "moral circles."[67] That refers to how broad or narrow our universe of "moral regard" is. People tend to fit into two general categories, the "universalists" and the "parochialists." The zone of concern for universalists extends well beyond their immediate family. Sometimes, their feelings for friends can be greater than for blood relatives. They care for their community, but they also can have a deep concern for those they've never met or will meet, humanity as a whole, and even other species. The care felt by universalists tends to get stronger as the objects of their concern become more distant from their immediate world. They can agonize quite a bit about the health of the planet.

And then there are the parochialists. They care very much about their families, those in their immediate social circle, and the groups with which they identify. Parochialists worry about the country much more than the world beyond national borders. Their emotional investment tends to diminish the further beyond their immediate circle others are. Humanity as a whole is not very compelling, and non-human animals and plants are even less so.

By now, it may be obvious how this data fits with everything else discussed in the chapter. If you think these differences in moral circles map closely onto liberalism and conservatism, you would be correct. And that is what the researchers found. While they don't reference Hibbing's work on unitarians and securitarians, the alignment between the two frameworks seems pretty clear. The primary difference is their focus. Hibbing identifies where conservatives and liberals locate threats, whereas the moral circles investigators show whom partisans care about. One conclusion we can draw from the work of these researchers is that most people have a bleeding heart. Where conservatives and liberals differ is in regard to whose suffering causes compassion to hemorrhage.

In the next four chapters, we look at how some of the psychological traits that differentiate partisans get expressed in Right and Left identity politics. While some of these manifestations are ludicrous and amusing, others are decidedly malignant and may be bringing us to the brink of a new civil war.

CHAPTER 3

Identity Politics on the Left— Cultural Purity and the Battle against Burrito Colonialism

The Pleasures and Perils of Ethnic Appropriation

In 2017, two Portland women were forced to shut down their food truck because of the bad press generated by the local guardians of cultural boundaries.[1] Many argued that their burritos were the fruits of the owners' shameful exploitation of the Mexican women whose recipes they used. Eliding the not-so-subtle distinction between colonial plunder and the use of a freely given tortilla recipe, one earnest online culture warrior said, "These appropriating businesses are erasing and exploiting [Mexican women's] already marginalized identities for the purpose of profit and praise." Of course, the real problem facing ethnic minorities in this type of situation is not so much cultural borrowing but discrimination in financial borrowing and low generational wealth, which make it much harder for members of non-white groups to start their own food trucks and restaurants.[2]

That tempest in a tortilla isn't the only time that liberal anguish over the moral hazard of identity appropriation has reached comic proportions. There is another well-known episode of Left identitarian silliness, the Chinese prom dress uproar, which made headlines across the United States and United Kingdom.[3] Keziah Daum, a white high school girl, wore a close-fitting Chinese-style dress called a qipao to her prom and posted pictures of herself on Twitter. Predictable outrage ensued. "I'm proud of my culture. For it to be subject to American consumerism and cater to a white audience is parallel to colonial ideology," proclaimed a tweet from an enraged putatively Asian-American commenter. Notably, this dress was a style that had already gone through multiple "appropriations" by different ethnic groups within China. A Beijing-based fashion writer, Hung Huang, said, "To Chinese, it's not sacred, and it's not that meaningful."

Notably, there were passionate white and non-white proponents on each side of these two controversies. Nevertheless, it does seem like the historical care taken by some white Western leftists not to disrespect non-white cultural traditions and ensure a nonexploitative relationship to those practices has mutated into an ironic form of Left cultural apartheid in which ethnic groups must remain in protective culinary and fashion Bantustans.

Appropriation: What Is It Good For?

A major problem with the Left identitarian notion of appropriation is that it conflates theft with influence. A white musician who falsely claims authorship of and profits from the music of a Black performer is a thief. A white musician who sings in the style of a Black vocalist is influenced. A white writer who plagiarizes a Black author's work is stealing. A white writer who applies and cites a Black intellectual's ideas is expressing the latter's influence.

Theft is generally unilateral, deliberate, and often facilitated by economic privilege, political power, and violent coercion. *Influence* is multilateral, requires no force, occurs without conscious effort, and is exerted without regard to boundaries of class, ethnicity, gender, or any other demographic trait. It is easy to see how influence is foundational to creativity.

Appropriation is also a sloppy term to refer to the varieties of performative racism—from drunken white frat boys who engage in mocking ethnic cosplay to cringy Caucasian stand-up comedians ridiculing the accents of immigrants for whom English is a second language. In addition, the term fails to capture the now out-of-fashion self-parodying envy of suburban white teens who, pants hanging down around their knees, strain to speak in what they believe to be Black urban argot and call each other the N-word. Appropriation, when deployed as a name for all those disparate phenomena, is hopelessly vague, incoherent, and, to answer my own question, not good for much.

It is indisputable that every culture incorporates and transforms aspects of other cultures, notwithstanding the absurd efforts to maintain unambiguous boundaries between groups distinguished by ethnicity, gender, religion, or class. Subordinate groups adopt and change traditions from dominant groups—and vice versa. Sometimes, the aim is to pattern one's group after another. At other times, the drive is to create practices designed to differentiate one's group from others nearby, which anthropologists call *schismogenesis*.[4]

One division on the frequently fractious Left is between those who adhere to the notion of cultural purity and those who enthusiastically embrace ever-mutating hybridity. Some want to maintain impermeable boundaries around race but celebrate a rainbow of infinite variation regarding gender and sexuality.

We on the Left tend to view ourselves as more freedom-loving, embracing of difference, and open-minded than those on the Right. Nevertheless, sometimes the best liberal intentions can result in profoundly illiberal outcomes. Take, for example, two universally endorsed principles of left-wing moral politics, the defense of civil liberties and opposition to autocratic rule. There are far too many cases, some of which I discuss later, in which activists abandon their egalitarian principles and ardent defense of public and private freedoms to maintain "solidarity" with politicians and world leaders who claim to be allies. That generally takes the form of turning a blind eye to abuses perpetrated by those who brand themselves as ideological kin or with whom there is a common enemy.

Many on the Left rightly advocate for the acceptance of fluidity when it comes to certain categories of identity but not others. Similarly, while most liberals celebrate cultural cross-fertilization, others go into paroxysms of moral outrage over "appropriation" and, as I've noted, can't distinguish respectful influence from rapacious colonialism.

You Talkin' to Me?

Speech is another domain in which rigid policing is in tension with the best liberal instincts. Many on the Left view language as shaping and being shaped by power relations, especially concerning race, gender, and class. Therefore, discourse is viewed as a potentially oppressive *action* that can reinforce subordinate groups' domination by those more privileged. It can, in this view, do actual harm to others. While that assumption holds some truth, it has sometimes been used to justify authoritarian censorship, notably in classrooms, university campuses, and various media. Particular ideas and speakers are seen as agents of spoken violence and, therefore, dangerous to oppressed and less powerful groups. Therefore, the thinking goes, to protect potential victims, such speech must be silenced.

Context is everything here. Students might find an author on a college syllabus offensive or disturbing. A thoughtful teacher can use that as an opportunity for a challenging but respectful scholarly debate. Confronting difficult or even ugly ideas is part of learning. When I was a professor, readings were included on syllabi because they served a pedagogical purpose, not because I necessarily agreed with their point of view.

But that is quite different from a non-white person being verbally harassed and threatened by a neo-Nazi or a woman being subjected to intrusive and intimidating behavior by some Cro-Magnon "Big Man on Campus." It seems self-evident that those speech situations should be criminally sanctioned, just as are other kinds of harassment or violent threats.

Unfortunately, as things stand now, principled classroom debate can sometimes be an identitarian minefield in which students are encouraged to retreat to their "safe spaces." In an ironic mirroring of the repressive ambiance promoted by Florida Governor Ron DeSantis's education policies, teachers and students in some progressive academic settings are cautioned to avoid even respectful discussions that might make others uncomfortable.

Louis Farrakhan, Promoting Bigotry to End Bigotry

One example that illustrates the difficulty some on the Left have with rejecting prejudiced and authoritarian leaders who claim to be allies is the case of Louis Farrakhan. A few prominent progressive activists have shown a profound aversion to criticizing the leader of the Nation of Islam. In citing the importance of maintaining a unified coalition against white supremacy, some have minimized or called for liberals to overlook his well-documented anti-Semitism, homophobia, and misogyny.

In journalist Adam Serwer's interview with Tamika Mallory, one of the original organizers of the Women's March, she speaks of "intersectionalism" and a "united front against racism" to justify her support of Farrakhan.[5] Unsurprisingly, those groups reviled by the Nation, like Jewish Americans, have not been especially mollified by her reasoning. Nor have they felt included in her intersectionalism. Nevertheless, Mallory says one should not use words like *anti-Semitic* to describe groups like Farrakhan's. Instead, they should be viewed as "misinformed." It's unclear if citing his ignorance is intended to make his bigotry more forgivable and benign. He may very well be "misinformed," like all bigots. But his ignorance seems motivated by hatred—just as his hatred is enabled by ignorance. The bigger problem with Mallory's rationale for overlooking Farrakhan's multiple prejudices is her call for a "united front."

We can do a thought experiment to see if this united front logic feels ethically persuasive. Imagine that Marjorie Taylor Greene had defended her appearance at that white supremacist conference in February 2022 by saying, "I certainly don't approve of their racism, but it is important to establish a united front with those who share our Christian values." Do we think liberal or African American Christians would find that acceptable? I suspect not. The central question in any call for a united front is: a unity of whom and against whom? Justifying bigotry as a strategy against bigotry seems like pretty Orwellian logic.

Mallory cites Farrakhan's various social services his organization offers to the Black community as a reason to support him. That is similar to the argument made by some on the Left in the 1970s for why certain "left" authoritarians, like Fidel Castro, should be admired or at least not criticized: They may be autocrats who tolerate no opposition and send dissidents to prison or execute them, but their regimes provide basic literacy and public health infrastructures. Sure, no one was permitted to publish any criticism of the government,[6] but leftists were encouraged to celebrate the literacy programs that enabled everyone to read the party newspaper. For some American leftists, repression was somehow leavened by the wide availability of health care. Again, a hypothetical right-wing example might sharpen the outlines of the issue. Suppose David Duke and the Klan began offering free medical care to working-class whites. In that case, it seems unlikely that the former Grand Wizard's charitable efforts would lead anyone on the Left to overlook cross burnings or break into a chorus of "Dixie."

I have mixed feelings about bringing up the case of Farrakhan and his group because little about him and his organization could justify placing him on the Left. Were it not for his African American and Muslim identities, he would fit right in with right-wing Christian fundamentalists. If he converted and accepted Jesus as his savior, Farrakhan might even be offered a position at Liberty University. However, the reasoning of his Left apologists and their identitarian rationalizations makes his example instructive.

My other apprehension about discussing him is that those on the Right point to his anti-Semitism and his few Left enablers to paint the Left as anti-Semitic. But it must be said that, with the exception of some notable recent examples soon discussed, Left anti-Semitism is primarily a myth. (Those who assert otherwise generally equate opposition to Israeli policy toward Palestinians with anti-Jewish hatred—a bizarre charge given the many American liberal Jews among the critics of Israeli human rights abuses and colonial practices like collective punishment and land seizures.[7] Prominent Jewish scholars have even argued that a state that privileges one ethnic/religious group above all others, in this case, Israel, cannot be a democracy.[8])

Unfortunately, embracing an organization like the Nation of Islam is consistent with a broader history on the part of some Left activists. Readers might be aware of the mid-twentieth century American communist idolatry of Stalin. Unfortunately, that began a long and ignominious tradition of credulous leftists overlooking, excusing, or normalizing oppressive actions by leaders who presented themselves as saviors of some oppressed constituency, spruced up their autocratic rule with a "socialist" gloss, or added "democratic" to their party name or movement.

For example, during an earlier era of American imperial interventions, there was a tendency for some opponents of US policy to proclaim the authoritarian regimes of North Vietnam, China, and Cuba to be exemplary models of socialism to which we should all aspire. Some argued that we should overlook the absence of democracy and civil liberties because citizens of these countries were given health care, housing, and other social services. Others framed oppression in these regimes in cultural terms, insisting that those who criticized the limits on fundamental freedoms were manifesting typical American ethnocentrism. Having lived in Berkeley, California, in the early and mid-1970s, I can assure the reader that the rhetorical air was thick with those cringe-worthy rationalizations for "Left" authoritarianism.

Fortunately, in the current era, apologists for tyrants, dictators, and bigots are much less common on the Left than in earlier times. However, when we look at "anti-imperialist" apologists for Putin's invasion of Ukraine, it is apparent that Left defenders of autocracy have not vacated the field of political discourse.[9]

Politically Correct Pogroms: Hamas Atrocities and Israeli Collective Punishment Meet Left Identity Politics

Following the mass murder, rapes, torture, mutilations, and beheadings of Israeli civilians, many of whom were left-wing advocates of Palestinian rights,[10] by Hamas jihadists along the border with Gaza, a "pro-Palestinian" rally was held in Manhattan. One "progressive" speaker described the attacks with a bemused snicker. "And as you might have seen, there was some sort of rave or desert party where they were having a great time until the resistance came in electrified hang gliders and took at least several dozen hipsters." That was followed by a chorus of marchers chanting, "From the river to the sea, Palestine will be free."[11]

The attendees at that Democratic Socialists of America (DSA) event echoed Hamas itself. They seemed to agree with Hamas's founding covenant that said Palestinian emancipation from Israeli control required "killing the Jews."[12] Similar sentiments were expressed online by erstwhile allies of those victimized by bigots and autocrats. Within days of the attack, Black Lives Matter Chicago posted an image of a Hamas paratrooper depicted as a liberator, accompanied by the caption, "I stand with Palestine."[13] At Columbia University, a campus organization comprised of earnest social justice warriors in the School of Social Work, promoted a teach-in on "the significance of the Palestinian counter-offensive on October 7 and the centrality of revolutionary violence to anti-imperialism."[14]

I am writing this about a month after the Israeli ground invasion. The architects of the Hamas incursion could easily have foreseen and probably planned that the sadistic horror show they visited upon Israeli civilians would induce a reciprocal blood lust for vengeance against the citizens of Gaza. The self-evident reality is that Hamas views their own people as expendable meat puppets as much as they do Israelis. As with all terrorists, people are things—utilitarian chess pieces to be moved around or sacrificed depending on the strategic advantage conferred. Hamas has a long history of abducting, torturing, and murdering its own people who are deemed political threats to its regime.[15]

On the surface, they warned Israel against attacking Palestinian noncombatants. But, clearly, on another level, their fondest wish was that the Israeli army would enter the Gazan briar patch where innocent civilians would be murdered directly or as "collateral damage" and thereby undermine any sympathy the October 7 pogrom might have generated, and, by extension, incite a multifront war on Israel. Hamas knew that Israel's aspiring autocrat, Netanyahu, was aligned with his country's fundamentalist, ethno-nationalist fringe and that their likely response would be a continuation of the policy of collective punishment[16] but with an exponentially higher body count.

So far, the Israel Defense Forces (IDF) has given Gaza's bloodthirsty but strategically smart holy warriors precisely what they wanted—an unrelenting spectacle of civilian slaughter and torment. For Hamas, the mass death of fellow Palestinians is simply a tactic for demolishing what little may be left of Israel's moral authority after decades of colonial behavior toward Palestinians.[17] Their hope was and is to excite a wider war,[18] just as the US invasion of Iraq squandered any goodwill engendered by the 9/11 attacks and created a state of war that lasted a generation. The IDF bombing of civilian neighborhoods and infrastructure produced a massive death toll for children alone, nearly two thousand[19] of the five thousand civilians[20] killed by the third week of October 2023. By November, events in Gaza had significantly eroded compassion for and eclipsed the fourteen hundred[21] Israeli victims, even for Americans who have been among the Jewish state's staunchest allies.[22] In that relatively brief period, deaths of women and children in Gaza were of such magnitude that they exceeded the number killed in Ukraine after two years of Russian attacks.[23] By December, an Israeli study found that 61 percent of those killed in the IDF's bombing campaign were civilian. That was a higher ratio of civilian to combatant deaths than all the armed conflicts in the twentieth century.[24]

Among the questions that plagued me was: how could leftists—activists devoted to fighting against oppression of all kinds—sign on to the aims of misogynist and anti-gay Islamic holy warriors seeking to ignite a region-wide jihad against non-Muslims and expand their authoritarian rule? How could they conflate Palestinian liberation with domination by Hamas? Similarly, how could so many Jewish Left advocates for social justice (as I will show), especially those descended from Holocaust survivors, remain indifferent to the suffering and death toll of Palestinian civilians? One answer can be found in the same dynamics that underlie the earlier examples of Left illiberalism and reverence for "Left" dictators—a fundamentalist frame of mind. There is a desperate longing for saints and devils, unambiguous good guys and bad guys, pure-hearted liberators and soulless and malevolent oppressors.

Of course, the current Middle East conflict does have clear victims and perpetrators. Palestinian and Israeli civilians are the victims of both regimes. Both governments have taken the position that civilians are not innocent. In their founding documents and most recent actions, Hamas has been explicit about that. Israeli President Isaac Herzog said of ordinary Gazans about the attacks, "It's an entire nation out there that is responsible."[25] Cutting off food and water to Palestinian residents, a punishment not even inflicted by most nations on death-row inmates, is a logical expression of that moral position. Those exterminationist moves were rightly condemned as war crimes[26] when implemented by Putin against Ukrainians.

Rather than face the nightmare of a war in which the leaders of each group are malignant and self-serving, a contest between Jewish and Islamic Jihadists, some on the Left feel compelled to construct one set as freedom fighters. In the wishful fantasy of the DSA, Hamas is the "resistance" devoted to Palestinian emancipation rather than the willing grave diggers of their fellow Gazans who are "honored" as martyrs. Similarly, they can't see Israelis in all their complexities and contradictions—a multiethnic people comprised of pro-democracy advocates of Palestinian rights as well as fascistic ethnic cleansers seeking to turn their country into a Jewish theocracy. Instead, some activists seem to prefer a two-dimensional enemy, a homogenous nation of racist colonizers down to the last baby, whose annihilation they can celebrate. The Left identitarian attachment to rigid notions of ethnic/racial identity—a longing for purity is more commonly seen in conservatives—can lead to essentialist stereotypes like the noble Palestinian victim and the genocidal Israeli Jew perpetrator.

Ironically, for a political tendency that fetishizes difference, differences *internal* to each tribe are elided, as are all tensions between their respective citizens and leaders. All conflict between those groups gets reduced to a war of opposing caricatures. I don't want to give the impression that left identitarians impose their black-and-white ethnic schemas only in ways that demonize Jewish Israelis and idealize Palestinians. In many cases, the dichotomy is reversed.

My own social media feed is certainly not a random sampling of Left opinion but may be revealing nonetheless. There have been multiple posts from fellow Jewish leftists that insisted there is no moral equivalence between Hamas and Netanyahu's military, and that only the former has committed war crimes. Somehow, they were able to construct an ethical distinction between decapitating a child with a blade and doing so with a bomb. In both cases, a larger emancipatory aim is cited as the rationale for the slaughter of civilian non-combatants. In both cases, those aims—the liberation of Palestinians and the security of Israelis—have been eclipsed by the global revulsion over the deployment of exterminationist means.

There is a counterfactual question that no one is asking of the official explainers for the IDF and that my liberal friends who seem indifferent to Palestinian deaths are not considering: If Hamas terrorists were hiding out in the homes and hospitals of a Jewish Israeli town and in a war zone where no safe exit was possible, would you be willing to kill tens of thousands of those civilians and reduce their community to rubble to achieve your military ends? Or, put more plainly, whose humanity matters? If the answer is "only those in my group," the justifying foundation for genocidal tribalism has been laid.

A shocking amount of my Left Jewish Facebook friends have found a way to accept the annihilation of Gazan civilians. One of the more common rationalizations is to view all residents there as Hamas. They seem to forget that Hamas is an armed dictatorship. The decision to commit war crimes against Israeli civilians was not something ordinary citizens of Gaza got to vote on. Polls conducted just before the October 7 attacks showed that more than two-thirds of the population opposed that regime.[27] (Thanks to Netanyahu's unrelenting ethnic cleansing operation, that is likely to reverse over time.)

And yet, my "liberal" friends could rationalize a politically powerless people being starved, deprived of water, and bombed into oblivion as punishment for the brutality of those who rule over them. These are leftists who until recently seemed to hold their Jewish identity and affinity for Israel lightly. But once an out-group threat became a reality, many not only became Israel jingoists but cultivated a shocking indifference toward Palestinian bodies.

Another Facebook friend, whom I don't know beyond his online persona, regularly posts impassioned screeds denouncing the endless assaults on America's multiracial democracy by MAGA politicians and their voter base, proclamations I could not argue with. But after Hamas's terror attacks, he published long, meandering posts attacking the notion that Palestinians even constituted a people with a history, a culture, or a legitimate claim to land and sovereignty. He posted a widely circulated map of ancient Israel/Palestine circa 1000 BCE. The implication was that contemporary Israel is entitled to claim all land within its current borders by virtue of that early history and the continuous presence of Jewish residents. And Palestinians, therefore, have no legitimate claim. The latter's expulsion and mass killing are simply acts of historical justice.

The argument that a people is a historical nonentity is a twist on the more common approach to devaluing a rival ethnic group, whereby the outsider tribe is the object of negative projections. Instead, the aim here is erasure, an ontological iteration of ethnic cleansing. Palestinians? They never existed. How can people who never existed claim rights to anything? The poster's assertion was not simply the idiosyncratic rantings of an isolated individual. Israeli Finance Minister Bezalel Smotrich said in March 2023, "There is no such thing as a Palestinian nation. There is no Palestinian history." He even called for the West Bank town of Hawara to be "erased" after right-wing settlers attacked it to avenge the killing of two Israelis.[28]

Some discerning readers may hear in that an echo of Russia's justification for colonizing Ukraine, put forth by Putin—another autocrat, as I noted previously, that some leftists[29] in the United States[30] and around the world[31] contort themselves into supporting (or at least not opposing), claiming he is a warrior against the worst depredations of the American empire. When not calling Ukrainians "Nazis," Putin argues for their nonexistence as a nation or a people with a history distinct from Russia.[32] What may look to the rest of us as genocide really isn't because you can't exterminate a group that was never there in the first place.

The mindless cheerleading of war crimes is certainly not specific to nor does it represent more than a minority of the Left. Nevertheless, it is an especially troubling paradox for those who espouse a political worldview that abjures coercive violence and is grounded in the values of empathy, compassion, and fairness.

Unfortunately, too many on the Left are embedded in a partition of the world that locates everyone into the binary camps of oppressor or oppressed. Some who are "pro-Palestinian" feel compelled to valorize Hamas and rationalize their atrocities; some who are "pro-Israel" feel the need to conflate Hamas with all Palestinians and sanitize their extermination as "collateral damage."

There is nothing contradictory about observing that any group, such as the European Zionists of the 1940s, could be persecuted refugees when fleeing one continent and colonial settlers once landing on another. However, it does challenge the Manichean dichotomies that all too often feature in the narratives of Left identity politics.

From the 1948 ethnic cleansing of Palestinian Arabs[33] to the present, it has been excruciatingly clear that having been part of a victim group does not inoculate anyone from becoming a perpetrator. As the Italian-Jewish scientist and Holocaust survivor Primo Levi said after the massacre of up to 3,500 Palestinian and Lebanese Shia Muslims by the Israeli-backed Phalange militia at the 1982 Sabra and Shatila refugee camps in Lebanon, "Everybody is somebody's Jew. And today, the Palestinians are the Jews of the Israelis."[34]

Becoming a perpetrator can be facilitated by being a victim. Psychotherapists who work with trauma victims have long noted this horrifying but commonplace irony. The clinical literature on the transgenerational transmission of trauma is a voluminous and compelling one, especially as expressed within the families of both Holocaust survivors and Nazi perpetrators.[35]

Perhaps we are all becoming inured to the deliberate killing of innocent civilians, which is an increasingly common feature of military conflicts worldwide. One way we can remain untroubled by the murdered babies of outside groups is by accepting a mental hierarchy of human worthiness, which renders certain people more expendable than others. The valuing of one group over another is part of how we can justify exercising power over them, a trait behavioral scientists call a social dominance orientation (SDO). As I argued in prior chapters, SDO is foundational to the psychology of conservatives. It is antithetical to liberal egalitarianism, even when expressed by nominal leftists.

Regardless of whose innocents are slaughtered, it sets in motion an endless cycle of vengeance and countervengeance, giving each new generation of victim-perpetrators what they see as a justification for terrorism. When it comes to the destruction of Israeli and Gazan civilians specifically, Hamas and Netanyahu's IDF share the same gaslighting proclamation: "Look what they made us do." But I find it hard to argue with the peace activists among both peoples who insist on the obvious moral and empirical truth that murders are the fault of those doing the killing.

Blame versus Responsibility

Another problem in contemporary progressive identity politics is the self-defeating way some approach those who occupy positions of demographic privilege in American society. Too many on the Left focus on blaming those in dominant or privileged groups for harm in the past. That leads those individuals to a defensive repudiation of any accountability. A more effective frame would be to make it clear that while we should not be blamed for the sins of our ancestors, say slavery in the United States, we continue to be the beneficiaries of that system and thereby bear a moral responsibility to mitigate its harms.

The unpaid labor of Africans helped to make the country rich. And that wealth continues to grow to this day, especially in the South. For most white people, privilege is mainly expressed in what *doesn't* happen to them—being denied loans, having their homes devalued by appraisers, followed, pulled over, arrested, beaten, and sometimes killed—all because of their color. White people who may not engage in racist behavior or hold conscious racist beliefs nevertheless benefit from having white skin. We enjoy its perks in terms of jobs, housing, better medical care, and greater respect from law enforcement. That is not to diminish the fact that many white people are economically disadvantaged. However, the poverty they struggle with and its associated injuries and humiliations are not derivative of racial bias.

An alternative to blame would be to advocate for responsibility. Members of high-status or privileged groups should not be punished or shamed for the passive, unbidden special treatment they enjoy but be presented with opportunities to help repair the damage caused by a system animated by racism and a history of slavery from which they still extract dividends.[36]

The Particular and the Universal in the Identity Politics of Left and Right

There is a tension *within* the Left between the particularism of identity politics and the universalism inherent in liberal values and policy goals. Before highlighting its excesses, I hasten to point out that critiques of white, male, and heterosexual privilege can provide a useful framework for reflecting on the unconscious context of the self, which might enable a bridge of empathy to the ethnic, gendered, or sexual other. Recognizing these unexamined privileges can also blunt the tendency to denigrate non-dominant groups and temper the impulse to arrogantly inflate the putative greatness of one's own ethnicity, gender, or class. While many of the values and practices of universalism may be laudable, they have often functioned as a projection of dominant group particularism, e.g., the assumption by some Caucasian liberals that folks of color are simply white people with more pigment. That is a form of "tolerance" founded on a narcissistic fantasy that obliterates the identity of groups outside one's own.

However, far too often, notions of privilege and hegemony have been used as sanctimonious and repressive bludgeons to silence others and affirm a monolithic tribal identity grounded chiefly in the experience of actual or perceived victimization. Moreover, Left identity politics warriors sometimes fail to appreciate that an attack on people as a group, such as white straight Christian males, is one of the most effective ways of consolidating a tribal identity in one's perceived opponents. Being vilified based on one's group membership only makes it harder to see and appreciate the commonalities we have with one another.

On the Right, this lesson was unlearned during the Bush-era "War on Terror." The same mistake was repeated by the Trump administration's insistence that "radical Islamic" be added as a modifier of terrorism. Ditto for the latter's "Muslim ban." A reliable way to strengthen the identity of out-group members and their determination to fight you is to attack them based on their identity.

White supremacist groups, especially those aggregated around neo-Nazi Richard Spencer, have constituted themselves as ironic racist doppelgangers of left-wing identitarian groups. They protest that the "white race" and "white culture" are targets of denigration and persecution and demand special consideration and a national homeland. Spencer uses and embraces the term *identity politics* to advance his "separate-but-equal" reframing of the white nationalist project.[37]

Crossing Identity Boundaries

Spencer's curious identification with the victimization of genuinely oppressed groups raises interesting questions about the unconscious envy of those he and his cohorts denigrate. We can find a surprising resonance on the other end of the racial politics spectrum in Rachel Dolezal. Her story highlights a curious contradiction in left-wing tribalism, centered on its own conflicts over cross-category identity. Dolezal, the former president of the Spokane, Washington, chapter of the NAACP, was famously outed in 2015 as a white woman after presenting herself as African American for many years. She was widely vilified for this masquerade, which most on the Left saw as a shameful case of cultural appropriation by someone wielding her white privilege. On the other hand, Dolezal argued that she was simply living out a deeply felt ethnic identity. Her cornrows and skin-darkening makeup merely rendered her external appearance congruent with her inner sense of self.

The objectionable nature of her claim to Black racial identity seems self-evident. Even if sincerely felt, it is hard not to think of the history of whites engaging in Black minstrelsy's racial mockery. Yet, there is another less well-known history of white people living and passing as Black, more akin to Dolezal's example. These are not cases of clownish ethnic burlesque that ended with the final curtain call, but white musicians, writers, journalists, and others who seemed to identify and were seen by others as Black. Reverse racial passing dates back to at least the 1830s in the United States. That phenomenon is riven with many contradictions, but an in-depth analysis of its compelling history, psychology, and sociology would be beyond the scope of this book. I recommend Baz Dreisinger's *Near Black* for the intrigued and curious reader.[38]

The complex nature of whites crossing racial boundaries presents many nagging questions. The Left revulsion toward the white appropriation of Blackness seems intuitive. But how does it square with what might seem like the isomorphic version of cross-category identity in terms of gender? What makes cross-*racial* identity wrong but cross-*gender* identity right? Why do we regard the former as an appalling example of ethnic colonization but view the latter as a respected, if not revered, case of personal choice and a courageous assertion of the right to identity self-determination?

Both involve a member of a dominant group taking on the identity of someone in a less powerful group. (Obviously, the latter point in the gender version of identity change applies only to male-to-female transitions, which had been more than three times as frequent as female-to-male transitions.[39] Although, currently, the ratio is reversing among adolescents.[40]) Both can include body modification (temporary in Dolezal's case) and the donning of identity-congruent clothing.

A subset of feminists who call themselves "gender-critical" (a group of activists that contains trans and non-trans people[41]) regards trans women as more akin to a third gender. Members of that gender, in the view of such feminists, certainly have the right to reject mainstream masculinity, femininity, and the oppressive constraints that come with those labels. And they have the right to use any pronouns that fit with their sense of self, to be free from harassment and violence, and enjoy all the civil liberties accorded to any other citizen. However, gender-critical feminists would view as fraudulent any claims trans women might make to an authentic understanding of biological females' life experience, whether or not they modify their bodies with hormones or surgery.[42] Moreover, those feminists reject any demand trans women might put forward to be considered legal women for the purpose of entering specific female-only spaces like single-sex bathrooms, domestic violence shelters, women's prisons, or locker rooms.

The argument made by other feminists against the gender-critical position is that the biology of sex itself is a continuum, encompassing complex and discontinuous aspects of self, such as gender, sexuality, chromosomes, hormones, anatomy, and identity. The gender-critical counterargument to that continuum notion is that the science affirming the binary nature of our reproductive biology is irrefutable. They argue that while there may be individual variations in hormone levels, secondary sex characteristics, and anatomy, there are only two types of gametes, eggs and sperm. Only egg producers can get pregnant, and only sperm makers can fertilize eggs. While "intersex" individuals exist, they are rare and thus could not be reasonably placed on a continuum of incremental shades of difference.[43] And unless the anomaly is mild, many of these people are sterile.[44] From that perspective, any framework that viewed them as a different sex and thereby a challenge to the binary notion of biological sex would be scientifically incoherent.

Scientists and clinicians aligned with the gender-critical view agree that the enormous variation in gender-role behavior and cultural notions of what it means to be male and female exist on a continuum. Still, they insist, it does not negate the biological reality of two sexes.[45] And, some would point out, in the current repressive political climate in which rights to reproductive health care

are undergoing a radical contraction, only natal females will be forced to carry pregnancies to term.

Nevertheless, the medical lexicon has changed to reflect an ethos of trans-inclusivity. "Pregnant mothers" and "breastfeeding" have been replaced by "pregnant people" and "chest-feeding."[46] Some celebrate that shift to a gender-neutral lexicon, like the American Civil Liberties Union. Others, like Dr. Sara Dahlen, are less sanguine. In the *British Medical Journal*, quoting feminist medical colleagues, she insists that "the same arguments that support gender-inclusive language for transgender people apply equally to women who may feel erased or dehumanized by terminology labeled 'neutral.' If the aim is to maximize respect for every person's sense of self, it must follow that [natal] female patients who simply understand themselves as women cannot either be expected to 'go along silently with language in which they do not exist.'"[47]

Unfortunately, the debate among those opposing factions of feminists has too often devolved into ad hominem and straw-man (or in some cases, straw-*woman*) arguments and, even on a few occasions, physical assault.[48] Trans activists are denounced as "misogynists," and gender-critical feminists are reviled as "transphobic TERFs" (trans exclusionary radical feminists). And, as so often happens on the Left, the conflict has obscured what these groups have in common, such as support for the freedom to be gender nonconforming and fierce resistance to the constraints of stereotypical masculinity and femininity.

My aim is not to settle that passionate dispute but to highlight it as a curious contradiction in Left notions of identity. In the case of race, a category with little coherent basis in biology, identity is spoken of as fixed and must not be breached through appropriation.[49] Those who do should be called out and shamed. With gender, identity is seen as fluid, and those who arrogate to themselves whatever label they want are to be respected, honored, and protected. Even biological sex is understood by some social constructionists as a normalizing fiction that has no utility.[50]

Racial vs. Gender Drag

As another example of the puzzling distinction made by those on the Left between racial and gendered identity, we can look at the different ways we regard drag performance. There is near universal agreement that racial drag performance is repellent and should remain in the dustbin of America's racist history. And yet, gendered drag by male performers is not only acceptable but celebrated. Nearly all gay pride parades feature hyper-fem harlequins playing femaleness for laughs. And for many decades, clubs in San Francisco's Broadway district have been sustained by the busloads of straight, otherwise conservative Midwest tourists flocking to the neighborhood's famous drag shows.

Viewed through a psychoanalytic lens, we could see female impersonation and an earlier generation's theatrical "blackface" racial mimicry as more than lighthearted play, caricature in the case of the former, or bigoted mockery in the case of the latter. We could also understand those theatrical displays as expressions of the performer's covetous envy of and identification with the traits projected onto the respective gendered or racial characters. Given the popularity of those shows, that interpretation might also apply to the audiences. Such a reading is not just theoretical. There is extensive scholarship on male womb and breast envy in the historical and cross-cultural literature on gender[51] Male rituals that mimic birth, breastfeeding, and menstruation are well described in multiple ethnographic accounts. And the same dynamic seems to operate along racial lines, as the life stories of some white people who have passed as Black indicate.

Rachel Dolezal is not the only person who's proclaimed cross-racial identity went far beyond a transient performance. The cases of white people living as Black men and women, described in Dreisinger's book mentioned earlier, suggest that envious racial appropriation is a more common psychological and social reality than we might have imagined. Laura Browder's study of "ethnic impersonators" in the United States, which covers a broad range of non-white identities—Black, brown, and native—adopted by whites, reveals a similar psychology.[52] Accounts in both books feature white people who have projected certain envied traits onto other ethnicities and then try to possess them by appropriating the identities of those racial groups.

If some white people view rhythmicity, musicality, or "cool" as traits limited to people of African origin, then those Caucasians may try to be "Black." In the case of gender, some males might perceive nurturance, generativity, or flamboyant seductiveness as the exclusive property of women. As a consequence, they may conclude that finding a way to be or present as a "woman" is a path to feeling whole. (That said, this framework is not an explanation of transgender identities, a phenomenon far too complex to reduce to any single account.)

Escaping the Traps of Essentialism

The problem with *biological* essentialism is that it reduces behavior and identity to matters of anatomy and physiology. In this view, what we can think, feel, and be are entirely dictated by the organs we are born with. For natal females in red states, for example, the ability to get pregnant, gestate a fetus, and nurse an infant *mandate*s childbirth. Abortion for any reason violates God's and nature's laws. And in those parts of the country, it is increasingly a violation of statutes. Thanks to Republican legislators, the law in those regions now requires that women's biology be their destiny. And women's uteruses have been declared property of the state. Beyond forced pregnancy laws, natal females everywhere must bear the burden of the maternal-instincts-fiction as authored by men.[53] For generations, that story led to white middle-class women's confinement to the gilded cage of domesticity. And even once they left to join the workforce, women were rebuked and often felt guilty for departing from their supposed proper caretaking role.

On the other hand, the problem of *psychocultural* essentialism is that it reduces biology to an inconsequential feature of human existence, a simple artifact of discourse. In other words, bodies are whatever we say they are. The *reductio ad absurdum* of this vulgar postmodernist notion can be seen in situations where anatomically intact male prisoners, some convicted of sexual assault, are allowed to serve their time in women's prisons simply because they *declare* themselves female.[54] Once inside these all-woman facilities, some have continued their prior pattern of sexual predation. Those rare instances certainly should not be read as a claim that trans women have any greater incidence of criminality or sexual offending than others of their natal sex. Indeed, the crime rate, including violent offenses, for males who undergo gender transition remains the same as cis men.[55]

However, this is an under-researched area. Future epidemiological studies may yield results that fit better with what many, including myself, would intuit, i.e., men who disidentify with the traditional dominance-based male role would seem less prone to violence. One major challenge of that research would be the growing acceptance of the idea that sex (and thus trans identity) is simply what one declares it to be. There are those whose trans identity is a genuine, long-standing, and deeply felt response to gender dysphoria. And there are those for whom it might be a fraudulent performance in pursuing another aim—like doing easier prison time in a woman's facility. Instantiating the idea of gender self-identification in law or policy would make it impossible to distinguish the two scenarios. In any case, the previously cited research does pose a challenge for those who claim that male socialization and a lifetime of hormonal priming are magically undone once a man identifies and lives as a woman.

One solution to avoid either form of essentialist reductionism that has emerged in various cultures has been the creation of third genders. These are identities that enable gender-nonconforming individuals of both biological sexes to live how they want and love whom they desire regardless of cultural expectation—in most cases, without having to modify their bodies or medically "transition" to a body that resembles the other sex.

One of the most well-known examples is the *berdache* gender among North American indigenous peoples.[56] This third gender identity has been documented in about 150 native groups and observed over five centuries of contact between Anglo-Europeans and Native societies. It endured in native cultures until about the first third of the twentieth century. The role was adopted equally by natal males and females. Non-native observers and early anthropologists strained to understand the *berdache* through the lenses of colonial categories. "Hermaphrodite," "sodomite," "homosexual," and "transsexual" were all labels that whites used in their efforts to capture an identity that persistently eluded their understanding. Even the term *berdache* was another colonial distortion and an insulting one borrowed from the Arabic word for "kept boy." As we might expect, the native word for that role came much closer to their self-understanding: *two-spirits*.

Of the *two-spirits*, some chose same-sex partners, but not all. Some were bisexual, others heterosexual (if we define sexual object choice in biological terms). Some cross-dressed but not all. Both male and female *two-spirits* modified their dress according to the gendering of the job that had to be performed, such as donning male attire to join a war party. Most engaged in labor more typically performed by the other sex. Male *two-spirits* specialized in domestic tasks and craft production. Female *two-spirits* were involved in hunting, warfare, and leadership roles usually held by men. Their identities and social roles were understood as spiritually endowed and thus highly respected. They were perceived as possessing supernatural powers.

Notably, no evidence suggests those native groups suffered from gender dysphoria. And no account of the *two-spirits* indicates they felt they had somehow been born into the "wrong body." That seems to be because they lived in a social world where their natal anatomy and physiology did not dictate their identity or social role. Their gender nonconformity and sexual object choices were not problems and required no medical solutions.

The Psychology of Liberal Partisans and the Trans Debate

At this point, readers might wonder why the "trans-inclusion" debate has split parts of the feminist Left and why conservatives are relatively unified in their exclusionary stance. The answer might lie in what we know about the moral psychology of partisanship.[57] Recall from the research cited earlier that liberals and conservatives tend to be driven by specific but different values that underlie their policy and candidate preferences. For partisans on the Left, those values are equality, fairness, openness to experience, and the embrace of outsiders. It is important to note that the argument on each side of the liberal split is framed in the same liberal values. The disagreement centers, in part, on who is the underdog/outsider subject to unfair treatment and unjust exclusion, whose rights are being abridged by whom, and who are the rigid bigots clinging to old dichotomous categories.

On one side, trans people are depicted as a minority targeted for discrimination and sometimes assault. So, their rights and safety must be ensured. Being open to new experiences means breaking out of binary notions of sex and gender. Fair treatment means more than just respecting whatever pronouns someone wants to use. In this view, biological natal sex should never be a consideration in matters of justice. Gender, what people call themselves, is all that should matter. Women who want to be in single-sex spaces and exclude trans women who may or may not have penises are seen as transphobic bigots.

Conversely, while gender-critical natal women would agree that they are not a minority, they would quickly point out the discrimination and risk of assault that women are subject to wherever they venture, day or night.[58] Their lifelong experiences of having to make room for and defer to men should be acknowledged and not repeated by demanding that they accommodate men who call themselves women. Fairness and equity for biological females mean supporting their need to feel and be safe, whether in lavatories, single-sex changing rooms, domestic violence shelters, or prison cells.

From that perspective, those who insist that gender-nonconforming behavior is a sign that someone was "born in the wrong body" and must be medically modified are the ones stuck in archaic, black-and-white categories. Pressuring gay or lesbian people to change their sex to make them no longer technically homosexual, such as in Iran and Pakistan, is viewed as an egregious form of homophobic oppression and a particularly malign iteration of "conversion therapy."[59] In both countries, being gay or lesbian could lead to a lengthy prison sentence or execution, but being surgically remodeled to resemble the sex opposite of the one you desire could save your life.

Conservatives, by contrast, are motivated by entirely different values—deference to traditional authority, in-group loyalty, purity/sanctity, discomfort with complexity and a predisposition toward black-and-white thinking, and wariness and hostility toward outsiders. Mostly, this translates into opposition to gender flexibility of any kind. Biological sex is real, but gendered behavior and sexual object choice must be dictated by it. Men must dominate. Women must defer to men. Homosexuals are sinners who choose their "disgusting" lifestyles. Transgender people are defying God's plan for them to live life in the bodies with which they were born.

However, there are some cases in which conservative Christian parents with gender-nonconforming children have channeled their effeminate boy, masculine girl, or suspected homosexual child toward hormone "therapy" and sex reassignment surgery as the other sex.[60] At least then, such parents figure, they will no longer suffer the shame of having a gay, lesbian, sissy-boy, or butch-girl child.

The Left Critique of Trans Ideology

Another way to view this split on the Left is to consider it as a debate over what some call trans ideology. Trans ideology is a mental framework for thinking about trans phenomena. It is a belief system held by a diverse range of individuals and includes those who embrace every conceivable gender and sexual identity, mainly by people on the progressive Left. The critique of trans ideology from the Left is that it is a belief comprised of an essentialist notion of gender and a social constructionist concept of biological sex. They challenge the view that holds that gender—our sense of self as male or female—is an unalterable essence with which we are born.

These critics also take issue with the trans ideology view of biological sex, which is seen not as an empirical reality but as an infinite rainbow of socially constructed possibilities—one that has no existence apart from how we name and stamp it on certificates of birth. And yet, somehow, essential gender identities can exist in bodies that are wrong and must be altered. This brings us to the heart of what some Left feminist critics would regard as one of trans ideology's core contradictions: bodies are at once nonmaterial social constructions *and* material realities that must be surgically and hormonally modified to be congruent with those essential identities.

Most Left critics of trans ideology do not see themselves as criticizing those who identify as trans. And yet, understandably, many trans folks do feel attacked and their very existence denied when the conceptual foundation of their identity is challenged. Nevertheless, as I've noted previously, there are even a few trans people who reject that ideology. Those on the Left who dispute it are certainly not arguing against protecting the civil rights of trans folks, nor do they aim to limit their freedom to call themselves by any label that suits them—except in those rare instances where that nomenclature, in the case of trans women, leads to policies that compromise the privacy and perceived safety of natal females.

That said, there are many on the Right who do seek the abolition of civil rights for sexual and gender minorities, including trans women and trans men. Those critics are mainly driven by ignorance and dehumanizing bigotry enhanced by religious demonology. For them, trans people comprise another group of despised others who are utilized by the MAGA Right to create politically useful culture war narratives. Christian conservatives are not simply opposed to medical solutions to gender nonconformity (as some on the Left might be) but view gender non-conformity itself as an abomination. In other words, their essentialism consists of conflating gender, sexual orientation, and natal sex. From that perspective, there is only one way to be or love a woman or a man. And, as is typical of the Right, their answer to any ambiguity in those pure categories is a repressive one, with measures designed to police stereotypes and cultural norms.

When Left Identity Politics Becomes Tyrannical

Some readers might assume that intellectual repression and censorious persecution have been confined to red state administrations, like that of the increasingly fascist reign of Florida's cynical culture war governor, Ron DeSantis.[61] Right-wing book bans, curricular surveillance, and the suppression of historical scholarship are epidemic across multiple red states. They can readily eclipse the pedagogical skirmishes over Left identity politics on American campuses.[62] And it can be tempting to trivialize the dramas associated with university cancel culture and the notorious battles over ideological purity or alleged failures to deploy the proper PC vocabulary du jure. But those conflicts are far more than tempests in the Left identitarian teapot. In many situations, those disputes have had life-altering and, in some cases, life-ending consequences.

Journalist and renowned scholar of authoritarianism Anne Applebaum wrote a troubling and well-documented report on academia's illiberal liberals.[63] Titled *The New Puritans*, we might expect it to refer to a priggish cloister of religious conservatives who see demons everywhere. Sadly, what once would have been a bracing oxymoron, "puritanical progressives," has become a new reality. Her piece revealed that on some campuses, accusations, investigations, and tribunals are often initiated without due process, in some cases without evidence, and without the accused being able to know the identity of their accusers or confront them in a fair and open hearing. The decisions handed down in these academic Star Chamber proceedings destroy careers, tarnish reputations, impoverish its "defendants," and even lead to suicides.

In many cases, firing was unnecessary because trolling, threats, or shunning forced the resignation of those with minority opinions or whose non-bigoted scholarship violated some component of Left-identitarian catechism. Notably, the professors targeted were not Holocaust deniers, advocates of racial eugenics, homophobes, or perpetrators of sexual assault. Instead, they were liberal scholars who argued for intellectually heterodox positions, like the once ordinary but still evidence-based assertion that biological sexes are real and that there are only two of them.[64] The latter case involved Dr. Colin Wright, an evolutionary biologist who, exhausted by harassment and false accusations of bigotry, opted to leave his position and, ultimately, his career.[65] He is not a conservative and certainly not a MAGA Republican. A militant atheist, he spent years debating and writing against religious deniers of evolution, only to be driven out of academia by science-denying leftists. And remaining behind in the wake of these expulsions and resignations are those still employed but who have learned through the example of others that self-censorship is crucial to a scholar's professional survival.

Dr. Wright's story brings to mind a related area of Left identity politics, which also concerns the most hotly contested domain of sex and gender—gender self-identification (GSI). That refers to the concept and now a legal principle whereby gender identity is conflated with natal sex. In practice, it means that all one needs to do to be legally considered a member of the other sex is to declare it so. No body modification, hormonal treatment, psychological evaluation, or transition is required.

Some trans activists, who are not necessarily trans, have moved far beyond defending the right for people to call themselves what they want, be safe from harassment and violence, and be treated with respect and fairness. For example, activists worldwide have sought to extend the GSI principle to all public records so personal histories can be rewritten on birth certificates or data on natal sex can be removed from all government documents.[66] That post-truth move would damage public health epidemiology and our collective ability to track disease and violent crime incidence, among many other phenomena that vary profoundly by natal sex.

In addition, under the GSI rubric, no natal male needs to do anything but declare himself a woman to enter single-sex female spaces legally. While an important goal of many trans activists, it has not yet been inscribed in American law. However, it is written into the legal code of a few other countries.[67] In some places, natal women who protest against being exposed to the intact male genitals of a trans woman or undressing in front of one risk being demeaned as "transphobic" or subject to legal sanction. Ironically, the right to privacy was the foundational principle of the now-overturned *Roe v. Wade* decision to grant reproductive choice to women and was fiercely defended by the political Left. Yet, that right seldom arises in discussions among liberals regarding the unlimited extension of gender self-identification.

Lastly, there is the controversy over the entry of trans women into female sporting competitions. Some cis women have been concerned about competing with natal males whose musculature has enjoyed the enduring benefits of pubertal androgens before transition. They point to research that shows that there is a significant athletic advantage that is only slightly attenuated by suppressing testosterone.[68] Natal women and girls who have protested what they perceive as the clear and unfair edge that gives to trans women athletes have been shamed, threatened, and denounced as bigots.[69] Gender-critical women say they are not arguing for trans people to be excluded from sports, only that competition takes place on an even playing field.

Unfortunately, conservative politicians have adopted this issue as a culture war bludgeon, not necessarily because of any abiding concern for women's rights. Liberal failure to develop a creative, fair, and science-based resolution has created an exploitable opportunity for the Right. Despite viewing gender nonconformity as disgusting and evil and consistently pushing policies that limit women's freedom, congressional Republicans have been allowed to don feminist drag and proclaim themselves allies of natal female athletes.

The hallmarks of the most limiting versions of conservative psychology (though not characteristic of every conservative) include: shunning heretics, cognitive rigidity, incuriousness about the different views of others, bullying, intolerance of ambiguity, and a defensive adherence to fundamentalist dogma over factuality. It is heartbreaking and fills me with despair when I see friends and colleagues on the Left aping those traits. Those who comfort themselves with the assumption that only right-wingers form literal or virtual lynch mobs need only look closely at the demonization and persecution of J. K. Rowling.[70] A liberal feminist supporter of gender nonconformity and the rights of sexual and gender minorities, she has committed the unpardonable heresy of arguing for the salience of biology, especially concerning the right of natal women to be in specific female-only spaces. For that, she lives with non-stop harassment and death threats.

I realize that some of my readers may be shocked to hear me question the conventional Left wisdom about Rowling—that she is a hateful and transphobic bigot. I would only implore you to read or listen to her yourself before accepting that hearsay as truth. An excellent place to start would be her interviews featured in the podcast series, *The Witch Trials of J. K. Rowling*.[71]" The series documents the central role she played for many years in the baroque demonology of the Christian Right due to the explosive popularity of her *Harry Potter* books. That was then followed by years of misogynist hatred and willful misrepresentation by some on the identitarian Left, who essentially issued a secular but no less life-threatening fatwa against Rowling for her apostasy on certain matters of sex and gender. Unfortunately, her years of battle against identitarian lynch mobs appear to have hardened her in ways that seem to invite even more antagonism. In a feud with one militant trans woman, Rowling's refusal to refer to that activist by her preferred pronouns came off as gratuitously combative.[72] It also illustrates one of the casualties of spending so much of one's life being under siege—the collapse of empathy.

Finally, some caveats are in order here. There is a risk of painting college cancel culture with a broad partisan brush, giving the impression that it is primarily a problem of the Left. However, if we look more closely at politically motivated academic censorship, the emerging picture is complex. In 2018, more liberal than conservative scholars were sanctioned for their views.[73] Turning Point USA, a right-wing pro-Trump advocacy group, maintains an academic enemies list of professors targeted for their perceived liberal views.[74] In 2021, they were the force behind a substantial plurality of sanction attempts.[75]

An extensive study of efforts between 2020 and 2022 to censor or fire university faculty revealed interesting partisan and demographic differences.[76] More than 75 percent of *on*-campus efforts to punish or censor faculty came from student and academic peers to the left of the targeted professor. An equal percentage of *off*-campus pressure campaigns to ban specific courses and teachers arose from right-wing citizen groups and politicians. That may reflect a growing political gulf between "town and gown" on a national level—at least in red regions of the country.

Identity on the Right vs. the Left

Right-wing identity politics around race and gender, which will be the focus of the next chapter, are more uniform and far less conflicted than we see on the Left. Conservatives tend to eschew ambiguity in all identity categories. That is especially apparent when it comes to race and ethnicity. Unlike those on the Left, who generally seek to preserve the integrity of cultural and ethnic boundaries out of respect and care (however misplaced at times), white conservatives see safety in the conceptual and physical barriers that separate them from non-white races.

Right-wing partisans tend to view qualities like race as being automatically contiguous with many other aspects of a person or group. In other words, they are more likely to traffic in stereotypes and find comfort in them because such beliefs organize the social world into understandable and discreet categories. However, as described in the previous chapter, those on the Right are more likely to view other races as threatening and embodying a moral and biological impurity that must be kept on the other side of the tribal boundary.

As troubling as Left illiberalism can be, there are ways in which the politically powerful and well-armed partisans of right-wing identity politics are far more concerning. They are represented by a large plurality in Congress. They have neofascist militias ready to deploy if Trump gives the word. And they have control of over half of the state houses across the country. Right identitarians in the United States are also explicitly committed to ending democracy, denaturing civil rights protections, and replacing science and history education with religious doctrine.

In contrast to liberals, conservatives wield economic and political power far out of proportion to their numbers in the population. We need only look at the tax structure, the Electoral College, the Senate filibuster rule, and how Senate representation is allocated. Those structural inequities show that American democracy has long been hampered by a bias that gives a conservative minority of citizens what amounts to veto power over the more moderate and liberal majority. As will be shown later in the next chapter, that right-wing minority has caused enormous harm to the American people and the democracy that enables their voice to matter. Promoting racial hatred and injustice is one area where that harm has been particularly discernible. And behind that lies the psychology that undergirds white conservative identity politics, a politics rapidly being codified in law by red state legislatures nationwide.

CHAPTER 4

Identity Politics on the Right — Race, Class, and the Freedom to Harm

Ricky Thompson, a pipe fitter from Mobile, Alabama, told a *New York Times* reporter, "He's neither-nor. He's other. It's in the Bible. Come as one. Don't create other breeds."[1] Another denizen of the GOP's "real America" shared his spiritual insights with the same interviewer. Glenn Reynolds of Martinsdale, Virginia, pointed out, "God taught the children of Israel not to intermarry." Such guileless proclamations of pious bigotry reveal something obvious but easily overlooked: It was not Obama's Blackness that disturbed the devout great-grandchildren of the Confederacy, but his grayness.

Why They Hated Obama: Miscegenation and Other Nightmares of the Racist Political Imagination

The frank comments of unapologetic anti-Obama racists across the country found a broad national audience during his presidency. Their discomfort with the permeability of racial boundaries was evident in the right-wing response to Barack Obama's mixed-race background and identity. Most on the Right no longer argue for legal segregation, although their flight to conservative white enclaves has been another way to achieve that. Well before Trump, there was an anxiety about the erosion of the wall, marked by melanin, that kept the category of race unambiguous. The psychological barriers foundational to America's apartheid system have been far more enduring than those inscribed in law.

Ideas that now seem like crackpot notions of race were, not long ago, regarded as common sense and were codified as statute. The "one-drop rule" asserted that a single drop of Black blood in an otherwise white citizen rendered that person Black. Blackness was widely viewed as a contaminant that sullied white purity. (On the other hand, in the antebellum period, the rape and impregnation of enslaved African women was justified as "racial improvement" for Black people.) The rule was adopted by numerous state legislators in the first third of the twentieth century and used as the basis for Jim Crow laws.

In 1924, Dr. Walter Plecker, a public health advocate who worked for Virginia's Vital Statistics Department, said, "Two races as materially divergent as the White and Negro, in morals, mental powers, and cultural fitness, cannot live in close contact without injury to the higher."[2] It wasn't until 1967 that the US Supreme Court proclaimed Plecker's *Virginia Racial Integrity Act* and the one-drop rule unconstitutional. This decision, which eliminated the ban on interracial marriage, bore the wonderfully apt title of *Loving v. Virginia*.

Sadly, but not surprisingly, such legal victories have not kept Plecker's sentiments from being embraced by contemporary guardians of racial boundaries. And Barack Obama, the child of a Black African father and a white American mother, was, for these folks, the very embodiment of what must not be brought together.

While legally sanctioned racial segregation in public life may be moldering in history's dustbin, corresponding segregation in our inner lives has continued to structure our thoughts and emotions. Some people consciously, but most unconsciously, hold on dearly to the pure and invariant categories of "good" and "bad." Keeping them apart and unambiguously distinct helps us retain a reassuring fantasy of safety, order, and certainty. "Race" lends itself well to that process psychoanalysts call splitting. Imagined as fundamentally unlike us, the racialized other becomes the perfect receptacle into which we are free to project all the wishes, impulses, and longings we cannot bear to see in our ethnic group or individual selves. In other words, racism allows us to be all-good because there is someplace outside of us to put the bad.

Of course, this ruse we perpetrate on ourselves only works if we can sustain the delusion of absolute difference. Those who are more consciously racist rely on what Erik Erickson called "pseudospeciation," viewing other racial groups as separate species, a notion discussed in the earlier chapters. "Interbreeding" becomes a psychological, biological, and, for some, a theological abomination. The fundamentalist Christian Bob Jones University didn't overturn its ban on interracial dating until 2000. This was done with considerable reluctance and primarily to save George W. Bush from political embarrassment after giving a campaign stump speech in their chapel.

Speaking of spiritual matters, we should not be surprised that the racism of right-wing religious fundamentalists tends to be more explicit.[3] Many biblical fables endorse slavery, ethnic warfare, and genocide, and some preachers inveigh against "race mixing." Not only is sanguinary brutality sanctioned by the celestial autocrat in their holy book, but authoritarian aggression turns out to be a trait quite common in fundamentalists.[4]

The bigotry of the ardently evangelical is also implicit. Christian fundamentalists tend to score high on measures of implicit or unconscious racism.[5]

In addition, the *structure*—not just the content—of fundamentalist theology and racism are quite similar—both rely on splitting and a low tolerance for ambiguity.[6] The dogmatically devout literally and metaphorically think in black-and-white terms.

All of that brings us back to the Right's contempt for Barack Obama. His very visibility—let alone his candidacy for the most powerful and, before Donald Trump, the most esteemed job in the world—created a category crisis of epic proportions. He not only mouthed rhetoric of transcending division but is himself a seamless physical and cultural integration of what should be immiscible. We might imagine that certain unanswerable questions plagued upstanding, God-fearing racists: What is this incomprehensible hybrid of badness and goodness? How can the same person contain that with which I identify and that which I despise?

In the 2008 presidential campaign, we heard Republican ads and saw GOP viral emails that posed more rational-seeming derivatives of these questions: Who is Barack Obama? Do we actually know him? Doesn't he sound kind of uppity and elitist? Is he a Christian or a Muslim? Is he really like us? Didn't he grow up in Hawaii, one of those un-American parts of America?

His mixed heritage elicited white racial tribal anxieties more than if he were comprised of unalloyed Blackness because his racial amalgam blurred tribal boundaries. Obama was a picture of intolerable ambiguity. Birtherism, the conspiracy theory that Obama was a "secret Muslim" born in Kenya, was promoted by Trump and others who see the world from the other side of the Fox News looking glass. We can think of the promotion of the Birther lie as a desperate attempt to confer an absolute otherness onto the former president. For the MAGA right, the birther fantasy was a trifecta of tribalist slurs; he was "pure" Black, non-Christian, and foreign.

In July 2022, Hungary's Christian fascist prime minister, Viktor Orbán, vowed to prevent the abomination of mixed-race Europeans.[7] In the same speech, the avuncular autocrat expressed his appreciation for the lighter side of mass murder. While discussing the European Union's plan to ration natural gas, Orbán jokingly referenced the Nazi gas chambers, saying, "The past shows us German know-how on that." That was enough to get a longtime advisor, Zsuzsa Hegedüs, to resign in protest. She described her former boss's speech as "a pure Nazi text worthy of Goebbels."[8] However, the 2022 Conservative Political Action Conference (CPAC) organizers in Dallas, Texas, were not dissuaded from welcoming him as a keynote speaker. Indeed, Orbán received a wholehearted embrace from the CPAC crowd.[9]

Most Americans are not consciously racist and tend to abhor explicit proclamations of bigotry. Like Orbán, they would reject "racism" as a label for their conscious beliefs and emotions.[10] However, as Drew Westen and other researchers have shown, the majority of people—Black as well as white—harbor an unconscious negative bias against anyone perceived as Black.[11] At a deep level, most of us use racial categories to navigate the world, manage its vague and unseen threats, and define our worth and that of others.

And why should we expect otherwise? Every person in this country is embedded in a culture and history founded on racist beliefs, practices, and emotions. American slavery was not only a normal and acceptable tradition for centuries but was accompanied by a legal, physical, and mental infrastructure that protected and justified it. There is no place to stand outside this psychological, social, and historical reality. It saturates our national sense of self and structures our neural networks.

However, it is possible to acknowledge and remain mindful of this ugly and disturbing legacy, enabling us to minimize its influence on how we treat others and elect leaders to public office. And, as the enthusiastic throngs of citizens who attended Obama's speeches, here and abroad, demonstrated, it is even possible to move beyond "tolerance"—to embrace and celebrate the fluidity of categories, cultures, and identities that his candidacy and presidency came to represent for many.

By noting that, I am not speaking of Obama, the politician, who remained a cautious moderate and harbored various wishful illusions about his critics' integrity and good faith. Nor am I arguing that his policies were much more than well-intentioned half-measures designed in the naïve and doomed hope that "moderate" Republicans would endorse them. Instead, it was Obama, the symbol, that had the most radical impact—his role as a signifier of integration, multiplicity, and hybrid identity.

Disappearing Race from Contemporary Right-Wing Narratives

Adam Serwer discusses the Senatorial campaign of David Duke, the former KKK Grand Wizard who won 43 percent of the Louisiana vote in his 1990 run for office.[12] Counterintuitively, Duke, in ads and photo ops, made what appeared to be an attempt to appeal to Black voters. That effort brings to mind how Trump rallies feature the few Black attendees posing with their "Blacks for Trump" T-shirts just behind the podium so TV cameras can easily capture them. It is absurd to suppose that either Duke or Trump had or expected to get many African American supporters. What is far more plausible is that the target audience for that racial choreography was racially resentful whites who would like to feel less conflicted about voting for white supremacist xenophobic candidates. In other words, they would like to act on racist impulses while believing themselves to be virtuous people who favor racial equality.

That may be one of Trump's more effective cons, convincing his white supporters that voting for him was not about white supremacy. The news media worked hard to promote this fiction. He convinced them that to speak of the MAGA base as racist would alienate their readership. To name race as a motive driving Trump's support was a kind of journalistic third rail, a dangerous taboo. The opprobrium visited upon Hillary Clinton for daring to tell the truth about the MAGA basket of racially resentful deplorables further muzzled an already timid press fearful of offending right-wing viewers and losing ad money.

Serwer's critique of civility in this regard is critical. He points out how hard mainstream journalists worked to avoid attributions of racism to Trump or his followers. That is despite the robust data showing that racism had been a significant motive for the base to support him.[13] While Hillary's comment about the deplorable plurality of racists among his supporters became the scandal, extraordinary efforts were made to avoid acknowledging the truth of her remarks. Her impolitic and indelicate honesty was derided, not the quite evident truth behind it. Journalists and commentators strained to conjure up every possible explanation for Trump support—economic, cultural, "West Coast elite" snobbery—to avoid naming the obvious white racial resentment. Serwer uses the apposite analogy of a pothole in the road. Everybody can be seen swerving to avoid it, but no one talks about it.

The story Republicans prefer to tell about Trump's support among their base revolves around economic concerns, as if he were some kind of working-class hero. Serwer cites data showing that in 2016 the most economically vulnerable citizens voted for Clinton over Trump by a considerable margin. But when you look at white voters, the research is mixed. Among whites, there was greater support for Trump at every economic level. Yet it wasn't so much economic suffering that pushed white voters toward Trump but the attribution of that suffering to non-white people.

A common notion in conservative political discourse is that no one is racist unless they say they are or they are caught attending a cross burning bedecked in a Klan robe. To argue that racism is a motivating factor driving membership in the MAGA faction is not to say that liberals are without racist beliefs or emotions. The main difference is that most liberals will acknowledge the reality of implicit or unconscious racism and its hold over everyone, including those who are its victims. Readers may not be surprised that animosity toward racial, religious, and sexual minorities assessed in 2011 predicted Trump support a decade later.[14] Individual and collective racism exists on a continuum of conscious and unconscious racism. Conservatives resist recognizing or addressing *systemic* racism, which can operate without personal bigotry or deliberate racist intent.[15] But, to make matters even more complicated, it is not just that racists are drawn to the GOP. It is also the case that membership in the party helps its members become racist.

Partisan Belonging Creates Partisan Attitudes—The Complex Nature of Racism on the Right

The research of political scientists Peter K. Enns and Ashley Jardina found that there was indeed a strong association between Trump support and holding racist attitudes.[16] Yet, that was not just because bigots could find a welcoming home in the Republican Party. Their study showed that identifying as a MAGA Republican can be an incentive to change your racial attitudes to be more congruent with those held by Trump. In other words, tribal membership can be a force for attitude change, rather than simply attracting people who already share the group's partisan beliefs. The same holds for religiosity and bigotry against sexual and gender minorities, according to the research of Andrew M. Engelhardt.[17]

Another study found that racial attitudes have become the leading indicator of a whole cluster of political stances[18] They predict opinions about gun safety regulations, police procedures, election access, health care, and international trade. For conservatives, non-racial issues have become saturated with racial resentment. That is primarily the result of the misperception by those on the Right that the Democratic Party comprises mostly non-white voters. The sense that the party of liberals represents ethnic outsiders makes identifying with the entire package of GOP attitudes easier. So, once adopted, racial bigotry appears to become a gateway drug that facilitates embracing other elements of a right-wing worldview.

Perhaps that is because the root of the American conservative worldview, libertarianism, not only dates from the early centuries of US white supremacy but was formulated as a justification for its central practice, slavery. Libertarianism was and remains an ideology from which a particularly conservative notion of freedom and a corresponding concept of tyranny were derived. The history of the Right's understanding of liberty and its relevance to the present will be unpacked at the end of this chapter and in the following one.

Conservatives of Color and Their Fantasies of Racial Transcendence

One of conservative racial psychology's most intriguing but puzzling features is its new iteration of ethnic minority passing. Rather than trying to look white, Black and Hispanic conservatives seem to have pursued an *ideological* path to transracial identity. From MAGA warrior Candace Owens to Afrocuban Proud Boys leader Enrico Tarrio, a prominent minority of people of color has aligned with openly white supremacists. Some conservatives of color, like Owens,[19] deny the reality of white supremacy and insist the GOP Southern Strategy is a myth. Yet others, like Tarrio, belong to or head a white nationalist organization.[20]

The fantasy of assimilation through collaboration with racists can never be realized, primarily because white supremacists view race as a concrete and immutable trait. Their right-wing peers may very well overlook the obvious and hold to their "color blindness"—the cognitive self-deception that is really an erasure of non-whiteness, i.e., "We're the same; you're just like me." But the rest of the world remains saturated with systemic and implicit racism.

To be clear, there is nothing pathological about people of color adopting a conservative ideology. What seems hobbling for them is the expectation that joining the MAGA cult will be a magical entry into a post-racial world. The GOP of the present moment is an undisguised white nationalist movement led by a fascist ex-president determined to overthrow democracy and who praises and dines with avowed neo-Nazis.[21] To invert Groucho Marx's famous assertion, non-white Republicans are happy members of a club that despises members like them.

Conservative Principles, Then and Now

It is startling to consider the issues and principles that once seemed to define pre-MAGA US conservatism, politically and culturally, but *no longer* do. A short and incomplete list would have to include: suspicion and fear of Russia, adamant insistence on law and order, reverence for government agencies charged with law enforcement like the FBI and the CIA (institutions whose *stated* purpose at least has always been to protect the country from those who would seek to attack or subvert it), harsh disapproval of those who fail to uphold the bonds of marital fidelity, commitment to democratic and fair elections, and passionate opposition to the accumulating national debt. It has been remarkable how quickly the latter concern, in particular, evaporates once a Republican enters the

White House. That was especially observable under Trump.[22] The conventional wisdom, endlessly repeated by stenographic reporters, that the current GOP is the party of fiscal conservatism is one that defies readily observable reality.

A well-researched analysis in an *Axios* article shows government discretionary spending goes up dramatically when Republicans are in power.[23] They are quite willing to send the national debt into the stratosphere as long it serves the interest of their corporate and wealthy benefactors. When Democrats hold power, GOP politicians do whatever they can to prevent spending, especially on constituencies that vote for Democrats. So, contrary to conservatives' claims, it is a well-documented empirical fact that contemporary Republicans do not govern as if they care about government spending. But they want to limit it when it could benefit Democrats.

In recent decades, whenever there is a Democratic president and the debt limit has to be raised to pay for spending already allocated, Congressional Republicans predictably hold the national and global economy hostage. It is essential to point out that hostage-taking is not a pejorative metaphor for the GOP. Matt Gaetz made that clear when he said, "I don't think we should negotiate with our hostage."[24] In the 2023 iteration of that ritual, they wanted to force Biden to sign on to budget cuts designed to hurt a large plurality of citizens. By threatening to devastate the financial security of many millions of Americans, they revealed a sociopathic indifference to all but their own political self-interest.

Their demand was, in essence, "immiserate ordinary citizens with draconian budget cuts, or we blow up the economy." Either path could cost Biden the 2024 election, which, of course, was their aim. But what can easily get overlooked is the collateral damage Republicans were comfortable delivering to many of their constituents. The economy they were willing to destroy would have devastated the social security recipients, veterans, and potential homebuyers among the GOP base.

As I noted, the debate over the national debt has never been about "government spending" but on whom tax dollars are spent. It can induce a kind of cognitive whiplash when we consider that within the relatively short time that the MAGA faction has come to define American and, to some extent, global conservatism, every one of the Right's supposedly foundational principles has been abandoned. There are almost no stances that Trump's Republican Party did not surrender or reverse once those positions conflicted with the shifting caprices of their leader. Perhaps the most unexpected GOP value to unceremoniously disappear has been its unwavering and obdurate patriotism (not that their performative flag-waving and "America first" rhetoric has abated).

The latter is particularly notable because what the Right has traditionally cherished most about the United States has not been its purple mountain majesty, civil liberties, or demographic diversity but its *sovereignty*—its freedom from foreign control and domination. Of course, conservative concern about the vulnerable nature of our sovereignty, especially during the Cold War, has been driven by paranoid fantasies and defended with various military misadventures abroad and repression of dissent at home. It turns out that this defining and enduring feature of the Republican worldview, along with the others, has been astonishingly mutable when it impedes more fundamental tribal interests like holding power, preserving economic privilege, and pushing back against the demographic tide of racial and ethnic heterogeneity. It is not that MAGA conservatives don't love "America;" they just hate *Americans*—or at least the majority of their fellow citizens who are not members of their tribe.

During the 2016 presidential campaign, according to a consensus of US intelligence agencies, America suffered the most severe attack ever by a foreign adversary on our sovereignty. Russia's attempt to corrupt our electoral process, which given the closeness of the election, cannot be dismissed as unsuccessful.[25] We know from the open testimony in Trump's first impeachment trial that his campaign asked for Putin's help, received it, and then tried to cover it up.[26]

Al-Qaeda's destruction of the World Trade Center in 2001, the Japanese surprise attack at Pearl Harbor in 1941, and the British immolation of Washington in 1812 destroyed buildings and killed many. Yet, none of those horrible assaults damaged what defines our democracy—the electoral process and confidence in its fairness. (Although the 9/11 attacks *were* used as an opportunity to limit civil liberties.)

For psychological and legal reasons, the former president could not acknowledge Russia's impact on his 2016 election win. It would have been too great a narcissistic wound for Trump to countenance. We should not be surprised that he and his administration, along with his enablers in Congress, took no action to prevent the reoccurrence of the Russian attack on our elections in 2020.

He views democracy as an impediment rather than something to defend. Whatever places him in power is good. And since his narrow first-term win, Trump has never sought to cover up his affinity for and emulation of dictators, his autocratic ambitions, his apparent conviction that the judicial and legislative branches of government worked for *him*, and his efforts to overturn the election he lost.

Trump's theft of top-secret government documents revealed his unsurprising indifference to the conservative value that Republicans once regarded as the most sacred, national security.[27] Even after leaving the White House, he regarded those highly classified files as presidential swag to which he was entitled to show off to foreign Mar-a-Lago visitors, brag about possessing, or perhaps even monetize. As of this writing, the national security consequences of his actions have yet to be fully assessed or at least revealed publicly.

That 2022 betrayal of the United States was so egregious it might eclipse the memory of the notorious 2017 episode in which he displayed an equally shocking disregard for his oath to protect the country. While entertaining a Russian delegation to the Oval Office, the former president blithely revealed classified information to Putin's representatives. That so alarmed US intelligence officials that they had to extract a Kremlin asset to prevent him or her from succumbing to one of Vlad's special polonium cocktails or taking an involuntary shortcut to the ground floor plaza of a Moscow high-rise.[28]

While brown asylum seekers were kept at bay during Trump's presidency, we know that Putin's army of cyber-saboteurs, hackers, Facebook fantasists, and Twitter bots were welcomed and did not stop their political trolling and propaganda efforts in the United States once their preferred candidate was elected. And they continued to be greeted with glee by the MAGA regime, since their interventions supported the Republican president and his party. Of course, it wasn't just those who stood to gain power and resources who made peace with Russian disinformation.

The Republican base had been easily persuaded to forsake national sovereignty and numerous other defining conservative principles to maintain tribal loyalty and fidelity to the leader. Pro-Putin T-shirts did not take long to appear at MAGA rally souvenir emporiums. "I'd Rather be Russian than a Democrat," blared the chests of several "America Firsters."[29]

Despite their incessant flag display, the sovereignty that the former president's supporters really privilege is *individual* sovereignty, especially that of their leader. That is what it means to be a sovereign—to not only be above the law but to *be* the law. That Trump should rule as a king, accountable to no one, has been a conviction shared by the former president himself, his minions in Congress, and his voter base. As former Energy Secretary Rick Perry proclaimed, Trump was God's "chosen one" to govern the United States.[30] And if you are acting in his name, as were the January 6 coup plotters, you, too, are doing God's work. A Trump devotee echoed these sentiments at a rally organized by MAGA necromancer Steve Bannon. She declared, "Never in my life did I think I'd like to see a dictator. But if there is going to be one, I want it to be Trump!"[31]

At this point, any attempt by Putin to undermine American democracy would be redundant of the GOP's own efforts. The Republican Party has completed the transformation it began in 2016 into an explicitly anti-democracy, post-truth cult of Trump. Denial of Biden's 2020 electoral victory has become a compulsory declaration for any candidate running for office on the GOP ticket. Up to at least May 2022, legal efforts to decertify Biden's election continued.[32]

Like all the others, this attempt to sanctify the Big Lie in the courts will probably fail. Nevertheless, endorsement of the stolen election fantasy has become the new bar MAGA candidates must meet if they want Trump's blessing.[33]

The numerous criminal investigations into the former president's business and political dealings have so far resulted in four criminal indictments. Many of the actions that led to charges look to many outside observers as acts of corruption and treason that have unfolded in plain sight. The outcomes of the trials will likely only be known after this book sees print. But even if he is convicted, it is unclear if that will impact his standing among the MAGA base, who take their ethical guidance from their revered leader. As Chris Hayes noted in a March 2018 *New York Times* editorial on Trump's highly selective outrage over criminality, "[C]rime is not defined by a specific offense. Crime is defined by who commits it."[34] By all appearances, his base employs the same moral reasoning.

That brings the conservative notions of freedom and tyranny into sharp relief. Of course, the kind of sovereignty to which Trump has happily become accustomed is not just the property of individuals but is a quality that marks the class of which he has been a lifelong member. It seems that economic class can, in some ways, function as a tribe.

Political Identity and Class

Among the ironies of class most puzzling to many journalists and social scientists is that the ones flying the "Don't Tread on Me" flags have been most willing to throw themselves under the limousine tires of the wealthy. In modern American society and elsewhere in the West, political identity has gradually shifted from class and issues associated with disparities in wealth, power, and status to a sense of group membership defined by taste, ethnicity, education level, and religion. This shift has been quite congenial to the economic elite, whose disproportionate political power has always been uncomfortably apparent. Nativist, xenophobic, and anti-democratic politicians have been there to help by offering fantasy threats—immigrants and ethnic, gender, and sexual minorities—that can distract a receptive plurality of the population and give them a target on which to displace their rage over economic and other pains. It's been a centuries-long game of "Let's you and them fight."

Of course, two different ways of crafting identity—race and class—have been present from America's infancy—grounded in the enslavement and extermination of non-white peoples *and* passionate and sometimes violent struggles between the business elite and labor. And both ways of structuring political selves remain to this day. This move from class-based tribalism to cultural/racial tribalism began roughly in the nineteenth century.[35] It becomes starker in the Tea Party movement of the early 2000s and reaches its fullest expression in the right-wing "populism" of Donald Trump's MAGA faction. Under that banner, millions of working- and middle-class citizens expressed their hatred of "elites" by idealizing, emulating, and empowering a billionaire developer who rarely paid taxes, relied on inherited wealth, was bailed out of multiple business failures by his wealthy father, and was notorious for stiffing his workers.

Part of what consolidates the wealthy class as a tribe with shared interests, identity, in-group affinity, and out-group hostilities is that material riches in the contemporary capitalist West translate into greater political and legal power, unlike certain early forms of society. However, the economically privileged cannot simply relax and cuddle with their pots of gold and all that can be bought with them. That is because their power involves a ceaseless battle against the forces of equity and the common good. They must contend with annoying out-groups such as organized labor, advocates of tax fairness, anti-corruption organizations, and environmentalists who insist on air, water, and food without toxic corporate effluents.

Fortunately for industry titans, the legal system they so effectively influence has made their position quite a bit more secure. Money, as the US Supreme Court has established, is now speech.[36] And corporations have rights accorded to human persons.[37] More than ever, political power and justice are commodities that go to the highest bidder. Correspondingly, those with little or no wealth are regarded and regard themselves as less worthy and, therefore, far less powerful. We have reached the point where not only do the economic elite buy politicians, but through entities like ALEC (the American Legislative Exchange Council), they write laws, which their Congressional vassals introduce as bills.[38] As the concentration of wealth is proceeding at a dizzying pace, the notion of capitalist democracy is becoming increasingly oxymoronic.

To put a finer point on my argument here, the *commodification of power*, not wealth itself, makes capitalism incompatible with democracy. In Graeber and Wengrow's *The Dawn of Everything*, they cite multiple examples of early Native American cultures where individuals were not stopped from accumulating wealth.[39] However, that wealth did not enable the rich to purchase greater influence or dominate others. In other words, power over material goods did not translate into power over other humans. Contrary to the conservative fiction, it is not that a more egalitarian social order would require the wealthy to give up a significant portion of their riches. (Although, exceptionally few ordinary citizens would likely shed tears over that.) Instead, as with some indigenous societies, we could choose to disallow economic privilege from becoming a currency for political privilege.

White Working-Class Support for Rule by the Rich: An Identity Conundrum

Only a minority of non–college educated working-class members tend to derive a sense of identity from their work.[40] The majority see jobs as tasks you have to perform to survive, provide for the family, and be able to afford endeavors that offer more meaning or at least more pleasure. That isn't because physical labor or service work could not be experienced as meaningful or rewarding. Instead, the social and economic *context* of working-class jobs makes them feel like low-status drudgery.

The conditions of physical labor often involve menial or routinized tasks under conditions of command-and-control hierarchies. Workers generally occupy the inferior position in these relationships of dominance and submission. With few exceptions, nonconsensual sadomasochism has become normalized for people of all classes working for bosses.[41] It is very revealing that libertarians who rant about the regulatory power of elected governments are entirely silent regarding the tyranny of the unelected private governments that run corporations. While workers are free to leave and risk their economic survival, the structure of nearly *every* workplace is autocratic.[42] Fleeing to another dictatorship holds little promise beyond the possibility of longer "bathroom breaks." In many settings, obedience is even more critical than competence for job retention.

And for those in the working class, in particular, the lifetime employment that one could have assumed in the 1950s no longer exists. While job security has disappeared for nearly everyone who can be fired at will, working-class employees live much closer to the edge. Losing a job means one is vulnerable to homelessness, starvation, and the ravages of illness from loss of health insurance. During the Trump government shutdown, many federal workers had to resort to food banks after missing only one paycheck. (In an interesting side note to that episode, the former president's billionaire Commerce Secretary Wilber Ross claimed he couldn't understand why hungry workers didn't just take out loans.[43] While finance is not my expertise, I suspect banks would regard food as somewhat unreliable collateral.)

Working-class members live with both the daily humiliation of following orders and the perpetual anxiety of unemployment. That makes white workers vulnerable to ethnonationalist appeals that can promise racial dominance to compensate for class subordination. They are susceptible to the wishful delusion of restoring lost esteem by joining the white supremacist tribe—esteem that may be harder to achieve through their work. When we add in the chronic anxiety of their daily lives, they are prime targets for conservative threat appeals, revenge fantasies directed at the "liberal elites," and anti-immigrant scapegoating. That strategy of working-class pacification can be traced as far back as the nineteenth century.

The postbellum Southern white elite used racialized status anxiety much like the contemporary GOP deploys it—to eclipse the real economic disparity among whites, fight unions, and keep wages low.[44] Agrarian populists threatened to disrupt this twin domination strategy by advocating greater racial and economic equality. Reuben Kolb, the leader of the populist movement in 1890s Alabama, had elections stolen from him on three occasions through ballot stuffing and voter suppression.[45] Moreover, there were no legal mechanisms for contesting an election. So, elections, like many resources garnered through theft, went to whoever could most effectively steal them. The third stolen election effectively killed genuine populism in the state from then on.

Since that period, iterations of racialized pseudo-populism discussed in this and other chapters have replaced genuine populist politics in Alabama and across the country. Consequently, economic privilege has often been left unnamed, untouched, and secure. In many ways, segregationist crusader George Wallace founded that new right-wing "populism." He seduced white working-class voters by conjuring and directing hatred toward a two-headed demon comprised of Black people and the federal government. That gave birth to what historian Jefferson Cowie calls "racialized anti-statism," which masqueraded as anti-elitist but remained silent about class.[46]

The Self-Defeating Defiance of the White Working Class

Joan Williams, the author of *White Working Class*, comments on a pro-Trump rally sign saying, "We vote with our middle finger." She notes that Trump was their middle finger.[47] While they can't say "Fuck you!" to their superiors, they can form an identification with an apparent Übermensch whose life of impunity has enabled *him* to say it for them. The irony of this bond cemented by rage is that the source of their fury is the conditions created by the economic elite, of which Trump is a member and whose interests he actually represents.

Class violence is regularly perpetrated by the wealthy. That is done by lobbying against affordable health care, using the legal bribery of campaign donations to get politicians to create a regressive tax system, and resisting efforts to ensure companies pay a living wage. In addition, they push to deregulate away public health and environmental protection, thus enabling poisoned water, air, and food. The problem is that people feel the pain that results from those actions while being bewildered about their origin. Instead, they are experienced as an ambient state of affairs, in which agency is mystified, and therefore no one is held to account. Those who suffer are frequently blamed by others, even family and friends, and often blame themselves. To lose health care, develop an environmentally induced disease, or have one's home repossessed due to job loss tend to get interpreted as signs of personal failure or inadequacy. In other words, the damage one suffers is not just physical or economic; it is also psychological and can feel self-inflicted.

The "hidden injuries of class," a phrase coined by sociologists Jonathan Cobb and Richard Sennett, generally refers to the psychological wounds and assaults on dignity that are features of everyday life in modern capitalist society experienced by those in the middle and working classes.[48] It is not so much the injuries that are hidden but their origins in class hierarchy—an etiology that remains enveloped in a fog of mystification. We could add to those afflictions the ways in which working-class individuals are enlisted through various right-wing propaganda outlets to identify with and fight for the ruling elite's interests, trapping them in a kind of class-based Stockholm Syndrome.

Popular culture narratives often depict the working class, especially men, as having a profound aversion to psychotherapy and a near-allergy to interiority, i.e., a desperate avoidance of one's thoughts, emotions, regrets, and doubts. I wish that could be dismissed as yet another media stereotype. Unfortunately, my clinical experience does bear it out. Memoirist J. D. Vance transitioned from being a child of the Appalachian working poor to a professor and eventually to an amoral Trump Big Lie–endorsing GOP senator.[49] After attempting psychotherapy, he said that "talking to some stranger about my feelings made me want to vomit."[50] Antipathy to reflecting on one's inner life is another hidden injury of class. That aversion could be conceived as a psychological autoimmune condition in which the qualities of mind that evoke a sense of vulnerability are viewed as threats to one's survival and attacked. The fear is that taking time to contemplate, let alone honor one's thoughts and emotions, might jeopardize the ability to accommodate the demands of the external world, obey the authorities on whom one is dependent, and normalize the everyday suffering and humiliations of class.

Under some circumstances, an effective demagogue can mobilize and channel this suffering and transform it into rage at various projective targets, especially those lower on the social hierarchy of race or gender. Another fantasy target is the "liberal elite," a straw man villain frequently featured in right-wing narratives. In the alternative universe of Fox News, the Democratic voter base is reduced to the familiar caricature of snooty, condescending, and contemptuous professors and students from elite Ivy League colleges, along with Hollywood celebrities, who fancy themselves better than their working-class inferiors. They love to deride physical laborers as pathetic and laughable primitives. But, unlike those smug, soft-handed liberals, Angry Man (insert the right-wing pseudo-populist of the moment) understands and respects you. He will fight for you and keep the criminal darkies out of your neighborhood. Left out of these pseudo-populist narratives are the elite university backgrounds of the right-wing demagogues pushing them.[51]

Conservatives have always preferred to battle over taste and consumer choices—croissants, cappuccinos, Volvos, arugula, and the *New York Times*—than to talk about corporate power, the wealth gap, or other realities of class. Currently, the most popular diversionary right-wing culture war bogies are those coded as ethnic and sexual threats. We have "critical race theory" (the dangerous concept of systemic racism), "MS13" (the gang that all brown immigrants belong to), and "pedophilia" (the true sexual preference of gay and trans people, and recently, all Democratic politicians).

When pain is inflicted by policy, it is harder to identify the agent, and the consequent injury, illness, or death may take time to manifest. Stories of liberal condescension, criminal minorities, job-stealing immigrants, and pedophilic gay and trans people are widely circulated public meanings. Those fictions take up residence in the conservative imagination as suspects in search of a crime. They perpetually exist in-waiting, to be blamed for a yet-to-be-determined problem.

For the most part, physical, economic, and psychological suffering are pains felt in *private* life, often understood as personal woes reflecting individual bad luck, weakness, or moral failure. While many experience shame, there is frequently no discernible humiliating agent. Economic trauma can take the form of losing one's home, being without adequate health insurance in the face of a cancer diagnosis, or having a foot amputated from uncontrolled diabetes because the price of insulin has been jacked up. The role of the ruling elite and the policies that privilege their interests might have played in these personal tragedies often remain shrouded in mystery. There are no eyewitnesses or fingerprints to identify the perpetrator. That is when the line-up of the usual right-wing suspects offers a choice of culprits.

Beyond the evil-doers mentioned, Republicans also deploy the non-white poor as a target for the displaced rage at conditions created by the wealthy. That has been a pretty successful divide-and-conquer strategy for the Right—presenting those who live in abject poverty as the enemies of the working class. The working poor are rendered invisible by acting as if these categories are entirely distinct. Also obscured is that most who are poor enough to receive food assistance are white,[52] like most welfare recipients.[53] The result is that many white working-class individuals vote for cuts in social services and in favor of deficit-busting tax cuts for the super-rich, which everyone but the wealthy will be paying for in the ensuing years.

Jonathon M. Metzl, a public health physician and researcher, has conducted the most thorough and compelling analysis of white backlash politics' destructive impact on white people.[54] The deliberate promotion of racial resentment by conservative policymakers to push through laws defunding health care, preventing gun safety legislation, and reducing the tax burden of the rich has devastated white Americans. It has led to death by suicide, murder, and disease. Metzl makes an irrefutable case that white identity politics is lethal to white people.

According to the ethnographic research of Arlie Hochschild, conservative workers tend to see the underemployed poor, especially those of color, as cutting in line, getting benefits and "free stuff" they don't deserve, and for which they haven't worked.[55] These workers are more likely to accept the conservative view that capitalists are simply the "job creators" and that the pollution that caused their environmentally induced diseases is the acceptable price they have to pay for a good job. One way that working-class voters—in fact, voters of all classes—internalize and identify with the worldview of the economic elite is by accepting the conservative notion of freedom and tyranny.

What Freedom and Tyranny Mean in the Conservative Moral Universe

It is no coincidence that Confederate flags, pro-Trump banners, and assault weapons featured prominently at anti-vaccine and anti-mask demonstrations over the grim years of the pandemic. They were ways of signaling the right-wing conception of freedom—the inalienable right to harm and dominate others in the pursuit of self-interest. That principle is one of those identity-saturated issues mentioned in earlier chapters foundational to conservative political selfhood. It is a notion of freedom that those on the Right have unwaveringly abided by from the antebellum period to the present.

The crude propagandists in George Orwell's dystopian nightmare, *1984*, declared, "Freedom is slavery." Orwell may not have realized at the time that he penned the slogan that much of the US population had already embraced that notion—but without any of his intended irony or sense of absurdity. For the nineteenth-century Confederate apostles of human bondage, freedom meant the freedom of white Southern men to enslave non-whites.

In an 1864 speech, Abraham Lincoln described two very different notions of freedom: "We all declare for liberty, but in using the same *word*, we do not all mean the same *thing*. With some, the word liberty may mean for each man to do as he pleases with himself and the product of his labor, while with others, the same word may mean for some to do as they please with other men and the product of other men's labor."[56] In this passage, he succinctly summarized the psychological and moral fault line that marked the cleavage between two deeply antagonistic halves of the country, one that continues to divide us today. The division is no longer structured around slavery but more broadly between two radically opposing ideas of freedom—the right to be free from harm and control by those with more power vs. the right by those with greater power to impose their will on others.

Historian Jefferson Cowie, mentioned previously, has written a rich and vivid account of the actions that flowed from Lincoln's second definition of freedom—the freedom to dominate others. It is a definition I would call conservative because those on the Right have consistently endorsed it, whether by Democrats in the nineteenth century or Republicans in the current era. While Cowie's narrative is a local story set in one county of antebellum Alabama, it is repeated throughout the country and across the centuries. He begins his etymology of freedom with the arguments put forward to justify the theft by white invaders of land given by treaty to the Creek Nation—an appropriation made possible through swindle, occupation, forced exile, and mass murder. He moves from there to the rationales offered up to justify slavery, secession from the Union, postbellum Black voter suppression, neo-slavery in the form of convict leasing, Jim Crow laws, and George Wallace's defiant celebration of racial segregation.

While we cannot administer psychological tests to the Confederate antecedents of the current GOP, one of the most replicated research findings in studies of present-day conservatives is that they often exhibit a social dominance orientation. During every period in the American South, domination of others by any means necessary was framed as a fundamental freedom to which all white males were entitled. In other words, freedom was the right to deprive others of freedom. Should harm be necessary to exercise that freedom, then causing harm is a liberty no one should abridge. The primary threat to the freedom to dominate in the periods Cowie studied was understood to be the federal government. Then and now, "Washington" has been the chief villain in conservative demonology. Government forces, military and legal, were always sticking their noses where they were unwanted, constantly placing fetters on the free exercise of terror and conquest by white elites. The federal infringement on the freedom to hurt and subordinate spawned racialized anti-statism.

Of course, the fact that federal power was viewed as a nefarious usurper of white entitlement did not mean it was a force that reliably protected the human rights of Native, Black, or even poor white communities. But it was enough of a constraint on the depredations of the Southern white elite that emissaries and troops from Washington continued to be seen as the enemy long after the formal end of the Civil War.

That sentiment continues in the present day and well beyond the South as the anti-government outcry of the Tea Party and later the MAGA Right, who in many ways seemed like political descendants of nineteenth- and twentieth-century white Alabamians. Over three centuries, the racial component of that crusade against federal power has oscillated between a dog whistle and a bull-horn. It was a bullhorn from the antebellum to the postbellum period, mutating into a dog whistle in the Nixon, Reagan, and Bush eras (at least outside the South), and became an unapologetic bullhorn again in the period of Trump, Tucker Carlson, Steve Bannon, and the neofascist coup supporters who now have seats in Congress.[57]

A side note: As I write this, Alabama (along with Mississippi) is celebrating King-Lee Day.[58] This holiday commemorates the life and actions of civil rights leader Martin Luther King Jr. *and* the treasonous defender of slavery, General Robert E. Lee. Perhaps this neo-Confederate notion of diversity will be extended to other holidays. Should that trend become national, our calendars might mark the day we celebrate the birthdays of George Washington and Benedict Arnold together or the week we observe Hanukkah *and* the grand achievements of Hitler. If you, my thoughtful reader, regard that as *reductio ad absurdum* overreach, I invite you to ponder the example of Indigenous Peoples-Columbus Day.[59] That is a joint national holiday in which we honor the original inhabitants of the American continent *and* one of the figures central to their enslavement and near extermination. That the Columbus component of this hybrid holiday remains even after his predatory exploits have become common knowledge is a testament to the valorization that rapacious domination can still earn in the United States, or at least our continuing ability to be inured to cognitive dissonance. As I will show, the freedom to dominate is not limited to the effort to subordinate racial or ethnic minorities.

"Fuck Your Feelings!"

On January 6, 2021, MAGA "patriots" defecated on the floor of the Capitol Building.[60] Other insurrectionists carried a large banner that blared, "Fuck your feelings."[61] In 2008, with the slogan, "drill baby drill," the McCain-Palin campaign trumpeted the freedom of polluting industries to increase their dominance over and exploitation of natural resources.[62] It was a green light for those corporations to continue asserting an unrestricted right to extract from, contaminate, and even eradicate the flora, fauna, and mineral deposits of the global commons. Planetary ecocide was reframed as a form of untrammeled liberty.

During the former president's administration, Trump-loving neofascist militias made death threats against governors for imposing public health mandates.[63] The COVID pandemic and the right-wing resistance to government efforts to blunt the spread of the virus showed how the freedom to dominate was not just proclaimed by large institutions or groups but also expressed on a microcosmic, interpersonal level. Pandemic libertarians essentially argued, "I should have the freedom to sicken you if that enables me to enjoy the pleasures of unmasked pubic life. If there is a common space I want to occupy, I should be able to do so at your expense. Government mandates that insist I protect you are an unbearable infringement on my liberties." The same argument has long been made about secondhand smoke, a position still embraced by Congressional Republicans who, once they regained the House majority in 2023, repealed the rule against forcing staff members to breathe the smoke of their bosses.[64]

What do these seemingly disparate events have in common? They each exemplify the right-wing version of freedom. While they can be prettied up with Ayn Rand and Koch-brother sophistries, we are left with nothing more than libertarian lipstick on the pig of sociopathy. Over the centuries of American conservatism, that has meant the freedom to dominate, which has included the right to enslave, discriminate, coerce, disenfranchise, censor, injure, exploit, attack, pollute, starve, invade, rape, colonize, infect, abduct, shoot, murder, and, recently, mandate full-term pregnancy. When we look at the broad sweep of history, there appears to be one expression of domination that links all the others: theft.

It may involve the theft of land, water, labor and its fruits, culture, identity, agency, the right to vote, health, and life itself. The notion proffered by the French anarchist Proudhon that "property is theft" can be extended to include much of existence in a social order founded on the dominance of one group over another. Domination is about stealing that which either belongs to others or everyone. It is about declaring that all you covet belongs to you. You can take it if you have the weapons and a large enough army. And once you take it, it is transformed into your property. That is the unspoken ethos that underlays the enclosure of the commons that began in the seventeenth century and continues to this day, the foundational theft that created the space of capitalism.[65] It is also the moral reasoning that transmuted the enslavement of others into entrepreneurial freedom, at least in the minds of plantation owners and, more broadly, the entire Confederacy. And it remains the intuitive logic of today's MAGA Right.

The Violence of Conservative Freedom

Like the nineteenth century, in the present day most threats and acts of politically motivated violence emanate from the Right.[66] Offensive violence, which is harm in the service of domination, is and has always been fundamental to the conservative notion of freedom. Without physical coercion, theft would not be possible. Of course, some segments of the radical Left, from John Brown to the Black Panthers to the Weathermen to the anti-clearcutting monkey-wrenching of the Earth Liberation Front, have deployed violence to achieve political ends. In the latter case, it was limited to property destruction. As misguided and self-defeating as some of those efforts may have been, the aim was mostly self-protection, protection of the environment, or the emancipation of less powerful groups. For reasons outlined in the introduction, I am leaving out the "Left" history's various Leninist and Stalinist movements and governments. Like others in the global Right, their aim has been domination and theft, facilitated by violence. Similarly, the freedom they have sought has been the freedom to deprive others of freedom.

The Right vs. the Right

It is crucial not to lose sight of the heterogeneity and multiple squabbling factions within the American conservative movement.[67] While drawing comparisons between the nineteenth-century post-Confederate white supremacist Right and the current neofascist iteration of the Republican Party, it is essential to acknowledge that the GOP is not a monolith. In particular, they are riven by a tension between their two very different wings.[68] There is its corporatist faction with its central concerns of low or zero taxes for the wealthy, unregulated profit-taking, and the unrestrained ability to pass on the environmental, health, and other costs to the rest of society. Then there is the patriarchal ethnonationalist Christian fascist white base driven by racial resentment and paranoid fantasies about replacement by non-white immigrants. Periodic tensions have erupted between these two wings.

The belief that domination over others is a fundamental freedom has linked these two disparate tendencies from the antebellum period to the present. The primary difference between the two wings of the conservative movement is the sphere in which domination is exercised. For corporatists like the Kochs and fossil fuel barons, it is economic domination, including unrestrained resource extraction. For the ethnonationalists, it is domination over non-white, non-Christian, non-heterosexual, and gender-nonconforming citizens. Their ire and need for control also extend to women who refuse to have their gestational status regulated by men. That is the America they seek to make "great again." Both wings are willing to inflict unlimited legal and extralegal harm to arrogate to themselves the freedom to which they feel entitled. That harm may include ecocide, incarceration, job loss, death threats, or lynching.

Regardless of their domain of concern, economic or cultural, both varieties of conservatives want to conserve traditional status hierarchies and the impunity that comes with them. The social dominance actions I've described are the means to achieve that restoration, whether refusing to protect others by wearing a mask or deregulating industrial pollution. When it comes to the hoary adage, "Your right to swing your fist ends where my nose begins," conservatives consistently side with the fist. For the MAGA faction in particular, what excites their political passion is the freedom of predators.

For those who might regard these assertions as tendentious overstatements, consider Donald Trump, now the GOP's apostle for entitled libertarian freedom and its ethical lodestar. Though numerous election losses have tarnished the magic of a Trump endorsement, it is still the case that many Republican candidates who hope to survive their party's primary feel they must repeat the canonical MAGA lies[69] and mimic their leader's defiant swagger.[70] If not incarcerated by then, and given Nikki Haley's withdrawal from the race, Trump will likely be his party's 2024 presidential candidate. We cannot forget his frequent idealizing praise for Putin's murderous reign and "genius" in implementing genocide in Ukraine.[71] Beyond his admiration for Russia's war-criminal-in-chief, the former president openly revealed his affinity for other violent autocrats.[72]

Many of us heard his call to police officers to smash suspects' heads as they were placed in the back of squad cars.[73] And in the infamous *Access Hollywood* tape, the nation witnessed the snickering pride he expressed in using his celebrity to get away with sexual predation.[74] His open and enthusiastic embrace of thuggery has not been something his base and collaborators had to overlook, even if it were possible. It has been central to his brand and foundational to his popularity. (I'll have more to say about this in the section on cruelty next and in chapter 10.) Parallel to the libertarian idea of freedom has been a complementary notion of tyranny.

"Sic temper tyranis!"—thus always to tyrants—bellowed Confederate sympathizer John Wilkes Booth in Ford's Theater after putting a bullet in the brain of Abraham Lincoln in 1865. It was not just the president's emancipation of enslaved people that infuriated Booth but Lincoln's promise to grant suffrage to those formerly held in bondage. From the post–Civil War period forward, tyranny was a label applied by the Right to any government policy directed at the common good, whether aimed at political equality or providing goods and services to the needy. Under the rubric of combatting "socialism," conservatives fought hard against any policy or program that sought to allocate shared resources to projects aimed at the well-being of society as a whole.[75]

Until law enforcement began to hold Trump accountable and most members of the armed forces showed more loyalty to the country than him, police and military spending has been exempted from the Right's aversion to funding the general welfare. (Although, since the FBI began investigating the former president's potential crimes, Congressional Republicans are vowing to defund it.)[76] Just as conservatives have almost always embraced the freedom to harm, they have been allergic to nearly every policy founded on the common good. That has included the abolition of slavery, the expansion of voting rights to non-whites and women, public education, child labor laws, the eight-hour workday, Social Security, Medicare, unemployment insurance, progressive taxation, public libraries, environmental protection, seat belts, indoor smoking bans, gun safety legislation, police accountability, programs to support renewable energy and reduce fossil fuel dependency, publicly funded highways, hospitals, and, recently, mask requirements and vaccination. Each of these policies has been viewed as tyrannical because they required a collective financial contribution for the benefit of all. Or they involved a mandate that citizens consider the well-being of others. Or they challenged privileges based on wealth, gender, race, or religion. Or they placed limits on the ability of businesses to externalize the environmental and social costs of production.

It should come as no surprise, then, that a study of 1,130 subjects found that COVID vaccine refusal (a position adopted disproportionately by Republican politicians and their constituencies[77]) was highly associated with a low score on a measure of prosocial attitudes.[78] And as we might expect, these same individuals were much more likely to embrace conspiracy thinking and exhibit authoritarian personality traits.

One of the terrible ironies of the right-wing comfort with harm and opposition to caretaking policies of government is that it hurts white conservatives more than any other group. A study conducted before the pandemic by Brigham and Women's Hospital found a significant "death gap" between Democratic and Republican areas across the country. Residents of red counties died from multiple causes at twice the rate as blue counties. While the death rates of non-white citizens were higher, they did not vary between partisan districts. Mortality among whites, however, showed marked differences that depended on political affiliation.[79]

There are many reasons for the partisan discrepancy in death rates. GOP representatives have tended to oppose Medicaid expansion under the Affordable Care Act, regulating environmental toxicants, establishing workplace safety rules, and funding healthcare services generally. In addition, Republican-driven media deregulation has led to red-county news deserts. And driven by the seductions of confirmation bias, conservative voters have largely self-segregated into information ghettos of right-wing post-truth. That has deprived them of the facts they need to make healthy choices regarding food, vaccinations, and exercise. So, in general, as I noted in the Introduction, the policies promoted by Republican politicians are most lethal to GOP voters.

What about the Harm of Abortion?

One plausible counterexample to the claim that conservative freedom is based on the right to cause harm would be the issue of abortion. From the perspective of right-to-life advocates, pro-choice liberals are the ones who rationalize harm. In this view, they are willing to torture and kill developing fetuses so potential parents can exercise the freedom to lead a more convenient life.

Let's look more closely at that argument. There is no objective or exact formula to measure the hypothetical suffering experienced by aborted fetuses. For example, there is no scientific consensus on the precise point in development when a fetus can experience pain. Unlike verbal children and adults, fetuses cannot offer subjective reports. There is some agreement among scientists that the closer to the third trimester a mother gets, the greater the likelihood that the fetus can register and suffer pain.[80]

On the other hand, the mental and physical harm to women or girls forced to give birth in areas without legal abortion services is measurable and profound.[81] Women denied an abortion suffer enduring negative impacts, including higher anxiety, lower self-esteem and life satisfaction, and increased risk of exposure to interpersonal violence.[82] Long-term adverse mental health outcomes for women who sought but could not obtain an abortion were found even in studies that controlled for socioeconomic status and in which the subjects were white and married.[83] Forced pregnancy is considered a criminal human rights violation under international law.[84] And the harm is not limited to those carrying unwanted fetuses to term. The children born to mothers denied an abortion suffer various developmental impairments[85] and are at greater risk of depression.[86] None of this data should be interpreted as meaning that the decision to seek an abortion is not agonizing for many women. It can be an excruciating choice beset with intense conflictual emotions. But those are reasons to leave such choices in the hands of the women they affect rather than politicians.

Let's assume good faith on the part of those who seek to ban abortion— that they do want to save "babies." We are still left with some glaring contradictions. Their positions on policies relevant to child and maternal well-being seem to affirm the old meme from the Reagan era: For conservatives, life begins at conception and ends at birth.[87] They shed copious tears for aborted fetuses but make no secret of their opposition to the social supports designed to help infants develop healthfully. Republican politicians, now almost uniformly anti-choice, have long opposed government funding for food assistance, preschool, health care, and family leave to care for newborns.[88] In 2022, when the shortage of infant formula became an acute crisis for mothers and babies for whom breastfeeding was not an option, 192 House Republicans voted against supplying emergency funds to the Food and Drug Administration to save those infants from starvation.[89] States that prohibit abortion provide the lowest level of support for mothers and babies.[90] While anti-choice conservatives adamantly deny that their motive is to control women's bodies, many in the GOP are also entertaining a ban on contraception, which, if enacted, would only increase the demand for abortion.[91] It seems pretty apparent that right-wing opposition to abortion rights is a position that maximizes harm rather than limiting it.

The Liberal Notion of Freedom

Those on the Left have tended to endorse policies founded on a very different set of freedoms, which are fundamental to contemporary liberal identity. A shortlist would have to include the following:

- The freedom to breathe, drink, and eat in a healthy world;
- The freedom to make reproductive health choices and exercise bodily autonomy;
- The freedom to select representatives in an electoral system based on majority rule;
- The freedom to move through cities where skin color doesn't determine whether the police protect or prey upon citizens;
- The freedom to get high-quality food, health care, housing, and education regardless of income;
- The freedom to live in a country where racial, economic, sexual, and other forms of bigotry are not codified in law;
- And the freedom to spend one's remaining days on a vitalized planet teeming with plants, animals, and robust ecosystems—one we can bequeath to those who come after us.

Conservatives might appreciate many things on that list, like breathable air and potable water. But they don't view them as freedoms to which all are entitled. And given their social dominance orientation, it is unclear which freedoms they are willing to share with out-groups. And even regarding the rights they prize, like gun ownership and the ability to pray loudly in state-funded schools, do they really want them extended to other ethnic groups? I may be presumptuous, but it seems unlikely that many right-wingers would like to see mosques on school campuses or ethnic minorities carrying assault weapons into Starbucks.

Fear and Loathing of the Nanny State: The Federal Government in Right-Wing Demonology

One conservative objection to the state playing any role in the protection and welfare of the general public is their putative aversion to "big government." However, even a cursory examination of this argument reveals its absurdity. To cite a few examples, politicians on the Right consistently seek to beef up the martial components of the state—such as a militarized police apparatus and border patrol—provided they are directed against pro-democracy and pro-racial justice advocates or immigrants. The "size" aspect of government is a conservative red herring. Their real concern is ensuring government policy and budgets serve the interests of their most important constituency, the economic elite. This latter point is brought into sharp relief whenever erstwhile "fiscal conservatives" celebrate deficit spending, as they did in the Trump era, as long as the wealthy are the beneficiaries. They detest the caretaking functions of government, especially when directed at the middle- and underclass or ethnic minorities.

And there is nothing small or freedom-loving about GOP state governments either. They do not hesitate to crush municipal self-governance,[92] especially when cities pass ordinances that burden businesses, such as raising local wages, enforcing public health guidelines, or protecting the environment. As we have witnessed, Republican state big governments have been quite active in suppressing voting rights, stopping local municipalities from enacting anti-discrimination measures, and implementing indoor mask mandates.

In Ron DeSantis's Florida, the "freedom" to infect others was not only expressed through policy but was manifest in the personal behavior of the administration. His anti-vax surgeon general, Joseph Ladapo, could not get a letter of recommendation from his UCLA training supervisor because Ladapo was assessed as exercising poor medical judgment and not being guided by science in his decisions. So, in many ways, he was a good fit to implement DeSantis's anti-public health policies. At one point, a state legislator undergoing cancer treatment requested that Ladapo wear a mask for their meeting. He refused, saying that doing so would inhibit his self-expression.[93] Experts estimated that about half of the 175,000 Floridians that perished from COVID would still be alive had the state government implemented standard public health measures.

Florida Republicans have not been shy about dictating local school curricula and instituting book bans. DeSantis has even prevented businesses from imposing public health measures within their own companies to protect their workers and customers. As of this writing, he is on a crusade to ban any school books, including math textbooks, that make any mention of the experience of non-white people or non-heterosexuals.[94] These laws give the lie to the Republican claim that they are concerned about "government overreach." Once again, the government "intrusion" conservatives object to is that which is directed at the common good.

As some readers may recall, libertarian politicians were instrumental in the right-wing takeover of the Black-majority city of Flint, Michigan, in a state government coup.[95] The occupiers, believing that too much money was being spent to provide city services, and ignoring the warnings of technical and medical experts, presided over the infamous water supply switch from a clean source to a polluted river. That, in turn, created an epidemic of lead poisoning. As is commonly the case with lead, its most significant impact was on children's developing brains. Conveniently, the scholars at the Koch-funded libertarian think tank, the Michigan Mackinac Center, came up with statutory rationales that they hoped would exempt the perpetrators from legal liability.[96] It wasn't enough that the "fiscal conservatives" who took over the city could exercise the freedom to poison the population; they had to ensure their impunity, too.

Sadly, there is nothing anomalous about the water debacle in Flint. A very similar crisis afflicted Jackson, Mississippi. An 80 percent Black city with a quarter of its residents struggling below the poverty line, Jackson's water crisis in the summer of 2022 resulted partly from the chronic underfunding of its water purification and delivery infrastructure.[97] When climate change-induced apocalyptic rains hit, the fragile system was not resilient enough to manage it and broke. Citizens were faced with undrinkable water. Only the emergency delivery of bottled water kept them alive. Even once water pressure was restored and residents could flush their toilets, they were told to shower with their mouths closed to avoid ingesting contaminants. There were proximal and distal causes of that catastrophe. All of them could be understood as derivatives of a right-wing libertarian ethos—especially the Republican denial of and inaction in the face of climate change, racism, and the refusal to mobilize social resources to fund public infrastructure maintenance.

Mississippi's GOP Governor Tate Reeves vetoed a bipartisan bill in June 2020 that would have helped impoverished Jackson residents pay their past-due water bills.[98] In March 2021, Republican statehouse lawmakers blocked a plan that would have allowed the city to raise a one-cent sales tax to repair the water and sewer infrastructure.[99] Reeves explained his and his colleagues' actions by arguing, "Other cities have problems too. Why should Jackson get a carve-out?

There are needy Mississippians who would rather not pay their bills all over."[100]
Apparently, Reeves believed that the poor citizens of Jackson were expressing
a *preference* not to pay for water and exercising their fundamental freedom to
choose dehydration over starvation. One local activist noted what she saw as
the main reason the state resisted funding infrastructure repairs, "[T]here are
no white people there."[101]

Libertarian Identity

So far, I've referred to "libertarian " as a generic descriptor for a set of attitudes
and positions expressed by conservatives. It names a worldview central to right-
wing politics, a sense of entitlement to act in the world without regard for
others, rationalized as "liberty." But in using libertarian as an adjective, we can
forget it is also an identity for a vocal minority of Americans. And since many
of them are wealthy, their voices get heard. Libertarianism is a set of beliefs and
attitudes that overlaps with conservatism and shares some perspectives with
liberalism. Yet, as an identity, it is distinct from both.

While often personified by the work of Ayn Rand, the philosophical origins of contemporary libertarianism can be traced back to John Locke and
other seventeenth- and eighteenth-century thinkers. For those writers, the liberty of the individual was the preeminent moral value. It was liberty understood as negative freedom—freedom from intrusion, which included rejecting
the notion that there was any moral duty to others. Any policy that required
one to consider and contribute to the well-being of fellow citizens would be a
tyrannical impingement. That notion has expanded in the contemporary libertarian moral universe to include opposition to the social safety net, taxation,
Medicare, and Social Security.

They reject any interference with individual liberty and the state's attempts
to impose morality on its citizens. In the late 1950s and early 1960s, that argument girded the segregationist resistance to federally mandated segregation
and Supreme Court decisions favoring civil rights. Currently, however, many
libertarians have made common cause with liberals. Like those on the Left,
libertarians repudiate government efforts to impose religious values and beliefs
and insist citizens should be free to make their own choices regarding sexual
partners, reproductive health care, and drug use. Also, like liberals, they now
prize civil liberties and have been ardent defenders of unpopular speech and
decry censorship.

While libertarians are passionate opponents of governmental infringement
on freedom, they exhibit a curious political blindness concerning corporations'
coercive and liberty-denying behavior; they don't see it or seem unconcerned.

That appears to stem from their view of business as an extension of individual personhood and property ownership as an inviolable and sacred prerogative.

The privileges accorded property owners have varied over time as the definition of property has shifted. Women, enslaved Africans, and various components of the commons—land, water, minerals, and, more recently, DNA—have been considered property. And a sense of entitlement to pollute the resources they do *not* own has often come along with the prerogatives of property ownership.

Readers might be surprised to learn that libertarianism is not just a political belief system but a self-conscious identity driven by a distinct psychology. That psychology has been studied extensively by a group of American social scientists. In that work, only individuals who self-identified as libertarians were accepted as subjects.[102] While libertarians reject conservatism's traditional moral constraints on sexuality and religion, especially their preoccupation with purity, they retain and even enhance other aspects of the right-wing worldview.

Social psychologists have identified a set of "moral foundations" or values that predictably differentiate liberals from conservatives. These are often the unexamined and unconscious assumptions and emotions that motivate political thinking and acting. In the research, those foundations have been measured using a test called the Moral Foundations Questionnaire. According to the study, liberals tend to be impelled principally by a concern to avoid *harm* and offer *care* and a desire for *fairness and equity*. Conservatives typically score low on harm avoidance/care and fairness/equity. Their primary drivers are *in-group loyalty* (what I call in this book exclusionary tribalism), deference to traditional *authority*, and concern with *purity and sanctity*.[103]

Among the most astonishing findings in this body of research is that the terrorist groups most effective in recruiting new members deploy propaganda that (intuitively, it seems) frames their messages in terms of the same moral foundations. Appeals to in-group loyalty and fairness were found in all the samples analyzed. However, terrorist groups that emphasized purity and loyalty engaged in attacks that had the highest number of fatalities.[104] As even the most casual observer of modern history can attest, fascists, ethnic cleansers, and fundamentalist holy warriors have often framed mass murder as a kind of purification and a way of showing fealty to the tribe.

In extending moral foundations research to include libertarians, they were found to be even less motivated than conservatives by a desire to avoid harm and ensure care, scoring even lower than traditional conservatives. And like others on the Right, libertarians have little concern for fairness and equity. But like liberals, they tend to score lower on in-group loyalty, deference to authority, and purity/sanctity.[105]

What that study on libertarians has added to the moral foundations research is a sixth moral value, *liberty*. There are two components of that liberty, *economic* (being free to use your wealth in any way you want) and *lifestyle* (being free to live as you see fit). Libertarians had higher scores on both forms of liberty. Liberals came close to them on lifestyle liberty. And conservatives scored slightly lower than libertarians on economic liberty. That last finding may help explain extreme conservative Florida Governor Ron DeSantis's eagerness to regulate corporate behavior and limit free speech to keep it aligned with right-wing cultural values around sexual and gender "purity" and his holy war against "wokeness."[106]

Perhaps the most revealing part of the study on libertarians concerns the psychology that seems to underlie their political morality. Of particular note, libertarians scored the lowest on empathic concern for others, emotionality, desire for social connection, and loving feelings for all types of people, including family and romantic partners. In addition, libertarians scored high on measures showing a "need for cognition" and "systematizing." Respectively, those traits describe a tendency to intellectualize and a drive to "analyze variables in a system."

These findings, taken together, evoke a picture of libertarians as conservatives on "the spectrum." Perhaps this may explain the attraction of so many tech bros to libertarian politics. The study finds that males tend to make up the majority of libertarians *and* individuals with autistic spectrum disorders. Libertarian CEO billionaire Elon Musk seems like the paradigmatic example. He's made no secret of his Randian worldview.[107] And we know of his Asperger's diagnosis because he once announced it while hosting *Saturday Night Live*.[108]

Because of libertarians' attenuated attachment to others, tribal bonds are not compelling motivators for political action. That trait might also contribute to their tendency to be socially liberal. It's not that they have much concern for the liberty of others; clearly, they are not that invested in people. They just want to be left alone. Libertarians don't want to be policed, nor do they want the job of policing others. Unlike traditional conservatives, they're indifferent to issues of purity, perhaps because of their low disgust sensitivity.[109]

Given the well-documented psychological dispositions of self-identified libertarians, it is unsurprising to find them taking the positions they do. Of course, they oppose most regulations, demands for public accountability, and the use of tax revenue to help those in need. Because libertarians imagine themselves, and all people, as disconnected monads in an unlinked universe, they deny their negative impacts on others and their dependency on the people and collective resources that help make them who they are.

Libertarian "Freedom" and American Slavery

As documented in Jefferson Cowie's historical study described earlier, one crucial origin of the broad libertarian ethos in the American context is the institution of slavery, especially the confident entitlement of the wealthy to own and abuse other humans. Nancy MacLean, in her insightful and well-researched history of right-wing libertarian economic theory and policy, *Democracy in Chains*, identifies John C. Calhoun, a passionate defender of slavery, as the founding thinker of this tendency among the ruling elite of his day.[110] He was an enslaver whose ideas turned the common understanding of class conflict on its head. In Calhoun's view, the wealthy were exploited by the majority through the extraction of tax revenue. Of course, he would not be the last among his class to spin this tale. To this day, that is the story told by those who lobby for America's contemporary right-wing oligarchy of wealth—that economic elites are somehow victims of exploitation by others. They alone produce wealth, while everyone else is somehow a "taker."

Calhoun's was a truly breathtaking inversion. In this view, slavery, the ultimate form of expropriation, was nothing compared to taxing the wealth garnered from the unpaid servitude of others. In that era, opposition by the economic elite to taxation in the interest of public good was primarily confined to the slave-owning South.

And the riches he and his peers accumulated through the forced labor of others were considerable. South Carolina was the wealthiest in the slave-owning South, which held two-thirds of the nation's financial resources. Slavery was such a significant investment that it eclipsed the railroads or other infrastructure. As historian Edward E. Baptist has painstakingly documented, slavery and the forced migration and torture that maintained it were the most significant factors in American capitalism's success and competitive advantage.[111]

The US economy became an enduring powerhouse in world markets, not so much because of the creative bootstrapping of hardworking business owners, but mainly due to the straps applied to the bleeding backs of captive Africans. Baptist shows how even long after slavery's formal end, the wealth it generated continued to grow and enrich the descendants of enslavers and the communities and states in which they lived. It is a bloody legacy that all white citizens still benefit from, while remaining a lingering economic impediment and source of transgenerational trauma for Black Americans. Even after slavery's official demise, structural racism continued and has taken a multiplicity of new forms.[112]

Calhoun and his cohorts were some of the earliest advocates of wealth-based oligarchy. And since slavery was the source of their lucre, any attempt to abridge their prerogative to own, exploit, beat, and murder their human property was an intolerable infringement of their freedom. As described previously, they reviled the federal government and its supposedly intrusive efforts to regulate business, like Republicans of the present day. They were no more sympathetic to local authorities than to the power in Washington. As with the current GOP, state government was far preferable because it was easier to influence. Controlling the levers of the state enabled one's group to provide a bulwark against federal authority. At the same time, it offered the means of suppressing the obstreperous but less powerful local rabble. By monopolizing state power, neither national nor local democratic forces could impede oligarchic ambitions.

MacLean describes the early Southern elite's attempts to suppress the vote. This history links the anti-democracy efforts of the nineteenth century to the present moment, although the methods have changed. In the past, there was a concerted effort to keep working people from being able to influence government practices. The slave-owning oligarchy suppressed unions and instituted poll taxes and other measures. Then as now, anti-democratic conservative efforts to block and nullify the vote were primarily concentrated in state legislatures where the wealthy could maximize their influence. The next chapter will look more closely at the resonances between antebellum and contemporary right-wing identity politics.

CHAPTER 5

From Slave and Free States to Red and Blue States—Historical Continuities in the Politics of Identity

"Being a southerner is no longer geographic. It's a philosophy and an attitude," militant segregationist George Wallace noted with considerable satisfaction in 1964. His troubling observation not only captured the sensibility of more white Northerners than we might want to acknowledge, but it has turned out to be quite prescient.[1] The white supremacist worldview, once primarily limited to the Confederacy and later the Jim Crow South, at least in law, has come to define one of America's two national parties. Voter suppression measures targeting the non-white electorate have been enacted nationwide, primarily where Republicans control a trifecta of state government bodies—the two legislative houses and the governorship.

Some might object that any apparent continuity between the politicians who represented the interests of the nineteenth-century Southern slave-owning oligarchy and today's GOP is purely coincidental and does not represent any genuine ideological kinship. And, any attempt at such a comparison could only be a strenuous exercise in reductionism. As Ricky Ricardo might say to those proffering such an objection, "You've got some 'splaining to do."

There is more than a cartographic overlap between the old Confederacy and current red states.[2] That is especially clear when we look at the South itself. According to a 2021 survey, two-thirds of Southern Republicans want to secede from the rest of the country.[3] They share with their forebears an ethos of white supremacy, a commitment to right-wing libertarian economic policy, a social dominance orientation, and an impulse to deploy coercive violence to solve personal and political conflicts. In the past, the latter was often expressed as hypermasculine bluster and with the conspicuous display of guns—much as it is today.

Southern slavers were unapologetic about the source of their riches and that their desire to retain it was the chief motive for leaving the Union. Nevertheless, some of today's conservatives feel compelled to either minimize the harms of slavery or deny its role in secession. According to the architects of Florida's middle school education curriculum, slavery was essentially a benign jobs program, an internship that prepared the enslaved for the labor market.[4] Prominent Republicans have also argued that secession of the Confederacy wasn't as much about slavery as "Southern culture," high taxes, and federal government infringements on states' rights.[5] That last point is not wrong; the national government did seek to interfere in states' rights to abduct and enslave Africans. Despite many attempts to rewrite the history of the Civil War, the rationalizations offered up by today's apologists for the Southern slaveocracy have been soundly refuted by historians[6] and the Confederate state constitutions themselves.[7]

One particularly twisted attempt to distort the past has been the claim by contemporary Republicans that the infamous "Three-Fifths Compromise" was a good thing. That was an agreement reached during the 1797 Constitutional Convention that allowed slave states to count the enslaved as three-fifths of a person, which, even though they could not vote, enabled those states to use their captives to increase Congressional representation. By legally inscribing the diminished humanity of enslaved persons, it was a law that legitimated slavery. However, those historical facts did not stop MAGA Republicans from describing this provision as an anti-slavery law.[8]

By counting the enslaved as three-fifths of a person to determine population-based electoral representation, slavery continues to contribute to the most profound distortion of American democracy, the over-representation of less populated and conservative states, and the growing problem of minority rule. The Three-Fifths Compromise became the foundation for the Electoral College system. In the nineteenth century, that meant that although enslaved people could not vote, the white slave-labor oligarchy had more say in government than other Americans. As historian Akhil Reed Amar notes, eight of the first nine presidents came from Virginia, a state with a large enslaved population.[9] Virginia had fewer actual voters but more electors than states with a larger electorate, like Pennsylvania. But the long-term psychosocial implications, though rarely named, have been profound.

To enslave others, to see them as suitable for exploitation and torture, requires a psychology and ethical framework that renders domination by one group over another an acceptable, natural, and, for many nineteenth-century enslavers, a divinely ordained practice. As I've noted throughout this book, social scientists call this a social dominance orientation (SDO), one of the most consistent findings in the research on the psychology of conservatives.

While most on the contemporary Right would not embrace slavery per se, the rhetoric and policy of the Republican Party—especially that which emanates from its predominant MAGA faction—are saturated with the discourse of domination.

On issue after issue, the GOP has opposed racial, gender, and economic equity, especially in the form of legal protections. Correspondingly, it has consistently defended the privileges of those already privileged and fought for the freedom to deprive others of freedom. So, while slavery is no more, the perversions of democracy it engendered remain. The plantation system may be gone, but its corrupting ethos is embedded in the electoral system.

Social dominance is also evident in public life more broadly. Due to the Trumpian normalization of bigotry against multiple minority groups, homicidal trolling, assault, and even murder of those with less power and status has increased dramatically. It would be reductionist to attribute all of this to the Three-Fifths Compromise and its resulting institution, the Electoral College—especially since racist violence and anti-democracy efforts are global in scope. But it would not be wrong to say those measures have contributed to the enduring legacy of domination and hobbled democracy that could end the country as we know it.

This catalog of similarities between the slave-holding South of yore and the current GOP must include the frequent appearance of Confederate flags at Trump rallies, and the January 6 attempted coup and assault on the Capitol. The former president's fans have made it apparent that the MAGA hat is the sartorial equivalent of the enslavers' stars and bars. Unlike the hooded Klansmen of an earlier time, those donning the red cap have felt no need to hide their identity. After all, the MAGA Grand Wizard was the president of the United States, who not only encouraged violence[10] but told his base whom to target.[11] They could not find a more permissive superego for racist aggression. And with his many self-serving pardons, he implied that his followers might enjoy a kind of impunity for acting on his wishes.[12]

Are there any indications that the nineteenth-century politicians who fought legislatively and literally for the interests of slave states were the political and psychological ancestors of today's Republican Party? Is there evidence of that in the conduct of antebellum identity politics? That is certainly a very plausible reading of what historian Joanne B. Freeman has uncovered in her lively and painstakingly researched account of Congressional violence that led up to the Civil War, *The Field of Blood*.[13]

Relying on primary sources and, unlike me, eschewing any comparison to the present, the documents she unearthed have an extraordinary resemblance to our current era. What follows in the next few sections is based primarily on her material. My overview and interpretation of Freeman's work cannot do justice to its depth and scope. I encourage those seeking a more comprehensive exploration of this period to read her study. My interest in her work is in the insights it may offer into some of the unexamined origins of our current politics of identity, an interpretive leap she did not make in her writing. Nevertheless, in spite of Freeman's scrupulous confinement to her historical lane, in 2023 she could not ignore the belligerence and violent threats that have become so commonplace among contemporary Republicans. She joked that their behavior was so strikingly resonant with the pugilistic antebellum conservatives of her study that she had enough material to write a second volume of her book.[14]

In highlighting the resemblance between antebellum slave-holding politicians and MAGA conservatives, I am not arguing for a straightforward political genealogy. We can only speculate about the role that geographical, ideological, and familial factors may have played. Perhaps there has been transgenerational transmission of a social dominance orientation through multiple influences. Those might have included childrearing patterns, education, fundamentalist religion, folklore, the persistence of local cultural psychology across the generations, and a desire sustained across the centuries to see one's economic or racial privileges as just and divinely sanctioned.

Likewise, antebellum northerners did not magically give birth to contemporary Democrats. While Democrats of the Old South in many ways resemble the GOP of the current era, over the centuries, each party evolved into a complicated mix of different and sometimes conflicting tendencies. Nineteenth-century northerners were not uniformly abolitionist. And they were undoubtedly embedded in their own forms of racism. There were multiple turning points that led the polarity of the past to resemble the current one. A landmark moment that established the battle lines for contemporary partisan conflict was Democratic President Lyndon B. Johnson's 1960s conversion to a passionate and forceful civil rights advocate. The racist, pro-segregationist wing of the Democratic Party found a new home in the GOP. And the rest is history.

It is not my intention to offer a definitive explanation for the similarities between then and now but merely to call attention to them and consider what lessons we can draw from the past that might help us respond to the intractable divisions of the present. Based on Freeman's description of the political parties that represented nineteenth-century southern slavers, they sound a lot like what Hibbing calls securitarians, people who guarded group/racial boundaries with great vigilance.[15] They were also comfortable with aggression and physical violence, embedded in a brittle, defensive hypermasculinity and resistant to compromise with their opponents—a picture that brings today's GOP to mind.

In contrast, her depiction of the parties representing abolitionist northerners is one of a faction that embraced racial equality (to varying degrees) and was primarily unitarian, as Hibbing would describe them, with more permeable group boundaries. They were politicians who prized the unity of Congress and the nation, did not countenance threats or acts of violence, and often sought compromise and bipartisan collaboration. Their resemblance to today's Democrats is hard to overlook.

From the War on Civility to the Civil War

The nineteenth century was a bloody one in America—even before the Civil War. There were fistfights and deaths at polling places perpetrated by various nativist groups trying to stop legal immigrants from voting. One group of xenophobic vigilantes called themselves the Pug Uglies, as if to embrace the repellent face they presented to the world. But the most notorious violence of the antebellum period occurred between members of Congress.

Especially noteworthy were duels. They were highly rule-bound and ritualized. To challenge a peer to a duel, accept or refuse a challenge, and stipulate the precise process in which it would be conducted required elaborate and painstaking negotiations. As common as these episodes of violence were, the media of the era, newspapers, were under tremendous pressure not to cover too many details and to render the vitriol more benign and gentlemanly. These prohibitions were enforced through coercion by interested parties as well as self-censorship.

Importantly, duels were only fought between perceived status equals. So, a congressman (they were all men at the time) would not challenge a newspaper editor nor accept one from such a person. Journalists could be threatened or assaulted but not in the rule-bound context of a duel, as they were not considered worthy of such an honor.

Slavery was the primary area of dispute between members of Congress. Unsurprisingly, this debate mapped onto regional identity (North vs. South). Then, as today, the white supremacist/red states held much more power in proportion to their numbers than did advocates of equality. Similar to the present, several structural biases built into the system favored the southern conservative states. In the nineteenth century, the Three-fifths Compromise described earlier gave southerners a disproportionate political representation advantage.

One of the most contentious issues in the 1850s was whether new states entering the Union would permit slavery. As enslaved people were property, property owners had the right to do with their property whatever they wished. As described in the previous chapter, to engage in the slave trade was regarded, without any sense of irony, as a cherished freedom. Being able to enslave others—the freedom to deprive others of freedom—was seen as a fundamental right by white southerners. And in this period, "states' rights" were synonymous with slave-holding rights. And they fought furiously, sometimes with guns, to ensure new states were permitted to put Africans in bondage. For northerners, freedom was the *absence* of bondage; hence the label "free states" applied to the North. While slavery is no longer legal, those radically disparate concepts of freedom, as noted earlier, have continued to define political battle lines into the present day.

Slaveholders in Congress approached politics as they approached their role as owners of other humans—asserting dominance through threats, beatings, and other forms of coercion. And some of the same implements of the trade were employed—fists, canes, whips, knives, and guns. These methods were quite effective as political tools against the northern "non-combatants" (as their Congressional peers called them) until the late 1850s. That's when the Republican Party was born, and slavery opponents began to fight back more aggressively, physically and politically.

Before that transition, the weapons of choice for northern politicians were rules, procedures, and calls to order. But even in the domain of procedure, southerners were more ruthless. For example, they established a gag rule prohibiting any discussion of abolitionist petitions submitted to Congress, with which northerners dutifully complied. Interestingly, the word abolitionist was, for some, a term of derision, much like the way "liberal" is now, which led the "moderates" among northern slavery opponents to avoid that label. It seems those on the Right back then were as effective at getting their opponents to adopt pro-slavery framing as contemporary conservatives have gotten liberals to use Republican frames.

Nineteenth-century southern politicians played to the base as much as red-state representatives do now. Impassioned diatribes by a North Carolina congressman directed to his home county of Buncombe became the paradigmatic example of performative bombast. That led to the coinage of the term *bunkum* or *bunk* to describe such melodramatic appeals directed at an audience of one's constituents.

The physical fights between representatives of the North and South over slavery in the antebellum Congress turned out to be the first battles of the Civil War. The country was so regionally divided that individual state banks printed their own currency, making interstate travel a challenge requiring considerable preparation. Fighting for one's constituency was quite literal. Voters in home districts would send their representatives guns to give them an edge in the surrogate warfare.

Freeman's depiction of the different collective character traits of the politicians that represented northern critics of slavery (mostly Whigs and, later, Republicans) and its southern defenders (mostly Democrats) resemble, to a striking degree, the differences between contemporary Democrats and Republicans. Among the qualities that link the nineteenth-century partisans of slavery and twenty-first-century Republicans, beyond overlapping geography, include conduct and rhetoric that imply a shared understanding of freedom—the freedom to harm with impunity, which was in the service of the freedom to dominate others. That translated into a propensity toward the use of threats, coercion, and violence to achieve goals (they were often called "fighting men"). Another link between the two is spurious patriotism manifested in a willingness to betray the country if their regional/tribal interests are served. For the nineteenth-century South, that was manifested in their secession from and military assault on the United States. For the contemporary MAGA faction, that was expressed most obviously in their alignment with a foreign dictator, Putin, whose explicit aim was the weakening and ultimate destruction of America.[16]

Anti-slavery politicians of the North resembled contemporary Democrats in their conflict-avoidant tendency toward capitulation. Their designation as "non-combatants" referred to their disinclination to duel, which their fellow party members and constituents viewed as barbaric, and their care to avoid offending slave-holding colleagues. Some were so compliant with southern bullies that they were mocked by both members of their own party and those to whom they caved.

The common term of abuse for being so squishy was "doughface." It initially referred to those northerners who voted with the South when issues of slavery were up for a vote. Over time, its meaning expanded to include any politician too weak to stand up to coercion. The Webster's Dictionary of 1847 defined it as "The willingness to be led about by one of stronger mind and will."[17] As with contemporary Democrats (at least those in power before the Trump era), nineteenth-century northerners tended to be uncomfortable with contentious politics and anxiously sought compromise with opponents who relished all manner of combat, physical and political, and, like today's GOP, had no interest in comity.

Nevertheless, while eschewing duels, some northerners, such as John Quincy Adams, were capable of blistering verbal retorts to their Southern opponents. With the birth of the Republican Party just before the war, northern abolitionists grew stiffer spines and gradually became as politically pugilistic as the southern slavers. I'll say more about that soon.

One interesting feature of that period in Washington was the legal impunity that southerners seemed to have for their violent acting out, even on the floor of Congress. Those who engaged in bullying and physical coercion were undaunted by the occasional wrist slap from those charged with enforcing order. Indeed, such behavior was a source of pride for the slavery-defending perpetrators, especially when others perceived it as a defense of one's manly honor. Upholding the shared honor code was a central feature of southern regional identity.

Contemporary Republican politicians don't seem to have a code of honor. Loyalty is their driving motive. They are committed to promoting all fictive utterings that emanate from their party leader, Donald Trump, and supporting any GOP colleague, no matter how treasonous, corrupt, or mendacious. Unwavering fidelity to the former president and the MAGA faction is the closest they come to a code. We could think of this new right-wing tribal ethos as an extreme extension of the Reagan code, his "Eleventh Commandment": "Thou shall not speak ill of another Republican."[18] However, that commandment is readily violated in the face of perceived disloyalty or inadequate displays of reverence toward Trump.

The GOP's resemblance to their violent antebellum forebears is more in the ease with which they subtly and not so subtly threaten violence against their political opponents with apparent impunity and how those threats are celebrated in the right-wing media echo chamber. Posing with assault weapons in campaign ads and family Christmas cards, combat cosplay at MAGA rallies, and other violent vogueing have become de rigueur for GOP politicians and their constituents. As of this writing, Congressional Republicans are defending the violent January 6 coup plotters as patriots, and those few who have been incarcerated are being described as "political prisoners."[19]

The familiar aphorism that politics is warfare by other means is also true in the other direction; warfare is politics by other means. That was the case when the first physical battles of the Civil War occurred between Congressional combatants in Washington—and on the floor of Congress itself. From 1855 forward, politics *was* war.

That was also evident in the MAGA faction's assault on the Capitol and their readiness to lynch those who stood in their way of overturning American democracy. In the same period, Trump-base terrorists made death threats against many election workers across the country because they failed to "find" enough votes for their leader.[20] While the present era has come to resemble nineteenth-century conflicts more than ever since the antebellum period, it remains to be seen if those episodes foreshadow a second civil war, which would look very different than the first one.[21]

While the new Republican Party of the 1850s was primarily and explicitly abolitionist, it was in some ways like the contemporary Democratic Party. By that, I mean it was a big tent. It contained "moderates" who were opposed to slavery but supported the Fugitive Slave Act, the provision that mandated that northern states return runaway slaves to their enslavers. It also contained unapologetic racists and radical abolitionists. Freeman points out that many of the northerners were more disturbed by the bullying political tactics of the slavers than slavery itself. Southerners' methods to exercise political dominance over the North did not compare to the relentless brutality used to control enslaved people. Yet, both were driven by a similar zero-sum approach to power. Both relied on violence and intimidation. That resemblance was not lost on Congressional northerners.

The antebellum Democratic Party was similar to today's GOP in its homogeneity. It comprised "states' rights" advocates and passionate defenders of slavery that tolerated little diversity and was held together by an unbending expectation of loyalty. Regional/tribal interests generally eclipsed considerations of national unity.

The most famous episode of antebellum Congressional violence was the near-fatal caning of Massachusetts abolitionist Senator Charles Sumner by South Carolina pro-slavery Representative Preston Brooks. The beating followed a five-hour fulmination against slavery and those who benefitted from it, delivered by Sumner in the Senate chambers. It marked the final breakdown of Congress' ability to engage in debate. It was an attack, not just on unarmed Sumner, but on the remnants of free speech itself, a right that pro-slavery gag rules had already hobbled.

That assault was, in many ways, the first skirmish of the Civil War. It was a source of pride for Brooks, who bragged about restoring southern "honor." Feeling so emboldened by the beating of Sumner, he challenged other Congressional abolitionists to duels whose speeches he also found offensive. Unsurprisingly, Brooks's southern colleagues insisted that Congress give him impunity for his actions and threatened even worse violence should there be any attempt to hold him to account.

Northerners framed the attack as a testament to the unmodifiable brutality of slavery's political wing, the Democratic Party, and their inability to be governing partners in a democracy. Civil discourse was impossible with opponents who could not reign in their "plantation manors."[22] The event also catalyzed the arming of the northern members of Congress, who finally threw off the appellation of "non-combatants" and prepared for the battle to come.

Freeman argues that part of what led to the literal arming of members of Congress and ultimately to the full expression of civil war was that existing institutions were not strong enough to prevent violence. Thus, there was no force outside the disputing parties to enforce accountability. That sounds like our recent history, when violent, anti-democratic forces, including the former president and the terrorist wing of his party, were not stopped on January 6 by the National Guard. Finally, and much belatedly, the high-level planners of the coup plot, including Donald Trump, have been indicted by the Justice Department's Special Counsel Jack Smith.

Americans of an egalitarian bent may find comfort in knowing that slavery came to a formal end after the Confederacy lost the war. However, some may be surprised to learn that it did not take long for slave labor to be replaced by its functional equivalent, the "convict leasing" system. Newly emancipated Black people in the South were arrested on dubious charges, such as "vagrancy." They were then convicted, incarcerated, and leased to agricultural and industrial enterprises. Prison operators made money, and businesses got very cheap labor. It was a win-win—except for those who did the unpaid work.

Unfortunately, that new penal plantation system was not limited to the states of the former Confederacy. Slavery as punishment was written into the constitution of many states. Even in 2022, that statutory language remained on the books across the United States. It was such a source of embarrassment to some that multiple state midterm ballots featured measures to remove that language. While the measure passed in three of the four states that had initiatives (it lost in Louisiana), a large plurality of Republican voters wanted to retain slavery as a punishment for crime. Even in my bright blue state of Oregon, nearly 45 percent of voters (all in red counties) voted to keep slavery on the books.[23] In light of the social dominance orientation that characterizes conservative psychology, we might be troubled but not shocked that so many on the Right could accept forced labor as a form of punishment. It would be hard to imagine an expression of domination more undisguised and absolute than the enslavement of other humans.

Of course, racial domination has persisted well beyond slavery—convict leasing in the postbellum era, voter suppression, gerrymandering, and systemic discrimination more broadly. But that leaves us with a disturbing question: To what extent can we say that the Confederacy lost the war? Black Americans remain disenfranchised in so many ways, despite laws and constitutional amendments, like the Fifteenth, to the contrary. Currently, one of this country's two major parties, the GOP, is an unabashed white supremacist party with open racists and anti-Semites serving on House committees. To add irony to injury, then as now, the loudest voices decrying "voter fraud"—the rationale for voter suppression—have come from those who were perpetrating it.[24]

The South Rises Again: The Birth of the "Southern Strategy"

At the 1948 Democratic Party Convention, the liberal wing of the party was particularly bold in its support for civil rights. That predictably enraged southern segregationists who formed the State's Rights Democratic Party, the Dixiecrats." Strom Thurmond was nominated as their presidential candidate and won in four states. However, those were states where he and his allies could keep Truman off the ballot—a little-known episode in the long history of conservative hostility to democracy. That cleavage among the Democrats presages the profound political realignment that would follow. While Dixiecrats would not endure as a separate party, they formed the substrate that, over many decades, would morph into the openly white supremacist GOP of the present day.

In historian Kevin Kruse's enlightening account of that realignment, he describes some incremental steps toward that transformation.[25] In 1949, Dixiecrat J. Harvie Williams from North Carolina proclaimed at a fund-raising event that a "formal alliance between Republicans and Southern Democrats" would motivate "white, English-speaking stocks" to propel a "conservative president" into the White House.[26] Senator John W. Bricker of Ohio was another Dixiecrat who advocated the merger. Anticipating the rhetoric of the future GOP, he said, "Voters may have a chance to decide whether they believe in all this big government, high taxes and profligate spending, or believe in conservation of resources, of human energy and opportunity for the individual." Coming from an avowed segregationist, we don't have to guess which individuals he thinks should be granted an opportunity, whose rights government should protect, or who should be the beneficiaries of tax revenue and other resources. From the postbellum period forward, conservatives framed the federal government as a tyrannical force precisely because of their efforts to enforce civil rights for Black people in the South.

The courtship between those two political parties began to heat up in 1952. That was just the beginning of the romance between southern racists and elements of the GOP. It would be many years before it fully flowered. The GOP was not then explicitly racist or segregationist and just starting to use the rhetoric of "states' rights." To all parties involved in the political realignment of southern Dixiecrats, it was explicitly understood that being pro-segregation was a conservative position. It was labeled as such by both the supporters and opponents of Jim Crow laws and policies.

The ideological gulf between Republicans and Democrats was not the yawning chasm it is now. And, while Republicans began to "moderate" their enthusiasm for civil rights, the Democrats were not exactly passionate about it then. Adlai Stevenson, who ran against Eisenhower in 1952 and 1956 on the Democratic ticket, attempted to court both Dixiecrats and African Americans.

The Southern Strategy, the conscious but coded appeal to white racial anxieties, was embryonic in the Eisenhower era and more explicit during Goldwater's campaign. While efforts have been underway to rehabilitate the image of Barry Goldwater as a more mainstream conservative, his political star rose following his opposition to *Brown v. Board of Education* and declaration of his allegiance to states' rights and in favor of segregation.

At the 1964 Republican convention, where Goldwater was ultimately nominated as the party's presidential candidate, liberal Republican Nelson Rockefeller attempted to introduce an amendment to the party platform that repudiated the Klan and the John Birch Society. He was loudly denounced and defeated. In 1964, when Bill Dickinson, a segregationist from Alabama, switched from the Democratic to the Republican Party, he proudly declared, "I have joined the white man's party."[27]

Some of the few Black Republicans that attended that event were told to stay in their place, physically assaulted, and even set on fire. Black baseball icon Jackie Robinson, at the time a Republican, was quite shaken after attending the convention and said, "I now believe I know how it felt to be a Jew in Hitler's Germany."[28]

It is worth pointing out, if unsurprising, that Robinson could not evade racism in the North. My father became good friends with him when they played together in the Southern California minor leagues. He would come over for dinner at our home in Glendale but had to rush home before dark to avoid arrest for violating the racial "Sundown" ordinance, a Black curfew law adopted in thousands of US cities. Glendale was notorious for bigotry and was home to the headquarters of the American Nazi Party.[29]

Richard Nixon, whom most associate with the Southern Strategy, made the pitch to Dixiecrats based on their shared "conservative" values.[30] When forced to take a stand on an explicit segregationist plank in the GOP platform, he declared his opposition to it. But then he turned around and praised Strom Thurmond as "a man of courage and integrity." While the plank was apparently a bit too explicit for Nixon, he promised to soften school desegregation enforcement. The final party platform did not mention civil rights but vowed "law and order." And from that point forward, the Republican discourse on crime became a reliable way to activate the securitarian neurocircuitry and associated racial representations of white conservatives.

A decade later, Ronald Reagan denied employing any race-based Southern Strategy. However, when he campaigned in Mississippi, the GOP candidate proclaimed, "I believe in states' rights," and promised to "restore to states and local government the power that properly belongs to them."[31] Many Americans of a certain age may recall his coded Jeremiads against "welfare queens." In Reagan's 1984 reelection campaign, his Southern Strategy got more explicit. In a speech before the Sons of Confederate Veterans, Mississippi GOP Senator Trent Lott said, "The spirit of Jefferson Davis lives in the 1984 Republican platform."

George H. W. Bush's "Willie Horton" campaign ad was among the most explicit expressions of the Southern Strategy, which, at this point, was a national one, given its efficacy in turning the tide toward Bush's election. The ad told the story of Horton, a Black murderer, who was released on a furlough by then Massachusetts governor and later Democratic presidential candidate Michael Dukakis. During that furlough (made possible by a prisoner release program enacted by the former Republican governor), he stole a white Maryland couple's car, knifed and pistol-whipped the man, and raped and beat the woman. That narrative was custom-made to trigger and direct primitive racial paranoia and white male anxiety. The ad, created by campaign attack dog Roger Ailes, who would later go on to found Fox News, succeeded in depicting Dukakis as a weak and feckless castrato, unable to protect white women from the depredations of the predatory Black males who constantly roam the streets looking for victims.[32]

Republican efforts to exploit and exacerbate racist sentiments in the country have only gotten more brazen over time. But there have been brief departures from that strategy, such as under George W. Bush. Not to diminish the ethnic targeting of individuals from Arab countries and the creation of "Black site" torture facilities, Bush created a more racially diverse cabinet and made some gestures toward a more just and less punitive immigration system. In a 2005 speech to the NAACP, RNC chairman Ken Mehlman even apologized for the Southern Strategy. He acknowledged that his party was guilty of "looking the other way or trying to benefit politically from racial polarization."[33]

Perhaps unsurprisingly, that fleeting moment of GOP self-reflection and regret ended abruptly when Rush Limbaugh reminded the male Republican base of the psychosexual meaning that apology, especially for racism, carried for conservatives. As Limbaugh saw it, Mehlman's speech was the political equivalent of submitting to anal rape. "Once again, Republicans are going to bend over and grab the ankles," he said.[34]

Limbaugh, the proud misogynist and bigoted OG pit bull provocateur of the modern Right, has been the role model for the legion of others that have followed in his wake. Conservative shock jocks and politicians alike have learned that slander, doxing, rumor mongering, puerile insults, verbal bullying, racist rants, and punching down can boost their MAGA audience share. We might wonder: what makes that so gratifying and politically mobilizing? To answer that, we have to take a deep dive into one of the Right's affective weapons of choice, cruelty.

CHAPTER 6

The Tribal Politics of Sadism

At a 2016 St. Louis campaign rally, then-candidate Donald Trump had enough of the protesters in the audience and was frustrated at how long it took for his MAGA muscle to throw them out. "Part of the problem and part of the reason it takes so long is that nobody wants to hurt each other anymore," he declared.[1] It wasn't just syntax he sought to torture. Seeing protesters beaten to a pulp would be even more gratifying. The bloodied Black man was ultimately dragged away by security.[2] That was just one of numerous calls for violence, against administration critics, immigrants, and those in government who dared to hold the former president accountable for his actions. For the next seven years, many of his followers heeded those appeals for cruelty and sanguinary retribution.

George W. Bush made a valiant but unpersuasive and unsuccessful attempt to repackage the Republican worldview by coining the oxymoronic term "compassionate conservatism."[3] That conservatism required the modifier *compassionate* revealed what conservatism had been all along—an outlook and value system grounded in the ruthless and callous pursuit of self-interest and domination. But with the rise of Trump, cruelty became more than a mildly unfortunate side effect of the privileged consolidating their privilege and dominating those with fewer resources. It became an end in itself.

Jeff Sharlet compares and contrasts Trump's shtick to that of a Borscht Belt comedian.[4] While there are some similarities in style, the humor of those Jewish comedians is, in some ways, a means of managing tragedy. But for Trump, "humor" is a delivery system for cruelty. Laughter makes it easier for his audience to delight in fantasies of mayhem and suffering directed at their leader's enemies. That has been a part of the sadistic call-and-response animating his rallies from the very beginning of his first presidential campaign.

I am not arguing that the Left is incapable of organized sadism and ideologically driven lynch mobs. Rather, what is unique to those on the Right is that for today's MAGA conservatives, cruelty is woven into their identity and even celebrated. One of the most popular items sold at Trump rally concession stands is a cup emblazoned with the words "Liberal Tears." Sadism on the Right is more common, acceptable, and even viewed as virtuous. Psychologists refer to it as "ego-syntonic"—impulses and behaviors that are compatible with one's sense of self, values, and worldview.

For the MAGA faction, the political utility of sadism and cruelty has not been simply to inflict suffering on tribal outsiders—whether the victims are non-white people, immigrants, or women. As Adam Serwer has argued, the most critical aspect is that perpetrators do it together.[5] Thus, cruelty becomes a bonding ritual that consolidates tribal identity and boundaries. It is a *collective* action.

That is what links political gang rapes seen in wars across the globe, lynching of ethnic minorities, police assaults on demonstrators, racial taunts against opposing sports teams (many of which were inspired by the rhetoric of former President Trump[6]), and border patrol attacks on immigrants.[7] Each is a form of coordinated sadism enacted by in-groups and perpetrated against out-groups. They are shared rituals that establish who belongs *inside* the tribal boundary and should be protected and who belongs *outside* and should be subject to torment.

In chapter 1, I described research showing that for political torturers, their victim's outsider status gets reinforced by virtue of their victimization. The tautological reasoning goes like this: "We hurt them because they are not like us. And the fact that they are the ones being tortured is proof that they are not like us."

During his time in office, Donald Trump gave the presidential bully pulpit a new and more literal meaning. ABC News alone documented forty-one cases of violent assaults, vandalism, and threats that explicitly invoked the former president's name or echoed his rhetoric.[8] The number has doubtless grown exponentially since that report was done. The perpetrators were mostly white males, and the victims were predominantly racial minorities and gay men. Although lone individuals committed some of those attacks, it is clear that they experienced themselves as part of a collective effort. Even while acting in isolation, their tribal signaling made it clear they felt themselves to be part of a national lynch mob led by the highest authority in the land.[9]

Beyond those cases of freelance MAGA cruelty, there has been an explosion in more organized forms of right-wing terrorism. A series of reports issued in 2020 showed that far-right militias committed most acts of political violence.[10] The Department of Homeland Security warned that white supremacist groups constituted the "most persistent and lethal threat to the homeland." And none of us can forget the brutal assaults directed against the Capitol police by the Trump-inspired putschists on January 6 and their determined but unsuccessful efforts to lynch Vice President Mike Pence and House Speaker Nancy Pelosi.

Not all manifestations of ultraconservative tribal cruelty have been carried out by non-government perpetrators. Some were features of administration policy. But occasionally, right-wing sadism has been off-target. During a Trump-facilitated government shutdown, workers at a prison in a deep-red rural area were severely affected. Contrary to the president's assurance that "most of the workers not getting paid are Democrats," one ardent Trump supporter complained, "He's not hurting the people he needs to be hurting."[11] However, the administration did not take long to determine how to inflict pain on the correct targets.

Especially disturbing in that regard was Trump's immigrant child abduction program. Rather than give a hearing to non-white immigrants seeking asylum, immigration officials responded with punishment to refugees' flight from lethal threats in their home countries. And what better punishment than systematic and legally sanctioned kidnapping? "We need to take away children. If they care about kids, don't bring them in," declared then-Attorney General Jeff Sessions.[12] "Separation," the term used then, seems far too anodyne for the enduring trauma inflicted on families, many of whose children were permanently lost in the system, some of whom were infants at the time.[13] One administration lawyer who helped design White House immigration policy excused their actions by saying, "Justice Department officials merely took direction from the president." Apparently, the Nuremberg defense has not exhausted its utility regarding governmental sadism driven by tribal race hatred.[14]

Trump's child abduction policy was not something he and his administration invented. It was part of a long history of such practices by authoritarian leaders and imperial conquerors, particularly common during European and American colonial expansion. Under the rubric of "kill the Indian, save the man,"[15] the kidnapping and forced relocation of native children into church-run reeducation camps, euphemistically known as "boarding schools," was a form of soft genocide. Abduction of the children of minority or dissident groups and adopting them out to members of the regime's own ethnic or political tribe has been a practice implemented by a variety of fascist governments. It was carried out by Franco's Spain,[16] the Nazis,[17] the Argentine junta[18] in the late 1970s, and Pinochet's Chile.[19] It is a policy currently enacted against Ukrainian children in Putin's[20] effort to erase Ukraine as a distinct nation and people.

We could think of this as a fascist or authoritarian resolution to Hegel's master-slave conundrum. The master wants to subordinate the enslaved person, to deprive him or her of all agency and subjectivity. But he (a male in Hegel's story) depends on the enslaved person for recognition of his mastery. The problem is that someone who is reduced to a thing cannot give recognition. In the real-life example of children whose culture and identity have been denatured and replaced with those of the abducting group, the children grow up to become adults who can give recognition—albeit with a colonized self. This repressive assimilation renders mass murder unnecessary, at least for the children of the enemy group. The otherness of ethnic or political enemies has been killed while preserving their bodies.

Not all attempts by the Trump administration to codify cruelty in policy could be implemented. The former president's unfulfilled wish list included plans to have migrants shot in the legs, devoured by alligators in border moats, impaled by electrified wall spikes, and other creative ways to welcome the huddled masses seeking refuge in the United States.[21] To his considerable frustration, Mr. Trump's advisors informed him that these approaches were not currently legal.

Especially galling to the former president was being upstaged years later by the neo-MAGA GOP governor of Florida, Ron DeSantis, who implemented an anti-immigrant act of cruelty Trump insisted was "my idea."[22] In September 2022, DeSantis's functionaries conned a group of Venezuelan migrants in Texas who had pending asylum claims with promises of jobs, food, and housing, put them on a privately charted plane, and deposited them on Martha's Vineyard with no notice to local officials.[23] They could twist the knives in their backs even further by arranging to have the refugees' asylum claims heard at distant ends of the country. Because the traumatized claimants could not possibly get there in time, they would risk losing their cases by being no-shows. DeSantis was stealing the limelight from Trump and other Republican governors who had engaged in similar anti-immigrant sadistic trolling of Democratic areas.[24]

The essential political question raised by those acts of cruelty is what their utility might be. I think there are three possible answers to that. One, it occurred only a few months before the 2022 midterms and after GOP politicians had made it clear that they intended to adopt the Gilead approach to women's reproductive freedom, i.e., criminalize it nationwide. The actions of Republican governors were attempts to put the immigration "threat" back in the foreground. Two, the dumping of refugees like so much garbage at the doorstep of Democrats was a sadistic two-fer. It could gratify the MAGA base's hatred and disgust toward non-white immigrants—a punch down. And it could be imagined as an attack on the liberal "elite"—a punch up. And three, it raised the national profile of DeSantis, who could depict himself as the principal MAGA antagonist, with the hope of eclipsing Trump in the 2024 Republican primary race.

Trumpian Trolls In-Training

Children have not only been the victims of MAGA cruelty but have internalized its ethos and enacted it against their peers. While causality might be complicated and not always straightforward, one study found that bullying increased in areas that voted for Trump.[25] The National Education Association issued a report based on teacher surveys that cited increased bullying episodes among students in demographic groups targeted by the former president.[26] In another study, researchers looked at differences between pre-and post-election bullying in districts of Virginia that voted for Trump. Following his election in 2016, incidents of abuse based on ethnicity and perceived sexual orientation by children of other children increased significantly.[27]

Should the reader be tempted to dismiss these findings as mere correlations, one report found that white children engaged in harassing children of color often used versions of Trump's own words and phrases in the verbal attacks.[28] Maine teenagers yelled, "Ban Muslims," at a girl wearing a hijab. Two kindergartners in Utah told a Latino boy that Trump would send him back to Mexico. A mixed-race middle-school girl in Ohio was told by other kids, "This is Trump country." After unfurling a Make America Great banner, white students at a Washington state high school yelled, "Build the wall," at a Mexican-American boy. These and many similar incidents strongly suggest that the associations established between MAGA-faction rhetoric and bullying among children are causal, not random. However, another factor has long preceded the rise of Trump that links conservative values and psychology with abusive behavior—the use of physical punishment to discipline children.

The Red Bottoms of Red Staters

Nearly all of the states in which it is legal for school authorities to inflict corporal punishment on children are in the South.[29] According to a study jointly authored by Human Rights Watch and the American Civil Liberties Union, not only is it acceptable to hit students in these Republican strongholds, but disabled children receive a disproportionate amount of the beatings.[30] In one North Carolina high school, students caught breaking the rules can choose between in-school suspension or being paddled.[31] Perhaps because of the resulting academic disadvantage and parental ire over missing class, "Most kids will tell you they prefer paddling," said the school principal. While permission from parents is required, that does not impede school beatings in that part of the country. For example, one student whose crime was an errant cell phone ring in class said, "And my dad was like, 'Just paddle her.' Because down here in the mountains, we do it the old-school way." A parent who also teaches at the school explained, "A lot of parents hold to the traditional values of corporal punishment. They use it at home, and so the school is an extension of home."

A North Carolina child advocacy organization showed the principal at that high school research demonstrating that corporal punishment leads to various troubling outcomes.[32] The list included increased incidence of depression, high dropout rates, drug abuse, and a greater likelihood of being a perpetrator of violence in the future. The principal was indifferent to the evidence, insisting, "I think if more schools did it, we'd have a better society."

Okay, so folks in red states like to "discipline" children by raising welts on their buttocks and find the derrières of disabled people a particularly tempting target. Does this story of corporal punishment in schools tell us anything new about right-wing politics? We already know conservatives are comfortable with cruelty, can feel contempt for the vulnerable, and score lower on empathy measures. Well, as it turns out, right-wing ideology not only justifies and facilitates spanking, but spanking also helps to create future right-wing ideologues.

Two University of Massachusetts research psychologists, Michael A. Milburn and Sheree D. Conrad, studied the developmental impact of authoritarian and physically punitive parenting and described the results in their book *The Politics of Denial*.[33] Controlling for the known effects of education and income, they found that a history of this sort of childrearing predicted conservative political attitudes in adulthood. If we attend to the affective register of Republican "street" politics (however fueled by K Street), it is driven by fury, grievance, and lust for revenge. And there is a sense that a malevolent authority responsible for caring for them is really out to humiliate, hurt, and destroy those dependent on its ministrations. We should not be surprised that GOP propagandists and wordsmiths have gotten such a high political yield from conjuring up the evil parental bogey of "Big Government." (In chapter 10, I will have a lot more to say about the political consequences of that fusion between love and terror, especially the role that "trauma bonding" plays in recruiting and retaining members of the Trump cult.)

To be clear, I am not arguing for a single variable responsible for conservative identity. There are numerous interacting factors—psychological, economic, and sociological—that contribute to the adoption of right-wing values and ideas. A history of harsh childhood punishment that includes spanking is only one. But there's a well-known public figure whose history is quite illustrative.

Occasionally, far-right pundits reveal more truth than they might have intended. Michael Savage, the bigoted, shrieking rage-monger of ultraconservative talk radio, offered up a moment of rare if still rationalizing candor in his 2003 book, *Savage Nation: Saving America from the Liberal Assault on Our Borders, Language, and Culture*.[34] In a passage referencing his childhood, he said, "Things were tough every day of our lives. And we made the best of it. Frankly, that's why I'm driven the way I am. I was raised on neglect, anger, and hate. I was raised the old-fashioned way." Whether he was beaten with fists, words, or both, Savage echoes the paddled North Carolina student. Like her, he illustrates how abuse can be reframed as an ennobling conservative family value. Savage also shows how it can be recalled in adulthood through the haze of wistful nostalgia as a character-building expression of "tough love." It prepares one for the imagined Hobbesian future by excusing and identifying with the aggressor.

In one interview, Savage delivers his usual rant against "turd-world immigration," "left-wing pinko vermin in high places," and the uppity women of the "she-ocracy."[35] Then he warns his readers, "Only a more savage nation can survive—not a more compassionate nation." Perhaps feeling a particularly acute need to cultivate a hypermasculine exoskeleton, in the late 1980s, he shifted his identity from a mild-mannered North Beach bohemian herbalist to a snarling reborn conservative, changing his last name from Weiner to Savage. If you accept power as a zero-sum game—the Republican worldview, and one that parental violence makes quite persuasive—it's far more compelling to identify with perpetrators than victims.

Putin Enters the MAGA Pantheon of Sadistic Saints

Given the above, we should not have been surprised to see so many Republicans initially side with Putin over Ukraine. The political winds shifted once the 2022 Russian invasion brought images of mass murder into American living rooms. Even then, a shocking plurality of the MAGA faction did not abandon their role as apologists for Russian genocide.[36]

Republican support for the Putin dictatorship was particularly discernible after Trump's undisguised extortion of Zelenskyy over the former president's demand that the Ukrainian leader open an investigation into Joe Biden's son. Threatening to withhold military aid to Zelenskyy, Trump said, in essence, "You've got such a nice little country there. It would be a shame if something were to happen to it." As we all witnessed, House Republicans not only refused to hold their party's leader to account but, while defending him during the ensuing impeachment hearing, pushed various conspiracy theories authored by Russian intelligence.[37] It wasn't until Russia began its widely televised 2022 war on Ukrainian civilians that it became politically inconvenient to side with the world's most visible war criminal. Even then, Trump, who remains the clear leader of the Republican Party, called for Putin to do him the favor Zelenskyy refused to deliver on—releasing any available dirt on Joe Biden and his son.[38]

Trump's palpable dictator envy makes perfect sense in light of this framework. Overturning the 2020 election would have been his path to surpassing Putin's autocratic ambitions. Now he was condemned to being a mere spectator as the Russian dictator got to lock up purveyors of unflattering news and expand his dominion with impunity. Scorched-earth conquest is the ultimate expression of conservative freedom. Sovereignty is the prerogative of the conqueror, not the conquered—the enslaver, not the enslaved person.

Anyone who doubts that the right-wing libertarian notion of freedom is, in small and large ways, a justification for the sovereignty of predators, let me introduce you to my expert witness on the matter, Kentucky Senator Rand Paul. Although suckled at the teat of Ayn Rand's "Objectivism," he was not named after her.[39] An early adopter of Tea Party crackpottery, an avid Trump supporter, and a vociferous opponent of anti-COVID public health measures, Paul distinguished himself by his dissemination of pro-Putin propaganda. In a dialogue with Secretary of State Anthony Blinken, Paul repeated Putin's claim that Ukraine isn't actually a separate state entitled to national sovereignty.[40] Because it was once a captive country in the Russian empire, Putin was the sovereign to whom the world should defer. Paul was not ignorant about what he was defending. His comments were made many weeks after Russian war crimes—mass murder, rapes, torture, and the deliberate targeting of civilians— were a nonstop feature in America's newsfeed.

In those and many other examples too numerous to name, modern conservativism is revealed to be a coherent value system that sees predation, mistreatment, and exploitation as "rights" worth fighting for. Issue positions and candidate endorsements might vary with the political winds. And rhetoric and linguistic framing will always reflect the latest poll and focus group data. Nevertheless, their social dominance orientation described in the earlier chapters remains a constant. Narrow group and individual self-interest and the subjugation of those who impede it continue to be their guiding ethos. Theirs is a world in which Hobbes's famous "war of all against all" is the only one possible and one over which they are determined to triumph, without mercy or restraint. It is no wonder that until it became an image problem, Putin was so revered by the MAGA Right and the mentor of his chief acolyte, Donald Trump.

Schadenfreude and Domination

As I mentioned, at Trump rallies, among the most popular souvenir items peddled by MAGA merchants, also available on eBay at the time of writing, have been cups embossed with "Liberal Tears." In addition, the text on the cup mocks those on the Left for displaying "equality bumper stickers." At first glance, the co-occurrence of these two messages makes no sense. But a moment's reflection makes it clear that this novelty item is a revealing artifact of MAGA culture. For one thing, it tells us that the fantasy of causing emotional pain in their political enemies is gratifying. And for another, it lets us know just how absurd and offensive the notion of equality is to those on the Right. That cup is more than just a silly piece of Trumpworld kitsch; it is a trinket that betrays the conservative conjoining of sadism and their preoccupation with dominance.

It seems to be easier for right-wingers to endorse the freedom to harm when those they might harm are tribal outsiders. Social science research shows that conservatives are far less troubled than liberals by out-group members' suffering.[41] They are also more likely to experience schadenfreude (pleasure at another's suffering) over the losses endured by political opponents and *gluckschmerz* (pain from another's pleasure).[42] Comfort with harming political out-groups and pleasure in their suffering is highly associated with a social dominance orientation (SDO). Readers may recall that that much-studied personality trait refers to a preference for group-based inequality and a belief that one's own group is superior, and should therefore dominate others. Social dominants, as those who score high on measures of SDO are called by researchers, often embrace xenophobic, sexist, and racist policies and candidates. In the next chapter, I'll discuss SDO as a factor in the politics of anxious masculinity.

As might be expected from that description, conservatives tend to score higher on SDO than liberals. Perhaps equally unsurprising, those with this personality trait are also low in out-group empathy and perspective-taking (the ability to see the world through the eyes of others).[43] If you aim to subordinate "inferior" groups, it helps to not only be indifferent to their pain but to take pleasure in it. In other words, schadenfreude makes the work of domination more rewarding. That is especially so when out-group loss is perceived as necessary for an in-group win, otherwise known as a "zero-sum" competition. And, to be a social dominant is to live in a zero-sum world. So, harm is not just an acceptable cost of right-wing "freedom" but is an incentive to subjugate others. For those with an SDO, feeling good about oneself may require the shame of others. In other words, schadenfreude would have to be part of the experience of self-esteem. From this perspective, having a degraded other is necessary to feel elevated. When one is embedded in an SDO, self-worth, like all other rewards of life, gets absorbed into an all-or-nothing economy of value. Anyone observing the dramas of the MAGA-verse cannot help but notice that, in that world, winners require losers.

SDO intersects with another framework for understanding inter-tribal enmity, the stereotype content model. Researchers, principally Susan T. Fiske and her colleagues, found out-group stereotypes operate on two dimensions, each being a continuum.[44] With the first, tribal others are viewed on a scale of cold to warm. With the second, out-group members are ranked from highly competent to incompetent. Particular emotions accompany each combination of stereotypes. If we take as examples the attributions directed at out-groups by some white conservative American Christians, the model becomes clear.

Those seen as highly competent and cold tend to be objects of envy (Jews, Asians, feminists, Black professionals, and liberals). These are people who figure prominently in the conspiracy narratives of the Right. Other African Americans tend to be subject to different sets of stereotypes. Poor Blacks, in addition to welfare recipients, homeless people, and non-white immigrants, are more likely to be perceived as incompetent and cold. They often generate disgust, contempt, anger, and resentment. In the past, some Black Americans were seen as incompetent and warm. They tended to evoke bemused paternalism. Think of the happy slave characters in *Gone with the Wind*.

Older people can be viewed that way as well. They are often treated with condescension and cruel mockery. And sometimes, they are targeted by con artists because their perception as incompetent and warm makes them look like easy marks. There is an illustrative and repellent example of this from the Enron scandal decades ago. The company had created artificial energy shortages, price gouging poor and vulnerable customers. The scam led to multiple blackouts. Rarely does the public get to listen in on corporate sociopaths discussing their craft, but somehow a recording surfaced of two Enron operatives at the end of 2001 laughing and boasting about their con.[45] Here is a brief excerpt of their conversation:

> **Kevin:** So, the rumor's true? They're fuckin' taking all the money back from you guys? All the money you guys stole from those poor grandmothers in California? [Laughter]
>
> **Bob:** Yeah, Grandma Millie, man. But she's the one who couldn't figure out how to fuckin' vote on the butterfly ballot. [Laughter]
>
> **Kevin:** Yeah, now she wants her fuckin' money back for the power you've charged right up. Jammed right up her ass for fuckin' 250 million dollars a megawatt hour. [Laughter]
>
> **Bob:** You know Grandma Millie. She's the one that Al Gore is fightin' for, you know? [Laughter]

They go on to praise George W. Bush, and mock liberals, Al Gore, and the supposedly laughable idea of defending the vulnerable rather than exploiting them.[46] The exchange condenses many of the themes discussed here. Predation is one form of dominating others. And we can see the sadistic joy they get at the idea of defrauding their imagined elderly victim. Because she is presumed ineffectual, helpless, and benign, they depict her as a grandma—a figure often portrayed in cultural narratives as kindly but vulnerable. They are the favored victims of fairy-tale and Enron wolves. Then, as if they anticipated the argument I would make decades later, they add a partisan dimension to their cruel swindle. Democrats protect the weak, which is why they're the loser party. Republicans take advantage of opportunity, even if it means plundering those with minimal resources. And in the zero-sum universe where they reside, *that* is what makes them winners. And what fun it is.

There are other groups that get stereotyped as incompetent and cold, such as underclass African Americans. They feature as the foot soldiers of conniving Jews in neo-Nazi fantasies of white persecution. The most dangerous groups (and in reality, the most endangered) are those perceived as competent and cold. They evoke envy, fear, and hatred and are more likely to be on the receiving end of terrorist violence.

As it turns out, envied groups are those most subject to schadenfreude.[47] Researchers occasionally employ *primes*, which are subtle, sometimes subliminal or unconscious messages used to trigger certain thoughts or emotions. When socially dominant subjects are exposed to primes that imply that they are in competition with or threatened by a racial out-group, especially those perceived as competent and cold, they express more schadenfreude.[48] And the higher the subjects scored on SDO, the more they showed pleasure at the misfortune of the non-white out-group.

Right-Wing Trolls and their Conformist Rebellion

Online trolling—the harassment, humiliation, and threating of perceived political opponents—could be considered a kind of rehearsal for the cruelty of real-world violence. It is a practice of dehumanization, a way of making the despised other a nonperson who ceases to exist as soon as one's screen goes dark. If the first step in killing an enemy is killing off one's empathy and compassion for them, trolling can facilitate that.

Culture warriors on the Right tend to celebrate the violation of modernity's taboos—those against the elevation of superstition over science and the undisguised expression of cruelty, racism, and misogyny. They see themselves as rebels. But, as I described in the introduction, they are *conformist* rebels who seek a return to an earlier tradition of authoritarian rule, normative bigotry, Christian theocracy, and white male hegemony. Their defiance of existing authority is driven by an urge to obey more archaic ones. MAGA faction militias are dissident disruptors in the same way that ISIS and the Taliban have been. They share an enemy in Enlightenment liberalism and a common dream of returning to the reassuring hierarchies of their respective Dark Ages.

A related manifestation of that right-wing "rebellion" is their glee over being "politically incorrect." They complain bitterly about the "intolerant" Left's sanctimonious virtue signaling. That is their excuse for undisguised expressions of racism, sexism, and their sadistic punching down. At base, this is another iteration of the Right's assertion of their freedom to harm. The joy proclaimed by MAGA members over evoking liberal tears or "triggering" them with smirking "politically incorrect" insults (i.e., bigotry) is real. But there is another, more profound example of the relationship between social dominance, threat priming, and inter-tribal sadism. That would be the now mainstreamed white supremacist "Great Replacement" conspiracy theory, which will be explored in more depth later.

That belief was initially promoted by neo-Nazis and subsequently wholly endorsed by Trump's GOP and his Fox News mouthpieces. It refers to the idea that the liberal Jewish elite is conspiring with racial minorities to smooth the path into the country of non-white immigrants so they can outvote, out-work and outbreed white conservative Christians. Conservatives have used this story as one of many rationales for GOP efforts to write and pass laws designed to undermine and overturn elections. Multiple mass murderers have cited that delusion to explain their passion for slaughtering Black and brown citizens nationwide. You have, in this scenario, which will likely be repeated, a lethal mixture. There is a high SDO population that is well-armed, envi-ous, angry, and aggrieved (MAGA faction members), a threat prime (Great Replacement theory), and a collection of minorities and political opponents perceived as competent and cold—a trifecta of factors that has already led to multiple atrocities.

The Adaptive Advantages of Cruelty in a Capitalist Moral Universe

Before leaving the topic of the political utility of sadism, bullying, and author-itarian belligerence, it must be said that we live in a world in which those traits can be quite adaptive. Conscience, empathy, and compassion can impede financial or political success in business and politics. In the context of amoral global capitalism, the greatest spoils often redound to the most ruthless. That environment of normative sociopathy seems far more congenial to the predis-position of conservatives outlined in this book. Of course, even though the unfettered pursuit of narrow and short-term self-interest at the expense of oth-ers can be materially enriching, it leaves one in the wake of an impoverished and degraded world. Indeed, the accumulation of those pyrrhic victories ulti-mately may lead humans to their own extinction.

One particularly striking and consistent feature of right wing identity politics, not unrelated to its celebration of cruelty, is the many risible performances of hypermasculinity by Trumpworld men. The bluster and bloviating so central to these dominance displays belie a timorous vulnerability that occasionally shows through. That is what we will unpack in the next chapter.

CHAPTER 7

The Brittle Manhood
of MAGA Males

These Stilts Are Made for Walkin', and They're Gonna Walk All over You

Former Fox News pundit Tucker Carlson, the most prominent purveyor of the Great Replacement theory, is also the creator of a documentary, *The End of Men*, which is dense with images of homoerotic beefcake and saturated with dread of the feminine.[1] It is the latest in a long line of right-wing Jeremiads about the "crisis of masculinity." The film features such fatuous remedies for flagging manhood as testicle tanning, which he describes as a form of "bro-meopathic" therapy. Drawing on his deep understanding of endocrinology, Carlson concludes that liberalism in men is the unfortunate consequence of declining testosterone.

Carlson's antecedents among the men of the Ku Klux Klan, back when they donned robes instead of MAGA caps, used to move about on stilts to make themselves look taller.[2] Looking down on others is much easier if you tower above them. That is more than an amusing episode in the history of American white supremacy. It is a strikingly apt metaphor for the brittleness and precariousness of the hypermasculine preoccupation with dominance, which remains so prominent on the Right and is exemplified by Carlson.

In light of that history, it is interesting that, in a notorious pissing contest with comedian-come-activist Jon Stewart, Carlson tweeted a bizarre and clunky ad hominem against Stewart. He argued that his nemesis was "Really short. Too short to date. Was he always that short?"[3] In his view, having diminished stature is the only thing more unmanly than being undatable. Watching Carlson on Fox, it was apparent that his position at the network functioned as *his* stilts. It was a perch from which he expressed smarmy contempt, condescension, and fantasies of racial superiority without challenge. Although being propped up on stilts places you above "inferior" others, it is easy to be knocked over, as Stewart's blistering retorts over the twenty-plus years of their feuding attests.[4]

Similarly, in her study of white supremacist groups, Cynthia Miller-Idriss describes a neo-Nazi fight club named "Rise Above," which refers to the urge to "rise above the weak."[5] From Klan stilts to Carlson's condescension and aversion to shortness to the need for neo-Nazi brawlers to be on top, we are dealing with iterations of social dominance orientation expressed in spatial metaphors.

The right-wing male obsession with manliness does not reflect their greater masculinity (whatever that is) but their fear of not being "real" men. As I documented in my last book, *The Wimp Factor: Gender Gaps, Holy Wars, and the Politics of Anxious Masculinity*, the most crippling gender dysphoria is suffered by conservative males. So much of their time and energy is taken up with the endless task of affirming manhood and disproving their greatest fear, feminization. Weakness and vulnerability are read as feminine and must therefore be purged from the self. In light of that, hypermasculinity is best viewed as an anxiety disorder, not an exalted state of extreme virility.

The Linguistic Tells of the Masculine Bluff

He-man is a curious redundancy. Somehow, it is necessary to say it twice. It suggests that being born with male anatomy, the capacity to make androgens, and XY chromosomes are not enough to confer masculinity. For some cis males, manhood must be constantly proven and asserted at every turn—because it is continually endangered. And what is that danger? If we tune our ears to the subtext of everyday macho invective, the answer becomes startlingly clear. Straight men must be careful not to become someone's *bitch*. Deferring to women's concerns in a relationship could lead to being *pussy-whipped*. Conservative men insufficiently obdurate in their MAGA-mania can be dismissed as a *cuckservative*, which denotes a kind of political eunuch for the Right.[6] In the world of the online neofascist and misogynist "manosphere" documented by Jeff Sharlet,[7] liberal males are derided as *manginas*.

Males of earlier generations had to guard against being seen as a *pansy*, *sissy*, or *mama's boy*. George H. W. Bush's most significant political liability was supposedly the *wimp factor*.[8] Masculinity is such an ephemeral achievement that if not performed constantly and convincingly, one could readily become feminized. That being seen as womanlike would be such a shameful loss of status tells us that we still reside in an iteration of patriarchy, despite the considerable advances of feminism and the ever-expanding rainbow of gendered identities. The rhetoric of misogyny also reveals the extent to which all things feminine have been linked with subordination, an association evident in the earliest versions of Western civilization.

Anxious Warriors of Antiquity

"Fucked male" is how classics scholar John Winkler translates the ancient Greek word *binoumenos.*[9] Athenian men of the fourth century BCE, as is well known, had no problem with homoerotic practices. They were, however, embedded in an elaborate matrix of gender and class codes that regulated who could have sex with whom and in what way. Following these rules mattered because gender was a terrifyingly mutable trait for them, not fused to biological sex. You might begin your day as a man but end it as a woman. The Greeks defined manhood, in part, as being a penetrator, which was read as domination. Male genitals were necessary but far from sufficient to be a real man. That required being and remaining a dominator. And getting penetrated, especially if one took pleasure in it, made you the social equivalent of a female or an enslaved person.

To be seen as the receptive partner in sex was a fast track to feminization. Had transgender surgery been available then, it would have been redundant. Sexual "submission" was viewed as the interpersonal equivalent of a scalpel. The threat of such an emasculating metamorphosis was the ultimate "character issue" for Athenian politicians. If believed, accusations that one violated the male dominator code could lead to an abrupt end to a career in public life. The same slander was directed against foreign enemies as a form of psychological warfare designed to humiliate and demoralize them. Ancient Greeks would commemorate a military victory by issuing special conquest crockery that featured triumphant soldiers with erect penises preparing to rape the losing army.

Those rigid gender codes were a problem for master-apprentice relationships, which were always between males and often involved an erotic bond. Since penetrative sex feminized the "receptive" partner, that would create a perilous situation for an apprentice who sought a future life in politics, for whom unambiguous masculinity was an inflexible prerequisite. The solution they devised was to have face-to-face intercrural (between thighs) intercourse. It was as if these sexual positions had concrete, objective, and unalterable effects on the participants rather than physical acts saturated with cultural meanings.

At first glance, the fusty kinks of ancient Greece's quirky patriarchs may seem like an odd way to begin examining the tribal politics of gender in the present era. But a moment's reflection makes it clear that the continuities with the distant past are far greater than the differences. The most significant similarity to that early Aegean version of patriarchal masculinity is that we still equate manhood with domination. That makes maleness an inherently unstable condition. You may be on top today, but tomorrow someone could come along and knock you off your throne. The regal metaphor is particularly apt. Autocrats have almost always been male. The essence of their rule is domination. While powerful, they know a coup is always possible. That breeds paranoia, which leads to a police state. Vigilant attention to the possibility of losing power and status becomes a way of life.

Masculinity is a similarly unstable achievement. It is not just something you could lose to a usurper in a gang, a prison, or a sadomasochistic corporate hierarchy. It could dissipate by violating the unwritten but well-known gender codes—dress, voice, emotion, gait, and political identity. That is why "proving manhood" is a Sisyphean endeavor; it can never be a permanent state. Like our anxious Athenian forebears, code violations can lead to a feminizing loss of status.

The Gendering of Domination in Modern Politics

Significant moves in the direction of gender equality aside, we remain a male-dominant culture in which most things female are still devalued, and all manner of inequities persist. The anti-feminist backlash has gained renewed force and influence with the political merger of the Christian Right and the MAGA faction. There is an urgent effort to make male domination great again. With the increasing loss of reproductive choice and contraception rights, half the country is on the verge of turning into Gilead, Margaret Atwood's misogynist dystopia.

A powerful confirmation of the notion that domination is intrinsic to the prevailing definition of masculinity comes from extensive research on social dominance orientation (SDO), a personality trait discussed throughout this book. SDO refers to a preference for inequalities between groups, and a tendency to proclaim the superiority of those one belongs to, whether based on race, gender, or national identity. It includes a willingness to employ all necessary coercion to establish and maintain that dominance. Few readers would be shocked to learn that men invariably score higher than women on that measure.[10] But there is a revealing variation among men themselves. Males who identify the most strongly with other men are likely to score even higher on SDO than those whose masculine sense of self is less tied to being like their male peers.[11] That suggests that the most significant variable in this association—between maleness and domination—is not necessarily having a male body but a conventional masculine identity.

Hearing that psychological research has confirmed conservative men's tendency to be preoccupied with proving manhood through ceaseless efforts at asserting dominance may be as newsworthy as learning that physicists have finally proven the existence of gravity. Both are expectable findings to most observers of the world. The link between right-wing macho posturing and efforts to subjugate others will surprise neither liberals (who seem appalled by it) nor conservatives (who appear to be proud of it). But that is only half the story. Men who feel compelled to perform belligerent masculinity don't do so because they are more "manly." More than attempting to prove their manhood, these men are trying to *disprove* their femininity. In the current world, like the patriarchal ancients, the most important thing about being a man is not being a woman. That is what I call femiphobia, the male fear of the feminine.

Dating from at least the warrior male citizens of ancient Greece, patriarchal manhood has always been driven by that anxiety. The threat that men must perpetually ward off is a feminine one. In the external world, it may take the form of an enemy who, by defeating you, turns you into a feminized loser. That can be a fear generated by actual combat or merely the battlefield of everyday life. Because of the cultural gendering of subordination as a feminine condition, such men live in dread of being someone's bitch, as I mentioned earlier. Alternatively, the threat can present as women who fail to defer to men or honor male assertions of privilege.

In the inner world, it can appear as failed efforts to disidentify with women or to repudiate aspects of the self that the culture codes as feminine. Unwanted emotions like sadness, envy, or longing—pretty much any feeling other than anger and vengeance—can feel perilous. Similarly, unbidden taboo desires, whether an urge to submit to the sexual agency of women or erotic and romantic feelings toward other men, must be banished from consciousness if possible. We could think of all those internal manifestations of femiphobia as misogyny turned against the self. They are attempts to subordinate and strangle in one's inner world what must be constrained and sometimes crushed in the external world, femaleness.

Top Dogs Don't Get Humped

While winning (coming out "on top") is a vital, if transient, path to male identity, losing is a fast track to feminization. That may explain Trump and his base's twin obsessions, being a "winner" and denying his 2020 election loss against all evidence to the contrary. As political psychologist Lilliana Mason has shown in her research, winning and losing are the outcomes with which political tribalists are most concerned.[12] That may help us understand why homoeroticized losing (being fucked, penetrated, dominated) has become so central to propagandists on the Right, from Putin's Russia to the MAGA faction in the United States.

As historian Timothy Snyder has described, Putin found it politically useful to manufacture a homophobic moral panic about a global Western conspiracy to promote gay rights.[13] He argued that that was designed to depress the Russian birth rate and soften up his nation for rapacious exploitation. The gay peril and the European Union are merged in Putin's imagination as a hybrid monstrosity. In this fantasy, homosexual rape is envisioned as the means by which the European Union and United States want to unman Russia. Putin presented the West as a sodomizing force with voting as their penetrating phallus seeking to defile the Fatherland's traditional values.[14]

One of Putin's openly fascist allies, Alexander Prokhanov, described the democratic European enemy as a vector for infections.[15] He blamed Russia's extraordinarily high rate of HIV infections on outside threats like the European Union and their supposed strategy of deliberately spreading venereal disease instead of blaming his nation's absence of sex education.[16] Not only has Putin's regime homosexualized domestic protesters, but it also depicted the Ukrainian defenders against Russia's 2014 invasion of Crimea similarly. Pro-European crowds assembled on the Maidan were campaigning for a "homodictatorship."[17] The leader of a Putinist paramilitary biker gang said that the slogan of their imperial war should be "death to faggots."[18]

While the Republican Party in the United States has not needed any mentoring in malignant homophobia, the resemblance between the Russian campaign to depict gay people as pedophiles and GOP efforts is striking.[19] Both have gone after "gay propaganda" and instituted a strategy of censorship and slander of political opponents. In a rhetorical approach that makes them indistinguishable from the right-wing post-truth cult of QAnon, Republicans have accused multiple Democratic representatives of being pedophilic "groomers."[20] There is no reason to think that spreaders of this slander believe what they say. But there is every reason to assume that they think saying it would have political utility. What we know about the GOP base is that they are highly motivated to believe whatever their leaders tell them, especially if it seems to represent the prevailing beliefs of their peers. And the male members of the MAGA faction are especially vulnerable to appeals based on threats to their masculinity.

Manly Victim or Feminized Mark?

In the MAGA-verse, there is an essential difference between being a victim and being a mark. Being a victim is celebrated in Trumpworld. Rageful grievance is the primary psychic energy source that powers contemporary GOP politics, stoked by its members of Congress and its militia allies.

In 2023, *Politico* conducted a survey to access the relationship between men's beliefs about gender, especially masculinity, and support for Trump in the 2024 presidential race. Unremarkably, one of the highest correlations with support for the former president was with the endorsement of a variety of sexist attitudes. But the factor that was the *most* associated with the decision to reelect Trump was the view that men are victims of persecution in politics and the culture. Seventy-seven percent of men who held that belief said they were voting for Trump.[21] That was in contrast to only 7 percent of male Biden supporters.

The delusion that they are being persecuted for being white, male, and Christian is the bottomless wellspring of MAGA men's animating resentment. As I mentioned earlier in the book, what they love most about Jesus and identify with is his crucifixion. The fantasy that there is a plot to replace them with swarthy immigrants gets them up in the morning and keeps them locked and loaded.

However, as anyone unblinkered by Trump worship can see, they are indeed victims—because they are *marks*. And those victimizing them include the various Fox News and political con artists crafting, promoting, and profiting from the narratives of persecution. Of course, Trump is the preeminent con man responsible for turning the MAGA faction into America's largest collection of marks. He has taken their money, devotion, assumptions of good faith, freedom (by being imprisoned for being his January 6 coup cannon fodder), and in some cases, their lives (by dying at his altar of COVID minimization)— all to expand his wealth, power, and sense of omnipotence. In addition, the former president has enabled his apprentice grifters, like Steve Bannon, to fleece the flock for even more.[22] The psychic and physical cost the Trump base has paid for their loyalty is a theme I'll return to later.

As revealed at the second of the January 6 congressional hearings, Trump knew he'd lost to Biden.[23] He'd been told that from the most authoritative legal experts in his inner circle. But he saw political and financial utility in promoting the Big Lie. It has now reached the point that the "stolen election" conspiracy has become such an article of faith almost no Republicans can get elected unless they endorse it. It has also been an incredibly lucrative con. As of June 2022, Trump was able to extract $250 million from his followers for the putative purpose of funding legal efforts to overturn the 2020 election. In reality, it went to fill the coffers of his political action committee.[24]

Unlike the ennobling status of being a victim of the Great Replacement or the "woke mob," being a mark, especially for right-wing males, can be experienced as a feminizing humiliation. To be a mark is to be a loser—the most lacerating insult in the MAGA tribe, as described earlier. And for a femiphobic man to be a loser is essentially to be a woman. Like all con men, Trump can count on those he's conned to defend against recognizing that they've been manipulated, against seeing themselves as marks. Ironically, their denial of being fooled sets them up to be defrauded by the next hoax.

That denial is aided by Trump's deployment of the time-tested technique of "cooling out the mark," first formulated by sociologist Erving Goffman.[25] When caught in a lie, and his or her grift is exposed, the con artist lies even more brazenly, and redirects blame. The pain of the mark's financial losses is rationalized, and the mark gets to preempt the humiliation of having his or her misplaced faith exposed. But to avoid feeling like a sucker, trust in the con artist is redoubled. That process has helped Trump engage in political profiteering and open corruption without consequence since he first campaigned for office. He effectively applied many techniques honed in his decades of corrupt business practices and interpersonal predation.[26] As of this writing, which the former president faces indictments in four criminal cases, it remains to be seen if he will actually be held accountable. And he has his marks, in part, to thank for that.

From Gender Gap to Gender Gulf

In preparation for my 2004 book, *The Wimp Factor: Gender Gaps, Holy Wars, and the Politics of Anxious Masculinity*, I conducted a study involving both sexes to identify the psychological variables associated with the ever-increasing political differences between women and men. Participants completed three measures: 1) A political attitude questionnaire that assessed the strength and partisan nature of their opinions on various issues, 2) a gender role scale that tested subjects' degree of flexibility in notions of how to be a man or a woman, and 3) for men, a measure of their fear of femininity. As the reader may have already intuited, men who scored in the conservative direction on political attitudes tended to adhere more rigidly to masculine gender stereotypes and struggled with a greater fear of being feminine.

Since my book was published, all the dynamics associated with male femiphobia have persisted and, in many cases, become more pronounced. In a 2019 study, investigators found that men with a precarious sense of masculine identity were much more likely to support Republican politicians and endorse aggressive policies.[27] Trump, in particular, is appealing to such insecure men.[28] While those findings may be precisely what many readers might intuit, having empirical confirmation of that speculation is essential. It helps to explode the myth held by many, especially the men themselves, that Republican identity can somehow offer talismanic protection against gender self-doubt. As it turns out, the MAGA hat is another form of male drag, a perfect way to accessorize conservative men's openly-carried assault weapons.

There is a vital caveat that must be included here. None of this research should suggest that liberal men are "more masculine," just that they seem to have less of a need to affirm it. I believe it would be more accurate to say that right-wing males tend to have greater anxiety about their gender identity due to trying to live within a much more restricted range of emotions and behaviors deemed "manly." They tend to suppress a variety of ordinary human experiences because, to them, they are gendered feminine. In addition, as I said earlier, if maleness is predicated on always being a dominator, that is a precarious condition upon which to base one's sense of gender.

The gap between the political attitudes and identities of women and men is another area that can help us understand the dynamics at play in tribal politics. In a 2016 study comparing women and men in their first year of college, 41.1 percent of women identified as liberal and far left, in contrast to 28.9 percent of men, the largest gap since the survey began in 1966.[29] For context, the greatest plurality of both sexes identified as "middle-of-the-road" (44 percent), followed by "liberal" (32.3 percent) and "far-left" (4.5 percent), "conservative" (17.8 percent), and "far-right" (1.9 percent). Of course, the gender gap is not limited to first-year college students. A Pew Research study found that 56 percent of women in general identified as a Democrat, whereas only 42 percent of men did.[30] Only 38 percent of women aligned themselves with the GOP, compared to 50 percent of men.

The largest difference in attitudes turns out to be between Republican and Democratic men. In one study, subjects were asked whether they thought the United States had become "too soft and feminine."[31] For non-college-educated men, 41 percent of Democrats endorsed the statement, but 80 percent of Republicans did. When the researchers only looked at those with college degrees, just 9 percent of Democrats believed that was so, whereas 73 percent of Republicans held that concern. Interestingly, education profoundly affected the Democratic men, rendering them less worried about America's supposed feminization than their less-educated peers. For Republican males, not so much. The impact of education seems to have only minimally modulated their concern. It appears that their anxieties about the fragile masculinity of the nation (likely a projection of their own sense of manhood) were so deeply etched that any amount of cognitive learning could not assuage them.

Green Is the New Pink

I and others have found a profound gender gap in attitudes toward the non-human natural world. Conservative men tend to gender it female and thus view "nature" as something that should be dominated and serve their interests. For men, engaging in green behaviors generally tends to activate femiphobic anxieties.[32] Researchers could observe that when they placed male subjects in a masculinity-threat situation. The men were given pink gift cards with a frou-frou floral design. That was enough to get them to make environmentally hostile choices, such as littering and wasting water, in hypothetical scenarios. Imagining trashing the natural world was an unconscious strategy to diminish their sense of fragile manhood. The researchers did not examine partisan differences in their male subjects' responses. However, given what we know from other studies, it might not be groundless speculation to suppose that conservative men would be more susceptible to a gender threat and, thus, more likely to take anti-environment actions. Those gendered meanings for right-wing men date back to 1992 when Montana Republican Ron Marlenee called male environmentalists "prairie fairies."[33]

Conservative males tend to see plants, animals, and other aspects of nature as feminine resources over which men should have dominion. Those who stand in the way of that control and exploitation are hated impediments. That can help us understand the extraordinary misogynist vitriol directed against female environmental advocates like Greta Thunberg and Alexandria Ocasio-Cortez.[34] As self-authorizing women, they are feminine enemies twice over—uppity females who resist the male dominance over and exploitation of plant and animal life.

Empirical research on climate change denial has shown that conservative white males in the United States are much more likely than other demographic groups to be deniers.[35] Other researchers replicated that work in Norway.[36] And years later, similar results were obtained in a survey among twenty-nine thousand subjects from twenty-one European countries.[37] In the US study, the relationship was the strongest among men who believed themselves to have the most significant level of expertise in climate science. That is one of many examples of identity-protective cognition—irrational beliefs we hold because they are shared by other members of a group and thus vital to our identity.

Gender and the Freedom to Harm

One central factor in the growth of the gender gap is the apparent increase among conservatives in the acceptability of harm to others to ensure "freedom."

That was a primary focus of the chapters on right-wing identity politics. So, I won't repeat that argument here. Nevertheless, it would be instructive to cite a few examples that illustrate the hypertrophy of this tendency. The list would have to include the willingness to tolerate the exponential increase in mass gun murders of children.[38] The GOP's ballistic libertarians seem to believe that recurring episodes of mass slaughter are a small price to pay to preserve the freedom of eighteen-year-old teenagers to purchase assault weapons whenever the impulse strikes them, regardless of their predictably fledgling prefrontal cortices.[39]

Then there was the call by a prominent Republican for older people to sacrifice themselves to COVID to preserve the freedom of others to shop maskless during a pandemic.[40] Last but surely not least in this short catalog of harms right-wing male freedom lovers find unproblematic is rape. Well before GOP voters found it easy to overlook a presidential candidate who bragged about getting away with sexual assault, numerous male Republican politicians let it be known that they thought rape was either no big deal or a good topic for jocular male bonding.[41] And now, after the attempted Trump coup on January 6, 2021, 40 percent of GOP voters find it acceptable to direct violence against the government, in contrast to 23 percent of registered Democrats.[42]

You may be wondering what that has to do with the gender gap. For men, the willingness to harm is linked to their greater social dominance orientation (SDO). A significant component of that trait is comfort with coercion as a means to dominate "inferior" others. Researchers have found the gender gap in political attitudes is highly associated with SDO.[43] In other words, the specific conservative positions men are more likely to take on political issues are consistent with social dominance. That includes embracing punitive approaches to social problems, military intervention, racist attitudes, and police violence (if directed at out-groups). And as my research found, men tend to oppose programs that comprise the social safety net or other caretaking functions of government. Moreover, the most conservative men score higher on measures of SDO.

Female MAGA warriors aside, women, on *average*, are more concerned with mitigating harm and have a stronger urge to ensure fairness, collaboration, and the well-being of others.[44] In forced-choice tests, they would be more willing than men to limit speech that produces suffering for others. Women are far less inclined than men to see violent coercion as an acceptable means of achieving goals, be preoccupied with social status, or jockey for position in dominance hierarchies. While there may be bio-evolutionary contributions to that difference,[45] many modern environmental factors have led to the expression of those predispositions in the voting booth.

Since the nineteenth century, women's participation in public life has grown substantially, from being central to the temperance and abolition movements to gaining the right to vote and ultimately running for and holding political office. So, as their engagement in politics increases, the more the values they bring with them impact political discourse. That includes not just the ability to influence policy but also to trigger conservative male backlash attacks.[46]

What we are experiencing at the present moment is a collision between two powerful forces. On the one hand, there is the radical expansion of women's political agency and resulting public moral authority. On the other hand, that is being met by attempts on the part of conservative men (and a minority of women) to reassert patriarchal entitlement, especially the freedom to harm when it serves the interests of dominant or privileged groups. That led to the unprecedented expansion of the gender gap in politics, especially the presidential vote, first observed by pollsters in 1980.[47]

Of course, those gender dynamics don't apply to all men and women. One significant variable for people of both sexes is how they align themselves with feminism. In fact, among male and female anti-feminists, there is no gender gap.[48] Unsurprisingly, Republicans, stay-at-home moms, and born-again churchgoers are likelier to identify as anti-feminists.

The notion of anti-feminist women may seem like an oxymoron. But one needs only to spend five minutes watching Fox News or listen to those at the GOP podium in Congress to witness many examples. There seem to be at least two varieties. Most prominent nowadays are those who seek to ape right-wing males' arrogance, aggressive ignorance, gun fetishism, and comfort with harm as the price of freedom. That would include notable conservative pugilists such as Laura Ingraham, Ann Coulter, Marjorie Taylor Green, Lauren Boebert, and Candace Owens.

Then there are the paradoxically self-authorizing spokeswomen for female subordination.[49] They speak forcefully about the need for women to whisper and seek permission. Since the era of Phyllis Schlafly, Anita Bryant, and Beverly LaHaye, the mantle of holy warriors against women's equality has been picked up by Concerned Women for America.[50] The Bay Area street theater group, Ladies Against Women, effectively satirized that self-contradictory political identity and posted their "Ladyfesto," featuring a list of "requests." Near the top of that list was "Abolish the Environment. It takes up too much space and is almost impossible to clean."[51]

The most counterintuitive iteration of these warriors for women's subservience are the self-identified "Honey Badgers."[52] They comprise the militant women's auxiliary of Trumpworld's misogynist "men's rights" movement. The name is adopted from a fierce and unrelentingly aggressive African weasel that can't be stopped even by the piercing fangs of an attacking cobra. They are ready to protect their men from all perils, from feminists to the putative roving gangs of female rapists looking for vulnerable boys to infect with venereal disease. Both varieties of anti-feminist women are avid admirers of Donald Trump, the Right's most revered exemplar of male entitlement.

Pride and Prejudice: The Proud Boys and the Battle for White Manhood

Their venerated leader, Donald Trump, told them to "stand back and stand by." The Proud Boys, the former president's personal Brown Shirts, did as instructed and even affixed that mandate as patches onto their gang uniforms. Then, on the morning of January 6, 2021, they heeded the call to conduct a reconnaissance mission at the entrance to the Capitol Building that the Ellipse mob would breach hours later.[53] Testimony given by several witnesses on the first day of the January 6 committee hearing made it clear that they were merely one part of the multipronged and well-planned coup strategy to keep the former president in office despite losing the election.[54] According to an FBI informant in the group, had they managed to reach their targets that day, Proud Boy terrorists would have murdered Mike Pence,[55] whom Trump called a "pussy" for being unwilling to do Trump's bidding by refusing to certify the election.[56]

The Proud Boys see themselves as more than MAGA stormtroopers.[57] As warriors for whiteness, these self-described "Western chauvinists" detest the "Marxist myth of ubiquitous equality." They have also been on a Christian holy war against Islam and the fictive spread of Sharia law across the United States. And Trump is not the only authoritarian who has earned their veneration. The late Chilean fascist dictator, Augusto Pinochet, is one of their heroes because of his murderous efficiency in exterminating many leftists. Some of the group's more avid fanboys have sported T-shirts reading, "Pinochet Did Nothing Wrong."[58] Referring admiringly to the dictator's fondness for dropping opponents from helicopters, Proud Boy posts have featured memes like "Make Rotary Aircraft Great Again."[59]

Their enemies list includes more than non-whites and liberals. According to the group's founder, Gavin McInnes, women who don't know their place, "at home with the kids," earn particular contempt. In one of his YouTube videos, he describes feminism as a "war on masculinity."[60] Echoing the anxious males of ancient Greece, he sees bold, self-authorizing women as "taking masculinity away from men," as if it were a precariously attached appendage. Interestingly, McInnes performs his anti-feminist rant in quasi-drag, mocking male effeminacy while seeming to savor its pleasures.

For femiphobic males, being a *proud* boy requires being a *bad* boy. That is especially so for men who have suffered the humiliation of being at the bottom of class hierarchies, but it can operate in men at all socioeconomic levels. Social class scholar Joan Williams has examined the conflict among working-class males between a *good* man and a *real* man.[61] In my last book, I traced that dichotomy back at least to the nineteenth century when there was a culture-wide moral panic over male feminization.[62] Virtue was and continues to be coded feminine. That is one of many factors that contributes to male support for Trump. A real man is a dominator, and Trump's impunity (being a "winner") confirms his dominant status. Humiliating, subordinating, and abusing others—being a "bad" man—highlights Trump's masculinity to himself and his followers. These notions also find expression in Proud Boy religiosity.

Given the centrality of hypermasculine fundamentalist Christian theology to the belief system of MAGA males, some readers may be reminded of the nineteenth century gospel of muscular Christianity.[63] That was the movement to take back religiosity from the "feminine" version of Jesus's teaching, which emphasized pacifism, temperance, and love for others. Femiphobic males of that period strained to rewrite the character of Christ as a tough, hardened warrior against evil who would never turn the other cheek and was depicted as "the Supremely Manly Man" and "no Prince of Peace-at-any-price."[64]

Back then, spiritual machismo was less wedded to politics than now. Trump cult religious practice is more of a fusion of Nazi hypermasculinity[65] with Christian fundamentalism. In the MAGA imagination, the defeminized Christ is joined by Donald Trump as comrades in a joint holy war. Jesus is even more of a martial figure now, a kind of Rambo redeemer. As journalist Jeff Sharlet describes in his peripatetic ethnography of the "Trumpocene," the sword has replaced the cross as a signifier in a modern fascist version of the Crusades. Masculine vengeance and the smiting of tribal others are replacing sacrifice. But what has not changed in 150 years is femiphobic anxiety. MAGA males are just as besieged as their forebears by the terror of softness, which could, at any moment, turn one into a woman if one's vigilant attention to performing masculinity flags. To that end, Trump, their spiritual leader, points the way.

The former president's open corruption has not interfered with his sanctification. In fact, it has been a particularly effective way for him to be a manly bad boy, which his base does not find troubling and even finds admirable.[66] For Trump and other male authoritarians, corruption props up their manhood by demonstrating an ability to subordinate others, including those seeking to enforce laws or accountability. Getting away with crimes enables autocratic leaders like Trump to function as a permissive superego for the predatory and corrupt behavior of others.[67] His example is a psychic pardon he grants to his followers, echoing the legal ones that have blessed his treasonous and criminal underlings with impunity.

Trump has been the sadistic troll-in-chief, uber-bully of the nation, and the one who sanctifies the cruelty of his followers. Without any apparent sense of irony, his wife, Melania, took up the other side of the conservative gender dichotomy in her tepid campaign against cyberbullying.[68] So, there you have in one relationship and over the same issue, the split between "masculine" badness and "feminine" virtue. Of course, neither have been more than unconvincing, if not laughable, poses.

The Proud Boys are not content to merely trash the seats of government; they are also seeking to occupy them. In various regions of the country, their members attempt to insert themselves into local political bodies and contests. They are showing up at school board meetings to speak out against COVID public health measures and the teaching of history,[69] running for city council in Topeka, Kansas,[70] and competing in an Oregon state house primary battle.[71] As we might expect, they are campaigning as Republicans in all electoral contests. Their most successful attempt at mainstreaming has been in the Miami-Dade County GOP. Several Proud Boy members have been elected committee members in the local party organization.[72] Others are running for legislative and city government jobs.

Along with the Republican Party's groveling and wholehearted submission to Donald Trump, the rise and assimilation of the Proud Boys into the GOP's mainstream is another powerful indicator that misogyny and hypermasculine acting out are intrinsic to the tribal identity of the American Right. Their passion for sadistic violence and hatred for multi-ethnic democracy has not impeded their absorption into one of America's two major parties. Indeed, it seems to have made them more welcome. We don't yet know if that greater institutional legitimacy will discourage or inspire the Proud Boys, Oath Keepers, and other MAGA militias to light the fires of a new civil war.

Then there are fascist freelancers, like former industrial oligarch Charles Haywood, who are less well known than the organizers of those other Trumpian armies. Financially supported by the fringe-right Claremont Institute, he is working strenuously at recruiting "shooters" for his national all-male fraternal order/militia over which he intends to preside as "warlord." Haywood rails against those who seek to estrange "men from family, community and God" and vows to "counter and conquer this poison." He refers to himself as "Maximum Leader" and his national chain of lodges, which has been awarded 501(c)(10) non-profit status, as an "armed patronage network." Apparently, the IRS was not troubled by Haywood's frank and irony-free declaration that he expects to engage in "open warfare with the federal government, or some subset or remnant of it."[73]

Whether militia recruiters can induce ordinary non-militant Republican voters to enlist in that battle will probably depend, in part, on how much the partisan self-segregation of the population described in the next chapter continues to grow.

CHAPTER 8

It's a Partisan Day in the Neighborhood—The Geography of Political Tribalism

"We are going to Montana to fight! The Mountain States just might become The Alamo of the twenty-first century, with, hopefully, much better results. But if not, I would rather die fighting for Freedom with liberty-loving patriots by my side than be shuttled off to some FEMA camp," declared Pastor Chuck Baldwin in 2010.[1] Pastor Baldwin is the founder of Liberty Fellowship in Kalispell, Montana. He is credited by several conservative "relocation consultants" as the inspiration behind a relatively new niche market in the real estate business. In 2011, it was dubbed "The American Redoubt" by James Wesley, Rawles [sic]. Presumably, he decided to add the comma to his name to show his independence from the tyranny of conventional punctuation.

Rawles later found SurvivalRealty.com to help conservatives from across the country create their own rural fortresses against the malevolent encroachments of big-city liberalism. "As our society fragments further, the imperative to find a like-minded community becomes stronger," his website proclaims.[2] His business is part of a consortium of right-wing real estate rebels, including Todd Savage of Black Rifle Real Estate, whose motto is "Ready, Aim, Move."[3] One of the most prominent members of this group is Conservative Move, based in Dallas, Texas. CEO Paul Chabot saw a need and devoted himself to filling it.[4] He concluded that those on the Right needed a safe space to flee from the unbearable oppression of their progressive urban overlords, who imposed such nanny-state abominations as "forced masking."

Those highly organized and presumably profitable efforts to facilitate conservative geographical self-segregation are just the tip of the pitchfork, as it were. While regional partisan sorting is not limited to those on the Right, I made a strenuous effort (as strenuous as googling can be) to find a liberal equivalent to those real estate companies. There was nothing. When I used the search term "real estate firms for liberals," what came up were all those companies that served customers seeking to *get away* from liberals.

While the antipathy that Republicans and Democrats feel for one another is substantial, growing, and bilateral, conservatives seem to feel a greater need to be with their partisan brethren and physically distant from those unlike them.[5] And they not only want to move away from liberals but tend to seek greater distance from people more generally.[6] Conservatives are drawn to bigger houses and seek neighborhoods with homes as far from one another as possible. They are content to travel miles to reach shopping, schools, and other forms of public life. Thus, they are drawn to ethnically and politically homogenous rural, suburban, and exurban areas.

Liberals, by contrast, prefer smaller homes in culturally cacophonous urban neighborhoods that are walkable to stores, schools, and restaurants. One interesting preference of left-wing home buyers is their attraction to houses with front porches.[7] That expresses a desire to be open to the social world passing by and constitutes a kind of semipermeable membrane that marks off a more graduated boundary between public and private life. That is an intentional design element of architect Ross Chapin's charming (to liberals) and community-friendly "pocket neighborhoods."[8]

Location, Location, Location: Xenophobia on the Move

At this point, readers may be struck by how closely the issue of partisan geographical self-segregation maps onto Hibbing's framework described in earlier chapters.[9] To appreciate how his model can help us understand the partisan sorting sweeping the country, it may be helpful to briefly review his schema of "unitarians" and "securitarians." While empirically derived, his framework is best viewed as comprising ideal types. As with any typology, they are far less complicated and contradictory than individual people. Unitarians tend to be drawn to urban life in all its multiplicity. They are xenophilic and attracted to difference in many forms—ethnic, musical, culinary, artistic, literary, and linguistic. For them, there is a process for outsiders to become insiders, which doesn't require that all expressions of "outsiderness" be forsaken, such as language, ritual, and costume. Bureaucratically, in the case of citizenship, this would include "naturalization." Ideally, the assimilation would be mutual, a reciprocal exercise in empathy that could enable all parties to understand and accept their differences and the similarities that could bridge them. A sincere embrace of pluralistic democracy and mutual respect is the primary ticket to Americanness in this worldview.

In contrast, securitarians feel it would be foolish to relax one's vigilance against the hazards of human difference. They tend to think, "Those who don't look, speak, worship, or eat like us cannot be assumed to have our interests at heart and pose various inchoate risks. Immigrants, in particular, could never be fully like us. They have accents, eat odd food, engage in foreign religious practices, and, most disturbing of all, they don't look like 'legacy Americans.'[10] They have designs on our jobs, want to crowd into our neighborhoods and vote against the conservative candidates for office that we need to protect us. It just makes sense to regard them with suspicion. Whether it is the risk of disease or crime, it's safer to be as far away from them as possible.

"What's worse is that liberals are constantly promoting the interests of for-eigners against those of straight, white, Christian conservatives. The left-wing woke police always try to reprimand us for defending our values and insist we speak using only their politically correct language. School teachers confuse our children by teaching science that contradicts the Biblical truths they hear at home. And they're forced to listen to lectures about aspects of our history that make them question the timeless virtue of America. The best way to secure our safety, way of life, and children's happiness would be to move somewhere surrounded (but not too closely) by people like us. Since Trump didn't get a chance to build the wall, geographic distance will have to do."

However, simply moving to a safe white Christian enclave may not provide sufficient racial and ideological purity. Georgia Representative Marjorie Taylor Greene, one of the more visible members of the MAGA caucus's Cro-Magnon contingent, suggested that liberals from blue states should not be allowed to vote if they move to a red one. In a February 2023 tweet, she called for a "national divorce."[11] During an interview the following day, Greene explained that the danger to red state homogeneity occurred "when Democrat voters leave their Democrat states and bring their Democrat votes with them."[12] Her solution to partisan differences is closer to the lived reality of Jim Crow—separate and unequal.

Partisan Self-Segregation and the Twilight of Democracy

Given the nearly irreconcilable differences in psychological orientation, it is unsurprising that the urban-rural partisan gap has grown ever more pro-found.[13] As regrettable as Americans' estrangement from one another might be, the reader may wonder why we should be so concerned that our politi-cal identities are increasingly reflected in our geographical segregation. Maybe we'd all be happier if our neighbors were like us. Unfortunately, as Marjorie Taylor Greene's fantasy illustrates, ideological sorting by region renders our democracy more precarious. Also, as I'll discuss later, it leads to corresponding information ghettos.

Partisan self-segregation has reached a point where near one-party monopolies now rule whole states.[14] As of this writing, Republicans dominate government in twenty-five states (45 percent of the US population), whereas Democrats have near total control in fifteen states (about 40 percent of the citizens). So, even in the absence of formal secession of half the country, we are approaching the functional equivalent of the nineteenth-century division between the United States of America and the Confederate States of America. The laws of each "country" are driven by different values and focused on different ends. However, in fundamental ways, they are not symmetrical. That is because Republicans have pursued and achieved a much more unified agenda across the United States, not just in their predictable culture war crusades. Yes, they are rolling back rights for sexual and gender minorities, reasserting patriarchal dominance over women's bodies, ensuring that mass killers have easy access to the tools of their trade, and censoring history curricula that depart from triumphalist accounts of American greatness. But as I've described in various parts of this book, they have also succeeded in passing laws to end democratic governance effectively. GOP officials have tacitly and at times explicitly agreed that any election they lose is by definition fraudulent and will therefore be overturned by state legislative fiat.[15] (Readers interested in just how conservatives and their wealthy funders achieved such thoroughgoing political dominance at the state level, from school boards to legislatures, should read Alexander Hertel-Fernandez's comprehensive analysis in his book, *State Capture*.[16])

That anti-democracy agenda is made even more impactful by the tribal political bias built into the very structure of American governance. Those who live in more rural, less populated areas have far more representation than those in urban areas. That shows up in the Senate in dramatic ways. For example, blue California, with a population of nearly forty million, and beet red Wyoming, with a population of about 580,000, have two senators each. The discrepancies in the representation ratios between other blue and red states may be less, but the pattern is the same. Rural bias is inherent in the Electoral College as well. When these foundational features of the American system are combined with bad-faith and race-based right-wing gerrymandering, along with voter suppression and election nullification laws passed in GOP-dominated state legislatures throughout the country, a small minority can rule over the majority with even less accountability. Add to that the growing conservative homogeneity of rural areas—more formerly purple areas turning red—the result may be an irreversible power shift to the minority and the disenfranchisement of the rest of the nation.

One example among many is the proliferation and deregulation of military assault weapons. I'm writing this section shortly after two mass murders, one of ten Black shoppers in a grocery store in Buffalo, New York, and the other of nineteen fourth-graders and two teachers in Uvalde, Texas. A poll conducted within a few days of those atrocities found that 67 percent of those surveyed said they supported an assault weapons ban.[17] Only 25 percent stood against such a ban. As of June 2022, congressional Republicans, seamlessly aligned with the National Rifle Association (NRA), have refused to consider any limit on anyone purchasing such weapons, which, given the filibuster limitations, means that, once again, nothing will be done. They suggest that teachers, who, in red states, are not trusted to recommend library books or teach history, be given weapons to "harden" schools against killers that even the police are afraid to take on.[18] All this implies that the 25 percent opposed are the ones whose voices matter and who get to determine policy. The other 67 percent will have to ensure their children are up to date on their active shooter-evasion training and don't attend school without being swaddled in Kevlar backpacks.

The Recent History of America's Voluntary Partisan Apartheid

In their 2008 book, *The Big Sort*, journalist Bill Bishop and his sociologist collaborator, Robert Cushing, were the first to publish a major study of political self-segregation in the United States.[19] According to their analysis, 1976 was the last year in this country when a citizen was likely to live next door to someone who voted differently than he or she did in a presidential election. "Landslide counties" are counties where national elections resulted in local landslides. We can think of them as tribally homogenous. By 2004, they had become half of all counties in the United States, doubling a few years before. And the magnitude of that phenomenon has only grown in the years since Bishop's book was released.[20] As racial segregation was declining, political segregation was increasing. While the South often comes to mind when thinking about stark polarization, Bishop convincingly shows that it characterizes the entire country.

He found that Republican counties became more politically segregated than Democratic counties.[21] That would be consistent with the frequent observation that *exclusionary* tribalism is more characteristic of the Right. But, of course, the problem is bipartisan. Bishop cites studies and natural experiments showing that members of like-minded groups, regardless of the issues around which they are like-minded or to which party they belong, tend to adopt more extreme positions.[22] That is in contrast to the more moderate positions members of heterogeneous groups take. In other words, a mixed group moderates opinion; a collection of like-minded people polarizes opinion or skews it to one extreme. In homogenous groups, individuals seek to become more ardent and extreme adherents of the perceived group position to demonstrate tribal loyalty and thus consolidate group membership.

That is not to argue that moderation is necessarily good quality. But these findings help us understand the conclusions of other studies on partisan geographic sorting that appear to disconfirm or call the interpretation of Bishop's findings into question. Those critics argue that a politically sorted area makes its residence more partisan. It is not a simple case of partisans moving to like-minded locations.[23] In my view, it is clearly both. The migration of partisan individuals and the preexisting political identity of residents in the desired destination exert a synergistic effect that makes areas hyper-partisan.

Jesus vs. Jesus: Partisan Pulpits in a Divided America

One of the intriguing themes throughout Bishop's study is the tribal battle line between two modes of Christianity in the United States, which also tends to map onto geographical sorting. On the one hand, there is *public* Protestantism, which emphasizes the "social gospel." (Think of Jimmy Carter.) In this tradition, communitarian social values are central to what it means to be a Christian. Those adherents tend to be centered in urban areas.

On the other hand, *private* Protestantism privileges individual morality as the most critical path to spiritual salvation. Think of the gold-plated piety of right-wing megachurches preaching the prosperity gospel and the divinity of Donald Trump.[24] While comprised of devoted true believers who see themselves as uncompromising holy warriors against private immorality, they nevertheless wholeheartedly endorsed Donald Trump, a living embodiment of the seven deadly sins, if ever there was one. This iteration of Christianity transcends geographical regions, linking areas as varied as Orange County, California, to the coal country of West Virginia.

These lines of division are visible around the world. In multiple countries, the adherents of fundamentalist private Christianity tend to support authoritarian and fascist regimes and align with their various moral "purity" campaigns. Anathema to them are laws protecting the environment, public health measures, any form of social safety net, progressive taxation, funds for secular education, and any legislation that might mandate corporate accountability to the public. They have also tended to remain silent in the face of the political murder of "subversives" and the suffering wrought by austerity measures and elite class war policies that punish the poor.[25] In contrast, Christian advocates of the social gospel, Protestant and Catholic alike, are more likely to protest these regimes and policies and sometimes have been the victims of state tyranny.[26] They also support laws that place the public interest above private profit and power.

It is easy to dismiss the perspective of right-wing Christians, given their paranoid demonology, violent tropes of spiritual warfare, theology of wealth as a mark of God's favor, and canonization of amoral hustlers like Donald Trump. Nevertheless, it must be said that their anger at and bitter rejection of big-city liberals are not without foundation.

How Urban Liberals Have Earned Rural Conservative Resentment

Near the top of this list has to be the tendency of big-city progressives to vote for property tax increases to pay for infrastructure and vital social programs from which those in the hinterlands don't always benefit. Even those country folks with land have less cash than those in cities. Job growth is far slower, wages are lower, and credit is harder to get.[27] Even when rural populations benefit from tax-funded programs, liberal politicians do a terrible job communicating that.

That had been a much bigger messaging problem for the Democratic Party, which had had a lot to brag about over many decades when providing much-needed resources, benefits, and infrastructure. But they rarely touted that, which created space for Republican politicians to take credit for programs they had struggled mightily to crush at the outset.[28] That has led to such a dissociation between policy and partisan identity that Tea Party protesters in the Obama era carried oxymoronic placards reading "Keep Your Government Hands Off My Medicare."[29]

Democrats also did a terrible job communicating to America's agricultural regions how damaging the former Republican president's trade policy was to farmers.[30] That made it much easier for GOP politicians to use culture war boogeyman and right-wing identity politics to blunt the awareness of Trump-induced economic pain in rural areas.

Perhaps the most egregious political malpractice by liberal representatives has been not showing up. In Oregon, other than our two senators' brief annual visits, liberal state politicians commonly do not visit or campaign. Often, the state Democratic Party does not even run candidates in purple or red rural areas. Living in one of those areas, that oversight and its effects have been hard to miss. The 2022 state gubernatorial election was much closer than it should have been. I did not see a single television ad for the Democrat, Tina Kotek.

In contrast, the GOP candidate, Christine Drazan, ran ads nearly every twenty minutes—on liberal MSNBC, no less. The belief that red counties are homogenously conservative and can be safely written off has become a self-fulfilling assumption. Now that she is governor, Ms. Kotek has made an effort to have a presence in rural parts of the state, as have our two Democratic senators.

In 1960, most of Wallowa County in the northeast corner of the state voted for the Democratic presidential candidate, John F. Kennedy.[31] In 2020, only 32 percent of voters chose Biden in the last presidential election, whereas 66 percent voted for Trump.[32] But the conservative shift is starkly illustrated by the fact that in 1966, Multnomah County, the location of deep-blue Portland, was 59 percent registered Democrats. Eastern Oregon counties were 56 percent Democrat. That 3 percent gap has grown to over 30 percent in the current period. Many variables are at play in that change, some of which have been outlined in this chapter. But clearly, a major one is feeling written off.

That sense has led many here to join the "Greater Idaho" campaign, a conservative secession movement to cleave off a significant chunk of Eastern and Central Oregon and merge with Idaho, which is imagined as a welcoming right-wing homeland populated by a majority of people like them.[33] In the previous election, Wallowa County voters rejected by a slim majority a ballot measure to join that effort. However, the 2023 iteration of the same measure—a mandate for the county commissioners to discuss secession every year—won by a surprisingly close majority of seven votes. The ultimate success of secessionist ambitions is improbable because of the many legal, legislative, and constitutional hurdles advocates would have to overcome. But whether or not that movement ever triumphs, Idaho is well on its way to becoming a Christian fascist dystopia, not far from Margaret Atwood's vision of Gilead.[34] Among the many disturbing developments in that state is a bill allowing rapists and their families to sue victims who obtain an abortion.[35] In any case, Oregon as a state remains quite blue. It has allocated funds and other resources to accommodate the anticipated flood of Idaho women seeking reproductive health asylum and medical services. Nevertheless, we are still left with a vexing question: what makes a place like Idaho—with lower wages, declining health care, and diminishing freedoms—such a compelling conservative dreamscape?

Landscapes of the Mind and Right-Wing Tribal Homelands

There is physical geography and imagined geography. White supremacists fantasize about a white ethnostate—a utopian space where racial, religious, and cultural others are banished.[36] It is a place of such homogeneity that one need not ever encounter those unlike them. Ethnonationists are driven by more than negative emotions—vengeance for perceived persecution, hatred of non-white people, fear of being pushed out of "their" territory by foreigners, and blood lust against "race traitors." They are also impelled by positive feelings, such as a yearning for a monochromatic homeland where all will be bliss, and racial kinship will heal all ruptures.

Before people embark on actual geographical migration based on political identity, there is a mental migration to a fantasized geography. We imagine a land where we might belong. That could be based on a location we know something about or a place we wish existed.

Nazis expressed that through the slogan "blood and soil." It brought together notions of pure race and pure land as a melding of racial pseudo-science with agrarian romanticism. Unsullied Aryan bodies belonged in geographies untainted by liberal/Jewish cosmopolitanism, which meant rural areas.

It is interesting that, like the German Nazis before them, contemporary white supremacists identify with Native Americans.[37] They can overlook their non-whiteness and perceive precolonial native people as an embodiment of the blood-and-soil fantasy. Their identification is driven by the paranoid belief that, as whites, they risk being put on reservations once they move into minority status demographically. Multiple white supremacist groups share this delusion in the United States and Europe and see it as part of a larger imagined plot to perpetrate white genocide.

MAGA's Marketplace: The Rise of the Right-Wing Tribal Economy

It seems that geographic self-segregation may no longer provide conservatives sufficient distance from their tribal enemies. Beyond literal secession, there are other ways one can "build the wall." It is not necessary to move to a red neighborhood or state to be with one's "own kind." For example, MAGA millennials can sign up for dating apps like The Right Stuff[38] that enable subscribers to screen partners for their support of the January 6 coup attempt or opposition to various "liberal lies."[39] However, lonely Proud Boys had better act soon because the dearth of women on the site may lead to its demise. (As of this writing, the start-up funding provided by right-wing libertarian billionaire Peter Theil is about to run dry,[40] though its website remains up.) But there are other options for avoiding the tribal other.

Conservatives seeking a workplace barricade against the progressive threat can utilize Red Balloon,[41] a right-wing job board to help the unemployed or those toiling in enemy territory find companies that won't abridge their employees' "freedoms" with COVID prevention policies (which, in any case, have mostly disappeared) or "woke" mandates against bigoted or harassing speech. Perhaps the most promising and durable rampart for those on the Right will be the *monetary* barriers against political outsiders.

As *The Economist* has documented, the Trump/DeSantis base has provided companies with a new niche market—consumers who don't want their dollars going to "liberal" products and their "woke" stockholders.[42] Alongside the parallel universe of right-wing "alternative facts," there is a parallel economy driven by alternative marketing.

PublicSq is an online MAGA marketplace comprised of forty thousand companies that offer a wide range of products and services sold in ideological packaging designed to appeal to the discerning Christian nationalist consumer. Commodities are coated in a patina of "freedom," "family values," biblical certainties, and 2020 election denial. PublicSq's founder, Michael Seifert, claims that, based on GDP alone, his site comprises the third-largest economy in the world.[43] It's unclear if that is a boast akin to Trump's inaugural crowd size or his popular vote count. But there is no question that many conservative Americans do not want to patronize companies like Disney, Microsoft, and Coca-Cola because they refuse to stay in the business lane and make "controversial" statements, such as declaring their opposition to voter suppression laws or support for civil rights.[44]

Of course, PublicSq is not the only virtual or brick-and-mortar shopping venue for consumers looking for products that affirm their tribal identity. The gun industry is an unsurprising marketplace for right-wing identitarians. The ideological inscriptions borne by their products can be literal. Soldiers in the Jesus army can vanquish liberals and other heathens by purchasing an assault rifle with factory-engraved bible verses.[45] That is a killing machine made in heaven for right-wing holy warriors fond of "Second Amendment remedies" to political problems.[46]

Conservatives are not alone in wanting companies they patronize to share their values. Liberals started a corporate rating service, BuyBlue, that scored the progressiveness of businesses based on their political donations. [47] Yet, by all appearances, those ratings were not determined by something as insubstantial as branding but by the real-world political impacts of corporate behavior.

Unlike the secessionist economy of the Right, those on the Left seem less driven by culture war phantoms and a need for their own well-armed enclaves than by policies that concretely affect the lives of citizens. Corporations that only engage in virtue signaling, such as polluters that launch greenwashing PR campaigns, come in for particularly harsh criticism from liberals.[48] Apparently, BuyBlue's service was not compelling enough to be sustained; it shut its virtual doors in 2007. But perhaps what is less compelling for those on the Left is the need to build real or imaginary walls to keep out those who are different, to swaddle themselves in the comforts of tribal homogeneity.

There is another wall I will shortly discuss that protects conservatives from discomfort but incarcerates them in the solitary confinement of disinformation.

It is a barrier that is sometimes invisible to those it isolates. But it is also one with which tribal members seek to surround themselves because it confirms their worldview. Unfortunately, by selectively keeping out factual information, that wall prevents the country's partisan camps from being able to share at least some of the same reality.

From Geographical to Information Silos

Many rural areas are "news deserts," regions of the country with few independent news sources, and which, not coincidentally, went for Trump by large margins.[49] Interestingly, the same parts of the nation that constitute *food* deserts, where fast-food chains and consequent chronic disease predominate, are limited to information junk food, such as Fox News, Sinclair, and right-wing talk radio.[50] Maintaining such a news diet can exacerbate the chronic afflictions associated with disinformation, such as conspiracy thinking.

But even when diverse media and news sources are available, the information landscape is subject to the same partisan self-segregation as the geographical one. Conservatives are far more isolated from liberal opinions than liberals are from conservative views. There are many reasons for this, which the next chapter will reveal. One is that conservative ideas tend to be hegemonic. In other words, they are likely to have wider circulation and carry greater legitimacy because they represent the world view of the wealthy and powerful—social forces that have both the means and the status to broadcast their ideas and render them acceptable.

Fox often has the largest audience in national cable news. And Sinclair Broadcasting controls many "local" stations to the point of centrally scripting their anchors' newscasts.[51] Like other right-wing media, they are primarily driven by ideology and tribal loyalty, in addition to a business model that pays literal dividends for inciting fear, rage, and disinformation.[52] And based on the behavior of Fox News in the Trump era, conservative outlets tend to be indifferent to evidence. Thus, their viewers are unlikely to be exposed to information that might challenge their worldview.

There is another, more ironic reason that conservative ideas have wider distribution. Because of the greater journalistic integrity of mainstream and left-of-center media, they seek to give voice to multiple perspectives, including those on the center-right. They also endeavor to be fact-based in their reporting and support most claims with solid and careful sourcing. However, many mainstream news outfits undermine their noble deference to factuality by engaging in stenographic reporting. That can involve simply quoting the lies of MAGA mouthpieces without comment, presumably under the belief that by doing so, they are being unbiased and neutral. Or, even more egregious, they might cover right-wing speeches and other events by turning on the cameras and microphones and letting them run for the duration. For example, even center-left networks CNN and MSNBC gave the 2016 Trump campaign many hours of free advertising by broadcasting Trump's rallies from beginning to end.[53] Similarly, they covered live, without real-time correction, the former president's lie-filled coronavirus briefings.[54]

Sadly, CNN did not learn from or try to make amends for their mercenary abandonment of journalistic standards. Instead, the lesson they learned was that providing a venue for entertaining right-wing thuggery could be quite lucrative. The network began to covet Fox's MAGA market share. Exhibit A of that sentiment was their decision to give over a chunk of prime time to an "interview" with the former president. In short order, the host lost control of the event, which devolved into a campaign dis-infomercial.[55] The rapturous preselected audience of Trump super fans applauded every slander against his critics and laughed at each cruel, misogynistic "joke."

While liberals may be just as likely to be encased in their tribal information silo, it is more permeable than that of conservatives, something I'll be saying more about shortly. In addition, fundamental to the liberal ethos (alas, not always abided) is critical thinking—a skeptical stance toward received wisdom and conventional authority. It also includes curiosity about and pursuit of other perspectives. We could think of that as a kind of information xenophilia, in contrast to conservatives' more xenophobic stance toward non-tribal knowledge. The next chapter will examine the complicated relationship between truth and partisan identity.

CHAPTER 9

Post-Truth, Autocracy, and the Tribalization of "News"

It took only one day after the mass murder of nineteen young school children in Uvalde, Texas, for a Republican member of Congress to declare the culprit a "transsexual leftist illegal alien."[1] Arizona Representative Paul Gosar's tweet fantasy hit the trifecta of usual right-wing suspects: a rumor plucked directly from the fascist hive mind of 4chan. The person in the photo posted along with the tweet, someone unrelated to the shootings, now has to worry about a MAGA posse—one unlikely to do any fact-checking before grabbing their own assault weapons.

"Anyone who has the power to make you believe absurdities has the power to make you commit injustices," Voltaire warned us.[2] His 1765 aphorism is well-worn but ever-relevant. Rather than being chastened by that declaration, the world has since affirmed its prescience. Genocide against multiple ethnic groups—Jews in Germany, Muslims in Serbia, the Tutsi in Rwanda, and the Rohingya in Myanmar—had the ground laid by lies, slanders, and "fake news." In Trump's America, the former president's multiple demonizing fictions led to threatened and actual violence against Hispanic, Black, and Asian Americans and protesters more generally.[3] His lies about protesters led to several attempted and actual murders.[4] The death toll of the widely circulated and GOP-embraced neo-Nazi "Great Replacement" delusion about non-white immigrants smuggled into the United States to throw elections is rapidly escalating.[5]

There was never a golden age of propaganda-free news media, reporters devoid of bias, or politicians who never told lies to promote their careers, cover up corruption, or advance racist or colonial policies. But post-truth refers to more than lies. It names an epoch in which truth no longer matters. In this world, experts are devalued, imagined as villains, and then given starring roles in various conspiracy narratives. Likewise, data are disregarded because they emanate from these despised experts. Assertions known as false are promoted if they are consonant with a group's belief system and increase its chance of "winning."

"Post-truth is pre-fascism," historian Timothy Snyder sagely observed.[6] Trump telegraphed in 2018 what he would later claim about his loss in 2020, that Democrats were conspiring to commit voter fraud. In a survey of Republican voters at the time, half said that they would support a Trump coup if their leader declared there had been fraud.[7] The projective slogan for the movement to overturn the election results, "Stop the Steal," became the Big Lie that animated the January 6 coup attempt. Of course, Democratic voter fraud has long been fiction but one that has reliably animated the MAGA base.[8] It remains the case that the distance from delusion to dictatorship is a short one.[9]

The Politics of Epistemological Nihilism

The end goal of lying as a political strategy is not just to disseminate false ideas and fake news but to instill a kind of numb docility in the population. Anything *could* be true. And if anything could be true, then nothing is really true.[10] When so many dubious truth claims get thrown up, lies and facts blur together. Both Putin and Trump have utilized active campaigns of information chaos, consisting of rapidly oscillating official lies and gaslighting. That has supplemented and, to some extent, replaced the crude censorship strategies of old-world approaches to autocratic rule.

The phrase "flooding the zone" was coined by Trump's post-truth Rasputin Steve Bannon. It refers to throwing out bogus stories, which debunkers then attempt to refute. But the debunking brings more attention to the fiction and increases its virality. That creates an obvious double bind for those invested in truth. If the false narrative is not debunked, it goes unchallenged. If it is debunked, the lie gets more widely circulated. George Lakoff describes a version of this dilemma when he notes that negating a linguistic frame strengthens it. To assert "I am not a tax and spend liberal" circulates the phrase "tax and spend liberal."[11]

The conventional wisdom on political communication is that you want your message signal to rise out of the noise so it can get attention and have influence. In the Bannon approach, the aim is to produce so much noise, no signal can be heard. The goal is to create a sense that truth cannot be known and thus induce a nihilistic indifference to factuality. The benefit redounds to whichever political performer captures the most attention.

A point is reached when the cognitive load imposed by the effort to disentangle fact from fantasy becomes unbearable.[12] All you have to guide you in this post-truth world is the leader, whose vague pronouncements, warnings of inchoate threats, constantly shifting assertions, and evocative but equivocal accusations against the enemy of the day take up the space once occupied by your mind. In this epistemological vertigo, the leader's utterances, however baffling, can feel like the only stabilizing crutch.

Vladislav Surkov was one of Putin's chief *political technologists*.[13] That is the term Russians use for those who aid the powerful by deploying their skills as propagandists, spinmeisters, spectacle creators, and Machiavellian dream weavers. They aim to mobilize or pacify the public, depending on the regime's needs at the moment. Among Surkov's outstanding achievements was developing an effective strategy to neutralize opposition in Russia. He created the fiction that diverse voices were welcome by promoting groups that could antagonize one another. In reality, he was playing off each side against every other side in a way that redounded to the benefit of Putin, who could be depicted as a stabilizing force in the moderate middle. Surkov also coined a head-spinning Orwellian title to describe his boss, "democratic dictator."

A similar approach was employed in Russia's US election disinformation campaigns, strategically detonating propaganda bombs along tribal fault lines and publishing social media posts favorable to Black Lives Matter *and* white supremacist groups. In such situations, the cacophony of dissonant voices produces a paralyzing mistrust of any truth claim. Even toward the leader's apparent lies, passivity and indifference rule the day. Truth becomes whatever assertion comforts, entertains, or makes us feel like our tribe is winning.

That approach to social control is especially effective when you have leaders who believe in nothing but their power. Trump, like Putin, is a post-ideological amoral authoritarian who can seduce ideological true believers into idolatrous followership. He focuses on engendering the ardent loyalty of traditional religious and xenophobic conservatives with nowhere else to turn and who thus view him as their only hope for salvation in an otherwise hopelessly decadent liberal world. Both leaders endeavor to consolidate their power and preside over a massive wealth transfer from the working and middle classes to themselves and other members of the economic elite that remain loyal to the leader. The hope is that the public will be kept busy chasing or running from post-truth phantoms so that the autocrat's corruption, however openly displayed, will be of little interest.

Post-Truth as the GOP Path to Power: The Case of Voter Fraud

Political and social fictions have long played a vital role in the Republican Party's approach to gaining and holding power. They comprise the content of GOP ideas and the process for inscribing them into policy. The most destructive myths have been those intended to achieve anti-democratic ends. Chief among those has been the voter fraud fable, a right-wing story designed to keep the "wrong people" (i.e., impoverished and non-white citizens) from voting, a racially-motivated post-truth meme that first emerged in the nineteenth century[14] but has remained in the conservative rhetorical arsenal ever since.

For centuries, what has worried white conservatives was not so much the counting of fraudulent votes, such as ballot box stuffing. The problem, in their view, was that fraudulent *people* were voting.[15] One nineteenth-century defender of white dominance, Judge J. J. Chrisman, acknowledged that all the voter fraud at the time was committed by white election workers and those who financed their actions. But, he insisted, the problem was that Black people were voting. If that could be fixed, electoral corruption would cease.[16] Under Jim Crow laws, the racial motivation for voter suppression remained relatively undisguised well into the twentieth century.

In 1964, conservatives ramped up their efforts to disenfranchise voters who were unlikely to check the R box on ballots. The appeal to white racial paranoia and bigotry shifted from bullhorn to dog whistle. The RNC initiated a ten thousand–person voter intimidation program called Operation Eagle Eye.[17] Once again, using the rationale of rooting out "voter fraud," they began a multipronged effort to frighten away what one GOP official described as "not the kind of people who would register and vote." Among their tactics include a hundred thousand–person "Ballot Security" force that donned official-looking armbands. Among the tactics of this anti-democracy militia was the placement of signs warning that anyone attempting to vote who had unpaid traffic tickets or was suspected of committing other minor offenses would be arrested. That operation did not succeed in getting Barry Goldwater elected, but it did have a modest effect in suppressing the Democratic vote among the non-white electorate.[18]

The results were encouraging enough that voter suppression became an enduring tactic in Republican electoral strategy from then on. After Jimmy Carter entered the White House in 1977, he attempted to push forward various election reforms to remedy the country's low voter turnout. Those proposals included designating Election Day as a national holiday and permitting same-day registration.

Predictably, that elicited a torrent of outrage among Republicans who didn't want the wrong sort of people casting a vote. Ronald Reagan clarified what was wrong with that slice of the electorate. He warned that it would comprise "those who get a whole lot more from the federal government in various kinds of income distribution than they contribute to it." Reagan conjured up such frightening scenarios as "labor organizations" in "metropolitan areas scooping up otherwise apathetic voters and rushing them to the polls to keep the benefit dispensers in power."[19] Needless to say, he was not referring to corporate welfare recipients or their mercenary allies in Congress. No, the danger was making it easier for poor and non-white folks to vote. Trotting out the GOP's tried-and-true meme, the RNC chairman dubbed Carter's proposed reforms "The Universal Voter Fraud Bill," which facilitated their defeat in Congress.

By 1980, at least one prominent Republican dispensed with euphemisms and plainly stated that the GOP's aim was not voter fraud prevention but voter suppression. In a bracing if fleeting moment of candor for the Right, Heritage Foundation co-founder Paul Weyrich made it clear that he was not one of those who wants "everybody to vote." Putting a finer point on the matter, Weyrich said, "Our leverage in the elections, quite candidly, goes up as the voting populace goes down."[20] ,

While the honesty of Weyrich did not persist in the GOP, the voter fraud lie was deployed in nearly every national election thereafter. Trump's 2020 loss was a profound injury to his brittle narcissism. In response to that wound, the former president unrelentingly pushed the voter fraud fiction in the courts. Despite his universal failure to get a favorable judgment in courtrooms across the country, including those presided over by his own appointees, the stolen election myth remains untarnished on the Right. Republican legislatures in thirty-nine states attempted to pass voter suppression bills to protect against the non-existent threat of "voter fraud."[21] As of this writing, efforts have been successful in eighteen states.[22] In total, since the *Shelby County v. Holder* Supreme Court decision in 2013 that gutted the Voting Rights Act, twenty-nine states have passed ninety-four laws restricting the ability to vote. Unsurprisingly, the most significant impact has been on non-white voters.[23] With the ascension of Trump to the de facto leader of the Republican Party, his role as permissive superego for bigotry becomes more pronounced. The GOP's appeal to white racial anxiety stops being a dog whistle and becomes a bullhorn again.

Those voter suppression efforts, partisan gerrymandering, the rural bias in Senate seat allocation, and the electoral college are primarily responsible for our current condition of minority rule. The GOP is not appreciably expanding its base, and the demographic atrophy of white, Christian, conservative political and cultural dominance is proceeding apace. That leaves the Republican Party little choice but to blunt democracy where possible and facilitate autocratic governance.

If His Lips Are Moving, He's Lying

It is undoubtedly true that before Trump, promoting the fantastical played a significant role in the rise of the Tea Party era and will continue long after he's gone. But his reign was extraordinary—an unrelenting and exhausting marathon of nonstop lying. While he was in office, quantifying Trump's lies had become a kind of journalistic parlor game akin to obsessive bird watchers competing for documented sightings of particular species. The ultimate champion was Glenn Kessler of the *Washington Post*, whose final count in January 2021 was 30,573 false statements.[24] However, there were particular qualitative distinctions left out of that quantitative assessment, namely the difference between Teleprompter Trump and Twitter Trump. Teleprompter lies were told in complete sentences because they were written out for him. Twitter lies appeared as a garnish on word salad and were thus more challenging to identify and fact-check. Let's dig into just a few of the specifics.

His administration was founded on biographical fictions, false accusations against opponents, conspiracy theories, science denial, and pseudo-problems like "voter fraud." Perhaps more fundamental, it brought onto the stage of public life a largely fictional character, Donald Trump himself. Rather than being the self-made real estate savant as portrayed on TV, Trump was a serial failure with multiple bankruptcies who squandered his daddy's money on various ill-conceived ventures.[25] Strong evidence indicates that to extricate him from those failures, the Russian mob made an offer he couldn't refuse—get financially rescued in exchange for money-laundering services.[26]

He was the consummate loser whose brand was winning. Thanks to his Russian benefactors and a diversified portfolio of grift, loan defaults, wage theft, and tax schemes, Trump did manage to obtain considerable wealth, which he garishly paraded as proof of his entrepreneurial genius.[27] The combination of arrogance, poor judgment, and corruption made Trump—the quintessential conman—into the perfect mark for a much wilier crook like Putin. By helping to turn this loser into a successful asset and facilitating his rise to power, Putin endeavored to make the United States a loser.[28]

Thus, Trump himself is a post-truth phenomenon. Not only does he *tell* lies, but he *is* a lie. Even his "autobiography," *The Art of the Deal*, was not written by him but by someone pretending to be him.[29] And it was not about Trump, the person, but Trump, the fictional character. Perhaps his tendency to refer to himself in the second and third person is a kind of unconscious recognition of the gap between his actual self and the character he plays. Multiple writers have scripted that character over the years.

Donald Trump, the Successful Businessman, was not the only MAGA fiction promoted by the Russians. The prolific fabulists of Putin's regime also authored many of Trump World's most notorious conspiracy theories.[30] The story sharing was bidirectional. Russian propagandists promoted the false narratives originating in the Trump-worshipping cult, QAnon.[31] That included the Obama birther fantasy, the story of the Hillary-run pedophilia ring that operated out of the non-existent basement of a pizza parlor, and the tale about the satanic ritual feast to which Hillary Clinton's campaign manager, John Podesta, was putatively invited.[32]

As this book goes to press, Trump has had to bear a consequence for his duplicity in the form of a $551 million judgment against him in the New York state civil fraud case for wildly inflating the size and value of his properties to get bank loans, although his bond was later reduced on appeal to $115 million. In some ways, it is the least serious of his trials. At another level, it names and concretizes the most self-evident feature of his life as a businessperson and politician—fraud. Fraud is the quintessential Trumpian crime—politically, economically, and rhetorically. As I have described, nearly every aspect of his being is fictional—who he claims to be and what he asserts as factual.

Of course, that was not his first conviction for fraud. In 2016, Trump was forced to pay a $25 million settlement to students defrauded by his fake university. Then, in 2019, he was required to pay two million dollars to eight charities his foundation had defrauded. He raised supposedly charitable funds that were actually used to pay personal debts and finance his campaign. Few of us can forget the more than fifty judicial rulings, some by his own appointees, against his fraudulent 2020 voter fraud claims. We could view his 2023 libel conviction in the E. Jean Carroll case as another conviction for fraud—in this case, a fraudulent and slanderous assertion against someone who dared to call him out for sexual assault.

However, it is the 2024 loan fraud conviction that could potentially bankrupt him financially and psychologically. Trump has long equated his value with his wealth. Unlike the possible criminal convictions he faces, the New York verdict, if upheld on appeal, could render him worthless literally and in his own eyes. He will become the loser he's struggled to project onto others.

Realpolitik vs the Politics of Unreality

There is another menace that haunts the right-wing conspiratorial imagination: the "deep state." A central part of MAGA catechism is the imperative to revile the professional, non-partisan layer of government that conservatives have designated the deep state.[33] The bureaucrats who staff it are the objects of particular vitriol by Trumpian flamethrowers like Steve Bannon. In their fevered imagination, government workers comprise the foot soldiers for a conspiracy of evil cabalistic liberals who run the world. For many readers, it might be a head-scratching puzzle that a stratum of largely faceless bland functionaries has come to embody such villainy in conservative demonology.

Why would nonideological civil servants be the recipients of such contempt? During Trump's first impeachment hearing, the country got to peek behind the curtain at the vicious campaign of harassment directed against former Ukraine Ambassador Marie Yovanovitch.[34] While speculative, it may be that right-wing tribalists hate her and other career public servants so fervently because they are trans-tribal. They resemble liberals in their tendency to have more permeable group boundaries and less constricted identities. Often serving in multiple administrations of both parties, their greatest loyalty is to factuality and the nation as a whole. That privileging of data over fealty to the ruler may earn them contempt by the MAGA Right.

Civil servants and professional bureaucrats are usually practitioners of *Realpolitik*. *Realpolitik* is often rightly criticized for being the amoral acceptance of what is feasible and for defending that which preserves elite power under the guise of advancing the national interest. But it is at least a politics informed by reality. Its projects may be benign, such as promoting public health or backchannel diplomatic negotiation. Or they may be malignant, such as facilitating domestic surveillance, black site prison camps, or war.

In one sense, the deep state can be thought of as the autonomic nervous system of the body politic. At its best, it maintains the equilibrium between the government and the larger society through reality-based assessments of threats and opportunities. Its charge, not easily achieved, is to enhance resilience by promoting the interests of the whole national organism rather than favoring one part at the expense of the rest.

As described earlier, the Trump administration was steeped in various fictions and evidence-free assertions that have ossified into the unquestionable MAGA theology. Unsurprisingly, they would be on a collision course with those in government whose primary allegiance is to the truth and the country's well-being rather than a tribe or its leader. That seems to be how competent but often unrecognized workers devoted to the common good ended up with targets on their backs. It may be that poll workers are targeted for the same reason; their job is to record data without regard for who benefits from the tabulation. Unfortunately, the attack on fact-based expertise has extended far beyond competent government workers and career diplomats.

Why Authoritarians Hate Experts, Journalists, and Scientists

You might assume that the greatest power wielded by autocrats or those aspiring to be one is being above the law—or, more precisely, to *be* the law. It's difficult to imagine a prerogative more total and consequential than being able to decide what is a crime, how it will be punished, and who gets prosecuted. And yet, there is an authority more profound and invasive, one that incarcerates minds and bodies. That is the power to define reality for others—to determine what is viewed as true or false, what counts as evidence, or whether evidence matters at all. We will revisit that theme in chapter 10 when I analyze the symbiotic relationship between Trump and his base.

Autocrats and their tribal followers predictably target experts, journalists, and scientists because the latter assert truth claims based on facts outside the leader's mind. They tend to be loyal to logic and empirical evidence and may contradict the scantily clad emperor's latest fashion statements. That's why authoritarians, from Stalin to Trump, often designated them as "enemies of the people." [35] In an echo of Putin's treatment of political prisoners, the former president even required journalists to be caged in metal pens[36] if they wanted to cover his rallies. This physical segregation from "the people" made it easier for the crowd to unleash a chorus of jeers and threats at reporters when prompted by their raving maestro at the podium.

Autocrats criminalize journalists because reporters position themselves between the leader's utterances and followers' ears. Questioning the autocrat's assertions is an intolerable mediation in the symbiotic bond aspiring or actual dictators seek with their subjects. Factuality is a treasonous challenge to the autocrat's brittle narcissism and claims of omniscience. To present objective data is, by definition, to defy his or her declarations of absolute sovereignty. That is why messengers get shot—figuratively and literally.

For authoritarian leaders, the notion that their information is incomplete can be hard for them to bear. Knowledge that they don't already possess is difficult to make use of. It challenges their intellectual solipsism, which masquerades as self-reliance and operates under the motto, "We don't need no stinkin' evidence." That is one reason that Trump, the narcissistic ignoramus par excellence, is a good fit for his faith-based followers.[37] He worships himself and believes in nothing. They worship him and will believe anything he says. Experts who don't affirm Trump are enemies. Besides, members of his base will often claim they do their "own research." So, who needs snooty scientists and their Godless methodologies?

Trump and his emulators are paradigmatic examples of the Dunning-Kruger effect—the finding that the least competent people tend to be those with the most faith in their abilities.[38] When this trait is combined with pathological narcissism, arrogant but fragile certainty is used to ward off reality. To know that they don't know is intolerable. The narcissist is too fragile to engage in the self-reflection necessary to make use of mistakes, failures, or critical feedback from the world. That renders learning from experience nearly impossible.

When that psychology is coupled with the economic and political ability to command social resources, the result is an informational police state. That is when we see censorship, book bans, regime takeover of media outlets, and the murder of journalists—autocratic prerogatives currently employed by Vladimir Putin and envied by Trump.[39]

Ordinary citizens also play a role in disseminating political lies and punishing truth tellers. They spread *dis*information (false narratives intentionally spread with malign intent) and *mis*information (false stories disseminated because their spreaders are misinformed). That can involve relatively independent centers of initiative—partisan social media networks, freelance trolls, and cult-like mass movements from which conspiracy theories emerge. But whether originating from political elites above or from the base below, conservative media is where deliberate lies and sincerely held delusions can find a welcoming home, and the truth is often exiled.

The Gated Information Communities of Right-Wing Media

Fundamental to disseminating tribal "truths" is the tribalization of information and the siloing of media. As described in the last chapter, you can live in a neighborhood where you never encounter someone who votes for the other party. It is also easy to limit your sources of information to those curated not to contain any point of view contrary to yours. That applies to both liberals and conservatives but not *equally* so.[40] Perhaps the most significant and apparent discrepancy between traditional fact-based journalism and right-wing media is the veracity of the information itself.

The more viewers watch Fox News, the less they know about the world. In fact, they know less than those who consume no news.[41] Not only does Fox fabricate stories, but they also alter photographs to make events they cover more congruent with right-wing ideology.[42] "News" on the Right is no longer about information. It is a hedonic commodity, like alcohol and pornography, cognitive cocaine designed to addict its consumers to small fleeting pleasures that make them want more and enrich their purveyors. In conservative media, the aim is to snare viewers with stories that shape and confirm their preferred worldview.[43] They have become platforms to sell back to their audience what they already think—to get them hooked on the dopamine of confirmation bias. (Of course, that pleasure is not limited to right-wing media. As a viewer of MSNBC, I am not immune to the lure of having my assumptions reflected back to me. But, in my observation, that network, CNN, and most in the broadcast mainstream make a good-faith effort to ground their coverage of events in the fact-based work of real journalists. And, when they do get a story wrong and become aware of it, they generally issue a correction.)

Tucker Carlson, once Fox's apical white nationalist demagogue and host of the most-watched cable show in the United States, had a libel suit dismissed in 2020.[44] He falsely accused former Trump mistress Karen McDougal of extorting the previous president. The Trump-appointed judge, Mary Kay Vyskocil, sided with the defense.[45] She agreed with Carlson's attorney's legal reasoning and used the latter's language in her decision. Vyskocil argued that Mr. Carlson "is not 'stating actual facts' about the topics he discusses and is instead engaging in 'exaggeration' and 'non-literal commentary.'" So, she concluded, despite telling lies about the plaintiff, "the statements are not actionable."

Here we have a bracingly frank official acknowledgment that truth-telling is an unreasonable expectation when watching Fox. (Unfortunately for them, that reasoning would not protect the network a few years later when a judge ruled against them in the Dominion voting machine libel case.) Audiences should have known, Vyskocil seemed to be arguing, that when they tuned in to Carlson, they would be fed just-so right-wing fables engineered to gratify their prejudices. Unlike cigarette packages, programs on that network do not feature warning labels about the toxic disinformation consumers are about to imbibe. Of course, like those tobacco cautions, a warning preceding a Fox program would do nothing to blunt the powerful urge to consume it. A product that can affirm your tribal identity, justify your prejudices, and demonize your hate objects is a powerful drug.

Sometimes the consequences of Carlson's fabrications are far more malignant than slander. He was America's most-viewed purveyor of the neo-Nazi "Great Replacement" conspiracy.[46] That is the belief that white women are not doing their job being broodmares for the race. Consequently, liberals are plotting to exploit the birthrate crisis by replacing white citizens, "Legacy Americans,"[47] as Carlson describes them, with dark-skinned immigrants to steal elections. That fascist fairy tale has a rapidly escalating body count. In 2019, a white supremacist citing that fantasy massacred fifty people attending a mosque in New Zealand.[48] The killer left behind a manifesto that repeated the mantra, "It's the birthrates," three times. Then, in May 2022, another deluded defender of the "master race" in Buffalo, New York, murdered ten people and injured three more, most of whom were Black. He, too, had posted a manifesto, which was essentially plagiarized from the New Zealand killer.[49] Until his 2023 firing for costing the broadcaster in the Dominion case, the lethality of Carlson's lies did not lead Fox to place any constraints on their top money maker. The network's mercenary pursuit of ratings had always eclipsed calls to have him terminated for peddling disinformation.[50]

Some readers might comfort themselves with the belief that the Great Replacement conspiracy theory is accepted by only the credulous few on the fringe of the American Right. Unfortunately, a third of the US public and nearly half of all Republicans embrace that Trumplandian tall tale.[51] Carlson's conspiratorial fiction has become increasingly mainstream. It seems likely that we will see more homicidal white supremacists act on it. One stunning indicator that the Right has normalized that myth is soon-to-retire Republican

Senate Minority Leader Mitch McConnell's refusal to disavow it following the Buffalo massacre.[52] It seems unlikely that he believes the popular racist fable. Instead, remaining silent about it appears to be just another Faustian bargain he has had to make with Trumpism to stay in power.

The tribal segmentation of the media has achieved what was only possible in North Korea through crude censorship techniques. Kim Jong-un's solution to the inconvenient truth problem has been to ban internet access and solder the dials of televisions and radios made outside the country so that only government broadcasts can be received.[53] In the United States, the same effect has been achieved voluntarily. Republican minds have been soldered to Fox, OAN, and Sinclair, even though fact-based news is widely available. Those on the production end of fake news seem to understand what is required to keep audiences welded to their creations. And the cynical purveyors of political lies can be surprisingly transparent about their craft.

Chris Ruddy, the CEO of the emerging right-wing media empire Newsmax, bragged to a *New York Times* reporter weeks after the 2020 election about how much his market share has grown since fabricating and promoting Democratic "voter fraud" narratives that suggest Donald Trump had really won the presidential contest.[54] Even though Ruddy is a Trumpworld insider and frequent guest at Mar-a-Lago, he doesn't believe that nonsense. "In this day and age, people want something that tends to affirm their views and opinions," he told an interviewer.[55] Ruddy and his cohorts see a need and are happy to fill it. Ka-ching. But this raises a crucial question: from where does that need come? What makes certain lies so compelling and some truths deeply threatening?

When Truth Threatens Individual and Tribal Identities

Republican voters comprise one of the nation's largest faith communities. And Trump is its high priest. Any call for empirical proof is apostasy. Faith, by definition, is belief in the absence of evidence. A complete list of delusions that comprise the ever-shifting Republican catechism would be unwieldy here and belabor what most readers already know. Nevertheless, a small sample of current MAGA fictions includes the belief that the 2020 election was stolen from Trump; critical race theory, a framework for understanding systemic racism, is an item featured in grammar school curricula and can be found in coded form in math books; Democrats run child sex trafficking rings; gay people seek to "convert" children into homosexuality; any firearm safety laws will lead to the confiscation of the guns; non-white immigrants are a physical and economic threat to Americans; and COVID vaccines are more dangerous than being infected with the virus and contain tracking chips. And those are the "moderate" delusions.

QAnon, the most vehemently unhinged sect of the MAGA faith, is only growing in adherents. As of February 2022, 41 million Americans—about 16 percent of the US population—embrace the gospel of Q.[56] Fifty-six percent of Republicans are at least partial believers.[57] They live in a dark phantasmic Boschian hellscape run by a cabal of cannibalistic Satanic pedophiles, primarily prominent Democrats, and await salvation from a reincarnated JFK Jr., who will be Trump's running mate in 2024.[58] Disciples constitute such a large percentage of the GOP constituency that, in 2020, twenty-four Republican politicians across the country were affiliated with QAnon.[59] Thirty-six QAnon members ran for Congress in 2022.[60] And the cult has found a welcoming sanctuary on Trump's social media platform, which bears the Orwellian name of "Truth Social."[61] As their principal deity, he is an avid promoter of their ideas.

Anyone who has attempted to challenge those or other false beliefs held by family members or friends has probably run into shockingly obdurate resistance and may have triggered the end of those relationships. One of the biggest reasons people cling so tenaciously to these notions is that they are inextricably woven into their individual and group identities. Psychological researcher Dan Kahan argues in an insightful review paper that the relationship between misinformation and partisan identity is, to some extent, the reverse of what we commonly think.[62] In other words, it is less that fake news can persuade us to align with one political tribe or another, although that can certainly occur. More significantly, we seek out information, fake or not, that is congruent with what we believe other members of our tribe hold.

What Kahan calls *identity-protective cognition* leads him to a strikingly counter-intuitive conclusion. People who readily believe rumors, fake news, and conspiratorial fictions that have no basis in evidence are not irrational. Instead, they are driven by a less obvious rationality, which is indifferent to truth-seeking. As individuals, our group attachments are far more compelling and precede our beliefs. As I argued in chapter 1, we have evolved to value our group membership above nearly every other consideration. So, securing our place in the tribe by thinking like our peers is far more critical than whether the facts support our understanding. Expressing the beliefs shared by our tribe is a way of signaling to others that we are members in good standing.

That raises questions mere observation cannot clarify. To what extent can we take a stated belief as a sincerely held opinion? And to what degree are we witnessing a *performance* of belief that functions as a behavioral declaration of group loyalty? I don't know if there is any empirical way of answering those questions. I speculate that both are operative to varying degrees in any given individual. We can have a genuine conviction that something is true but also be highly motivated to believe it. If one of those motives is to secure our tribal membership, then others need to know we are keepers of the faith—hence the imperative to *enact* our belief.

I could present factual rebuttals to the evidence-free fantasies uttered by the MAGA hat-wearing guy next door. However, regardless of where he fell on the sincerity-performance continuum, I would fail to persuade him that George Soros, the Chinese, and the late Hugo Chavez did not recruit Jewish lizard people to rig voting machines against Donald Trump in the 2020 election. He would not abandon a belief that makes him feel like an honored and recognized member of his beloved QAnon community. My neighbor would likely double down, cast a jaundiced eye at his rude, reality-based libtard interlocutor, and suspect me of reptilian sympathies. Even my lack of webbed toes would not dissuade him from concluding that I was an enemy of all he values.

That brings us to Kahan's most unexpected research finding. The sort of person most likely to adhere to a tribe-congruent false belief is not my caricature of the Cro-Magnon Trump supporter. It is a highly educated individual with a solid comprehension of science. That is because such people can recruit their scientific knowledge to refute other scientific notions that might threaten identification with their community of true believers. Kahan found that dynamic operates with particular intensity among those who deny or minimize the scientific consensus on human-caused climate change. Subjects most adamant in their denial and prone to misread the data are those who are the most scientifically literate.

Kahan's findings on identity-protective cognition help us understand the high psychological stakes that motivate some people to misread scientific research selectively. There are also personality traits that can be powerful drivers of science denial.[63] Chief among these is a social dominance orientation (SDO), which, as described in earlier chapters, is the tendency to embrace group-based hierarchy and a corresponding aversion to equality. One's tribe is not only viewed as superior, but that superiority justifies rule over other tribes seen as inferior.

An iteration of dominance is directed toward the natural world in particular. Nature is seen as separate from and subordinate to humans. It exists to be exploited for its extractable resources. Perhaps unsurprisingly, conservative white males display this attitude more than other demographic groups and thus are much more likely to deny climate change.[64]

In addition to believing misinformation about scientific matters, those with a high SDO are much more likely to share it via social media.[65] The relationship between those two factors, identity-protective cognition and SDO, seems intuitive. Those for whom their group's dominance over others is critical would likely be far more invested in protecting their tribal identity from the threat of evidence that might disconfirm shared beliefs that define them. That brings us to the most pernicious expression of misinformation, conspiracy theories.

One-Way Tickets to Dreamland

Creators of movies fashion dreams for their audiences to enter. The better the film, the more readily viewers can suspend disbelief. In front of two-dimensional screens, the ordinary human capacity for double consciousness is activated. On the one hand, audience members know they are in a building watching a visual illusion on a flat surface. Were there a fire or other disaster, they would immediately return to ordinary reality and head for the exits.

On the other hand, attendees can easily enter the dreamscape of the film-maker and feel sadness, anger, terror, and the thirst for revenge against villains. They might find themselves literally at the edge of their seats, gripping the arm-rests with anxious anticipation and fear. However, when the movie ends, they "wake up" and return to their relatively mundane lives without any confusion with the film's fantasy.

That capacity for double consciousness is the foundation of our ability to empathize—to enter the inner world of others while simultaneously holding on to our own. Without it, we could not engage in imaginative play—with children or other adults. We could neither act in nor enjoy watching a drama. But what happens when we enter another's dreamscape but lose the capacity to hold empirical reality or our own internal one concurrently? It looks like the political post-truth moment in which we now live. Partisans are invited into as-if narratives, but too often, the as-if quality is lost once inside. An increasing plurality of Americans have entered the theater of conspiracy fiction and cannot find the exits.

The Demographics of Delusion: Who is Vulnerable to Conspiracy Thinking?

Behind the stage set of mundane cause and effect lurk powerful forces of good and evil. While the backstage manipulations may go unseen, their impacts are felt. What may look like a random amoral universe obeying no laws beyond those of physics, chemistry, and biology is a battleground where invisible agents fight for supremacy. The machinations of clandestine cabals and villainous malefactors underly seemingly stochastic tragic events. Although no direct evidence of their control can be discerned, the bad things that happen are proof enough. We can assume that upstream from pandemics, mass shootings, and even natural disasters are omnipotent puppet masters who pull the strings of their minions in the mainstream media, write the scripts and choreograph the actions of their crisis actors in the streets.

That description of generic conspiracy thinking might sound very similar to the narrative structure of most religions, especially fundamentalist varieties. In that case, you might not be surprised to learn that evangelical Christians rank among the highest of those who accept conspiratorial explanations for world events. In one study, subjects were asked if they believed that "regardless of who is officially in charge, a single group of people secretly control events and rule the world together."[66] Fifty percent of born-again or evangelical Christians did. Interestingly, among those who got their news from conservative websites, the percentage was even higher, at 63 percent. Whether sitting in an evangelical pew or on a couch consuming right-wing media, one becomes a devout member of the faithful, conditioned to accept information without evidence. In contrast, one of the groups least likely to endorse such narratives was atheists (26 percent). Only 29 percent of CNN viewers believed in a controlling global cabal, while 48 percent of those who trust Fox were convinced that is how the world works.

Lies for Those Who Feel Lonely and the Powerless

Another demographic surveyed got my attention: "People who say they always lack companionship." At 57 percent, they matched the percentage of Trump voters and the "very conservative" who believe a secret group of master manipulators directs most global events. Among the fifty demographic categories studied, the socially isolated was the only one that revealed the relational world of conspiracy adherents. We know from the work on identity-protective cognition that an essential function of fake news and political fictions is to affirm one's membership in a community of fellow believers. While speculative, it may be that undergoing a conspiracy "conversion" and helping to disseminate those narratives to others on social media is a partial antidote to loneliness and an impoverished social life. It is also possible that the conviction that powerful forces care about manipulating you is preferable to believing others are indifferent to your existence.

Hannah Arendt's *Origins of Totalitarianism* explores how loneliness and the experience of social disconnection render people susceptible to the appeal of fascist propaganda. The experience of being "deserted by all others" leaves one feeling profoundly lost. That is because "for the confirmation of my identity, I depend entirely upon other people," she explains. Given the centrality of conspiracy narratives to the appeal of political and religious leader cults, her citation of Luther seems especially apt. A lonely person, she quotes Luther, "always deduces one thing from the other and thinks everything to be the worst."[67]

Arendt also talks about how loneliness takes particular forms under capitalist modernity. She alludes to conditions of work where people are crammed together in confined spaces while simultaneously feeling disconnected. Arendt may have had in mind the circumstances of physical labor in her era, under which human actions were reduced to the most efficient machine-like movements, and subjectivity and comradery were impediments to factory discipline. But as work has shifted from heavy industry, increasingly outsourced to the new proletarians of developing economies abroad, the growth of the service sector in the "first" world has meant an increase in *emotional* labor. These are jobs that involve performing affect to induce consumption-friendly emotions in customers. Sociologist Arlie Hochschild's 2012 book, *The Managed Heart: Commercialization of Human Feeling*, was an exemplary study of this new kind of work and its devastating impacts on those who must rely on it to survive.[68] The imperative to feign feeling can lead to another kind of isolation. Behind the falsified exterior is an inner world that must remain hidden and unrecognized. In such settings, scripts interact, not those performing them.

Isolation and loneliness can also be concentrated in sites of consumption and transportation. We are alone together in shopping malls, where things and their prices are far more salient than people. Even when our aim of going there is to connect with others, it is not easy to be as compelling as products. Collective isolation is the condition of both public and private transportation as well.

Subways and buses are often larger versions of the elevator experience. In other words, we manage the intrusion of other bodies into our personal space by creating *internally* the distance we can't achieve externally. Eye contact is an intrusive gesture that must be avoided. The private transportation space of crowded freeways is a different but harsher iteration of that dynamic. Everyone is jammed closely together with others, encased in their four-wheeled suits of armor. We try to avoid a lethal collision, while finding openings to pass others who are only impediments to getting where we want to go. That is both the lived experience of many and a grimly fitting metaphor for the worst of capitalist public life—a social physics in which like-objects repel.[69] These experiences of collective isolation are the normative background conditions of contemporary daily life, which we all struggle to manage or compensate for in various ways. Right-wing extremists have developed their own adaptions to the ambient estrangement of being alone around others.

We know where so-called "lone-wolf" neo-Nazi terrorists go to find affirmation, identity, and what passes for companionship—social media. They encounter a simulation of relationships, a placeholder taking up life space that might be otherwise populated with actual people. But the glue of those pseudo-communities and the commerce that enlivens them is the exchange and enhancement of conspiracy fictions. It is also where they brag about and get recognition for their occasionally enacted fantasies of cleansing violence.

Social media sites like 4chan turn smoldering paranoid grievance into bloody action.[70] Lone-wolf mass murderers, such as the explicitly racist Buffalo shooter, embody a paradox even a pre-internet philosopher like Arendt might recognize. He was alone with few actual friends yet a vital node in a quasi-relational network of the like-minded, bound together by their adherence to a fascist fable. In his case, it was the Great Replacement delusion. So, he and others like him may be lonely, but they're not "lone."[71] Behind each of them is a virtual pack.

Another intriguing category of people who scored somewhat high in acceptance of the fantasy of an all-powerful cabal was "people who say they lack control over their life." Forty-six percent of them endorsed the statement. Psychologists refer to the sense of possessing little agency as having an "external locus of control." It is an experience that can be both vexing and relieving. It is troubling to feel powerless to affect the fundamental conditions of one's life. Yet, it provides a forgiving narrative to explain away personal failures and disappointments as the actions caused by more powerful others.

People can lack agency over the good things that happen: "I got a promotion because the company needed another woman in management, not because I outperformed my peers on all measures." Or, they can see the bad events of their lives as the result of forces entirely beyond their control: "I was fired because I'm a white Christian man, not because the boss caught me spending several hours a day watching porn on my work computer." Readers may recognize the persecutory mindset of the latter example. It is not hard to see how having an external locus of control when it comes to the small-scale setbacks and misfortunes in one's individual life can be extended to the large-scale problems of our collective existence. The malevolent conspiratorial plots of more powerful others explain both.

That is not to negate the fact that there are very real power disparities in public life that can make acting on our agency quite daunting. We should not dismiss the evidence of real conspiracies that those with disproportionate political and economic resources can sometimes carry out. But conspiracy *thinking* is a psychological predisposition that can be refractory to evidence. That is because before there is a specific conspiracy theory to evaluate, there is a preexisting motivation to believe an all-powerful cabal is responsible for both one's shortcomings and the world's wretchedness. While an external locus of control is exonerating, it is also a belief that reinforces helplessness. Virtue is thus fused with victimization, an assumption, as I have argued throughout this book, that is foundational to the Christian story. One consequence of that narrative can be political passivity—either the quiet, paralytic passivity of despair, drug addiction, and voter apathy or the active passivity of surrendering one's agency to autocrats or cult leaders and marching in their armies.

Conspiracy Thinking and Credulity

As we might expect, in studies of those prone to believing in conspiracy theories, researchers found a significant association with reduced critical thinking ability.[72] Using a validated measure of critical thinking, low scores were correlated with the conviction that a clandestine group of powerful individuals "secretly manipulate world events." While such findings can only show an association and not causality, that ambiguity introduces the intriguing possibility that causality could be bidirectional.

Although this is entirely speculative, it may not be just that reduced critical thinking sets people up to believe conspiracy theories. It may also be that those who read, accept, and spread groundless conspiracy narratives because they are harmonious with tribal beliefs and identity are training their brains to disregard evidence and thus diminish their critical thinking ability. If we take seriously the widely accepted neuroplasticity aphorism that "neurons that fire together wire together," we would have a situation in which practice makes *im*perfect.

Belief in conspiracy stories seems to involve quite contradictory modes of thinking, paranoia and credulity—a tendency to be highly suspicious and, at the same time, shockingly gullible. However, the contradiction is only apparent. What links these cognitive traits is that they are both refractory to evidence. But this raises other challenging questions. Is there something beyond hobbled critical thinking at play here? What makes loudly proclaiming one's belief in and gleefully circulating a groundless conspiracy narrative so compelling?

Political Litmus Tests and Costly Signaling

The term *litmus test* is an interesting metaphor to describe the centrality of a particular issue position or candidate endorsement to tribal membership. After all, a literal litmus test is not only a marker visible to all, but it is also a signal coded by red or blue, the current colors of partisan identity. The message says, "I hold my tribe's defining beliefs, which shows my loyalty." But the best signal communicates your willingness to alienate and offend outsiders. It lets fellow group members know that your loyalty is so great that you are willing to burn bridges to all those beyond the tribal boundary. The name that social scientists call sending such messages is "costly signaling."

Questions always come up when a poll indicates the disturbing number of citizens who claim to believe a particularly unhinged and fact-free conspiracy narrative: Do they *really* think that? Or are they just trolling earnest pollsters because they hate all journalists? The answer is that both could be true. A third possibility is that they are engaged in costly signaling.[73] Regarding authenticity, genuine belief is usually more effectively signaled than a pretense of belief. Signals are most effective when hard to fake.[74] In addition, sincere belief is less of a cognitive load than subterfuge. There is a risk of one's deception being discovered, which could lead to punishment or exile.

In her paper, "The Signaling Function of Sharing Fake Stories," philosophy professor Marianna B. Ganapini doubts that people are simply gullible when they seem to believe fanciful tales.[75] Because it is unclear to what extent sharers of fake stories accept what they share as fact or how deeply they believe them, Ganapini directs her attention to the *function* of the sharing itself. She concludes that the aim is to signal that one is a member in good standing of the tribe. But to come across as sincere and not just as someone engaging in performative impression management, the signaling has to be costly. It has to cost them the support and respect of outside groups. A willingness to alienate other tribes is a testament to the sharer's authenticity. That is a situation where the more outrageous and implausible the fake story is, the more authentic and loyal the sharer can seem—as long as the fake story is congruent with the larger tribal narrative. Tribal villains can be accused of monstrous and unbelievable (to the outsider) crimes—the more extreme, the better for the sharer.

Signaling with fake stories serves many functions. Trump's numerous lies are not simple falsehoods but invitations to his base to demonstrate their submission to him by accepting (or seeming to accept) his fiction as truth. Every MAGA chant repeated at his rallies *shows loyalty* to the leader and especially to fellow Trump supporters. And whether or not a story is true, it can be a rallying cry (e.g., "Stop the Steal!" or "Lock Her Up!"). That process is readily visible in riots, lynch mobs, and the inciting rally on January 6. In other words, signaling can serve the function of *mobilizing action*.

The signal of a fake story can also function as an *alarm*. Evolution primes us to attend more to highly negative and threatening content, narratives that suggest a danger, especially one from outside the social and geographical boundaries of the tribe. That becomes a spur to approve of and obey tribal leaders (seen whenever the G. W. Bush administration raised the color-coded terrorism threat level) and promotes cooperative behavior among tribal members. Lastly, fake stories are especially suited to constructing group identities.

By asserting that those in power or leaders of competing tribes are out to harm us, those narratives help to create an "us."

Fake stories are saturated with what psychoanalyst Donald Spence called "narrative truth."[76] In other words, to get widely shared they don't need to be factually or literally true. They can be effective simply by being metaphorical carriers for powerful emotional truths—not so much reality but what *feels* like reality. To disseminate a fake story does not require that one believe it to be literally true, as long as it resonates with larger tribal narratives, i.e., it *could* be true. It is true-ish. Or, as comedian Stephen Colbert might say, it has an air of "truthiness." For example, Tea Party and now Trumpworld Republicans "know" the Clintons are ruthless evildoers who would not stop at murder to achieve their wicked ends. While one may not know with certainty that they have engaged in child sex trafficking and cannibalism in a pizza parlor basement, that is just the sort of thing they *would* do. Besides, it is what everyone at my church believes.

Projective Post-Truth

Sigmund Freud first coined the term *projection* in 1894. His daughter, Anna, further developed the concept in her masterwork, *The Ego and the Mechanisms of Defense*. In simplest terms, it could be understood as an unconscious psychological process in which we attribute to others aspects of ourselves we want to disavow. That can include desires, wishes, forbidden thoughts, or malignant intentions. Projection is seen as a defense because it protects us from certain kinds of self-knowledge that might be embarrassing, humiliating, or guilt-inducing. It is as if we are saying to the world, "I am not that sort of person, but *you* are!"

One way to understand projection more vividly is to return to the analogy of the movie theater, but this time to illustrate something different. While facing the screen, the projector containing the film is behind you. This being an old-fashioned cinema, the movie comes from the projection booth. Yet, it appears to be emanating from the screen. Even before we encounter the characters and their story, the first suspension of disbelief comes as we ignore the mechanical reality and keep our gaze fixed on the screen, from where the action seems to be arising. In life outside the theater, we are the projector and others are the screen.

Projective post-truth in politics is what happens when one group disavows its dishonorable or repugnant motives, feelings, and plans and attributes them to political opponents in the form of false accusations. It is a propaganda two-fer. One tribe can simultaneously depict itself as angelic while painting the enemy as demonic. It would seem more fair-minded to describe this as a "both sides" process. But political reality would not support such a "balanced" but wishful assessment. In the majority of examples, MAGA Republicans reside in the projection booth, and Democrats comprise the screen.

We can draw many lessons from the Trump era, which by all indications is not over. He could get reelected and many of his clones and surrogates still hold public office. One maxim retains its utility: if you want to know what crimes or ethical transgressions the former president has committed or is planning to commit, pay attention to the accusations he is directing at others. Projection is his tell. Before abducting and incarcerating Central American children, he ranted about vans of kidnapped Mexicans crossing into the United States.[77] Before attempting to defraud and overthrow American democracy by having votes thrown out and inciting a violent coup, he was warning of Democratic plots to steal the election, which morphed into the Big Lie after his 2020 loss.[78]

After leaving office, a Justice Department search of his Mar-a-Lago compound revealed that Trump had stolen and stored highly classified documents, including those pertaining to nuclear weapons, in a disheveled pile of boxes throughout his Florida resort and flushed others down the toilet. A few years earlier, he had gone on multiple Twitter tirades about putative security breaches that resulted from Hillary Clinton's use of a private email server while secretary of state.[79] (Notably, all the information in the government documents on her server was in the public domain, and the material had been classified only retroactively.)

After Trump denounced the Mar-a-Lago search as proof President Biden had politicized the Justice Department and FBI, the MAGA amen corner of Congress sang from the same hymnal of lies. Trump's second son, Eric, attempted to join the chorus but unintentionally revealed the projection behind his father's false accusation. In his Twitter (now X) post, he said, "I know the white house [sic] as well as anyone. I know the system. That did not happen without Joe Biden's explicit approval.[80] Projection translated: during the Trump administration, all government departments, including the Justice Department, worked for the president, not the country.

Before attempting to extort Ukraine into investigating Joe Biden's son by threatening to withhold essential defensive weaponry, Trump had promoted a fake story about Biden trying to extort Ukraine into covering up his son's supposed corruption. For three years, while he depicted the influx of immigrants seeking a haven in the United States as an "infestation," Florida health inspectors cited Trump's Mar-a-Lago for seventy-eight health violations for mold, parasites, and other unsanitary conditions in its restaurant's kitchens.[81]

Last but not least, in this partial catalog of Trump's projective post-truth was how he began his presidency. His inaugural jeremiad about "American carnage" referenced the metaphorical bodies left in the supposed rubble of what he implied was the disaster of the Obama years.[82] That dystopian contrivance would be followed a few years later by actual carnage—Trump's initial denial and consistent mismanagement of a pandemic that would constitute the largest preventable death toll in US history; the current count is about 1.2 million.[83] His lies and mixed messaging about masking, vaccines, and treatments still kill his followers disproportionately.[84]

The MAGA base has mirrored its leader's pattern of enacting what he falsely accuses others of doing. That has played mainly in their response to the Big Lie. The most notable example occurred a year after Trump's loss. In voting districts across the country, ardent followers of the former president, aided by Republican Party officials, were determined to act on their conviction that nefarious evildoers had attempted to steal the election from their presidential candidate by messing with voting machines. The top GOP election official in one location decided to mess with voting machines to gather evidence of that plot. He hacked into and copied data from the system drives.[85] That was only one of eight MAGA-faction attempts to break into voting machines to show they had been broken into. Much more than technology was damaged. The hackers also stole data on voters and their choices, violating one of the cardinal features of American elections, the secret ballot.[86] Among the enduring effects of these breaches has been replicating *their* mistrust of democracy by inducing suspicion in the electorate more broadly.

Lastly, we have the obviously projective aspects of the "White Replacement" fantasy mentioned previously. As it turns out, there was, in fact, a group of immigrants who sought to dispossess, disempower, and replace "legacy Americans." That would be white Europeans who, through genocide, incarceration, and legal disenfranchisement, replaced the native inhabitants.

Paleo-Paranoia: The Evolutionary Origins of Conspiracy Thinking

Up to this point, I've been discussing conspiracy theories as if they were entirely delusional. But there are and have long been actual conspiracies. The archeological, historical, and cross-cultural scholarship on such things shows that for two million years, humans have formed coalitions to raid, enslave, conquer, and murder other groups of humans.[87] Members of one tribe, most often men, coveting the human and material resources of other tribes or factions within their own group, have secretly plotted to attack them. Primatologists have observed the same behavior in one of our closest relatives, chimpanzees.[88] It is not hard to come up with numerous and familiar examples of real conspiracies in our lifetime and country—Pearl Harbor, Watergate, Iran-Contra, the 9/11 attacks, Trump's efforts to extort Ukraine, and the January 6 MAGA coup attempt, to name just a few. Then there are the ordinary business-as-usual conspiracies orchestrated by our nation's corporate oligarchy, such as the often-successful efforts of the American Legislative Exchange Council to inscribe the needs of the economic elite into law.[89]

The tendency to engage in conspiracy thinking is just as commonplace, perhaps unsurprisingly. (To my knowledge, the data on simian suspiciousness has not been gathered yet.) Given the longstanding and ordinary nature of actual conspiracies, it makes sense that the cognitive capacities to discern such plots would be adaptive. But being genetically adaptive doesn't mean such thinking is more than rarely accurate. It primarily produces false positives, i.e., paranoid fantasies like those discussed earlier.

Yet, from an evolutionary perspective, that's not as big a problem as false negatives. Failure to detect actual conspiracies would be and has been quite catastrophic. Overlooking actual wrong doers and misdirecting suspicion toward tribal scapegoats allows everyday corruption and malevolent schemes against the common good to go unchallenged. Those ancestors who were suspicious enough to foil lethal plots, even if they were wrong most of the time, got to pass on their genes. The ones who were insufficiently wary were less likely to produce many descendants. Psychologists sometimes call this vigilant attention to possible threats the *negativity bias*. Falsely identifying a stick on the road ahead as a snake might generate unnecessary anxiety. Falsely identifying a snake as just a stick could have more severe consequences for the individual and his or her chances of creating offspring. Speaking of herpetological perils, very young children can identify a snake more quickly than a flower.[90] Unfortunately, the evolved tendency to perceive danger and assume the worst has exacted a profound psychic cost, especially concerning the potential for severe anxiety.

Social scientists who have studied conspiracy theories have identified five key components: *pattern perception* (making meaning of seemingly random phenomena), *agency* (attributing intentionality to supposed plotters), *coalitional action* (members of the plot are seen as working together), *threat* (the perception that plotters intend to do harm), and *secrecy* (the plot is clandestine with little visible indicators of its operations.)[91] These elements are seen in mistakenly perceived and actual conspiracies. The clear difference between the two is supporting evidence. The ability to discern and evaluate evidence, my definition of critical thinking, leads to far fewer conspiracy false positives. That is why it can help inoculate people against the risk of slipping down delusional rabbit holes.

Conspiracy thinking that persists in the absence of evidence is paranoia. So, just because a trait has been adaptive over evolutionary time does not mean it continues to be or that it even remains useful. But usefulness is not such a straightforward quality. A bogus conspiracy theory may harm the larger society but be helpful to an individual's relationship with his or her small group. As humans are predisposed to pay attention to potential threats, someone who spreads even false information about danger can be rewarded with recognition and esteem.[92]

However, not every actual danger is imbued with the same sense of threat. There are those that natural selection has primed us to take more seriously—invasion by strangers, contamination, contagion, risks to offspring, and predation. The latter hazard, being another creature's tasty meal, was a feature of life for much of human existence on the planet—from saber-toothed cats to massive, bone-crushing, predatory kangaroos.[93] And it continues to exert a significant, if underappreciated, role in our everyday anxieties.[94]

Then there are dangers too recent in our evolutionary history to be inscribed in our DNA. That would include drunk driving, air pollution, cigarette smoking, deforestation, gun violence, nuclear weapons, and climate change—things liberals seem to care about more. While these newer hazards often threaten our well-being more than the older ones, they don't elicit the alarm they deserve. Appropriate anxiety about them is more dependent on learning than "instinct." So, we should not be surprised that conspiracy theories and much of right-wing propaganda more generally deploy language and symbols suggestive of those primitive threats: conniving others, marauding barbarians, pestilence, child abusers, and beastly predators. It makes sense that the threat narratives that go viral or turn into religious doctrines concern those archaic perils and not more recent ones.

There is every indication that the current level of political paranoia threatens the continuation of America's democratic experiment and even the continuation of mammalian life on Earth. There are delusions about the *presence* of a threat (believing that race-neutral voting rights are a vast conspiracy to replace white voters with illegal immigrants). And there are delusions concerning the *absence* of one (being convinced that we can dismiss the pessimistic conclusions of climate scientists because they are only motivated by grant money). When people harbor either type, the results could be disastrous.

Somewhat encouraging is that even though belief in various conspiracy theories is commonplace, only a minority appears vulnerable to them. However, they tend to be those in the country favored by the systemic political biases discussed earlier—52 percent of Republicans vs. 31 percent of Democrats.[95] To put a finer and more alarming point on it, when we consider the ratio of population to representation in the Senate and Electoral College, the votes of the paranoid count a lot more than those of critical thinkers.

Hatred in the Time of Coronavirus: Post-Truth in the Pandemic

At this point, some astute readers may be asking themselves a pertinent question. If contagion is one of those threats we are primed to take seriously, how could the GOP base be so easily persuaded to ignore or dismiss the public health warnings about the dangers of COVID-19? While speculative, this was likely achieved by intuitively exploiting another threat category primed for salience by our evolutionary history—invasion and abduction by strangers. In addition to China, the "foreign" threats here were Democrats and their oppressive "Big Government," Anthony Fauci (the Dr. Mengele of the anti-vax imagination), and malevolent funders such as Bill Gates and George Soros.

That level of suspicion also showed up in my clinical practice. One of my patients was a militant organizer of anti-vaccine protests. He spent several sessions excitedly discussing his preparations to evade attempts by FEMA agents to round him up and transport him and his family to special concentration camps for the unvaccinated. To be clear, other than that delusion, this patient exhibited no signs of psychosis and was highly functional in every other respect. He was not alone; other anti-vax patients shared the same belief. It should be noted that the fantasy of capture and transport to FEMA concentration camps has been a staple of right-wing conspiracy narratives for *many* decades.[96] So, it has not been difficult to append that threat to recent anti-vax stories.

My patient is a pro-choice liberal whose idea of protecting bodily autonomy included the "freedom" to reject masks and social distancing but coupled with a very unliberal indifference to protecting others more vulnerable than he. Notably, he is also a global warming denier and attributes climate-related weather disasters to government-sponsored weather-modification experiments on the population. Once I read Naomi Klein's account[97] of the bizarre but emergent coalition between the fascist fringe and a small subset of new agers and libertarian-adjacent leftists, it became apparent that this person was part of a new and disturbing partisan realignment. Klein and others refer to this as "diagonalism," an attempt to name a global trend that defies aspects of the more conventional left-right bifurcation. In some ways, this development seems like a variation of left post-truth discussed elsewhere in this book. My patient said that a significant source for his understanding of vaccines and the world more generally came from the right-wing social media platform Telegram,[98] where he proclaimed, "I finally found my tribe."

I hasten to add that my obligation to maintain my patients' confidentiality has not been breached here. Unfortunately, nothing shared in this account differentiates him from a number of other patients I worked with at the height of the pandemic and the associated epidemic of COVID disinformation. He was part of a shockingly wide trend.

The influence of social media here cannot be overemphasized. We are primed to take threat information on trust and tend to accept it if it comes from members of our group, even if that group is a virtual community. For Republicans, pandemic danger warnings came from the enemy tribe and should not have been trusted. Moreover, such alarms might disguise the "real" threat, an assault on our "freedom." So, the fantasy threat of FEMA (invasion and abduction by strangers) is recruited to eclipse an actual threat (contamination). I'm not suggesting that was intentional, just that it was another example of the Right's intuitive exploitation of primitive anxieties for political purposes. We can see derivatives of those fears reflected in the widespread pandemic-related delusions promoted in right-wing media.

They include nightmare visions of putting MAGA members in reeducation and internment camps, a variation of the FEMA plot endorsed by my patients.[99] As Klein reads it,[100] the middle-class anti-vaxxers' preoccupation with government internment camps was, in some ways, a delusional iteration of what many low-paid "essential workers" *actually* faced during the pandemic—wage labor "internment" in jobs they could not afford to leave. Especially before the COVID-19 vaccine, many employees faced the agonizing choice of risking their lives and those of their families by working unprotected in viral hothouse environments or losing their jobs and being unable to pay rent or buy food.

Other conspiracy stories claimed that Bill Gates arranged to have tracking devices embedded in vaccines.[101] Some argued that the point of public-health-driven shutdowns was to suppress worship services.[102] Still others insisted that liberals had created or faked the COVID outbreak to make Trump look bad, get rid of him, and crash the economy.[103] (Interestingly, House Republicans are currently engaging in actions that reveal the projection behind the latter fantasy: faking criminal accusations to make Biden look bad, trying to get rid of him through impeachment, and threatening an economy-damaging government shutdown and perhaps future debt default if they don't get their way.[104])

That brings us to the striking irony that, among the Republican base during the outbreak, protective masks were far more fearsome than the lethal virus kept out by those masks. It was not the respiratory straightjacket of ventilators that scared them but the relatively benign face coverings that rendered ICU coma induction far less likely. As we have come to understand, for them, masks were signifiers of tribal membership. The imperative to wear one was readily interpreted as a threat to freedom and imposition of an alien identity (invasion by strangers).[105] The threat of being placed in bondage by an enemy tribe seems to have eclipsed the actual danger posed by the pandemic. It starts to make sense of the extraordinary fury with which some MAGA cultists resisted public health mandates, whether as violence against hospital workers or as an incitement for a new civil war.[106]

My anti-vax, pandemic-minimizing patients evoked the most difficult countertransference I've ever struggled with as a psychoanalyst. Intellectually, I understood that challenging a true believer's group-identity-linked misinformation by interpreting their investment in it would be resisted passionately and likely lead to a doubling down on their mistaken beliefs and high-risk behavior. But emotionally, it was agonizing to witness them engage in life-threatening actions. It was nearly impossible to let go of my wishful fantasy that our long-developed rapport and therapeutic alliance could supersede any other influence.

Of course, their erroneous beliefs were unlike other notions about health or what constituted risky behavior. They had a firmer grip on their psyches than drug dependency. As compelling as opiates might be, addiction to them is usually seen by patients as a problem they want help with. Identity-saturated pandemic beliefs, by contrast, were more akin to deeply held religious convictions, which no well-trained clinician would ever dream of challenging, at least directly. There were a few occasions when my countertransference desire to pull them from the cliff they were cheerfully marching toward overshadowed what another part of my mind knew to be true. At those moments, my patients' defensive barricades of identity protection went up so quickly and with such ferocity, I abruptly abandoned my well-intentioned but foolish therapeutic ambitions.

"Sovereign immunity" was a term coined by Derek Beres, the host of the *Conspirituality* podcast, an exploration of the fascinating hybrid of right-wing conspiracy thinking and new-age spirituality, embodied perhaps most vividly by the now iconic buffalo-headed MAGA shaman who featured prominently in coverage of the January 6 assault on the Capitol.[107] The phrase refers to a belief among new-age anti-vaxxers and COVID minimizers that a healthy immune system can be somehow autonomous and walled off from the bodies of others and the pathogens they might carry. It strikes me as the importation of right-wing libertarian notions of the self into the magical physiology of new agers. The medical iteration of radically independent personhood is similar to other versions; it relies on the same fantasy of a decontextualized self, unaffected by and without impacting others.

The notion of sovereign immunity is embedded in the central meme of anti-vaxxers, "medical freedom." It imagines bodies as impenetrable fortresses that can keep out all invaders. Nothing unwanted can go in or out. That can be achieved through sheer will or perhaps the right supplement, off-label drug, bleach injection, or prayer to an intercessional deity. Anyone who *feels* good and is "healthy" cannot be infected. That stance repudiates one of the central premises of public health—that we are all linked by being embedded in a shared microbial ecology. In addition, it refutes the notion that protecting one another from infectious diseases is a social good and an obligation we should all take on.

The magical thinking goes beyond vaccine refusal. It includes the rejection of masking and social distancing, denying that diseases can be asymptomatic and communicated to others. Right-wing libertarian mask refusers manifested an obvious but perilous irony. In their effort to assert their "freedom," they opened up the unguarded portals of their bodies to the viruses of others who were imagined as outside their impermeable bunker of physiological autonomy.

That concept of medical freedom not only defies science, but it is also an ethic that operates in only one direction: I am free to reject masks, but you are not entitled to protection from infectious disease. Bodily autonomy is a prerogative I can claim but deny to you. Adherents to this belief ignore the fact that under vaccine or mask mandates, no one was forced to get the jab or wear protection. Immunization and masking were required to keep a job or remain in a classroom where close contact with vulnerable others would be unavoidable. Anti-vaxxers and mask refusers were free to avoid vaccination or face protection by finding other work or means of attending class. Like so many other forms of right-wing freedom, "medical freedom," in this sense, is the fundamental right to harm others if it is convenient or profitable.

Official GOP pandemic denialism and post-truth opposition to public health mandates took less flamboyant forms than right-wing militias and apoplectic grocery-store Karens exhibited. But they were far more lethal.[108] Redstate governors refused to issue stay-at-home orders, exempted churches from restrictions, disallowed mask mandates, and demanded a return to regular business without establishing safeguards to reduce disease risk. Many of them opposed widespread testing or contact tracing.

There was an obvious effort to align with the views and actions of Trump, their tribal leader—his denial, minimization, and privileging of economic concerns over public health. To enable the latter, his political allies accepted the former president's absurd dissociation of economics from disease prevention. That seemed driven by the now expectable deference to his every caprice and well-founded fear of tribal exile should they challenge him.

The Republican response to the pandemic was contiguous with past practices and policies of the party. Conservatives have long inveighed against the care-taking functions of the federal government, which they have reviled as the "nanny state" while revering its military and police responsibilities. Suspicion, if not hatred, of public health measures is not inconsistent with the history of the Right. Republicans have long viewed people experiencing poverty as undeserving of free health care and opposed workers getting paid sick leave. The problem for them and their wealthy allies is that those views also threaten the lives of the economically privileged, as we are all yoked together in a complex network of relationships, which include membership in the same viral communities.

Prematurely ending stay-at-home orders and other protective measures meant that the pandemic would continue through multiple resurgences. So, conservatives faced a difficult choice, change their worldview or engage in magical thinking until reality smacked them in the face. If the threat couldn't be denied, then scapegoats and projective targets had to be identified, as Trump did with the World Health Organization (WHO), China, and blue states. His stance toward China was a complicated and contradictory one, demonizing the nation while expressing admiration for the authoritarian power of its leader. In a move that revealed the right-wing homicidal fantasy behind the geriatric "death panel" lie about Obamacare (another example of projective post-truth), various Republican politicians and pundits called for the elderly to sacrifice themselves for the economy.[109]

Pandemic-related conspiracy theories expressed by GOP politicians and their base illustrated the role that disinformation and misinformation played in affirming tribal identity. Organized around the perception of a common threat (in this case, nanny-state public health measures), those delusions served to identify who was inside and outside the tribal boundary. For adherents to the MAGA cult, a mask in public marked one as an enemy. And the absence of one was a kind of invisible crucifix, a talismanic absence that indicated one was a loyal member of the faith and, in some cases, willing to die for it.

Appearing to refuse COVID vaccines became as crucial to tribal identity as publicly declaring belief in canonical MAGA conspiracy theories. And yet some in conservative communities tried to have it both ways, hoping to avoid both biological and social death. As I mentioned earlier in the book, this led some hospitals and clinics to create discrete backdoor entrances to inoculation rooms, enabling more reality-based Trump-world tribalists to protect themselves from the hazards of infection as well as exile.[110] Some even went so far as to don disguises, hiding their *individual* identity in order to preserve their group identity. Sadly, only a minority in conservative areas could manage that dilemma, leading most to bear a disproportionate burden of preventable deaths.

Those in the base who tried to calibrate their pandemic response to that of their leader must have struggled mightily to keep up with Trump's ever-shifting positions. Depending on what he thought would make him most popular, at one moment he would push the vaccine, announce his own jab, and even take credit for its development. The next moment he would repudiate vaccinations and promote a panoply of crackpot treatments, like bleach injections.

Right-wing mythologies surrounding COVID and the public health measures needed to manage it have resulted in Trump supporters being disproportionately represented among the over a million Americans dead.[111] It shows how lethal tribal incentives can be. The powerful drive to be a member in good standing can conflict with the instinct to stay alive. Viral post-truth should be considered as at least contributing to many COVID fatalities.

As I write this at the beginning of 2024, the virus is somewhat on the wane, though a winter resurgence is underway. However, mutations of anti-vax conspiracy thinking continue to spread. Consequences of vaccine disinformation are discernible across the nation, such as the steep decline in childhood immunization and the rise in preventable pediatric infections.[112] Even vaccinations for canine family members have fallen to alarming levels because of their owners' anti-vax beliefs.[113]

Some of the most bizarre iterations of pandemic tribalism have been manifested at a local level. Ultraconservative Shasta County, California, has been an area particularly congenial to MAGA anti-science policies. Following once-accepted and uncontroversial medical guidelines for managing infectious diseases led to the firing of their county public health officer.[114] Even the county's mosquito control board has become a platform for inveighing against chimerical threats and promoting right-wing fantasies. As soon as Jon Knight ascended to the board, he warned the community about the threat posed by genetically modified mosquitos unleashed by Bill Gates, which are actually "flying syringes that will mass-vaccinate populations."[115]

We have become so accustomed to anti-vax views and anti-public health violence on the Right that it might be easy to forget just how recent the partisan divide on vaccines is. Before 2020, polls did not show a split between Republicans and Democrats. But by October 2023, a survey conducted by *Politico* revealed a profound gap in approval of routine vaccinations for adults and children. The majority of Democrats appreciate the benefits of immunizations (76 percent), but only a minority of Republicans do (49 percent). The split in support for the COVID vaccine is even greater, with 98 percent of Democrats but only 48 percent of Republicans favoring it. Whether those numbers represent what respondents think is desirable by their partisan peers or genuine feelings, they are nevertheless striking indicators of the power of tribal identity.[116]

Postmodernism and Post-Truth, Right and Left

Some pundits have argued that Trump and his spokespeople are simply shrewd postmodernists rebutting the truth claims of authorities and pushing right-wing "alternative facts" relativism. The challenge of responding to that assertion is particularly ironic; there are so many conflicting definitions of postmodernism that it is impossible to argue for the validity of any of them.[117]

Postmodernism has been a convenient philosophical whipping boy for recent attacks on factuality and notions of objective truth, whether emanating from the Right or the Left. Jean-Francois Lyotard, the first to elaborate postmodernism as an epistemological framework, defined it as "incredulity toward grand narratives." [118] Those narratives refer to the big stories that seek to explain large domains of human experience. They might include grand ideas such as "history is a tale of relatively unbroken political, economic, and moral progress" or its right-wing antithesis, "life would be so much better if we could return to the good old days when power was wielded exclusively by white, male, Christians." Lyotard was not necessarily calling for rejecting all grand narratives, especially those with some factual basis. However, facts can be real and simultaneously folded into false narratives that serve the needs of capital, other private interests, religious institutions, and autocratic regimes. Those unnamed agents and vested interests often lurk behind claims of objective truth and the big stories they shore up.

Moreover, we are embedded in the reality we seek to understand objectively, which does not mean that reality would not exist without us. Class, ethnicity, gender, worldview, and group identities are among the many factors that comprise our embeddedness. It is difficult to see that reality without looking through our multiple unconscious interpretive lenses. Competing truth claims and the narratives they support do not mean that all stories are true or that there is no truth. There have certainly been postmodernist thinkers that preceded and followed the work of Lyotard, who went in a more nihilistic and solipsistic direction. But the version of Lyotard's postmodernism outlined here is a surprisingly mainstream notion.

Far from being recondite postmodern theorists, scientists operate from some of the same assumptions. Research methodology is deployed in large measure to control for the many known and unknown types of bias that can distort the results of empirical studies and lead to erroneous conclusions. Every journal article ends with a section on possible alternative explanations for its findings. While that tradition can undoubtedly be a perfunctory, self-serving exercise in knocking down epistemological straw men, it nevertheless exists as an essential practice that provides some brake on the impulse to overstate one's conclusion. However imperfect the efforts to control bias may be, scientists still make truth claims, which only get stronger as other researchers independently develop similar findings. Alternatively, one's exciting "discovery" can be disconfirmed by future research. So, like postmodernism, science can function as a discourse on how bias can impede our efforts to know reality.

Contrary to postmodernism's reductionist adherents and ill-informed critics, the context-dependent nature of truth claims does not translate into a denial of factuality or the repudiation of a real world that exists independent of our sensorium.[119] It is a fatuous leap of logic to argue, as some vulgar postmodernists do, that because powerful social and economic interests profoundly influence the truths we take as given, there is no truth.

In many ways, Trump and his enablers exemplify a kind of sociopathic inversion of postmodernism. Instead of exposing the self-interest behind truth claims, they deny any reality that does not serve their interests. Truth is whatever the leader needs his followers to believe at a given moment. As I argue at various points in this book, the ultimate manifestation of autocratic impunity is the ability to repudiate consensual reality and suffer no consequences. If the post-truth trolls and propagandists of Trumpworld are anything, they are *pre*-modern. Their stance on human rights, their racism, their efforts to revive male domination, and their anti-science policies and actions belong to pre-modernity. Instead of their biases quietly hiding behind some notion of universal truth, Trumpers defiantly and openly insist that whatever serves their interests is true.

Vulgar Postmodernism on the Left

A fundamentalist form of postmodernism seems to hold sway with an influential subset of left social constructionist thinkers. Instead of examining how social power *mediates* what we take as objective truth, those theorists argue that there is no knowable objective truth. In a linguistic reduction of truth, reality is simply a function of how we name and talk about it—discourse *über alles*. That is where some of the most arcane left-wing "high theory" meets the vulgar epistemology of Donald Trump. Neither needs empirical referents; it is enough to assert that "people are saying…" One place that gets expressed quite vividly is in the thinking of those who conflate sex with gender.

Earlier, I outlined some of the problems with that equation. Chief among those is a kind of post-truth denial of biological reality. How quickly that denial entered the larger culture's unexamined vocabulary is astonishing. Take, for example, the term "sex assigned at birth." The well-intentioned desire to create a safe social space for people to live as whatever gender suits them and to be called by their preferred pronouns has devolved into a bizarre attempt to rewrite reality. That phrase implies that the only reality that matters is the name we give to it. From that perspective, the sex of a neonate does not exist before bestowing a label upon it. The anatomy, physiology, and genetics that put an infant on a potential path to playing one of two roles in biological reproduction mean nothing. Driven by the noble wish to be inclusive, some activists have sought to extend the repudiation of reality to a movement aimed at abolishing the epidemiological utility of public records. The goal is for anyone to be able to retroactively alter birth certificates and all other data about biological sex.

Some who argue against the binary notion of biological sex take refuge in the continuum model. They point to the genetically driven variations in sexual morphology or biochemistry, called "disorders of sex development" (DSDs), as an indication that sex is really an infinitely variable rainbow of possibilities.[120] The problem with that account, as one feminist scholar shows in her review of the scientific literature on the topic, is that "A 'continuum' suggests adjacent entities that are only subtly distinguishable from one another, which is not the case here."[121] Significant DSDs, some of which used to be called "intersex," are rare statistical outliers (one in 4,500 to one in five thousand live births).[122] But even those numbers are misleading because relatively minor conditions, like hypospadias (abnormal location of the male urethra) and cryptorchidism (undescended testes), which are more common,[123] are lumped in with much more profound and rare conditions under the rubric of DSDs. Those variations do not support the concept of a sex continuum or justify the notion that applying a label to a female or male infant supersedes their biology.

It is possible to consider the empirical existence of sex *and* critique the misogynist and masculinist projections that mediate our understanding of it. One particularly striking example is the biology and social context of the ovum, the gamete that natal human females carry and, when combined with sperm from natal males, has the potential to create an embryo. If taken to term, a human infant is the result. To my knowledge, nothing about that biological reality can be altered if we call things by different names. That ovum exists independently of how we talk about it. At the same time, we understand it within the social discourse that reflects a history of power relations based on sex—patriarchy. In other words, we "read" that egg through a lens that justifies male domination by deploying a narrative saturated with stereotypes.

In 1991, in the journal *Signs*, feminist anthropologist Emily Martin published a fascinating analysis of the medical discourse concerning sexual reproduction, which she called a "scientific fairy tale."[124] Looking at medical textbooks as value-laden cultural artifacts rather than only objective accounts of reproductive biology, Martin could foreground the sex stereotypes projected onto female and male gametes. One textbook author marveled at how "femininely" eggs behave and how "masculinely" sperm moved about. Eggs never initiated motion but were passively "transported" or "drifted." By contrast, sperm were described as always active. They "burrowed" and "penetrated." The egg demurely waited for Prince Charming sperm to bring her to life.

Once fertilized, the Sleeping Beauty egg woke up. Ignored in this account was that ova, like women themselves, have agency. They grab a sperm and actively absorb it.

Over time, laboratory descriptions of gamete behavior changed along with the culture. Later laboratory observations even described a kind of mutuality, noting that the egg and sperm, as Martin notes, "recognize one another." So, we have compelling evidence, in case it is necessary, that shows how challenging it is to apprehend biological reality without the distorting effect of cultural lenses. Does it mean that eggs and sperm are cultural fictions? No. Does it mean that if we "assigned" natal males to a different category, they would then be able to produce eggs? Of course not. Should a person, regardless of their natal status, be able to embrace whatever identity they wish and live freely and safely with full civil rights? Absolutely. Does that freedom require a post-truth rewriting of epidemiological data? Obviously not.

The Deceit-Industrial Complex

No discussion of post-truth America would be complete without at least mentioning one of the *genuine* and barely disguised conspiracies—the ceaseless and well-funded corporate efforts to manufacture and disseminate lies congenial to profit-taking. As one lobbyist shamelessly acknowledged to the *New York Times*, "Once you have the study, you can point to it to prove your case—even if you paid to have it written."[125]

For the Fox News Channel, lying is foundational to their business model. You would be forgiven for dismissing that assertion as a tendentious and histrionic overstatement. However, that is what the Fox News anchors themselves have admitted. Readers may recall the false claim by the station's hosts and guests that not only was the 2020 presidential election stolen by the Democrats, but the Dominion voting machines played a central role in corruptly and intentionally switching votes from Trump to Biden.

Dominion did not take kindly to that slander and initiated a libel suit against the network. In the lawsuit's discovery phase, internal company emails were obtained in which the hosts acknowledged the fraudulent nature of what was being promoted on air.[126] Fox's star anchor, Tucker Carlson, said of one of the key figures close to Trump who pushed the conspiracy narrative, "Sidney Powell is lying, by the way. I caught her. It's insane."

Nevertheless, Carlson made it clear that were they to tell the truth, the network would lose viewers because the MAGA zealots who comprise most of their audience would move to a station like OAN (One America Network), where their conspiratorial fantasies could be more reliably affirmed. When one Fox reporter, Jacqui Heinrich, fact-checked a tweet from Donald Trump and issued her own tweet revealing that there was no evidence of voter fraud or supporting the accusations made against Dominion, Carlson went into a rage. In a group email, he said, "Please get her fired. It needs to stop immediately. It's measurably hurting the company. The stock price is down. Not a joke."

On air, Carlson worked assiduously to shore up the cult of personality around Trump that his employers helped to create. Privately, he revealed his unmodulated contempt for the former president, declaring, "I hate him passionately."[127] By implication, those sentiments suggest his disgust with and condescension towards the Trump-worshiping credulity of Fox viewers. Even after the disclosure of Carlson's cynical admission that the Big Lie was a fabrication, he could count on his audience to stay within his show's disinformation bubble and have little exposure to fact-based reporting beyond Fox. As a result, very few of his viewers are likely to learn of his con.

Consequently, Carlson produced and shamelessly aired the ultimate rewriting of recent history, a deliberately disingenuous re-edit of the footage of the bloody January 6 MAGA assault on the Capitol.[128] Cop beatings, Confederate flags, "Camp Auschwitz" sweatshirts, defecating rioters, and gallows were left on the cutting room floor. The new, improved version made the events look like a respectful, family-friendly, and peaceful assembly of Christian patriots.

A few errant viewers might wander beyond the right-wing media silo and get exposed to the original insurrection video clips made public during the congressional hearings on the coup attempt. However, their years of voluntary confinement to Fox's information ghetto would likely inoculate them against facts that threaten their identity-affirming beliefs. The revelations that emerged from the Dominion suit make it starkly apparent that feeding the insatiable confirmation bias of the Fox audience is fundamental to the network's economic vitality. That does not mean that propaganda for profit is an enterprise limited to Fox and its mendacious "news" anchors—just that owner Rupert Murdoch has done the most to develop it as a successful business model.

Unfortunately for Fox and Carlson, lies can occasionally result in an unanticipated cost. With the $800 million judgment against the network on behalf of Dominion, Fox's superstar prevaricator quickly went from mercenary money-maker to money-losing dumpster fire and *former* anchor. For the foreseeable future, he will be busking on Twitter's broadcast platform, now rebranded as "X."[129]

The well-established mendacity of Fox hosts and their incessant promotion of political fictions have even been invoked as a legal defense. The partner of Dominic Pezzola, a Proud Boy sentenced to ten years for his role in the January 6 coup attempt, tried to support him and diminish his criminal responsibility by claiming his MAGA zealotry resulted from getting drunk and watching Fox all day.[130] Her effort to blame Pezzola's actions on hooch and Hannity was ultimately unpersuasive. But we may have witnessed the birth of a new defense strategy for future right-wing terrorists: "Your honor, you must consider my client's action in light of the fact that he was DWI—drinking while indoctrinated."

In his encyclopedic and thoroughly documented book *Lies Incorporated*, Ari Rabin-Havt sheds a harsh and revealing light on the global economy's sophisticated and well-funded post-truth sector.[131] That deceit-industrial complex serves as a channel for anonymous donations on the receiving end and a multi-tentacled conduit for big and small lies on the distributive back end. The messages can concern tobacco, industrial chemicals, factory farming, foreign policy, or any other issue concerning the power and profiteering of big corporations. It comprises far more than lobbyists. Among the fake news sources are scientific journal articles ghostwritten by corporate propagandists, systematic trolling operations organized by Russia, Saudi Arabia, Turkey, China, or other countries with a vested interest in shaping Americans' opinions, and right-wing media empires like Fox and Sinclair.

The impact of their efforts on environmental policy is especially malignant. One of the most vital aims of the propagandists for big business is to render the actions of polluters benign and normal. Amoral corporate predators need to externalize the environmental costs of production and dump their industrial waste in the air, water, and forests we share. That means that the rest of us will pay for and clean up their mess. That creates a high demand for the services provided by the well-paid mercenaries of disinformation. After all, it takes a lot of persuasion to convince the public to accept turning the commons and their own bodies into a corporate toilet. Like the chemical excrement released into the environment by industrial polluters, the lies dumped into the public sphere do not appear to be coming from the companies themselves. As their agency is camouflaged, the spin shows up as ambient information. "People are saying…" as the former president is fond of repeating.

The *Citizens United v. FEC* Supreme Court decision consolidated the shift in our country from a weak partial democracy to an undisguised oligarchy of wealth. So, if money is speech, then the only effective opposition to the will of corporate power would be other superrich individuals willing to act contrary to their economic interests. There is little public speech without private wealth. That gives a new meaning to the need to "put your money where your mouth is." The effort of journalists to be good-faith truth-tellers is beset with its own challenges.

The Vital Bias of Factuality and the Fiction of Middle Ground

As journalism professor Jay Rosen has insightfully noted, there are few labels as saturated with ideology as "moderate" and "centrist."[132] Moderate connotes reasonable and reflective of a consensus. Centrist is a statistical metaphor, creating a picture of being positioned in the middle of a distribution. As terms applied to Joe Manchin and Kristen Sinema, they are starkly fictional distortions. Those two politicians were Democratic Party outliers (Sinema is now an "independent" who has announced she will not run for reelection in 2024)—two out of fifty who have blocked and denatured Biden's signature physical and social infrastructure and election integrity bills. They have operated as the GOP's fifth column, preventing the most important Democratic initiatives from being realized and increasing the chances for Republicans to take over the Senate and the White House in the next elections.

As Rosen pointed out, there is an inescapable dilemma for journalists who want to report on the Republican Party. As many have argued, lying is fundamental to the new Trumpian GOP.[133] It is now their default mode of public communication and central to the efforts to achieve and hold power. But here is the paradox: if journalism is about determining and reporting what is true, it cannot be objective and unbiased simultaneously. Factuality is the "bias" of journalism. If one side is lying, then truth-seeking prohibits neutrality. (As a scholar writing this book, I struggle with the same dilemma.) In other words, reporters can no longer argue that the truth lies somewhere between two polarities. In the era of Trump, the "both sides" trope is dead.

Republicans themselves seem far more aware of this paradox than do journalists. Trump and the GOP he leads have been running against "the media" for a long time. As the most determined standard-bearer of factuality, it has risen to the top of the pantheon of right-wing hate objects. Their long campaign against reality-based news has borne fruit. Nicole Hemmer, who interviewed Rosen, cited a Gallup poll from 2021 that showed that while 68 percent of Democrats trust the media, only 11 percent of Republican voters do.[134] The GOP base seems to have complied with Trump's mandate that they not believe what they read, only what they hear from him.[135]

CHAPTER 10

A Tribal *Folie à Deux*—Trump's Psychopathology and Those Who Love Him for It

Narcissus and Echo

In one of the most striking artistic renderings of the ancient myth of Narcissus and Echo, painted by John Waterhouse in 1903, our eyes go immediately to Narcissus, whose gaze is locked onto his reflection in a pool of water. Simultaneously, the lovely and adoring nymph, Echo, has her gaze fixed on him. Sadly, he appears utterly unaware of her presence. The image captures the tragic fate in which each character is imprisoned. Narcissus was cursed by the god Nemesis for a lifetime of arrogance and condemned to fall in love with his own reflection. As no other can receive his passion, he is doomed to isolation. And because he cannot perceive others, he cannot take whatever love they might offer.

Echo, whose exasperating volubility earned the goddess Juno's wrath, was punished by being deprived of the capacity to voice her own thoughts. Juno's curse would mandate that Echo be unable to articulate anything but the words of others. And so, her enchantment with Narcissus is entirely hopeless because he can love only himself. And whatever singular selfhood *she* possesses will be forever trapped inside. Narcissus and Echo are each left to pine away, tragically captivated by an impossible love – he with himself, and she with him.

At the risk of belaboring the obvious, the parallels between this myth and the Trump-base relationship are inescapable. This allegory may not give us new information about the mysterious bond between the president and those who adore him, but it might clarify what we see. There is an unmistakable quality of Greek tragedy to the relationship between Trump and his followers.

He cannot love anything but himself, but even that love leaves him empty and hungering for something he can never possess. Trump attempts to fill that yawning void with admiration, cheers, fawning servility, gushing praise, and high ratings. And yet, none of that sustains him. The delirious adulation available at his rallies and the oleaginous flattery reliably on offer from *Fox and Friends* provides no enduring sustenance. They are the empty calories that can only temporarily feed his narcissism before the inevitable crash and the desperate hunger for more. This frantic addiction to praise and veneration tells us he can neither love nor *receive* love. To do either—to give or take in—requires that others be psychologically real to him. What may look like self-sufficiency to his fans is a state of perpetual starvation. While cossetted by those who serve his well-financed solipsism, he is nevertheless cursed to spend his life in solitary confinement, with others nearby but perpetually out of reach.

On the other hand, his base, especially at rallies, evinces the heartbreakingly hopeless and masochistic love that makes them the Echo to his Narcissus. Unable to summon a voice of their own, they are condemned to utter the slogans and chants Trump feeds them. At rallies, he is a conductor of their inchoate and chaotic emotions. There, Trump evokes, affirms, and channels their hatred, envy, fear, and desperation to merge with a more powerful other, bringing it together into a cacophonous symphony of self-aggrandizement. He tells them who he needs them to be. They leave the rally with a strong, if fabricated, sense of group identity linked to Trump worship, compelling conspiratorial fictions about enemies that must be destroyed, and with their shame momentarily transmuted into a conviction that they will be winners. And he leaves buoyed by the transient satiety of a well-fed vampire.

Unfortunately, his followers must return to their derelict abodes, some still without health insurance or dependent on plans Trump tried to eliminate.[1] And, during the peak of the pandemic, due to the crowded and unmasked rally conditions, they found themselves unwittingly adding to the Trump COVID body count—succumbing to a virus he told them was no big deal.[2] Due to the Trump rally team's lack of care and preparedness, some attendees abruptly woke from their dreams of greatness to find themselves being transported directly to the hospital due to heat stroke or hypothermia.[3] Many of his most ardent fans found their unilateral love repaid with frank expressions of contempt by their revered leader. Veterans are "losers and suckers," and evangelicals are "all hustlers."[4] Like Echo, Trump's followers have kept returning for more, undaunted by their unreciprocated and unrewarded devotion.

The Problem of Diagnosis

Debates have raged in the increasingly politicized world of mental health clinicians about how to name and understand the psychology of Donald

Trump. Is he a narcissistic psychopath, a psychopathic narcissist, or simply a ruthless and evil con man who managed to grift his way into business and the White House? Should categories of mental illness even be applied to someone who has achieved great success in his fields of endeavor—in Trump's case, real estate and politics—and who evinces no apparent signs or symptoms of psychiatric suffering?

Psychoanalyst Steven Reisner has argued against using categories of pathology to explain Trump in favor of the notion of radical evil.[5] Trump isn't delusional but a masterful creator of delusions, what Reisner calls a "reality artist." He does this by shifting all arguments from factuality to feelings, a domain where evidence has no weight and prejudice is everything. Paradoxically, to pathologize Trump is to normalize him. To place him in the familiar realm of disorders and broken brains is to underestimate his extraordinary ruthlessness and how profoundly successful his con-artistry has been.

There is a lot of merit to Reisner's position. Although, as I will argue later, Trump's repudiation of empirical reality serves not just to con others but also, by all appearances, to convince himself that he is not subject to the constraints of the external world. Fortunately for him, his power, privilege, wealth, and psychopathic ruthlessness have helped him recruit or coerce others to make his solipsistic fantasy a reality. His 2020 electoral loss may be the first time his "artistry" has failed him.

There is still the question of what value diagnostic terms of art might have. A label doesn't tell us about the cause of pathology or offer a way to evade moral culpability for the harm one does when afflicted by it—nor does it give anything but a partial account of a person. In this, psychodiagnostic categories share the same limitations as physical diagnoses. But they are also useful in similar ways. Namely, they give us a shared vocabulary to help us talk about a condition and describe what it looks like.

There are those cautious souls who still abide by the "Goldwater Rule," a proscription against clinicians diagnosing politicians and others in public life who haven't been interviewed directly. This mandate was an attempt by the American Psychiatric Association to prevent the reductive and politically motivated pathologizing directed against Barry Goldwater in the 1964 presidential campaign from reoccurring. As it turns out, the rule was an overreaching corrective for an overreaching use of diagnosis. We have a wealth of data on what those in public life do and say in the world, something we clinicians don't have access to with our patients. Although patients behave in specific ways in treatment, we can only speculate how that translates to other settings.

Even though clinicians cannot know Trump through a personal therapeutic relationship, we have seen and heard him on the "psychoanalytic couch" of public life. His slips of the tongue, fantasies, evidence-free paranoid conspiracy theories, projections onto others, and many episodes of impulsive acting out have been visible for all to see. We have watched him openly betray American interests, reveal military secrets, engage in self-dealing and frank corruption, boast about getting away with sexual assault, express undisguised racism in word and deed, betray allies, break treaties, try to hide some crimes while bragging about others, lie compulsively, declare himself an enemy of democracy and an ardent fan of dictators, and announce his own autocratic ambitions. We have also witnessed the many responses he has invoked in others—initial harsh criticism followed eventually by groveling submission by fellow Republicans and unmitigated idolatry among his voter base. His famous talent for getting those under him to abandon any moral constraint when those morals interfere with serving his interests has been notable.

For example, in October 2017, we witnessed the supposed "adult in the room," presidential Chief of Staff General John Kelly, devolve into a more persuasive and articulate but no less mendacious Trumpian mini-me. A Florida congresswoman, Rep. Frederica Wilson, had overheard on speakerphone Trump's callous and thoughtless attempt to console the newly widowed wife of a slain soldier and dared to criticize the president for his stunning lack of emotional intelligence. Leaping to his boss's defense at a press conference, Kelly attacked Wilson's character and fabricated a story about her supposed outrageous behavior at a public event, despite readily available news footage showing Kelly's assertion to be an elaborate lie.[6]

In exile from Trumpworld, Kelly has joined the ranks of former sycophants and occasionally offers pointed criticism of his former boss. He is now one of the go-to MAGA apostates for journalists covering Trump's ongoing outrages.[7] There is nothing unique about him. As we have seen, he is part of a long line of aides and fixers whose efforts to please their leader have led to their own corruption, criminality, and in some cases, jail. While it may change in light of current indictments, the former president has largely evaded accountability for the corrupt acts committed in his name. Trump has shown a remarkable capacity to induce others to act as amoral agents of his ruthlessness, sadism, criminal ambitions, and petty retaliations (a theme I will return to later). It would not be an exaggeration to describe him as a "super-spreader" of corruption.[8]

Assessing Trump's psychology requires little speculation as we have a lifelong history of personal, romantic, business, and political relationships. As I described, much of his predatory, criminal, and corrupt behavior has unfolded in public. We know what he says and how he says it. Through his own words, Trump has even let us in on what provokes him to act—primarily vengeance, vainglory, envy, lust, greed, and an obsession with domination. It has been on this public stage, not behind closed doors, where we have witnessed him reward anyone who flatters him, withdraw that reward the moment fawning idolatry flagged (as happened with Chris Christie), and punish those who fail to do so. Before being temporarily banned from Twitter/X and shifting to his oxymoronically titled Truth Social, his daily tweet tantrums constituted a kind of ongoing characterological EEG reading, as if the vicissitudes of his personality disorder produced brain waves that could be converted into text form readable by all.

For an intimate portrait of the transgenerational transmission of sociopathy in the family of Donald Trump, one could not find a more compelling account than that of his psychologist niece, Mary Trump.[9] As a witness to and victim of the Trump brood, she deployed her clinical training to bring the family's pathology into sharp relief. While Dr. Trump's conclusions are congruent with my analysis here, I've decided not to refer to the details of her important work. Instead, I want to ground my analysis of the Trump-base relationship on the public record of readily observable behavior, data that is available to all. The reader can then judge how much the facts justify my interpretations.

To discuss and explore his apparent psychopathology—a malignant narcissism and psychopathy that has threatened us all—is not to adopt the Soviet-style use of psychiatric diagnosis in the service of political repression. Instead, it is a heuristic exercise that helps us name and understand his appeal to a significant plurality of Americans. Trump's pathology is isomorphic with his brand and the key to his political success. What may look to some of us as signs and symptoms of profound impairment make him the object of near deification on the part of his base. As he well understands, to them, he can do no wrong. Or, instead, every wrong he commits is righteous.

Does Trump Suffer?

Like Steven Reisner, Allen Frances, a former editor of the DSM, argues against the tendency of some inside and outside the mental health field to apply diagnostic labels to understand Trump.[10] He insists that because Trump's personality traits do not seem to bring him suffering and have made him quite successful, this militates against evaluating him through a psychopathological lens.

It is undoubtedly true that not all narcissists or sociopaths suffer. Many, if not most, are well-positioned for success in sadomasochistic corporate or political hierarchies. For them, the term *disorder* would certainly not apply. Evil would indeed be the correct appellation. Of course, those who seek treatment are, by definition, in some form of psychic pain. But even *they* don't show up complaining about a "personality disorder," regardless of whether it might be an upstream cause of their symptoms.

Trump, in some ways, is more confounding. There is no way to know whether or how, as a characterological narcissist/psychopath, he suffers. However, judging from his readily observable behavior, his sense of adequacy in the eyes of others and his control over them seems to be profoundly brittle. Trump may have been the most powerful person in the world. Still, he was ceaselessly paranoid about betrayal because he knew he couldn't command others' loyalty without some form of extortion. This nagging fear seems like a projection of his modus operandi—to betray others whenever convenient.

Trump's constant preoccupation with polls, ratings, and his status on the *Forbes* list of the super wealthy suggests pervasive anxiety over not staying on top. His narcissism requires continuous infusions of admiration because he can never really assuage his self-doubt. He evinces no sense of humor, let alone a capacity to laugh at himself. And Trump has good reason to worry about the low esteem in which others hold him. After all, he is profoundly unpopular and always has been since he won with only a minority of the vote. And in 2020, Trump lost the popular vote by a much larger margin than in 2016. He might like to pretend that polls are "fake news" but knows that he's never had even 50 percent approval. In the lead-up to his second impeachment trial, most Americans wanted him impeached and convicted.[11] What's the worst insult he thinks he can deliver? It is that his critics are unpopular losers with low ratings. While he sat on top of the world for four years in the White House, his perch turned out to have been a precarious one. After Biden's election triumph, Trump has become what he's feared the most, a big loser.

So, it is not that "successful" narcissists like Trump do not suffer distress. Instead, it is that their psychic pain is hidden behind the central preoccupations that mark their character: a ceaseless obsession with zero-sum status competition and a desperate Sisyphean pursuit of admiration that is never satisfied. There is also an unrelenting series of vendettas against those questioning his greatness. Like most narcissists, Trump would never seek treatment for his character—not because he doesn't suffer, but because he works hard to locate that suffering in the failures of others to affirm his most grandiose self-image.

As we have all witnessed, Trump is wealthy and privileged enough to get others to accommodate his pathology rather than challenge it. A December 2017 *New York Times* profile of Trump, drawn from sixty sources, advisors, aides, and political allies, fills in the details of a picture many can see from a distance: a petulant, brittle, and impulsive baby-man, a feckless king who must be managed by a large team of courtiers and sycophants whose main task is to protect him from his own actions.[12] Functioning as a funhouse mirror in reverse, they render his deficits and dysfunctions admirable virtues. For example, to counter the accusation that Trump is a perpetrator of fake news and a relentless fount of confabulation and conspiracy peddling, those who serve him affirm the notion that he is instead the long-suffering victim of and noble crusader against the "fake media" and lies of liberals. His loyal coterie of buffers and fluffers seems to operate as an auxiliary component of his personality disorder, ensuring that his impulses and actions remain free of regret or internal conflict and that his sense of self-importance remains perpetually inflated.

Trump's Defenses against Shame

I described the twin faces of right-wing mortification, shame, and shameless-ness in chapter 2. Those emotions can be powerful drivers of conservative policy and behavior. While they may, at first glance, appear as opposites, shameless-ness often functions as a defense against shame. That dynamic has been most discernible in the conduct of Donald Trump. At times, he presents as the par-adigmatic thin-skinned narcissist who evinces a desperate longing for approval and a famous inability to tolerate jokes about himself. He is readily wounded if the admiration he craves is not forthcoming. Any apparent criticism readily reveals an underlying well of shame.

But his defenses against that get quickly activated, like white blood cells rushing to the site of an injury. Trump retaliates with counter-shame and attempts to humiliate his perceived critics or those who threaten his ambitions. Inflamed with the determination not to be a "loser," he wards off collapse by puffing himself up. In defiance of those he fears would belittle him, he and all things Trump must be the biggest.

One manifestation of his shamelessness is moving through life holding a posture of unlimited entitlement. That which he covets—women, bank loans, votes, or political power—are his by virtue of wanting them. He claims the right to attack and use others and to violate any law that impedes the pursuit of his self-interest. That entitlement goes on full display whenever others, such as law enforcement agents or the court system, try to hold him accountable for his crimes. In other words, certain conditions lead him to shift from a thin-skinned to thick-skinned mode of narcissism.

One of Trump's major strengths as a cult leader is his success at invit-ing followers to share his experience of humiliating victimization and his determination to avenge it. The lines in his rally speeches that engender the most resounding applause are those that vow retaliation against tribal ene-mies through counter-humiliation and performative shamelessness. Living in a mental world of zero-sum power, their crusade is to make *them*—liberals, feminists, scientists, immigrants, and the entire rogues' gallery of MAGA villains—the losers.

From Personality Disorder to Brand to Political Regime

One of the noteworthy features of Trump's personality is how it has come to saturate and even define his brand as a businessman and later as a politician. As Naomi Klein pointed out in her 2017 book, the essence of the Trump brand is not simply wealth and power but *impunity*, which that wealth and power have bought him.[13]

"Sovereignty" is a quality asserted by various kings (the sovereigns) throughout the ages. It is an aristocratic declaration of impunity, essentially a claim to operate outside the moral order that others must abide by. We could think of it as the historical precursor to modern autocracy—an assertion that one is literally above the law. That has been such a discernible assumption behind Trump's conduct that a judge had to say in response to one of the former president's fatuous claims of executive privilege in the January 6 investigation, "Presidents are not kings."[14]

In many ways, impunity has been the essential quality signified by his political brand—the fantasy of being able to "do anything," as he bragged in the infamous *Access Hollywood* tape. Trumpian impunity has been manifest in many big and small ways; an entire catalog would require its own book. Nevertheless, I can highlight some of the more striking examples.

During the 2016 campaign, Trump expressed the now-infamous murderous vision of his moral, if not legal, indemnity when he said he could "stand in the middle of Fifth Avenue and shoot somebody" and "not lose voters."[15] That has become the go-to quote for all journalists trying to convey the impunity Trump enjoys. Ironically, this hypothetical rhetorical evocation of the president's insulation from consequences was superseded by many orders of magnitude in the pandemic. As hyperbolic as the Fifth Avenue murder fantasy may have seemed, reality has long overtaken it.

Trump's indifference toward and egregious mishandling of the pandemic led to thousands of unnecessary deaths. COVID denial, mask refusal, and vaccine resistance all became ways to signal MAGA tribal identity and loyalty to Trump. In addition, he has also been the architect of multiple super-spreader events, both before and after his own infection.[16] They led to the sickening and killing of many of his most ardent followers. He made it abundantly clear that he was perfectly willing to kill his admirers, and they made it quite apparent they were ready to die for him.

Even those in his immediate circle of advisors were not spared the consequences of the former president's indifference to their well-being. Days after knowing he was infected, he failed to disclose his positive test results to those around him, putting Chris Christie into intensive care within days after helping Trump with debate prep.[17]

Thanks to the former president and his messengers on Fox News, the tribalization of public health measures led to a dramatic and disproportionate increase in COVID morbidity and mortality in pro-Trump American counties.[18] Judging from the Republican voter turnout for the 2020 election, the carnage Trump presided over did nothing to diminish his supporters' enthusiasm. He got the second-largest number of votes in American history and nearly eleven million more in 2020 than in 2016 (even though, as I noted earlier, he lost by a larger margin.)[19]

Unlike people without his resources, impunity for Trump has not been a mere fantasy. While entitlement to evade all consequences seems deeply *felt* by Trump, it has also been realized in the external world. Naomi Klein detailed how his administration functioned as a brazen kleptocracy and a largely unconstrained one. And, of course, since her book, we have all witnessed the Republican Party and its voters refuse to hold him accountable for the numerous and flagrant episodes of criminality, impeachable offenses, and corruption committed in plain sight and without apology. Until 2023, that was also true of the legal system.

Trump transformed a personality disorder into a brand and, once in the White House, into a form of rule—an entire administration devoted to psychopathic self-dealing and operating through autocratic fiat. Now, that has been extended to the entire Republican Party, whose 2020 candidates ran not just against their Democratic opponents, but against democracy itself. As of this writing, the GOP attempts at voter suppression, and their multiple efforts to countermand voters' will through cynical and baseless accusations of fraud continue unimpeded in red states.

The fact that he and his family have enriched themselves by outsourcing their products and real estate development projects to manufacturers and builders that use sweatshops and slave labor in foreign countries[20] has not stopped him from depicting himself to his supporters as an America-Firster and a working-class hero.

As the entire country witnessed, Trump has shown obsequious deference to Putin, openly invited him to hack American elections, and worked assiduously to achieve Russian foreign policy aims, such as weakening NATO. Yet this has not impeded his ability to portray himself to his base as an uber-patriot. In 2020, Republican voters across the country flew their Trump banners alongside the American flag (and, in more than a few instances, the Confederate flag) as if there were no incongruity or contradiction in such displays.

His life of salacious debauchery, greed, and marital infidelity has not diminished the ecstatic enthusiasm with which the Christian Right greets him. In Trump's case, these good Christians do not merely defer to Caesar; they worship him. Some evangelical leaders compared him to Churchill, arguing that Trump "may be profane but ordained."[21]

The mantle of God's imperfect vessel was passed to former Alabama judge Roy Moore during his 2017 Senatorial race. He, like Trump, faced numerous sexual assault allegations. (In Moore's case, some involved underage girls.) And like Trump, Moore denied everything and attacked his accusers. As with many Trump clones on the Right, the Moore scandal illustrates how impunity, at least among pious Republicans, is conferred upon those who disclaim any accountability for their actions. While Moore lost the Senate race against Doug Jones, it was by a narrow margin. And, he enjoyed the enthusiastic support from the president, who made robocalls on Moore's behalf. The Republican National Committee, the executive arm of the "family values" party, resolved their earlier ambivalence about backing an accused pedophile and gave him a full-throated endorsement before the election.

In Trump's case, his Teflon exoskeleton is even slipperier than the one attributed to Ronald Reagan. The Trump "T" emblazoned across the top of his buildings could just as easily stand for Teflon. He is the spokesmodel for impunity—impunity for accusations of sexual assault and for admitting it, for stiffing contractors, for wage theft, for providing investment safe havens to laundered Russian mob money, for proudly embracing murderous autocrats around the world, for alternately inviting and denying Putin's corruption of our elections, and for facilitating the deaths of hundreds of thousands of Americans in a pandemic.[22]

A judge Trump appointed, Aileen M. Cannon, worked hard to repay the favor and, she seemed to be hoping, ensure her advancement as a potential MAGA Supreme Court nominee should a future Republican occupy the White House. She issued a much-criticized decision to block the Department of Justice from investigating his illegal retention and misuse of highly classified documents after leaving office.[23] A higher court vigorously rebuffed her efforts, but she is now the presiding judge as that case goes to trial.

Also, at least among his supporters, Trump evinces impunity for praising the virtues of Nazis and white supremacists, for blaming Puerto Rican hurricane victims for their suffering, and mocking their plight with Marie Antoinette–like "gifts" of paper towels tossed into a crowd desperate for an adequate government response, for exalting sadism and belligerence into noble virtues, and for compulsively and ceaselessly lying about both trivial and profound matters.[24] In some ways, the latter, the normalization and acceptance of his lying—his "reality artistry"—may be the most impactful and defining aspect of impunity in the present era.

By 2024, Trump's impunity moved well beyond a psychological stance, a political tactic, a business model, and a means to bypass any ethical accountability for the harm he has caused. It also became a central legal maneuver to defend himself against charges he conspired with others to overthrow the 2020 election and end American democracy in a coup. "Absolute immunity" is the term of art his lawyers offered up in their efforts to get the Supreme Court to protect him from prosecution for any crimes he committed while in office.[25] It echoed the claims of a previous crook who held the nation's highest office, Richard Nixon, when he said, "Well, when the president does it, that means that it is not illegal."[26] Notably, the Trumpian defense is not a denial of the charges but simply an assertion that he can't be held to account for anything he does. Whether the Supreme Court will grant Trump the impunity he feels entitled to won't be known until after this book goes to press. But even if they rule against him and he is convicted, a future Republican president may still pardon him. That was the promise made by Ron DeSantis before he dropped out of the 2024 primary race, along with Nikki Haley, the GOP candidate who ran second to Trump.[27]

"How Many Fingers, Winston?"

In the reign of Trump, we have witnessed the emergence of a paradoxical species of disinformation, the open cover-up. It is a lie about something we can all see. It attacks our capacity to know what is true and apprehend reality outside the regime's assertions. It can be about trivial matters, such as inaugural crowd sizes. It can also involve more substantive concerns, such as Don Jr.'s well-published glee over getting the dirt on Hillary Clinton from Putin surrogates, the fact that he lost the 2020 election, or the lethality of the COVID-19 pandemic.[28]

"Orwellian" is an appellation easily thrown around these days. But in the current moment, the descriptor seems especially apt. In one famous scene in *1984*, O'Brien, the interrogator, confronts the prisoner, Winston, insisting, "Whatever the Party holds to be the truth, is truth. It is impossible to see reality except by looking through the eyes of the Party." What follows is the nightmare exchange burned into our memories in which O'Brien holds up four fingers and insists, under the threat of escalating torture, that Winston must not only say that he sees five fingers but *believe* he does. We are now in a world where actual and aspiring autocrats demand obedience *and* hysterical blindness. Fortunately for Trump, he had an eager team of well-paid liars—Sean Spicer, Kellyanne Conway, Sarah Huckabee Sanders, and Kayleigh McEnany. They worked in concert with the Fox News rogues' gallery of fantasists to share the labor of rewriting reality.

Amazingly, in an episode that Orwell himself could have scripted, Trump even tried to assert, once elected, that the *Access Hollywood* tape mentioned previously, in which he gloated over his unique ability to get away with sexual assault, was fake.[29] That was despite his prior videotaped campaign admission and perfunctory apology.

An event in which Trump's attempt to rewrite reality took a literal form was the infamous Sharpie-modified map of Hurricane Dorian's path. Trump had tweeted that Alabama was precariously in the way of Dorian. However, this did not fit with the National Weather Service map of the hurricane's predicted trajectory. As it turned, Dorian did not strike Alabama, just as the Weather Service map anticipated but contrary to the president's tweet. Because being shown to err is a slippery slope to abject humiliation for him, Trump felt compelled to crudely and unpersuasively doctor the map with a Sharpie pen.[30] His narcissism is so exquisitely fragile that even being seen to get a weather forecast wrong was unbearable and required a disavowal of reality.

And we should not forget one of the biggest Trump lies that our eyes and ears could readily disconfirm. During the hearings for his first impeachment trial, the transcripts constituted the central unambiguous piece of evidence proving his attempt to extort political help from the president of Ukraine, Volodymyr Zelenskyy, by threatening to withhold vital military aid. And yet, to the astonishment of much of the non-MAGA segment of the population, that was precisely the document Trump and his team pointed to as exonerating evidence.[31]

Trumpian Corruption as Costly Signaling

As journalist Masha Gessen has pointed out, Donald Trump's corruption has not been duplicitous; it has been, to put it a bit oxymoronically, *transparent* corruption.[32] There are two critical things to say about this. One, it reveals his sense of entitlement to use public office to enrich himself and his confidence that he will continue to enjoy impunity for that. And two, the transparency of his corruption makes his actions a communication to others. By not hiding it and being frank about his right to do it, he essentially says to his base, "I am special, omnipotent, and deserve whatever I can gather to myself—wealth, power, and admiration. Moreover, liberals hate me for my special powers. And they hate you because you love me. I'm happy to endure their rage and persecution, which shows my loyalty to you."

In other words, Trump's openly corrupt practices in and out of office, his defiance of presidential norms, his willingness to insult and disrespect formerly honored individuals and agencies, his willingness to betray the country to enrich himself, his well-publicized acts of sexual predation, and his proud impunity in the face of all these actions could be viewed as the ultimate expressions of costly signaling. Because most non-Republicans have reviled him and seen him as a sadistic and remorseless psychopath and so dangerous to the country that he was impeached twice and criminally indicted four times, his bond with his base was strengthened with each charge. "Trigger the libs" has been the battle cry of the MAGA cult. That is negative partisanship at its most passionate. The more he is hated, attacked, and denounced, the more his followers adore him. In word and image, the Right has rendered him the crucified Christ of conservatism; thus, he is worshipped all the more fervently.

The now-famous mug shot taken following the Georgia indictment became the GOP's new crucifix. Emblazoned on T-shirts and coffee mugs, it became the hottest piece of MAGA merch.[33] His clearly well-rehearsed pose was supposed to signify defiance in the face of unjust persecution—unjust not because he didn't try to steal votes and overturn the Georgia election. He never denied that. But because he was *entitled* to do so. And Trump's claim to be his base's savior in all of this was not a subtle one. "I'm being indicted for you," he insisted.[34]

Just as Trump's open racism, affection for Nazis, willingness to kill Americans due to his COVID policies and rhetoric, and incitement to violence operated as costly signals to his base, so did his open corruption. The fact that this has led to indictments, trials, and at least the *threat* of prison time, is so much the better. It makes the signals costlier, consolidating the base's loyalty even further. During the period of the Republican primary race, his poll lead went up after each indictment.[35] Twenty percent of those who thought he committed crimes insisted they would still vote for him.[36]

As psychologist Joshua Green has noted, such behavior can function as the political equivalent of a prison gang tattoo.[37] Inking a swastika on your neck is not generally a reliable way to make friends—unless the friends you want to make are members of the White Aryan Resistance. The fact that non-white prisoners might hate you for it makes it an even better signal because it costs you the alienation of other tribes.

Everyone outside of the MAGA-verse wanting Trump tried and convicted for multiple crimes has only increased the adoration of those inside it. Consistent with this hypothesis is that those who voted for Trump in 2020 far exceeded his popular vote count in 2016.

Republican state legislatures around the country also exemplify costly signaling. The GOP realizes that they will likely lose every election unless they destroy what remains of majoritarian electoral processes. Their only hope for gaining and holding onto power is to cripple and nullify votes by Democrats. Those outside the Republican Party might decry the destruction of America's democratic traditions, making it an even more effective costly signal.

MAGA Post-Truth and the War against Factuality

There is a critical prehistory to the former administration's attack on the possibility of consensual reality. For many decades, right-wing pundits and politicians have not only lied whenever it suited their purposes but elevated lying itself to an admirable sign of Machiavellian mastery. Readers of a certain age may recall author Ron Suskind's interview with a senior presidential advisor employed by the George W. Bush administration who derided journalists as anachronistic members of the "reality-based community."[38] He insisted reporters only necessary function was to be stenographers of those in power—the movers and shakers whose stories were the only ones worth telling. That was the soil from which a thousand "alternative facts" would later bloom. There is no greater impunity than the ability to repudiate reality and suffer no consequences for that repudiation. However, there may yet be consequences. The crimes featured in Trump's first set of indictments brought forth by a grand jury under the supervision of Manhattan district attorney Alvin Bragg were all thirty-four incidents of lying[39]—each charge being a separate falsification of business records in the service of other crimes.

Trump has arrived at this post-truth moment in history bundled with the perfect psychopathological software to take nearly half the country through the looking glass with little resistance or protest from his party. For three weeks after Biden won, the former president elicited the collaboration or permissive silence of the entire GOP in his denial of the 2020 election results. And many helped to fund his mercenary legal teams across the country to push the voter fraud fiction and bogus legal narratives designed to overturn the results. Within two weeks after the election, and without a shred of evidence, 77 percent of Trump voters believed that Biden's victory was due to fraud.[40] While the Supreme Court unanimously rejected GOP efforts to throw out the votes in swing states, 126 Republican members of Congress signed on to this attempted judicial coup.[41]

Beyond his desire to retain power, Trump wanted to stop the 2020 vote count initially, and later overturn the results, for the same reason he wanted to stop the COVID case count and the testing that could enable it—to repudiate any marker that suggests that there is a reality outside of his own mind. All forms of objective measurement must be denigrated because they imply that he is not the measure of all things.

Statistics, biology, chemistry, physics, grammar, syntax, laws, contracts, traditions, journalism, daily presidential briefings, other selves, and even recordings of his own words must be ignored or disavowed as they suggest that the universe the rest of us occupy is not of his own making. And in his zero-sum world, failing to do so would make him a loser—a fate equivalent to annihilation.

As Trump administration policy and practice affirmed, pro-science is anti-Trump and, by extension, anti-Republican. His anti-science moves are legion—the firings of government experts and replacements with unqualified toadies, the executive orders to abolish science-based regulations, and the overall indifference to evidence as the basis for any policy.[42] These efforts by Trump and his appointees reinforce the half-serious maxim that facts have a liberal bias. John Matze, CEO and co-founder of the right-wing social media site Parler, which sought to replace Twitter/X, said, "Once you start ... fact-checking, you're introducing bias."[43] Even before Trump, public school teachers and textbook publishers had become timid about covering accepted scientific concepts like evolution and anthropogenic climate change.[44] Paradoxically, the assertion of objective truth had come to be viewed as an expression of political bias; and risked catalyzing the organized wrath of fundamentalist parents and advocacy groups.

In this light, we can even see Trump's consistent but random misspellings and garbled syntax, not just in tweets but also in official written White House statements, as expressions of his impunity and narcissism. The unspoken subtext seemed to be: if the president typed it, it was so. As with everything else, he made up his own rules of grammar and punctuation. The guidelines that might constrain others did not apply to him. There was no authority outside or above Trump's own inclinations. The "errors" in his writing, like the ubiquitous lies in his speeches and the crimes that have marked his life, evidence his domination over all of reality.

It is not as if the White House did not have access to proofreaders. The unspoken mandate seemed to be that there could be no limitation on the president's caprice, grammatical or otherwise. That is because correcting anything he did would result in firing. In other words, what he did was the standard because *he* did it. In grammar, as in every other aspect of his world, the rule of law is superseded by the law of the ruler.

Perhaps some of his staff were as worshipful as his base, believing that the Trumpian "mistakes" were marks of his special power and privilege. As one worshipful MAGA rally attendee insisted, Trump's tweets did not contain errors but profound, though coded, communications requiring painstaking Talmudic divination to discern their deep meaning. "The truth is right there in what the media think are his mistakes. He doesn't make mistakes," noted the superfan. To emphasize the point, the Trump follower pointed out the message embossed on one of the more popular articles of MAGA swag, a T-shirt that read: "Trump's. Tweets. Matter."[45]

While impunity for crimes against grammar and syntax may seem like an issue too laughably trivial to bother commenting on, the same dynamic operated in far more grave matters, like national intelligence. During Trump's presidency, we all observed his fondness for saber-rattling, his putative love of weapons and warriors, and a tendency to threaten his enemy of the moment with exterminationist martial rhetoric. Consequently, his attacks on America's intelligence services may have seemed counter-intuitive. However, it's not really surprising in light of the preceding.

Many would and should take issue with the malevolent policy aims and methods that sometimes drive intelligence gathering, whether by the FBI in domestic matters or the CIA in international affairs, such as supporting despotic allies, suppressing dissent at home and abroad, using torture, and pursuing wars of conquest. Nevertheless, at its best, intelligence is about data—facts that exist independently of any leader's policy goal, lust for power, or corrupt ambition (although facts certainly can be deployed to serve those malign ends). For this data to be weighed as evidence requires experts' discerning and well-informed interpretive capacities. That is fundamentally incompatible with the imperial whims of a single, unaccountable mind that imagines itself as the sovereign arbiter of reality—in other words, Trump's brain.

Given this, we should not be surprised to hear the former president's solipsistic defense against impending charges of stealing, hiding, and sharing classified documents upon leaving the White House. They were not classified because he had declassified them in his mind.[46]

The Base Behind the Man: The Psychology of Trump's Echo

Trump, who believes in nothing and will say anything, has been matched by followers who know little and believe anything. Authoritarian political tribalism is not simply about one person's character but the *relationship* between the leader and those who blindly follow him and the bond among the followers. So, in the case of Trump, we must ask what has made his solipsism, which has no room for the selfhood of others, so appealing to the MAGA base, which hasn't gone away since its leader left office. Here is one answer from James Hamblin in a piece he wrote for *The Atlantic* in 2020:

> This process, in extreme forms, leads to what some psychologists refer to as identity fusion. William Swann, a professor at the University of Texas at Austin, coined the term in 2009 while studying theories of individual identity. Once fused with a group or leader, he noticed that followers seemed tied to them, so things were true *because* the leader said them. Dystopian as that may seem, it can be a coping mechanism: Orienting your sense of truth around a person can be more comforting than doing so around a nebulous,

uncertain, or otherwise threatening reality. Fusion is not appealing because
it makes sense; **it is appealing because it alleviates the cognitive and emotional burden of thinking.**[47] [Emphasis added]

Hamblin attempts to explain Trump's enduring appeal to 74 million followers, even after his disastrous and incompetent response to the pandemic, by
looking at medical quackery's history and psychological dynamics. He looks
at Trump's progenitors in con artistry who purveyed their dubious wares long
before the president's own prescription for injectable bleach. The reader's unexpected conclusion from that account is that the psychological succor provided
by Trump's lies far outweighs the physical suffering resulting from believing
them. His conviction that no truth exists outside his own mind turns out to
be a reassuring delusion to those who find relief in no longer having to think
for themselves. The Trump base's credulity follows the structure of religious
faith—belief in the prophet's words despite all evidence to the contrary. As
I've noted, his evangelical fans often depict him as a Christ-like figure who
offers salvation to his flock if only they suspend all doubt or any other form of
cognitive autonomy.

That brings to mind the neuroscience research described in chapter 1 that
shows that conservativism is a mental path of least resistance.[48] The black-and-
white thinking that characterizes the right-wing cognitive style—not *what*
they think but *how* they think—has the advantage of being far less mentally
and emotionally demanding. It is a conservative mode of cognition, not just
in an ideological sense but also in the sense that it involves conserving mental
resources. One group of neuroscientists found that individuals who have suffered a traumatic brain injury resulting in damage to the prefrontal cortex were
more likely to adopt fundamentalist religious views due to impaired cognitive
flexibility.[49] Trumpian fundamentalism is an even more "efficient" use of one's
mind—the ultimate conservative framework. Everything can be reduced to a
binary: Trump thought or non-Trump thought. One doesn't have to wrestle
with the contradictions between what he said yesterday and tweeted today.
Trump thought is not what he is *recorded* as saying. It is what he is *currently*
saying he said. Any assertion to the contrary is fake news, even if supported by
a video or audio recording.

Trump and his enablers take advantage of a bioevolutionary predisposition in people to accept truth claims from their leaders and peers because it is
far less cognitively demanding than skepticism.[50] It requires a lot of time and
energy to constantly be looking for and evaluating evidence for the assertions
of others. In other words, disbelief comes at a considerable energetic cost. The
upside of our tendency toward credulity is that it facilitates quick and smooth

decision making. The obvious downside is that it can lead to decisions based on faulty data.

Few in the MAGA-sphere have expressed their fusion with the leader more unabashedly than Mellissa Carone, a costar in Rudy Giuliani's 2020 election denial roadshow. Following a brief stint as a Detroit election worker, which came on the heels of completing probation for the cyber-harassment of a boyfriend's ex-wife, she was recruited for Giuliani's quixotic campaign to overturn the election.

This spokesmodel for Trumpian post-factuality went beyond promoting the big lie of Biden's "fraudulent" victory but also shared her wisdom on the pandemic and the public health measures required to staunch it.[51] Carone was unperturbed at learning that she, unmasked, had sat close to an infected and unmasked Giuliani. "I would take it [the virus] seriously if it came from Trump because Trump cares about American lives." She acknowledged that a few Trump-aligned "news" sources would also get her attention. If OAN or Newsmax "told me to go get tested, I would do it."

Trauma Bonding to the Trump Cult

I have somewhat glibly referred to Trumpworld as a cult in various parts of this book. But the question deserves more serious consideration. Because if it is, the MAGA movement may be more enduring, malignant, and refractory to challenges than we might realize. If Trump is a cult leader, it is not because of the content of his ideas or positions (to the extent he has any). As with all leaders, the determination would be based on the nature of his relationship with his followers. When we look closely at that, it becomes evident that classic cultic dynamics are at play. His followers embrace every capricious change in his policies, claims, and proposals. They mock those he humiliates and applaud the objects of his fleeting and transactional praise. Trump's abrupt reversals or inversions of readily observable reality mean little. His base is like an exceedingly obedient dog trained to heel by their human's side regardless of the random pattern of the master's movement. It is not the destination that matters. Maintaining proximity to the holder of the leash is the only concern.

In cults, the leader-follower relationship echoes some aspects of the "get'em sick, get'em well" strategy seen in so much advertising. Many commercials begin with ominous music and a threatening message that generates anxiety about a troubling condition—body odor, obesity, disease, or unattractiveness. Then, as the music swells with uplift and hope, the cure is offered, which, of course, is the product. Cult leaders employ an analogous approach. They generate a sense of threat by conjuring an outside danger or by *being* a threat. Then, the leader insists he or she is the only one who can keep members safe. As the leader is both the source of fear and the protector against it, it generates what social psychologist and cult researcher Alexandra Stein[52] and others[53] have called a "trauma bond." Such a relationship resembles what child psychiatrist and psychoanalyst John Bowlby referred to as "disorganized attachment."[54] Fear and love become inextricably linked. Dependency is fused with terror. That concept has been applied to the dynamics of child abuse, domestic violence, sex trafficking, abductor-hostage bonds, and cultic relationships.

Various types of perpetrators share an intuitive understanding of and ability to exploit a core feature of our evolutionary nature—the predisposition to form powerful bonds with our early caregivers and seek close proximity to them. Our survival depends on that instinct, which we share with many other species, along with the corresponding drive of our caregivers to keep us close. Parent-child relationships are, in some ways, the templates upon which we build other kinds of attachments, like the tribal bonds discussed in this book. When frightened, children, and later adults, turn to their attachment figures for reassurance, comfort, and protection.

And here is the remarkable counterintuitive finding that researchers have noted: a proximity-seeking, comfort-craving response is even elicited when those to whom people are attached and on whom they are dependent are the *source* of the threat. In those situations, the frightened child or adult seeks a haven in the very person who is generating a sense of danger. That tortuous paradox and double bind can lead to dissociation—a kind of fragmentation of the self. This disintegration can significantly impair the ability to think, especially to link one thing with another.

As Stein describes this process on a brain level, sensory and emotional experiences become divorced from our capacity to reflect and verbalize. We are thus unable to understand or name what we feel. We cannot identify the attachment figure as the source of danger and what it would take to be genuinely safe, which would be to leave the relationship. Instead, we cling to it. That mental fragmentation is one reason attachment to such relationships is described as disorganized. The ultimate consequence is a kind of paralysis. It is not hard to see how such individuals, unable to think or exercise their own agency, would make ideal cult members eager to do the leader's bidding.

In discussing her research, Stein hastens to point out that people who get caught up in cults are not necessarily those with preexisting authoritarian personalities or histories of disordered attachment. In some ways, if cult membership was limited to those with unique vulnerabilities, it might be reassuring to those of us with relatively attuned, loving, and empathic parents who emerged from childhood capable of forming largely secure attachments. It would be relieving to think a healthy upbringing rendered us immune to the seductions of a totalitarian cult. Unfortunately, as Stein is quick to point out, such a history provides no guarantee against being captivated by charismatic, coercive, and authoritarian sociopaths. In cultic situations, anyone can develop a trauma bond with malign leaders and groups, which may exert a near-irresistible gravitational pull. In other words, the attachment style of our early life is not immutable. It can be modified as the social context of our lives changes. In that malleability lies the peril for those drawn to cults *and* the hope for those seeking to get out of them.

Like other cult leaders, Trump begins cultivating trauma bonds with his followers by conjuring multiple terrors. He tells them, in essence, immigrant murderers and rapists are out to get you, drag queens are grooming your children, non-white people want to replace you, and liberals want to leave you unarmed and defenseless. If you don't want to be a casualty of the coming "American carnage," Trump warned in his inaugural address,[55] you had better follow his lead. Only he can save you. But as someone known to hold a grudge for decades, Trump will also come after you without mercy. He lets his followers know he can be their savior *and* vengeful persecutor.

As leader, Trump knows better than the generals, the so-called experts, and public health authorities. When he instructs you to inject bleach for COVID, it is unimpeachable medical wisdom. His directives are the only reliable compass. "Don't believe what you're seeing, and what you're reading is not what's happening," he exhorted his followers.[56] Thinking for yourself will only get you killed. Those who criticize or challenge him are threats that must be vanquished by any means necessary.

In the DC appeals court hearing on Trump's claim of "absolute immunity" for crimes committed as president, his lawyers argued that he could legally order the assassination of his political opponents, providing he hadn't already been impeached and convicted in the Senate for it.[57] We would be justified in reading this as not only an absurd defense of his prior criminal actions but a threat against any current and future critics should he return to the White House after the 2024 election. Before dismissing that as unfounded hyperbolic speculation, consider that prior to the 2020 vote, Trump's self-proclaimed "dirty trickster" and grateful pardon recipient Roger Stone was recorded pushing for the assassination of Representatives Eric Swalwell and Jerry Nadler.[58] Stone had long detested them because of their role in Trump's first impeachment. He nevertheless claimed the tape was "AI manipulation." Stone similarly dismissed another audio recording in which he said to a cohort regarding Aaron Zelinsky, a Russia investigation prosecutor, "You have to abduct and punish him."[59]

When Trump denounces political rivals, however vaguely, the MAGA base intuitively understands its marching orders. They have never needed explicit instructions to issue death threats against those attempting to hold their leader to account, whether they be judges[60] presiding over an evidence-based trial and insisting no one is above the law or election workers[61] committed to facilitating a fair election by counting all the votes.

The delirious worshipers that fill Trump's rallies are not the only ones ensnared in that trauma bond. As noted throughout this book, it can also be seen across the Republican Party. GOP members of Congress know that compliance with the leader's wishes and granting him impunity for his many alleged high crimes and misdemeanors is the only way to maintain their positions of power. It is also necessary to stay alive. Enabling Trump's corruption and endorsing his lies are required if they and their families are to avoid becoming a target of sometimes lethal right-wing violence.[62] Whenever a Republican politician has dared to voice a mild criticism of the former president, it has been followed by a predictable sequence of events. Trump would retaliate by shaming them, insulting their family members, and signaling his base to troll them mercilessly and issue death threats to them and their loved ones.[63] Kim Ward, the Republican majority leader of the Pennsylvania state senate, said that if she failed to endorse Trump's stolen election big lie, "I'd get my house bombed tonight."[64]

Often, the humiliated and frightened apostate would eventually offer up a groveling plea for forgiveness, beg to kiss the ring, and seek reinstatement into the cult. Having been duly threatened, reprimanded, and publicly degraded, they would typically redouble their slavish fealty to Trump and return to vigilantly attending to his wishes. Kevin McCarthy is the paradigmatic example of that sort of mild Trump critic easily brought to heel. Three short weeks after the former house speaker blamed the ex-president for his role in the January 6 MAGA siege of the Capitol and lynching threats against Vice President Mike Pence, he realized it was better to be a suck-up than strung up and made the mandatory pilgrimage to Mar-a-Lago to earn back the master's blessing.[65] Sadly, for McCarthy, oleaginous servility was insufficient to keep his job and status in the cult.

Stein identifies isolation from the outside world as another central feature of cults. In the current era, the information silos enabled by the internet, in addition to the tribalization of network news, have rendered confinement to brick-and-mortar cult compounds redundant. The Jonestown commune in Guyana, the Mt. Carmel Branch Davidian property of David Koresh, and the hundred-acre remote Central Oregon cult city-state of Rajneeshpuram where the Bhagwan ministered over his flock of purple-adorned devotees are now historical anachronisms. Those quaint carceral compounds have been superseded by the self-enforcing isolation from factuality and non-cult viewpoints that MAGA cult members can achieve from their living rooms. Whether enveloped in Fox News, Newsmax, Truth Social, or Telegram, only the mouthpieces for Trump-thought can be heard or read. To seek any perspective outside that echo chamber would be treasonous disloyalty and risk tribal exile.

One way a cult leader can enhance their grandiose self-presentation and burnish their charisma is to appropriate and merge with something even grander. That is precisely what Trump has done with the American flag.

Branding Patriotism

It is standard performative conservatism for GOP politicians to wrap themselves in the American flag. However, before Trump, no Republicans had ever wrapped the flag in *themselves*. That is literally what the former president did at the 2019 CPAC conference, grabbing it close to him as if it were one of those women he thinks he can grope with impunity.[66] Should the reader be tempted to conclude that it was a one-off spontaneous gesture, it is worth noting that he had done the same thing on at least one other occasion.[67] Instead of using the flag to brand *him*, Trump appeared to be branding the flag with himself. For those who accepted the transfer of meaning, the flag became another iteration of the Trump brand. That may be one reason why so many in his base can simultaneously wave the stars and stripes along with the Confederate stars and bars and suffer no cognitive dissonance. Both flags have been reduced to MAGA signifiers.

We could think of his effort to colonize the red, white, and blue bit of the symbolic commons as his version of the tried-and-true trope of autocratic narcissism—*L'État, c'est moi* (The state, it is I). Widely attributed to the French king Louis XIV, some version is every dictator's spoken and unspoken stance regardless of ideological garb.

During the 2020 campaign, the MAGA zealots that attempted to run the Biden bus off a Texas road displayed both Trump and American flags.[68] Since then, a hybrid symbol has emerged. Now his followers can wave a banner that features the former president's image superimposed on the Stars and Stripes, conveniently available on Amazon.[69] For the base, allegiance to the country has become conflated with fealty to the former president. Perhaps that semiotic merger can help us understand the paradoxical passion of the January 6 terrorists who seemed to think they were defending the country by installing Trump as dictator.

That rhetorical conflation of the leader's self-interest with that of the group or nation turns complicity and obedience into heroic loyalty to the tribe. Correspondingly, any attack on the leader is depicted as an attack on members. As Trump told an audience in Georgia following the 2023 Florida indictments, "In the end, they're not coming after me. They're coming after you. And I'm just standing in the way."[70] Psychologically, the Trump brand carries far more symbolic freight than that merger fantasy.

The Appeal of the Trump Brand

Every brand makes a promise it cannot keep—that the qualities attributed to it, as with totem animals, can be bestowed upon those who purchase the associated products. In this sense, the brand functions as a kind of meta product. Think of a Harley Davidson T-shirt. You may be unable to afford an actual motorcycle or the time to savor the "freedom of the open road" it suggests. But you can own the T-shirt and taste a little of the promised frisson, or at least imagine it.

Products like Harleys are marketed as a form of currency. Once possessed, advertisers suggest, they can endow their owners with qualities and experiences consumers could never have on their own—power, sexiness, glamour, the admiration and envy of others, and freedom from moral or legal obligations. The brand—as a label, logo, fantasy, or reputation—can perform this magical transfer without needing an actual object or product. It can embody the same "spiritual essence" as the material thing once did—a fetish that has been liberated from the fetish object itself. For the MAGA cult, the red hat and the Trump-emblazoned American flag are talismanic carriers of their leader's perceived special power. And what is that power?

If the Trump brand signifies one quality above all others, it is impunity. As I described earlier, it is (so far) the story of his life and defines his character. In the wishful imagination of his customers and followers, it can be imparted as a kind of psychopathic grace. He is the permissive superego who says, "Since I can do it and not be held accountable, so can you." Thus, his brand offered a preemptive moral pardon (anticipating the legal one he offered for those convicted criminals who remained loyal to him, i.e., didn't snitch). The message was not just for his cabinet members, consiglieri, and official explainers but also for his base. The blessing of normalization is not limited to those white supremacist groups filled with "very fine people" but also conferred on ordinary Americans who no longer have to sublimate their ethnic hatred and misogyny.

Since the beginning of Trump's first campaign, racist verbal and physical assaults and vandalism have become increasingly commonplace. They had even featured his name in the language of those attacks.[71] As one businessman said to a John F. Kennedy International Airport worker in a hijab, "Trump is here now. He will get rid of all of you." As I mentioned in the earlier chapter on right-wing identity politics, in Connecticut, fans of an all-white high school basketball team hurled racist taunts at the opposing team, comprised mainly of Black and Latino players, and yelled, "Trump! Trump! Trump!"—as if they were casting a kind of fascist spell. This incident is one of many similar examples in which the president's name has joined the swastika and the Confederate flag as brands signifying unapologetic exterminationist white supremacy.[72]

At this point, some of my strenuously tolerant liberal readers might insist that not all Trump supporters are racist or contemptuous of various "others." And yet, they voted for someone who *was* and cheered rapturously at his rallies. What does it mean to say you are not a bigot but are happy to support someone who is?

Hitler analogies are often rightly criticized as a rhetorical third rail in any sort of argument. In particular, it would certainly be glib reductionism to argue that the former president is somehow a contemporary iteration of the infamous German chancellor, or that Trump's followers are all Nazis (though some clearly are). But I'd like to invite the reader to conduct a thought experiment: how might we have regarded "good Germans" in the post-Weimar era who looked upon the brash Austrian rabble-rouser and his party as simply the kind of nationalist disruptors the country needed? "Well," they might say, "I don't really think Jews are vermin, the principal vectors for all our economic and social maladies, but that Treaty of Versailles was a terrible deal. And I don't believe what the *Lügenpresse* [lying press] say about the Nazis. Hitler will 'make Germany great again,' [73] create jobs, and build that beautiful autobahn. So, I want his people in the Reichstag. Also, you've got to love that idea of *Lebensraum*. Who doesn't want to stretch out?" Whether you are a bigot or can overlook bigotry in your leaders, the distinction does not seem to constitute a meaningful difference, especially when the person you elect gets to enact policies like the abduction and imprisonment of Hispanic children described in chapter 6.

The Manufacture of Group Identity Threats and Obama-to-Trump Voters

One of the more vexing questions for pundits and the public is how seven to nine million voters who placed Barack Obama in office in 2012 could switch to voting for Donald Trump in 2016.[74] The short answer is that it wasn't the economy but Trump's ability to conjure a palpable racial threat to white voters.[75] But you rightly ask, how could it be race, given their prior willingness to elect and cheer an African American president? To answer that, we must understand how an out-group gets constructed as a danger to the tribe. We have learned from many decades of social psychology research that perceived or actual threats to one's group can increase and consolidate identification with that group, even if one is only loosely identified with it. That is one of the reasons that presenting uncomfortable, identity-threatening facts to a member of a religious or political cult only increases their bond to the group. Because those facts are experienced as a frightening challenge to their group identity, powerful defenses get mobilized to deny the facts and double down on their allegiance to the group. If the threat is vague and thus fails to provide a target or hate object, the resulting fear can lead to passivity. However, if the danger can be personified as another group or individual, that anxiety can be a powerful driver of action.

For many white people during the Obama administration, their white identity seemed loosely held and did not constitute a salient component of their sense of self. In the Obamaworld narrative, America was a glorious rainbow of ethnicities that wanted to work together as one people to make the world a better place. Then Trump came along and said, in essence, "Hold on, there are all these swarthy immigrants who want to take your jobs, steal your stuff, appropriate your tax money, rape, and ultimately replace you—and Democrats want to let them do it. Not me; I'll build a wall."

Trump may know little about history, statecraft, or law—areas in which politicians used to be knowledgeable. And he may have been so arrogantly incurious that he refused to read his daily intelligence briefing while president. Nevertheless, he did have a canny intuitive ability to read and target the psychological vulnerabilities of his base. One of his unique talents has been generating a sense of group threat from tribal out-groups. His threat message landed even with some former Obama voters. Suddenly, whiteness went from being an uninteresting background part of their self-concept to a vital foreground feature of their identity. Researchers have been able to replicate that process in social science laboratory settings. Under experimental conditions, when white subjects for whom white ethnic identity was important were reminded that they would eventually be a minority of the country, their support for Donald Trump and anti-immigrant policies increased.[76]

Group Identity Threats and Trump-Supporting Latinos*

Partisan efforts to appeal to Latino communities illustrate the different ways group identity and threats to it can be manipulated as well as how difficult it is. The main challenge to those efforts with Latinos is that both the Republican and Democratic parties tend to overlook the heterogeneity of those voters. A substantial plurality is socially conservative; most others are liberal.

---

* While Hispanic and Latino have somewhat distinct definitions, they are used interchangeably in common usage. So, I will continue doing so here.

They can be found in all socioeconomic classes. Some are devout Catholics. Others are evangelical Protestants. Still others are none of the above. Some are passionate pro-democracy advocates who want to expand voting opportunities. Others are right-wing Cubans whose lifelong opposition to the island nation's dictatorship somehow has not led them to oppose Trump's undisguised autocratic ambitions.

Some feel a deep connection to their brethren attempting to escape tyranny in their home countries and immigrate to the United States. Bilingual Latinos tend to favor Democrats over Republicans,[77] perhaps because they feel more of a kinship with those from Spanish-speaking countries. At the same time, monolingual English-speaking Latinos are more likely to align with Republicans.[78] Some of them share the GOP's opposition to immigration, disidentify with the label Hispanic, and see themselves as culturally undifferentiated Americans.[79]

Interestingly, the number of Hispanic Americans who identify as white has gone up exponentially since 1980. According to one study of census data, a majority now label themselves as white.[80] In many ways, that is the well-worn assimilationist path followed by other ethnicities, which was the case with Jewish, Italian, and Irish emigres who did not start their long process of Americanization as white. It is important to note that, then as now, having less melanin does not necessarily confer whiteness psychologically or culturally. In other words, it's not just how you look, but how you feel and how you're perceived that determines ethnic identity.

The white-identified segment of the diverse Latino demographic may constitute the most promising one for Republicans. It stands to reason that if you feel psychologically distant from others in your ethnic group, it's easier to feel unaffected by the travails of that group, especially their experience of race-based bigotry and persecution. That may even be a *motive* for disidentification. It's easy to understand the desire not to see oneself as part of a group openly denigrated by the country's former president and even targeted for mass murder by a white supremacist whose online manifesto echoed the rhetoric of the country's leader.[81]

There is one variable more than any other that drives Hispanic support for Donald Trump—the denial of racism.[82] *That* denial is like other forms of denial. It's a psychological defense against a threatening reality we want to wish away. The thinking might go: "I'm safe because I am not part of that target group. And even if I were, they're not being targeted anyway."

Conservatives have come a long way in their efforts to appeal to Latino voters. Their current approach is undoubtedly more sophisticated than Gerald Ford's botched photo op when he attempted to chomp down on a tamale still encased in its not-so-digestible husk.[83] Unfortunately, some Democrats are still engaging in cringy ethnic cuisine campaigns, such as when Pete Buttigieg proclaimed to his Latino audience the wonders of combining salsa with ranch dressing.[84] There's a fusion dish guaranteed to repel foodies from all cultures.

Republicans have moved well beyond that not-so-fruitful approach to wooing non-white voters. For example, the right-wing billionaire Koch family has been investing heavily in outreach to Hispanic communities across the country. They are trying to graft libertarian free-market ideology onto what they see as Latinos' conservative aspirational work ethic and bootstrapping determination to achieve the "American dream."[85] While the Koch network may have abandoned Trump as the most effective vehicle for their brand of free-market fundamentalism, their promotion of that soothing "post-racial" fantasy does seem to be driving a subset of Hispanic Americans to the GOP.

My less subtle translation of the Koch sub-textual message to Latinos is essentially, "You're different from those illegals who have come here to take your jobs. And you don't want to be like those Spanish-speaking anchor babies who grow up looking to the nanny state for a handout. We conservatives won't humiliate you with health care, low-cost college tuition, low-interest home loans, and government-subsidized child care. We'll make sure that unions stay off your back. And if you keep working hard at Walmart, save your pennies, praise Jesus, and vote Republican, one day, you'll be just like us—rich and accountable to no one. You'll be virtually white."

Despite Trump's racial targeting of Latin American immigrants, Republicans are making striking headway in those communities. Like they did with the Obama-to-Trump white voters, the former president and his campaign team are focused on generating a group threat. But ironically, in this case, they are conjuring the same one—evil Latinos. They are recycling the well-worn stereotype of "job-stealing, drug-smuggling, and murdering illegals" but marketing it to a new counterintuitive audience.

The aim seems to be to activate a kind of white and more conservative identity among a subset of Hispanics. It appears to be working. Latino support for Democrats has seen a measurable drop since 2018.[86] Trump enjoys record support among Hispanic Americans, significantly greater than he did in 2020.[87] As one Republican strategist noted, the GOP doesn't need to win a majority of the Hispanic vote.[88] Just a slightly larger plurality will enable them to take a number of swing states in the next election.

The Wall

Mind of State is a podcast examining politics through a psychoanalytic lens. In January 2019, the hosts interviewed Jungian analyst Thomas Singer to discuss the symbolism of Trump's much-vaunted but never-built border wall.[89] The panel pointed out that it quickly became *the* Wall, not just *a* wall. That gave it a psychic reality—a Platonic essence that existed before any physical wall. It seemed like the political battle was to bring it into material reality. But listening to that conversation, I realized that that *psychic* barrier might have been enough. It was the only wall Trump and his fellow xenophobic conjurors needed to erect to mobilize his base. Once this internal marker of tribal identity was built in the minds of his followers, any physical wall would have been redundant. In other words, Trump's political work was done once his followers located themselves on one side and the threatening non-white hordes on the other.

The psychic wall constituted an unambiguous and impermeable barrier between the clean and the dirty, the virtuous and the criminal, the revered and the reviled, the familiar and the foreign, and safety and annihilation. Once formed in the inner worlds of MAGA partisans, that mental wall provided a symbolic structure that made it easier to experience despised parts of the self as qualities of despised ethnic others. It obviated a challenge we are all confronted with—to come to terms with our complex and contradictory nature, to face and integrate the parts of us we love and are happy to own and the parts of us we dislike and fill us with guilt and shame. But using projections to bypass that struggle poses a major problem; they tend to function like boomerangs. The hated outsiders always seem to be threatening to breach the barriers we've erected.

On the surface, Trump's wall represents simple protection. But a closer reading of his rhetoric makes it clear that the wall is a central feature of his overall threat narrative, a story about the danger that outsiders pose to the survival of the tribe. Once he transmuted that threat into rage, he had an army of MAGA zealots who would die for him. And indeed, they did, in the pandemic and the January 6 coup attempt.

Symbols like the wall are not simply signifiers of the irrational; they are ways to represent the paleo-rational. In other words, they evoke archaic features of our species' nature, such as the importance of tribal identity and membership. Given how central this was to our survival for so many millennia, it is no surprise that we can readily find ways to symbolize it and that those symbols continue to be so activating. Though a symbol, in MAGA discourse, the wall is experienced as something concrete—a geographic suit of armor. It is perceived as literally keeping out the contaminating or attacking Other. The badness of the Other is viewed as an essence that outsiders actually possess. The very people who poo-pooed masks to keep out a real pathogen, embraced a border barrier to keep out fantastical disease vectors.

The internal tribal wall also functions as a border of compassion. It is a barrier that keeps the pain of the excluded from reaching us. As I described earlier, when a reporter asked Trump about his government shutdown's impact on federal workers, he said it was not a concern because they were Democrats. In other words, they were on the other side of the wall, so who cares? Many have remarked on the deliberate cruelty of his policies and rhetoric. We not only build a wall to separate us from those we fear and despise, but we also come to fear and despise those we've walled off. As Stanley Milgram found in his research, creating psychic distance from people makes inflicting suffering on them less troubling.[90] It even makes it easier to kill them.

In the spring of 2023, there was a shocking plethora of multiple fatal homeowner shootings of innocent people who crossed property boundaries.[91] Common benign mistakes, like driving up the wrong driveway or knocking on the wrong door, yielded a death sentence. In at least one of these cases, the role of Fox-fueled securitarian anxiety was explicit.[92] What seems to be happening is that, for some Americans, the threat boundary is moving from the national border to individual property lines.

Interestingly, when Trump talked about the border, it was either open and utterly permeable or closed and impermeable. That is a clear example of right-wing black-and-white thinking about personal, tribal, or national boundaries. Of course, the liberal idea of a healthy border is not "open" but a semi-permeable and selective membrane. The "open border" notion is a conservative straw man against which Republican politicians like to run.

Actual borders can divide, but they can also link. US-Mexico border towns show how the structures constituting a national boundary can function as a semi-permeable membrane instead of an impermeable barrier like the Trumpian wall fantasy. The zones that mark boundaries between real border cities are dynamic portals through which culture, food, trade, fauna, and flora move in both directions.

We could think of semi-permeable boundaries as a membrane analogous to our skin. Skin keeps in muscles, bones, and organs, thus ensuring bodily integrity. It contributes to the shape that makes us who we are as distinct individuals. But at the same time, it is porous. It releases constituents of our physiology into the world—sweat, heat, excrement, and the emotions conveyed through physical tenderness or aggression. It is also the pathway through which we take in aspects of the outside environment—sunlight, water, food, heat, and sensory input from the world, like the touch of others. Life itself depends on that selective, semi-permeable feature of skin and the two-way traffic that it enables.

The MAGA fantasy of a border is more akin to the Berlin Wall, through which few could pass except on pain of death. The regime designed it to keep people from getting out and prevent contraband and dangerous ideas from getting in. Arguably, it was, in part, that impermeability that led to the demise of East Germany.

A barrier through which little can pass is inimical to life, whether that organism is an individual or a nation-state. Of course, some states, like North Korea, have survived but in a profoundly hobbled condition. As little can go in or out, the insularity its government enforces has become toxic to its residents. And starvation, intellectual as well as caloric, has resulted.

Winning: The Imagined Antidote to Group Threat

Snake oil hucksters and advertisers generally follow the "get 'em-sick; get 'em well" script. First, generate anxiety about an imagined threat and then offer your product as the cure or antidote. Trump's fix for the group threat he effectively conjures is a zero-sum version of "winning." His life-long Sisyphean struggle to not feel like a loser, his obsession with ratings and approval, and his insatiable hunger to best others have been transformed into a strategy to wield power—turning his personal weakness into a political strength. That has involved making what was perhaps the most compelling promise he could to his base: electing him would make them winners. That meant they would triumph over enemies like Democrats and non-white ethnicities. The message could be heard in Trump's rally speeches and seen at MAGA swag stands, which featured "Own the Libs" T-shirts, the aforementioned "Drink Liberal Tears" beer mugs, along with Confederate flags. Apparently, the merchants peddling the stars and bars could count on their customers not recalling that the Confederacy was among history's biggest losers.

Of course, there are legitimate real-world contests with only one winner, such as elections and most sporting events. The winning at play in the fantasy Trump shares with his base is founded on a kind of sadomasochistic, top-down, winner-take-all model of recognition. The work of social psychologist Henri Tajfel can give us some insight into the power of this appeal.

In one of his studies, he divided individuals into groups using arbitrary and random criteria.[93] Nevertheless, subjects strongly identified with their group and, in various experiments, preferred to forsake greater individual rewards to ensure that members of the other group got a much smaller reward. So, rather than accept five dollars, they'd prefer four dollars if that meant that out-group members got only one dollar. In other words, a reward is far more satisfying if it enhances a status differential between groups.

While it is commonplace for individuals to derive a sense of value and esteem from the status of their group, among conservatives, that status tends to be evaluated in zero-sum terms, i.e., hierarchically relative to the status of other groups. As described in earlier chapters, this well-documented social dominance orientation (SDO) among those on the right is robust among Trump voters.[94]

Judging from their adoration of Trump, that high SDO seems to translate into a willingness of working- and middle-class white people to vote against their economic self-interest—as long as it means ensuring that those deemed less worthy, the poor and non-white, are deprived to a greater extent and kept in an even lower status.

Tajfel found that his subjects did not like compromise because it wasn't experienced as "winning." A win-win, where everybody gets more, is not nearly as desirable as when one's own group gets a smaller amount, but the out-group receives even less. The petty rewards of win-lose situations are preferred over the grand rewards of win-win conditions.

I hasten to add that there is nothing about that tendency that makes it unavoidable. But understanding it is vital for those invested in living in a more win-win world where our more egalitarian predispositions can be expressed. Like other urges we choose not to act on—murderous wishes, coveting the partners of our friends, or, more banally, lusting after an entire chocolate mousse cake—awareness allows a choice over our actions.

Winners Don't Apologize

For would-be autocrats like Trump and actual ones like Putin, corruption is a badge of honor because it is a consequence and expression of their impunity and, thus, an affirmative expression of their power. It says, "Look what I can get away with; I'm an important and dominating force. There is no limit to what I can do." That is the MAGA meaning of winning.

However, by boasting of his special privilege and criminal entitlement, there is the risk that he might induce envious resentment among followers. Unlike him, ordinary Americans can rarely evade the consequences for their actions. But Trump somehow avoids the hazard of his flock's envy through a kind of psychological alchemy; he transmutes any possible envy into idolatrous identification. Through the constant use of the first-person plural, "we," he invites his base to take credit for his triumphs—criminal and political—to feel the pain of "persecution" by those who would hold him to account, and to experience themselves as the actual beneficiaries of his self-serving scams. Thus, he and they are always either winners or defending their status as winners from those who would usurp it. But never are they losers.

In her book *Uncivil Agreement*, political psychologist Lilliana Mason points out that the overriding concern for those driven by identity-based (tribal) politics is winning.[95] Taking this formulation to its logical conclusion, those who get away with their crimes are winners. In this view, people who crush, humiliate, and even murder anyone who impedes a winner's advancement are to be celebrated. (That may explain Trump's fawning admiration for Putin, whose status as a "killer" does not trouble the former president.[96]) Perhaps the most compelling promise that Trump made to his base is that electing him would make them winners.

For people who see themselves as losers in society's seemingly rigged game, this was perhaps the salvific campaign message that moved them the most. Here is where Trump marshaled his singular native talent—the quality that determines all con artists' success—the ability to size up his marks well enough to tell them what they want to hear. In this case, they crave the message that they could be winners. But only *he* could make them winners. Of course, this would not be achieved by actually improving their lives. Instead, by electing him, he could be their savior and, like any good savior, transubstantiate their loser status through a fantasy merger with his greatness.

While that may sound like a rather fanciful interpretation, one only needs to listen to Trump supporters themselves. As one giddy MAGA rally attendee exclaimed, holding a Trump mask over his face, "I'm him, dude!" "He is God," insists another worshiper, a pastor, at the same Trump revival meeting.[97] As one scholar of the Christian Right described it, Trump's evangelical base doesn't see itself as engaging in a distasteful transaction—supporting someone with "unchristian" traits in exchange for lifetime appointments of theocratic judges. No, they love his autocratic and aggressive style because, like him, they hate democracy and want a king.[98] And nearly half of all Republicans believe the throne is his divine right because God put him in the White House.[99]

Trumpian Impunity Becomes the New Normal under MAGA Rule

Impunity for corruption is no longer the special prerogative of Donald Trump. (And, given all the criminal indictments, it could end for him.) It is now a feature of GOP governance nationwide, from the courts to legislatures. Few Americans any longer see the Supreme Court as a neutral body of the wise whose oracular utterances are untainted by politics. On the contrary, unethical behavior, like accepting money and special favors from right-wing billionaires who are invested in parties that have business before the Court, is on blatant display for all to see. Moreover, those justices seem to have impunity for that conduct.[100] As Senator Richard Blumenthal has referred to them, the MAGA justices are "corrupt politicians in robes."[101]

MAGA state legislators are also openly exempting themselves from accountability. Some of the more shocking examples took place in Iowa. The only state-wide elected Democrat is Auditor Rob Sand. One of the primary responsibilities of that position, which has not changed since the state's founding, is to investigate possible corruption and economic grift. Republican legislators and the governor decided they would rather not be subject to scrutiny. A majority of the state Senate passed, and the chief executive signed,[102] a bill disempowering the auditor position. That means that the legislature is no longer required to comply with Office of Auditor requests for records. Covering up potential crimes is now legal in Iowa. In addition, the preemptive impunity will cost the state billions in federal funds and place its bond rating in peril.

The Fictitious Moral Virginity of Trump Nation

MAGA America comprises an "innocence cult," as journalist Jeff Sharlet describes them.[103] In other words, they live in an imaginary nation, a fantasy from which slavery, indigenous genocide, Jim Crow, or any of the country's other complicating blemishes have been deleted. In red states like Florida, that delusion has been concretized in the mandate that only textbooks and lessons denatured of discomfiting facts be allowed in school curricula.[104]

That cult of innocence did not begin with the MAGA faction. It has been part of American conservatism's mythic self-understanding for centuries. One of its most vivid expressions is the fable of the "Lost Cause." In this story, the defeat of the Confederacy was and continues to be portrayed in GOP-controlled states as a kind of ennobling persecution. The Civil War was not a battle over slavery but an attempt to throw off the yolk of a repressive federal government that insisted on crushing state sovereignty. But despite the overwhelming defeat by Union forces, Southerners managed to hold onto their pride, unsullied virtue, and the purity of their Christian hearts.[105]

Moreover, the story goes, enslaved people were happy and well-treated. Persecution was something only the Confederacy suffered at the hands of malevolent and intrusive outsiders. Many years after the war, monuments to the defenders of slave labor camps that depicted them as heroes were built across the South. "Plantations" became sites of wistful nostalgia and romantic bed and breakfasts. Ten red states still celebrate Confederate holidays.[106] One political legacy of the Confederacy in states now ruled by Republicans is a profound mistrust, if not outright hostility, to democracy and racial equality. The other one is the enduring fantasy of secession as a solution to the problems majority rule poses for white dominance and Christian theocratic ambitions.[107] Texas Republican Representative Bryan Slayton has introduced a bill to place a referendum on the 2024 Texas ballot calling on a vote for secession.[108]

In contrast, after years of agonizing cultural and psychological self-examination, the post–World War II German population and their elected governments were able to express profound remorse, guilt, and shame.

Their schools teach the authentic, unflattering truth of Holocaust history and German culpability for it. Instead of erecting monuments to the architects and defenders of death camps or waxing nostalgic for the lost Reich, Germans built the Memorial to the Murdered Jews of Europe. Germans have preserved concentration camps as sites of industrial-scale horror and evidence of their collective criminality. They have not been remodeled to serve as cozy weekend getaways. The political legacy of the Nazi defeat has been a passionate commitment to defend and strengthen democracy in Germany and across Europe.

The denial of America's original sins may seem like an ironic conviction for a movement that claims to be driven by an ardent adherence to Christian theology. The MAGA cult lives in an alternate Edenic myth in which no apple was ever eaten, or more pertinent, where the fruits of others' labor, resources, and dignity were never stolen. That is a story that has periodically resurfaced throughout modern history. In particular, it has animated many fascist parties and crusades. They believe returning to their imagined pristine origins can vanish all present ills and threats. The solution is making Germany, Russia, or America "great again." The leader presents himself (generally, it has been a male) as the midwife to this national rebirth. In their efforts to understand the multiple iterations of that reappearing narrative, academics have deployed a variety of labels. Roger Griffin, an expert on fascism, refers to the myth as "palingenetic ultranationalism."[109] As retooled versions of this myth will likely be proffered by present and future autocrats, new scholarly terms of art will doubtless be coined to grapple with it.

As a cult of *persecution*, the Trump base is also more conventionally Christian. Mirroring their leader in his determined effort to ape the crucified Christ, the MAGA movement is deeply attached to a doctrine of victimization, just like the Christian Right has been for decades.[110] Since they see themselves as innocent, persecution only adds to their virtue. As I pointed out earlier, that is why the part of the Jesus story they most revere is his crucifixion. From the foundational assumption of primordial purity and unjust persecution, violence against perceived enemies is a righteous act of redemption. It is the *cri de coeur* of pious lynch mobs everywhere. As Trump said when announcing his 2024 reelection campaign, "I am your retribution."[111]

Manhattan: Trump's Mount Calvary

Trump has worked hard to cultivate the image of a persecuted savior. Confidential sources close to the former president's legal team revealed to *Rolling Stone* reporters in April 2023 how Trump wanted to choreograph his New York court appearance to hear the felony indictments associated with his hush money payments to Stormy Daniels.[112] Rejecting an offer to be arraigned by Zoom, he preferred the obsessive coverage of the long trip from Mar-a-Lago by plane, followed by the aerial photo-op, dutifully provided by numerous media outlets, of the multi-vehicle procession to New York—his own Stations of the Cross. Trump hoped his arrival at the Manhattan courthouse would be the MAGA cult's Mount Calvary.

Unlike Jesus, but like any other citizen accused of a crime, Trump has the right to a fair trial. To avoid the humiliation of being seen as an ordinary defendant, his attorneys successfully petitioned the court to keep video cameras and audio recordings out of the proceedings. Thus, despite the few still images to emerge, Trump could disguise his feet of clay and fix the gaze of his cult members on the nails he painted there.

As I described earlier, Trump is fond of conflating his interests with those of his followers. He also likes to blur the threat of his long-deferred *prosecutions* with the supposed *persecution* of the MAGA base. His handlers endeavored to depict any punishment Trump may have to endure as a salvific act on behalf of his worshipers. As the Trump legal team source said to *Rolling Stone*, "It's kind of a Jesus Christ thing. He is saying, 'I'm absorbing all this pain from all around, from everywhere, so you don't have to.'" The source elaborated, "'If they can do this to me, they can do this to you,' and that's a powerful message."[113]

You Knew I Was a Snake When You Met Me

Trump has been fond of sharing a poem from one of Aesop's fables at his rallies.[114] It is the tale of an injured snake who persuades a young woman to nurse him back to health. Once she does, and he is restored to vitality, he delivers a fatal bite to her. Shocked by his response to her kindness, before succumbing, she asks why he would repay her generosity this way. He replies with a sly grin that she knew he was a snake when she met him and that it is the nature of snakes to bite.

On one level, it is a story about the dangers inherent in the world and the perils of helping strangers—a recognizably conservative morality tale. Trump also used the story of the snake as a metaphorical stand-in for the mortal danger posed by immigrants. On another level, it is a narrative that normalizes predation and thus justifies his impunity—one more way he says the quiet part out loud. And we know from Trump's many reptilian and predatory moves that he is the snake. Over the years, Trump has turned on multiple allies, business associates, contractors, and wives whenever it served him. He demands loyalty from others but is incapable of offering it. Thus, we can view his frequent citing of this parable as a projection of his instinct for predatory betrayal.

Absolute Power, Absolute Impunity, and the Right-Wing Gospel of "Freedom"

Impunity preempts any need to perform, let alone feel, empathy and other emotions common to the rest of the species. As described in chapter 1, those who hold right-wing views do tend to score lower on various emotional intelligence measures, like the capacity to understand and care about the experience of others.[115] This quality is consonant with the conservative notion of "freedom," the "right" to harm others if it serves you or your group.

Trump is the current paradigmatic example of that long-standing right-wing ethos. His most admired superpower among the MAGA base is untrammeled entitlement, his iteration of libertarian freedom. He seems to live by a version of the medieval dictum of *le droit du seigneur*, the lord's right. Historically, this referred to the master's prerogative to rape any woman residing on the land he ruled. For Trump, it is a more inclusive privilege that applies to anyone and anything he covets.

That is why he must ward off and deny regret and remorse. Those emotions would be affective kryptonite to that singular superpower. They would render him a loser. He cannot learn from mistakes because he cannot acknowledge having made them. One of the roles the various disposable minions and enemies in his world perform is his psychological toilet, into which all badness, errors, and losses can be projected and discarded. So, unlike other politicians and CEOs, he can barely allow himself, even *insincerely*, to apologize, regardless of whatever short-term political or economic utility it might offer. The long-term damage to his brand would be too great.

Impunity is linked to another central feature of the Trumplandian universe—its authoritarianism and admiration of dictatorship. That may be why the Right was not just unperturbed by the Russian electoral espionage scandal but even saw it as a good thing. Their appreciation of the Russian autocrat went well beyond the electoral benefits he conferred on their 2016 presidential candidate. Even in the years before Trump entered politics, many conservatives viewed Putin as someone to be emulated, an icon of "manly" dominance whose central virtue was his ruthless proficiency at crushing those who impeded his pursuit of empire.[116]

Once Trump was in office, Putin's favorability ratings among Republicans increased even more.[117] GOP politicians have increasingly parroted Putin's talking points.[118] As we all observed during the first impeachment hearings, Republican senators, following Trump, strenuously promoted a fictitious conspiracy narrative about Joe and Hunter Biden known by American intelligence agencies (and thus also by Congress members) to have been crafted by Moscow. Trump has described Putin as "a strong leader" and "a genius."[119] When asked by Bill O'Reilly if he thought Putin was a "killer," Trump shrugged his shoulders and famously replied, "There are a lot of killers. Do you think our country is so innocent?"[120] Trump knows a lot about that, as his own body count was considerable even before his willful mismanagement of the COVID pandemic.[121]

While the Mueller investigation, the Senate intelligence report, and Trump's own statements showed that his campaign sought, received, and used the data derived from Russian electoral sabotage, and then tried to cover it up, many in Trumpworld reframed it as one more affirmation that the president is a virtuoso at the "art of the deal."[122] If betraying national interests leads to a win, it is an unalloyed good. Anticipating the obstruction of justice charge that finally made its way into the articles of impeachment, John Dowd, Trump's lawyer, said there was no reason to worry because the former president had impunity regarding that crime too.[123]

For his supporters, the fantasy of domination without limits, consequences, or regret can be an effective, if short-lived, antidote to feelings of impotence. So, while those outside the Trumpian universe may be filled with bilious revulsion, his base cheered every act of destruction: every attack on an Obama-era achievement, every arrogant pose on the global stage, every assault on public health, every puerile insult directed at the enemy of the day, every thinly veiled racist incantation, and every ludicrous denial of science. All his actions say, "I'm here to fuck things up and burn it down. And I can get away with it." And his brand is burnished further for those who feel powerless and enjoy little impunity in their own lives.

Impunity: It Takes a Village

What can challenge Trumpian entitlement? It will not be the invertebrate "mainstream" Republicans whose individual and collective Faustian bargains appear to have been offers they couldn't refuse. Prior to being ousted for the crime of working with Democrats to find a way to avoid a government shut-down at the end of September 2023, former Republican House Majority Leader Kevin McCarthy made a last-ditch effort to hold onto his position. He agreed to give Trump what he couldn't extort from Volodymyr Zelenskyy—an evidence-free "investigation" into Joe Biden.[124] Performed as an impeachment hearing, the obvious aim was to smear Biden and promote the narrative that everyone is corrupt, and thus diminish the moral taint of Trump's many alleged crimes.

Faced with the choice of standing up for the country and risking banishment from the GOP tribe, or enabling their leader's corruption and thereby keeping their status in the party, they chose the latter. Moreover, in addition to job security, Trump promised, while in office, to give them what they wanted politically—a world safe for unregulated corporate predation—in exchange for their loyalty to him. During his presidency, as long as they kept the praise coming and blocked any effort to impeach him or otherwise hold him accountable, they were assured that Bannonite deplorables with pitchforks would not be mobilized to primary them or issue the now-routine MAGA death threats against them and their families.[125] And now, even out of office, the same deals are in force. The few exceptions to GOP moral cowardice have been those whose belated courage had been born of impending retirement.

When it came to enabling Trump and his team to evade any consequences for their actions, a plurality of Republican members of Congress went well beyond looking the other way or uttering low-risk overdue and tepid protests as they exited public life. There developed a well-organized and determined effort among GOP politicians, Rupert Murdoch's *Wall Street Journal* editorial board, and Fox News (what became, in essence, Trump State TV) to subvert and delegitimate the Mueller investigation, discredit the Justice Department, and slander the FBI.[126] They are doing the same now in response to the current series of indictments by focusing on investigating the investigators and airing counterprogramming like their efforts to impeach President Biden.

As has been revealed over the last few years, multiple Republican politicians, primarily in swing states, attempted to help Trump overturn the results of the 2020 election, using a multipronged strategy—legal and illegal. However, their efforts got increasingly half-hearted as Trump lawyers' bogus "fraud" cases kept getting thrown out of court, even by Trump-appointed judges, and a growing number of states certified Biden's victory. One of the most clarifying developments of the Trump years is the extent to which the Republican Party has revealed itself utterly devoid of principles, even conservative ones. Supposedly the party of national security, traditional moral values, and fervid patriotism, they have publicly demonstrated their willingness to sell out these principles as soon they impair self-dealing or require taking a stand against a corrupt tribal leader on which their careers depend. As long their wealth and power are ensured, they have been happy to enable grift, bigotry, and an attempted coup. The party of moral absolutism now embraces the sociopathic version of situational ethics. Their frank opposition to democracy has earned the GOP Jonathan Alter's apt moniker, "banana Republicans."[127]

As I write these last few sentences, my impulse is to support those harsh assessments with more voluminous citations. However, I quickly realized how redundant that would be—akin to citing studies that proved heavy objects dropped from a great height tend to fall to the ground. All Americans watched these developments unfold in plain sight. In televised impeachment hearings, press conferences, and the many talk shows and courtroom calls to throw out votes, Republican politicians have strenuously argued for their leader's indemnity for multiple crimes and openly expressed their contempt for democracy. This behavior did not occur in secret or behind the closed doors of smoke-filled rooms—an obvious reflection of their sense of impunity for such actions.

MAGA Republicans do not simply object to particular charges against Trump but to the very notion that he could be charged with anything. In the days that passed at the end of March 2023, when Manhattan district attorney Alvin Bragg announced that the grand jury he empaneled voted to indict Trump, no one knew what the charges would be. That did not stop his GOP allies, along with the former president himself, from proclaiming his innocence and the proceeding a political witch hunt.[128] At that point, they made clear their passionate belief in his divine right to impunity; evidence is irrelevant.

When Treason Is Patriotism, and Betrayal Is Loyalty

On June 13, 2023, Donald Trump was arraigned on thirty-eight criminal counts in Florida related to mishandling classified documents and obstructing justice by refusing to return them. "Mishandling" seems a pretty tepid term for leaving nuclear and other military secrets lying around his faux luxury Mar-a-Lago bathroom for wandering Saudi, Chinese, or Russian agents to read on the toilet. But unsurprisingly, MAGA Republicans appear to see no problem in this episode other than the Justice Department's attempt to hold him accountable. Their fervid flag-waving has always been an unfunny joke. Since the former president's first open invitation to Russia to help him get elected, the GOP's fawning amen chorus in Congress has made it clear its allegiance rests with the leader, not the country. No praise could be too loud. Yet, given the magnitude of Trump's current disregard for national security, their fascist virtue-signaling could pose a moral dilemma.

Do they criticize their party's leader for his dangerous and treasonous actions and risk alienating the base and earning the condemnation of colleagues? Or do they stand behind Trump, regardless of his illegal and amoral conduct, as nearly all Republicans have done since 2016? As the research has established, in-group loyalty[129] is a fundamental moral intuition for conservatives. It is a core driver behind their policy positions and political choices. But what do they do when loyalty to the leader requires disloyalty to the nation?

Trump has long given his followers and collaborators an escape clause to help them evade that dilemma. He conjured an imaginary outside villain that has burrowed its way into the government's core, a kind of internal parasite eating away and corrupting the body politic. That evil entity is the "deep state." And to attack it is to love America. Trump must convince his true believers that the agents of that evil cabal are behind all attempts by law enforcement to limit his pursuit of self-enrichment. They are also the ones persecuting him by calling his actions criminal. And anyway, they couldn't be crimes because *he* is doing them. In an echo of the Republican denunciation of Alvin Bragg's investigation, the Florida indictments were denounced by former GOP House Speaker Kevin McCarthy and other Republicans *before* anyone knew what they contained. If the base can be convinced of that, then overthrowing elections, beating cops, and attempting to murder FBI agents are brave acts of patriotism.

Should he read it, Trump will likely be reassured by a survey conducted around the same time that the charges were unsealed. It found that more than 12 million US adults think violence is justified to return the former president to power.[130] In another post-indictment poll of Republican voters, 80 percent of the representative sample said that being convicted of violating the Espionage Act should not disqualify him from serving as president again. [131] Since Trump has so far been able to raise money off his alleged crimes, the country will have to look beyond the court system to interrupt the disturbing symbiosis between him and his base. Among other resistance tactics, America's tepid opposition party must develop a more muscular messaging approach.

The Democratic Party's Historical Role as GOP Enablers

While Democrats won the presidency in 2020, they have not won the framing war. They have persistently deployed language crafted by Republicans to put a positive spin on Trump's and the GOP's own self-dealing practices. For example, in the early part of the Biden administration, Dems tended to refer to Trump's foreign policy strategy using his phrase, "America First," even as they criticized it—as if an overzealous love of country were the main driver in the Trump approach to international affairs. All his domestic and foreign policies were *Trump* First, not America First actions, a point that Democrats are belatedly making as the 2024 election approaches. Democratic politicians knew this all along. And yet, they seemed unable to say it.

"The only things you'll find in the middle of the road are yellow stripes and dead armadillos . . . Voters want someone to kick ass on their behalf."

When the sagacious Lone Star populist, Jim Hightower, made that observation in 1990, it was as if he were anticipating the calls for then Barack Obama and now Joe Biden to "govern from the middle." Republicans painted those yellow stripes on the road's far-right shoulder at the dawn of the Reagan era. And Democrats, instead of defining the center for themselves and the country, struggled mightily to move to the center as stipulated by Republicans.

In addition to the impoverished rhetorical strategy of Democrats, much of the credit for the success of Republican propaganda efforts goes to the Machiavellian lexicographers of the GOP, such as Frank Luntz.[132] Among his greatest framing successes is popularizing the phrase "climate change." In a 2001 talking point memo to Republican officeholders, Luntz urged his clients to delete the words "global warming" from their rhetoric because it had unpleasantly "catastrophic connotations." Instead, they should adopt the "climate change" frame because it presented "a more controllable and less emotional challenge."[133]

Luntz eventually came to regret his mercenary offering to the fossil fuel lobby and their GOP collaborators. But that was too late to stop that phase from being incorporated like a virus into the linguistic DNA of everyone's discourse about the climate crisis, including that of environmental activists. We can only speculate on the role his bland reframe has had on Americans' shockingly minimal level of concern about the issue, even while whole towns are routinely incinerated, flooded, and blown away from ever-greater hurricanes. In 2023, only 38 percent of US residents surveyed view the climate emergency as a "critical issue" As many readers might presume, that average obscures the growing partisan gap in climate anxiety, greater than any other issue; 66 percent of Democrats but only 12 percent of Republicans expressed concern.[134]

Luntz also succeeded in redefining what was once regarded as mainstream American values and gave new meanings to old words. Of course, the nation's foundational moral principles have not always (or even often) been honored in the Realpolitik of governing. But until the current era of nearly uninterrupted conservative rule, these values were the moral yardstick by which politicians' and governments' actions were measured. For decades now, calls to honor such principles have been met with denunciations reflecting conservative framing.

Since at least the George W. Bush administration, the Republican edition of *The Devil's Dictionary* (apologies to Ambrose Bierce) has redefined the ethic of fairness that underlay Eisenhower-era progressive taxation as "socialism." That purple mountain majesty stuff? Just the sentimental whining of "tree-hugging dirt worshippers who oppose property rights." Are you bothered by torture as official state policy? You're a "terrorist sympathizer." Presidents no longer defy the principle of checks and balances; they merely exercise the prerogatives of the "unitary executive." Suppose you're a candidate who prefers diplomacy over military force and imperial occupation. In that case, you'd better prepare to fend off assertions that you're a "defeatocrat" and a "cut-and-runner."

Through the distorting filter of contemporary right-wing pseudo-populism, speaking well and with a command of the facts renders you an "elitist." Advocating the teaching of science in schools is "religious intolerance." Campaigning for equality under the law means you support "special rights for minorities." Government aid to citizens rendered unemployed and impoverished because of the economic devastation wrought by the pandemic is an attack on "personal responsibility." On the other hand, corporate bailouts are heroic "financial rescue plans." Social distancing and mask-wearing mandates, and other public health policies that have been shown to save lives, are depicted as totalitarian impositions on "personal and religious freedom" that require "patriots" to "liberate" the regions so "oppressed."

Rather than refuse that right-wing lexicon, Democrats have typically been either silent or adopted their opponents' vocabulary even while arguing against the policies that underlay it. It is not that liberals have not had their own versions of Frank Luntz. A short list of smart and canny Left messaging experts would have to include George Lakoff, Drew Westen, and Anat Shenker-Osorio.[135] The problem has been that, for the most part, these masters of persuasive language have not been listened to, at least not consistently enough to inform a national communication strategy.

The Democratic Party is not monolithic, either ideologically or stylistically. Yet, as an institution, they have made the same error for decades—mistaking accommodation for compromise, which had contributed to Republican impunity long before Trump. Too often, their idea of negotiation was to start out asking for very little and retreat from there. Preemptive submission had been their default tactic. We can all recall them declaring in negotiations with their Republican counterparts that certain items were "off the table" because they weren't "moderate" enough and would offend their political opponents. In the George W. Bush era, even with a congressional majority, there was very little Democrats would go to battle over. The mere whisper of a GOP filibuster would make them wet their pants and seek "compromise." They would begin most debates pleading for the usual half a loaf, only to end up toast—defeated by their own timidity.

Their linguistic surrender facilitated all the others. Regardless of Democratic beliefs to the contrary, over recent decades, the party has been quite willing to parrot phrases like "war on terror," "tax relief," "defense of marriage," "enemy combatant," and "regulatory reform." Even while railing against Trump's government-sanctioned kidnapping and torture of brown children,

Congressional Democrats deployed the administration's anodyne description, joining Trump in calling it a "child separation policy." It mattered little that the Democrats vigorously protested the policies. Using the terms preferred by the administration, they welcomed into the discourse a kind of linguistic Trojan horse. As a result, the emotional power of the issue was attenuated. By not introducing their own vocabulary, Democrats made it easier for the media to function as mere stenographers of government spokespersons. Consider how many years into the Trump administration it took for fact-based media to call his lies what they were, *lies*. In many cases, they were following the lead of conflict-averse Democrats.

Despite doing their share of warmongering over the years, Democrats have been readily depicted by Republicans as "weak on defense." It is no wonder. When congressional Democrats voiced their whining pleas for "bipartisanship" and "unity," voters correctly heard the creaking knees of capitulation. For too many of them, "reaching across the aisle" and "moving to the center" have been covers for a desperate, masochistic need for approval from GOP colleagues who seem to have felt nothing but contempt for their groveling Blue State suppli-cants. They wanted to "negotiate" with liberals like the lion wants to negotiate with the lamb. For too long, Democrats have agonized over what concessions to offer, while the only question Republicans wrestled with is which part of their opponents' shriveled viscera to eat first.

With the resounding 2020 victory of Joe Biden, Democrats were given the opportunity to reject their traditional role as docile collaborators of right-wing propagandists and use the profound moral authority granted them by an excited electorate. Even when Biden's poll numbers plummeted due to global inflation, the popularity of the congressional members of his party did not decline in parallel, at least early on. Had the Democrats defined the party's val-ues and policies in its own terms and put moral arguments up front, they would have had a greater chance of claiming the linguistic custody of the center. New political initiatives require a new rhetoric, one that conveys Democratic val-ues in an emotionally compelling way and leaves no one guessing, for exam-ple, what "building back better" means. Unfortunately, that did not happen. Despite Biden's successful efforts to improve the economy, voters have given him little credit for it.

In the first few months of Biden's presidency, there were many heartening signs that the Democratic Party had finally learned the linguistic lessons of the past. For example, they reframed "bipartisanship" to refer to the electorate as a whole rather than limiting that term to the DC zip code. As a result, they could say, in all honesty, that the American Rescue Plan had bipartisan support, even if congressional Republicans tried to block it.

Biden's explicit decision to allow the Justice Department to function independently marked a visible departure from the corrupt practices of former Attorney General William Barr, who dutifully complied with the former president's command to prosecute innocent political enemies and grant corrupt allies impunity.[136] Biden has neither mandated nor prohibited the DOJ from investigating and, if the evidence justified it, prosecuting Trump for his alleged crimes before becoming president,[137] while he was in office,[138] and upon leaving the White House.[139] Were Biden to "forgive and forget" the former president's open corruption and betrayals of the country, under the comforting delusion that would somehow "heal our divisions," it would be game over for the United States as a law-bound nation where citizens, especially leaders, are held to account for their actions.[140] Future autocrats-in-waiting would know that nothing and nobody will stand in their way.

Unfortunately, the Justice Department waited too long before finally investigating Trump's many apparent crimes. It might have been hard for Attorney General Merrick Garland to choose which among the Trump scandals, treasonous acts, and open corruption his staff should investigate first. But Garland's greatest impediment seems to have been his fear of appearing partisan, a concern Republicans at all levels of government have long abandoned. That fear has led to what may turn out to be a fatal delay in achieving justice. Sadly, Garland is part of a long embarrassing lineage of invertebrate Democrats. His hesitancy to investigate Trump has given the Republican candidate the delays he constantly seeks. And it may end up being the decisive factor in enabling the former president, should he be reelected, to cancel all federal indictments and trials.

Fortunately, his appointed special council, Jack Smith, seemed to suffer no hesitation about aggressively and unapologetically investigating and seeking justice for Trump's many alleged criminal acts, although, thanks to his boss, the process may have begun too late. The most dramatic and openly seditious act of the former president will surely be the Trump-inspired violent January 6, 2021, assault on the Capitol Building and coup attempt that ended in the death of five and the attempted murder of others perceived as enemies of the former president.

As of this writing, nearly half of Republican voters support the attempted coup.[141] In Trump's second impeachment trial, GOP senators again refused to hold him to account. The assault on the Capitol had likely collaborators in Congress, was joined by military veterans, and enjoyed financial support from wealthy donors who view democracy as an annoying impediment to untrammeled profit-taking.[142] Even though Trump's own Department of Homeland Security named white supremacist militias as America's most significant terrorism threat, it took the brutal assault on the Capitol to focus the country's attention on this issue.[143] Because of the GOP investment in MAGA impunity, it fell to Democrats in the House, Senate, and White House to name this danger, investigate, and take action to stop it. Alas, because the GOP in Congress privileged tribal loyalty and fear of MAGA retribution over patriotism, the Democrats alone could not make Trump accountable through the two impeachment hearings. It remains to be seen if upcoming trials can shine a light on the clay feet of the Right's deity, Donald Trump and end his lifetime of legal indemnity.

As a historian of dictatorship, Ruth Ben-Ghiat noted in a webcast event on April 8, 2022, that what causes leader cults to implode is not the exposure of their crimes—their theft, corruption, murders, rapes, etc.—but prosecution, conviction, and punishment for those crimes.[144] Shattering their impunity dissolves the illusion of their omnipotence. Part of the charisma of cult leaders is their apparent untouchability. Legal accountability explodes that fantasy, turning a seemingly all-powerful autocrat into the little man behind the curtain, or more specifically, behind bars.

Biden's Complicity with Israel's Trump

Sometimes, the Democrats' passivity and deference to the frameworks of domestic opponents also drive relationships with foreign leaders. Many of Biden's fellow Democrats, voters and members of Congress alike, have taken the president to task for his ineffectual response to Netanyahu's collective punishment of Palestinians in Gaza. In what has been an unrelenting horror show of human suffering, Biden seemed paralyzed and unable to mobilize the aggression necessary to lead in this international crisis. At least initially, he doubled down on the untenable position of decrying the enormous number of civilian deaths resulting from the IDF's campaign against Hamas while at the same time giving Israel the weapons used to implement the mass slaughter. Every week that went by in which the United States refused to use military aid as leverage, Biden's tears over Palestinian starvation and death looked increasingly crocodilian.

Biden and some of his congressional allies continually framed their policy as "support for Israel." But, as Israel's moral authority and alliances began to fray at an accelerating rate, it became clear that America's policy was actually support for Netanyahu and his war crimes, to the detriment of the nation the Israeli leader claimed to be defending. In the absence of any real consequences, Netanyahu could easily thumb his nose at his impotent benefactors. Biden was left in the absurd position of saying, in essence, to Israel, "Please be nice to Palestinian civilians. And here are the weapons to exterminate them." Sadly, that message is not new. Israel has long been granted exemptions to the human rights preconditions for receiving military aid from the US government that every other country must abide by.[145]

When seeking to modify the behavior of an autocratic psychopath like Netanyahu, Biden seemed unable to understand that moral pleading falls on deaf ears. There must be immediate and painful repercussions for not doing the right thing. Most Democrats and certainly Republicans have never been willing to impose such conditions on Israeli leaders. Whether the Biden administration will back up its exhortations for the IDF to respect human rights with an incentivizing consequence remains to be seen. One thing we can be certain of—if Trump is reelected, there will be no tears shed for Palestinians, crocodilian or otherwise.

The Fate of MAGA in the Near-Term

One of the soothing but hazardous fantasies to emerge from Trump's 2020 electoral beatdown was that he would disappear from the political stage and democracy would be safe from his influence. While Trump may never occupy the White House again, he consistently led by a wide margin in the 2024 GOP primary race. Now that other candidates have been defeated, he will surely be the Republican presidential nominee. A July 2023 poll on the general election contest had him in a dead heat with Joe Biden, each with 43 percent[146] Since then, he has edged ahead in many polls.[147] Numbers will doubtless fluctuate. But even if he doesn't win, the campaign will give him another opportunity to bilk his credulous base into supporting him into his golden years.[148] While his business career has been riddled with failures, by depicting himself as a persecuted victim, Trump has profited handsomely from attempts to hold him accountable for his crimes. For example, after the DOJ executed a search warrant of his Mar-a-Lago resort to recover illegally held classified documents, he turned that into another con, persuading his followers to help him fight the "deep state." In one week alone, Trump hauled a million dollars a day from his eager marks to defend against the FBI "invasion."[149]

Whether in or out of office, we can be sure that he will continue to function as the avatar of contemporary conservative tribalism. Some "Never Trump" Republicans would like to depict him as an aberrant departure from GOP tradition. However, his rhetoric and actions make it clear that style and performative excesses aside, he is the fullest expression of right-wing libertarian values and psychology. Most GOP politicians and voters seem to agree that the former president is the soul (however in hock to Lucifer) of the Republican Party and embodies its values.

Longtime Republican campaign operative Stuart Stevens penned a devastating analysis of the past fifty years of GOP politics.[150] Unlike his Never-Trumper colleagues, Stevens does not argue that Trump somehow corrupted the Republican Party. Instead, he makes a persuasive case that the party gave birth to Trump. The five decades of GOP hypocrisy, corruption, and racism created the perfect soil where a xenophobic, amoral authoritarian could thrive.

Similarly, but from outside the Republican universe, journalist David Corn wrote a history of the modern GOP and came to similar conclusions.[151] Namely, the Republican Party had long been a congenial place for white supremacists, promoters of conspiracy theories, and demagogues. From Joseph McCarthy to the Tea Party, all the elements of Trumpism had preceded the actual arrival of the former president. The GOP's rageful disgust with pluralistic and racially integrated democracy may have been more sotto voce under earlier administrations, but it was clearly there.

Embodying and carrying forward that extensive Republican pre-history, Trump is now the revered leader of an authoritarian mass movement comprised of antidemocratic militias and terrorist groups and a 74-million-member voter base that shows no sign of becoming disaffected.[152] That movement includes its conspiracy mongering, cannibal-hunting, pedophilic-deep-state-routing offshoot, QAnon members, which have already joined the Republican congressional "mainstream.[153] They remain attentive to Trump's every social media utterance as if he were some sort of fascist Yoda. Like the broader Trump base, they will continue to be a serious political force and comprise a significant threat to fact-based public policy and democracy itself. It would not be surprising to see Trump himself transition from thwarted dictator to an inspirational deity after his death.

One of the more disturbing developments of the last few years is the internationalization of Trumpism. We can't predict how soon Trump the person will disappear from the American political stage. As of this writing, it is also impossible to know the outcomes of the multiple investigations, indictments, and trials currently underway by national and state authorities. While he is facing trials for serious criminal charges, it is unclear if actual convictions and imprisonment would do anything but enhance the reverence of his base. But for years now, it has been apparent that he is the template for the electoral path to fascist rule in the United States and worldwide. His pugilistic style, xenophobia, endorsement of sadistic violence, and post-truth rhetorical tactics have been emulated across the globe—from Brazil, the Philippines, Peru,

New Zealand, and even Canada.[154] It remains to be seen if the defeat of the MAGA movement in America will weaken it abroad.

How Pro-Democracy Activists Can Challenge Trumpian Impunity

Trump's growing desperation and determination to defy the political gravity of his 2020 defeat and possible future indictments could lead to the self-immolation of his brand. If that doesn't happen, tarnishing it now may yield considerable benefits. For reasons cited earlier, this task cannot be reliably delegated to elected Democratic politicians. Grassroots efforts among pro-democracy citizen groups will be required. It might be fruitful to return to Naomi Klein's book and its compelling call to arms for possible interventions among the many that can be employed. In addition to local actions aimed at resisting the new fascism, she makes the case that one of the most effective forms of opposition to the destructive ambitions of the Trumpian right would be to undermine the Trump brand itself.

First, there needs to be an unrelenting campaign of semiotic guerilla warfare against his brand in which it becomes infused with meanings that displace the current symbolic freight that fills his base with such awe. The Trump T on his buildings and products must bring to mind a treasonous loser instead of a tough guy winner. Every effort must be made to recast his putative strengths as the weaknesses they are. As many have already done, his critics need to redefine his impulsivity. Instead of allowing his brand managers and the Trump priesthood to present his thoughtless acting out as bold frankness and authenticity, it must be portrayed as the infantile psychological incontinence it is.

Then there are the "luxury" attributions carried by his brand. Activists must render manifest the unconscious lexicography of the Trump name itself. In other words, few may know that the actual meaning of trumpery is "showy but worthless" (according to the America Heritage Dictionary)—an accurate description of everything Trump. Poetic justice can be done.

As the 2020 election has demonstrated, pro-democracy forces have grown in number and impact. If the resistance can unite across its many differences, and if we are creative, focused, and steadfast in our efforts, even his Success deodorant (once an actual Trump product) may not be able to cover up the stink.[155]

Once the brand's patina is tarnished and the products licensed to bear the ignominious T come to signify all that is vile and cheesy, a global effort could be undertaken to subvert its economic power, i.e., the ability to generate a profit for those who license it. Were there a worldwide boycott, it could turn a marker of pride and impunity into a symbol of shame and liability, and the stigmatization of Trump's brand could be one bankruptcy from which Russian mob money would not be able to rescue him.[156]

To be most effective, such a boycott would need to be extended to the financial holdings and products associated with the companies, corporate oligarchs, and politicians that have been complicit with and funded the MAGA assault on American democracy. It is an intervention that has already been proposed by one writer determined to abort Trump's autocratic ambitions.[157] And it may be the most promising of all ideas to stop him because it requires no moral or psychological change in his financial and political backers. If their support for the former president is driven primarily by economic greed and lust for power (which seems self-evident), the same mercenary motives potentially could be harnessed to efforts to protect the country from his stated aims[158] of anointing himself king, jailing opponents, and plundering the national and global commons.

Of course, this is not a strategy that his base will sign onto, at least not until his name, and thus his brand more fully connotes "loser." To reveal to his worshipers the small man behind the curtain, he must be electorally defeated, impoverished, imprisoned, and shamed. Until then, the non-MAGA majority in the world would have to bear the burden of enacting the approach I've outlined. But I would certainly not put all my subversive eggs in this basket. In the next chapter, I will explore other possible interventions for countering his influence, primarily by creating alliances with those whose partisan identity remains obdurately conservative, if not MAGA.

CHAPTER 11

From Tribal War to Tribal Collaboration—Turning Enemies into Allies

Confederate General Lewis Armistead was severely wounded in the Battle of Gettysburg. Desperate for help, he gave the secret sign of Masonic lodge membership, hoping to be rescued by a lodge brother. Union officer Hiram Bingham, also a Mason, saw this. Within moments, Bingham stopped seeing an enemy who had to be killed. Instead, he beheld a fraternal brother who had to be saved. The Union warrior immediately came to the aid of the fallen rebel, transported him to a hospital, and watched over his personal effects until Armistead died of his wounds days later.[1]

That is far more than an uplifting story about the unexpected eruption of kindness and compassion on a Civil War battlefield, a setting in which cruelty, hatred, and intimate brutality would be the predictable norm. It is a hopeful indication of the ease with which, under certain circumstances, seemingly impermeable boundaries of tribal identity can open up to grant a formerly detested outsider the status of an insider. Neuroscientist Robert Sapolsky calls this transformation "recategorization."[2] Not only can a tribal outsider suddenly be construed as a member of one's own group, but the affective valence can quickly change and even reverse. As with Armistead and Bingham, once the social context factors that drive enmity change, alliances suddenly become possible.

The preceding chapters focused on the opposite process—how readily members of certain groups, who had been insiders or benign outsiders, can transform into tribal enemies who must be destroyed. Readers may recall my earlier discussion of Obama-to-Trump voters. These were predominantly white voters for whom whiteness was not a salient aspect of their identity. It was part of them but not central to their sense of self or place in the social world. Along comes Trump and his white supremacist followers, who effectively mobilize a fear of racial and foreign outsiders, people who look different and speak other languages.

The message white Obama voters heard was: Those swarthy hordes from the big city and lands across the border are intent on raping and murdering you and your loved ones. Their ultimate aim is to replace you and all other white people. Trumpworld's recycling of that neo-Nazi "Great Replacement" paranoid fantasy moved it from the margins to the mainstream, at least in right-wing media. Thus, the growing perception of out-group threats turned a subgroup of the country's unitarians into securitarians, at least enough for Trump to win the Electoral College in 2016. People comfortable with equality and semipermeable group boundaries became citizens who felt safe only at the top of zero-sum dominance hierarchies and required impenetrable walls to protect them from dangerous outsiders.

But in that rapid and disturbing shift toward a more xenophobic outlook, there lies the hopeful possibility that political identities and orientations might be mutable in the other direction. A reverse paradigm change could occur if the context of political discourse changes. Liberals would have to learn to speak with provisional securitarians in a way that can activate a trans-tribal kinship with all of humanity. This chapter uses research findings and real-world examples to illustrate how enemies might be transformed into allies.

The Problem with Solutions

Throughout this book, I have presented evidence that exclusionary, dominance-oriented tribalism is the group psychology of conservatives. They have relatively minimal empathy and concern for those outside their tribal boundaries. I have also argued that, at the present world-historical moment, that form of tribalism is a growing and malignant force in the United States and across the planet. At a minimum, that emerging development may usher in the death of democratic governance. At its worst, it imperils the future of humankind and even the biosphere.

The problem with attempts to consider possible solutions is that those embedded in this group mentality do not see it as a problem. To them, what needs fixing are folks like me who identify with all of humanity and the non-human animate world. For right-wing securitarian tribalists, the problem is those who want to make tribal boundaries more permeable and undo the "natural" order of domination by shifting to more egalitarian power relations. In their zero-sum world, the choice is binary—to be an enslaver or an enslaved person. Ethnic, racial, and sexual inclusivity is a danger that invites contamination, invasion, murder, loss of identity, and subordination. Overthrowing class, race, gender, and religious hierarchy hazards chaos and the decapitation of traditional authority. Conservatives have difficulty imagining more than the *inversion* of power, not its more equitable distribution. As the January 6 MAGA coup plotters demonstrated, revolution, in the minds of today's conservatives, is replacing one form of perceived tyranny with one that bears their tribal brand.

That sensibility is based on a deeply held but unexamined assumption: mutuality is neither possible nor desirable. For me to win, you have to lose. Earlier in the book, I described the work of historian Jefferson Cowie, who has documented the antebellum origins of a specifically conservative idea of freedom that has reverberated across the centuries—the freedom to dominate others. He points out that southern white supremacists did not fear racial equality per se but were convinced that civil rights laws would bring about domination by Blacks over whites. In white conservatives' views, power relations could be nothing other than top-down.

Cowie largely stays in his historical lane and, until the end of his book, avoids making comparisons to the present moment. By being parsimonious in his analogizing, he allows his readers to see the apparent continuities on their own. They could not be more obvious when he finally and explicitly points out the similarities in his trenchant conclusion.[3] The freedom to dominate that incited the passions of America's class of enslavers in the nineteenth century is the same freedom that inspired the neo-Confederate insurrectionists on January 6. Moreover, it seems clear that the anxiety over *being* dominated also remains salient on the Right and is behind the contemporary MAGA cult's paranoid fantasy of the "Great Replacement."

To argue for the feasibility of egalitarian power relations is not to diminish the ubiquity or seriousness of interpersonal or inter-group conflict. Indeed, there are times when the self-interests of groups *are* mutually exclusive. The central problem is how such conflict is managed and resolved. From the dominator's perspective, solutions require coercion by one party and the submission of the other. For those who desire and can imagine mutuality, negotiation and compromise are preferred. But egalitarian solutions require political and legal systems that can engender enough confidence to function as good-faith arbiters of opposing interests. Unfortunately, what we have at the moment are systems rigged to favor the interests of those who already have disproportionate power and wealth. The solution is to understand and challenge the limits to mutuality, not to resign ourselves to its absence and accept the self-fulfilling belief that domination is inevitable.

In this chapter, as with the book as a whole, my argument is directed at those who might already share my values, especially those who can envision mutuality and find it to be a compelling and vital goal. But I also want to reach those like me who would like to find ways to bridge the gulf that separates us from securitarians and those who can only conceive of relations of domination.

We may be unlikely to persuade conservative tribalists to adopt our worldview. But it might be possible to find a way to share the planet, to create a psychic demilitarized zone where greater empathy can thrive and some of the worst consequences abated. We will have to figure out how to coexist, or we all cease to exist.

What may be hard for liberal tribalists to accept is that both of the two opposing ways of relating to outsiders have been selected by evolution, as I've argued throughout the book. Neither is more intrinsic to our nature than the other. The question is not which orientation is the best in some abstract sense. Instead, we should ask ourselves which approach to self and others is most adaptive to current conditions and more likely to enable humanity and the rest of animal and plant life to survive and thrive. There is no symmetry on those grounds.

The problem with evolutionary predispositions is that they were formed under entirely different conditions than those in which we live. The fact that some of them may no longer serve our interests does not make them fade away in the short run. So, right-wing tribalists are here for now. They will continue to be driven by the same psychology and see the world through the same moral lenses for generations. They will be guided by the same seemingly self-evident intuitions that have always made sense to them.

If those of us embedded in a very different psychology wish to enlist the cooperation of securitarians for the project of our mutual survival, it will require us to speak in a language of values that make sense to them. We have to enter their world of meaning and become morally bilingual.

How to Not Get Lost in Translation

Social scientists Matthew Feinberg and Robb Willer have done work that holds great promise. Readers may recall from chapter 4 an extensive discussion of the work on "moral foundations." Those are the intuitive moral principles upon which partisans base their positions on various policy issues and political candidates. Conservatives privilege in-group *loyalty*, respect for traditional and high-status *authority*, and *sanctity* (protecting purity and sacredness). While *liberty* (as they understand it) is also a central moral value for conservatives, libertarians value it more than anything else.

For liberals, the underlying moral concerns are *care* (preventing and alleviating the suffering of others) and *fairness* (ensuring equity and mitigating discrimination). Those moral frames are part of the deep structure of personality and are not easily altered. They are the foundations from which people reason about politics. That framework not only helps us understand why partisans take the positions they do, but it also makes sense of what may look like hypocrisy.

For example, many have puzzled over the striking contradiction in the conservative position on abortion and their opposition to nearly every child welfare program and legislation. They are supposedly very concerned about the life of embryos and fetuses ("unborn children," in their view). If so, why do Republican legislators oppose funding infant formula distribution during a shortage, health care for children, school lunch programs, and early childhood education? Why do they prefer "thoughts and prayers" *after* school children are shot instead of assault weapon bans and other gun safety measures that would *prevent* school shootings? And why do so many of them oppose the best way to preempt abortion, contraception? We may find the answer in the different moral frameworks that underlie those and other issues.

Embryos and fetuses should be saved because fertilization is sacred, and deference is due to the religious authorities who have designated it as such. And because the "pro-life" position is intrinsic to Republican and conservative Christian identity, tribal loyalty requires each community member to hold to that position. Not doing so would be an immoral betrayal of the group.

In contrast, programs that help postnatal babies and children are less deserving of support because they are linked to a *care* moral framework (at least how liberals argue for them), which plays a minimal role in conservative moral reasoning. Since the Second Amendment has taken on the status and aura of a biblical passage—a timeless statement that brooks only one interpretation, theirs—it has become sanctified. In addition, opposition to all constraints on gun possession and use has become another identity-saturated issue.

Like their "pro-life" belief, deviating from Second Amendment fundamentalism evokes concerns about violating the moral foundation of in-group loyalty. And for securitarians, loyalty also mandates weapons possession to protect family and tribe from multiple outsider threats. Lastly, contraception, even that which acts on preconception processes, is immoral because it allows nonprocreative female sexuality to be expressed without the constraints of patriarchal marriage or male supervision. It is a practice that violates purity, sanctity, and traditional authority.

Feinberg and Willer show that the only way to get those with opposing views to reconsider their position on an issue is to reframe it in terms of the moral foundations they already hold. For example, they found that if you want a right-wing Christian to feel concerned about the environment, the issue would have to be framed as a purity problem. Evoking disgust by speaking about the medical consequences of contamination and industrial pollution entering our bodies would be most effective. In contrast, a plea to care for plants and animals or an appeal to fairness by arguing we should share the planet with other species that are as entitled to life as we are would guarantee conservative indifference or outright opposition to any pro-environment policy.

They also note that presenting challenging ideas to members of groups with a moral foundation different from your own by using the language of *their* framework has the additional benefit of giving you greater credibility. Rather than coming across merely as an enemy spouting heresy, you are more likely to be viewed as a foreign diplomat who has at least bothered to learn the native language, customs, and beliefs. Such an act of translation would be particularly effective in communicating with conservatives. Being morally bilingual and respecting their value system enough to argue from inside may be less likely to activate their intuitive aversion to tribal disloyalty.

Some may bristle at this approach because it could sound like deceptive manipulation. On the contrary, nothing communicated in those imagined inter-tribal debates would be untrue. You are saying to those with different moral foundations, "This is why *you* should care about that issue." That hypothesis has been tested on real-world partisans.

In a set of experiments during the 2016 presidential campaign, researchers used moral reframing to argue against the two political candidates.[4] With Republican subjects, they attempted to make the case against Donald Trump using a conservative *loyalty* frame. With Democratic subjects, the experimenters tried to dissuade them from supporting Hilary Clinton using a liberal *fairness* frame. That approach was far more effective than using frames outside their moral foundation. In other words, Trump supporters were relatively unmoved by appeals to fairness. And Clinton supporters were no less unpersuaded by an argument based on in-group loyalty.

In another study, researchers attempted to resolve what some call the "progressive paradox." That refers to the fact that while there is often broad popular support for progressive economic policies, progressive *candidates* often lose. To test whether that might be attributable to moral framing, researchers conducted a series of experiments with a large nationally representative sample. They presented one hypothetical progressive candidate with an unambiguously progressive economic platform, but the argument for that platform was made using frames that might reach beyond a progressive base. Appeals for the policy were grounded in loyalty—to country and family—and respect for tradition. The researchers created another progressive candidate, but that fictitious person's platform was rendered more centrist to see if that pulled more support from conservative and moderate voters. By now, my discerning readers have likely guessed the outcome. Widening the moral frame elicited far more support from a broader range of potential voters than presenting a weaker, more "moderate" platform.

Those results go against what seems to be the intuitive and often unsuccessful approach of congressional Democrats—to water down a liberal policy to make it palatable to Republicans. It seems evident that arguing for a piece of legislation framed in the language of your own moral values will not be very effective with opponents who don't share those values. A more compelling approach would be to make the case that a particular bill or candidate would meet your adversary's moral ends.

Theoretically, that approach could be used by conservative or liberal parties. However, to speak from inside the alien moral framework of another requires the capacity to take the perspective of those quite different from one's group. As the research cited throughout this book implies, the ability to empathize is far more developed in liberals than conservatives, giving the former a significant advantage. We now turn to a very different and real-world attempt to challenge a conservative, securitarian frame, this time concerning non-white asylum seekers looking for refuge in a majority-white country.

Can Policy Rehumanize the Ethnic Other?

For Americans, the following story's most remarkable and counterintuitive part begins with Justin Trudeau's campaign promise leading up to the 2015 election. He vowed to bring twenty-five thousand Syrian refugees to Canada by the end of that year. You read that correctly. Trudeau did not promise to build a wall, abduct the children of asylum seekers, send people fleeing persecution back to their "shithole" countries, build a moat filled with alligators, seek to have refugees shot for seeking entry, or, as GOP governors did, dump them like so much human garbage at the doorstep of political opponents. That was *our* guy and those who have emulated him. Surprisingly, the Liberal Party candidate for prime minister thought compassion had political utility.

While Canada may seem like a liberal oasis, there is a sizable minority of anti-immigrant securitarians in that country. To them, refugees, especially non-white ones, can seem economically threatening, dirty, violent, a vector for repellent cultural practices, and not quite human. Aware of those sentiments, Trudeau's new administration rapidly began an aggressive program to rehumanize the incoming refugees.

They were met at the airport with the message, "You're safe at home now." Trudeau deployed the Twitter hashtag #WelcomeRefugees. News media captured and disseminated images of the prime minister embracing the new arrivals and giving them winter coats. The government set up a website titled "Open Hearts and Welcoming Communities: It's the Canadian Way." It featured photos of Syrian refugees, stories of their flight from persecution, and information about how Canadian citizens could assist their new neighbors. The *Toronto Star* published a message in English and Arabic proclaiming, "You're with family now. And your presence among us makes our Christmas season of peace and joy just that much brighter."[5]

The reader might think that none of those measures could work in the United States because Canadians live in a parallel universe of peace, love, and understanding. However, it is essential to know that Canada's prior Conservative administration put forth various anti-immigrant and xenophobic policies only a year earlier. Under former Prime Minister Stephen Harper, the government cut health benefits for asylum seekers, falsely claiming they were denied only to "bogus refugees." The Conservatives also proposed the Zero Tolerance for Barbaric Cultural Practices Act. It was transparently a piece of xenophobic propaganda, banning acts like honor killings and forced marriage, which were already crimes. The point was to depict refugees as barbarians on a mission to assault Canada's values and violate its laws.

The crucial question is whether the change in messaging about immigrants and the liberal government's efforts to rehumanize them yielded any change in attitudes. Within four months of initiating the new program, popular support for the refugee resettlement plan increased from 42 percent to 52 percent. In efforts to evaluate how immigrants themselves were perceived, researchers assessed Canadian attitudes just before, four months after, and eight months following the election.[6] They used the stereotype content model discussed in chapter 6 to measure any possible change.

As readers may recall, that is a well-established and empirically-validated framework for looking at how dominant groups view members of minority or cultural out-groups. It is comprised of two factors, warmth and competence. Those out-groups seen as low in warmth and competence are devalued and subject to dehumanizing projections. Ethnic groups perceived as cold but competent, like Jews and Asians, are more often seen as threats. This study found that the Trudeau government's efforts markedly increased the perception of refugees' warmth and competence.

The effect was especially notable among subjects motivated by a desire to justify the actions of government authority. Ordinarily, when a nation's leaders utilize xenophobic rhetoric, citizens who score high on "system justification" tend to adopt those attitudes more readily.[7] In this case, the same desire to see the socio-political system as legitimate and a force for justice led to the greater rehumanization of a previously devalued refugee group. Perhaps the most heartening outcome of the Trudeau government's approach is that it changed more than attitudes. It resulted in an increase in practical commitments by ordinary citizens to assist the Syrians, such as housing offers. Now viewed as fully human and individuated in the minds of Canadians, these traumatized immigrants were essentially adopted and treated like family.[8]

Does Familiarity Breed or Blunt Contempt?

For as long as racial, ethnic, and other forms of bigotry have caught the attention of social scientists, scholars have looked at various interventions with the potential to reduce, if not vanquish, prejudice. The work focused on the impact of in-group-out-group contact is particularly informative.[9] The question of whether structured interaction between hostile groups could reduce enmity has yielded complex answers. Some studies found that prejudice was reduced when members of opposing groups engaged in friendly interactions. But it was short-lived and did not generalize to other, unknown out-group members.[10] One of the challenges of researching that issue outside of the laboratory is that when people are prejudiced against out-groups, they are far less likely to seek contact. And correspondingly, reduced contact facilitates prejudice. As chapter 8 described, partisan geographical sorting exemplifies that positive feedback loop.

One benefit of studying intergroup contact in controlled settings is that it enables researchers to isolate the variables involved. For example, in one multinational longitudinal study, investigators found that increased contact reduced prejudice only if the groups had equal status in the setting, cooperated to achieve a common goal, and worked closely together.[11] It was also vital that in-groups perceived the out-group members with whom they interacted as typical of that out-group. That latter factor, typicality, was crucial for reduced bigotry to be generalized to all out-group members.

One of the more striking findings of that study is that the prejudice-reducing effect of contact was experienced mainly by majority groups. Ethnic minorities only felt reduced enmity if the ethnic majority members were considered typical of their group. Hostility toward ethnic majorities tends to be systemic—expressed not just in individual behavior but embedded in various policies and practices, including those governing education, health care, policing, and financial institutions. So, it makes sense that the apprehension of minority group members would not be easily modified. Only if there were an indication that their salutary contact wasn't limited to a few benign majority allies would it make sense to assume the best about all members of a dominant group.

From Humiliation to Humility

Early in the book, I described how shame and defenses against it function as motivating forces in politics, especially among conservatives. They live in a mental world divided into tops and bottoms, dominators and subjugated, humiliators and the humiliated, those who do unto others and those who are done to. These binaries of shame are iterations of a social dominance orientation (SDO). As discussed throughout this book, that is one of the most defining psychological traits of those on the right. While we who embrace a more egalitarian propensity could not delete this trait from the range of human predispositions, it may be possible to render it less reflexive by encouraging a more extensive range of responses to loss, misfortune, and defeat. We can experience failure or losing a competition as an adverse event instead of a measure of our character.

As psychoanalyst and political theorist Barry Richards has outlined in an insightful essay, humility is a state of mind that enables one to acknowledge and tolerate one's shortcomings, limitations, and setbacks without collapsing into shame.[12] Humility obviates the need to protect oneself from shame by humiliating others. Fantasies of omnipotence, which we are all subject to, especially in early childhood, are destined to collide with the needs of others and the impediments of reality outside our own minds. Only by allowing ourselves to be humbled by the constraints of the external world can we learn from experience. As Richards points out, humility does not foreclose pride, which we can think of as self-regard without hubris. With pride intact, feeling guilt, admitting wrongdoing, and engaging in reparative actions are easier.

In some ways, humility is an emotional prerequisite for democracy. It enables us to hold and respect the community's needs, which may have requirements that supersede our individual ambitions. The collectivity of others provides a necessary limitation on each individual's wishes to the extent that those wishes threaten to harm others. Refusal to consider others is one of the cardinal features of autocracy. In the SDO mindset, deferring to fellow citizens is a humiliating surrender of one's "freedom." That is the zero-sum framework that drives right-wing libertarian politics and the MAGA movement more broadly. By contrast, the defining feature of any democracy, acceding to majority rule, mandates humility.

For humility to be seen as a way out of the trap of humiliation and counter-humiliation—of shame and defensive shamelessness—there must be a multilevel and society-wide program of emotional literacy. Beginning with childrearing and early education and continuing in public discourse throughout life, citizens need to learn the difference between losing and being a loser, between disappointment and hopelessness, between failing and being a failure, between being defeated in an election and being humiliated victims of "voter fraud," and between including immigrants and asylum seekers in the national family and being "replaced" by them.

From Exclusivity to Inclusivity

It is tempting to view the problem of tribal enmity in politics as a bipartisan issue that equally afflicts liberals and conservatives. At least, it is tempting for liberals to view it that way. After all, fairness and equity are moral intuitions that drive liberal identity and policy. Alas, the research does not support this more comfortable and generous assumption. Liberals are more motivated to form connections with others, whereas conservatives are driven more by power—power *over*, not power *with*.[13] More to the point, liberals tend to feel more connected to those in outside groups, a dynamic researchers refer to as "intergroup interdependence."[14]

Another way to describe this is that liberals are likelier to form groups with relatively permeable boundaries. In contrast, conservative groups tend to seek more impermeable borders between themselves and out-groups. So, if conservatives, by definition, create and join exclusionary groups, intergroup collaboration will be a counterintuitive goal. As I've described in earlier chapters, those on the Right consistently score higher on social dominance orientation (SDO). And nothing could be more antithetical to intergroup interconnectedness than SDO.

Corresponding to those traits are other differences in motivation, especially different instincts about approaching or avoiding out-groups.[15] Liberals are driven by a desire to care for others they don't know, which leads them to err in the direction of approach. Conservatives, by contrast, are concerned about protecting the tribe from dangerous outsiders. So, avoidance is their default attitude toward strangers. That finding, left-wing xenophilia and right-wing xenophobia, should be unsurprising to readers of this book by now.

In my view, malignant tribalism results from the default assumption of in-groups that out-groups are either a threat, inferior, or both. The logic of that belief tends to lead to one of two remedies; outsiders must either be subjugated or destroyed. As the research indicates, that assumption is synonymous with the conservative worldview. If we accept the truth of those findings and the face validity of our observations of everyday political behavior, we are led to an inescapably asymmetrical solution. Conservatives must be rendered less xenophobic, i.e., less conservative, if we are to make political tribalism more benign and less driven by hatred.

Researchers have sketched out how such an approach might look. In experimental conditions, when conservative subjects are exposed to information that increases their perception of the interdependence of social groups, they become measurably more politically liberal.[16] That, in turn, leads them to have greater concern for the welfare of those outside their in-group. The obvious challenge would be translating that approach into a broad political communication strategy.

While currently confined to my speculative imagination, there is a potential approach to that problem, which could be described as a form of messaging Aikido. Rather than try to get conservatives to go against their "nature," it might be more effective to find a way to deliberately create what serendipitously happened to Lewis Armistead and Hiram Bingham. That is, devise circumstances allowing out-groups to be experienced as part of a larger in-group, i.e., to enable enemies to be recategorized as allies linked by common interests. So, the impulse to protect the in-group translates into caring for outsiders.

While no one, to my knowledge, has yet devised a methodology for achieving that, we know what traits tend to be associated with a much more inclusive kind of collective identity. Based on Sam McFarland's research on people who identify with all of humanity, it is clear that such individuals view the entire species as their tribe instead of seeing themselves solely as members of a partisan, sectarian, or ethnic subgroup.[17] They tend to show more empathy and compassion. But beyond that, they are more likely to act on those emotions. Panhuman identifiers make practical commitments to global human rights as volunteers or donors to aid organizations. McFarland's work has been limited to studying people who already see themselves as belonging to humanity as a whole. He has not studied approaches designed to engender that trait in those who have not already developed it.

It might be less threatening for some to feel part of all humanity if it were clear that joining a more inclusive group did not mandate dissolving one's smaller group identity. Intergroup connectedness is a relationship *across* boundaries, not the eradication of them. Research confirms that openly recognizing differences between groups promotes greater empathy than minimizing them.[18] For Black, white, Latino, Asian, multiracial, religious, secular, straight, LGBTQ, and perhaps even conservative and liberal Americans to join together as a superordinate group, as simply Americans, there must be a goal or a set of values shared by all.

Of course, many issues affect every citizen, which could be readily addressed if all Americans experienced themselves as part of a superordinate tribe. At the top of the list of possibilities, the most urgent would be the climate crisis and all its associated manifestations. It is the disaster that contains all the others. A short list would include killer heatwaves, droughts, megafires, toxic air, floods, increased hurricane severity and frequency, biodiversity loss, crop failures, starvation, lethal resource conflicts, social chaos and the consequent rise of autocracy, pestilence, disease, and shortened life spans. While some groups might be temporarily more insulated from the worst impacts than others, no one residing on Earth can escape.

That is the most catastrophic development in the history of our species. Yet, in one study (similar to the one cited in the previous chapter), it is viewed as a significant problem by only a modest portion of the population—39 percent.[19] But, as with other surveys, that average belies profound tribal differences. Only 13 percent of Republicans view it as important. In contrast, 69 percent of Democrats see addressing climate change as a high priority. Our species is famous for "future discounting," i.e., minimizing the severity and importance of future events, like environmental calamities.[20] But the climate crisis is not merely a future problem; it is unfolding now with devastating consequences. The persistence of humanity and other life forms depends on our ability to collaborate as a transcendent tribe that can readily communicate across the barrier of our different moral languages.

Pre-Bunking Post-Truth: Boosting Cognitive Immunity

Shared beliefs are foundational to tribal identity. And rigid ideas—inflexible and impervious to evidence—help consolidate rigid identities. One vital way to demonstrate our loyalty to the group is to embrace its defining narratives. Signaling fealty to tribal catechisms shows we belong inside, not outside, the group boundary—that we are allies, not enemies.

While the acceptance of tribal fictions could be faked and performed for the benefit of others, that sort of sham agreement would constitute a burdensome cognitive load. It is far more efficient and less taxing to internalize group beliefs—to be a true believer. But when an idea or worldview becomes part of one's identity, any challenge to the belief might feel like a perilous threat. That makes fact-based refutation of something like an anti-science conviction or a groundless conspiracy theory not merely ineffective. It can lead someone to double down, to hold the belief even more tenaciously because it is not just an idea at stake but the believer's sense of self and place in the world.

When groups do not share the same reality, collaboration on solving shared problems, such as our current ecocidal climate crisis, becomes nearly impossible. Liberals are certainly not immune to the internalization of false beliefs. But the problem is far from symmetrical. Conservatives, especially of the MAGA variety, are deeply wedded to various tribal fictions, many of which I've analyzed throughout this book.

Speaking to conservatives with empathy and patience is essential. And as I argue previously, so is enclosing one's message within the moral frameworks most meaningful to them, such as group loyalty, purity, and sanctity. We can think of this metaphorical code-switching as akin to speaking French to a native French speaker. It is a strategy for being understood. And when the aim is political bridge-building, it is an act of moral translation. But reaching people already embedded in a collective delusion is much more arduous than preventing the initial adoption of false beliefs. It is easier to "pre-bunk" than debunk.

Critical thinking must be learned as early in life as possible if we are to keep citizens from falling into the post-truth abyss. The encouraging news is that such a methodology has been researched and refined for decades. This pre-bunking process has been studied and developed under the rubric of "inoculation theory." As might be gathered by the name, it is a framework based on the metaphoric similarity between protecting against biological infection and an informational one. Resistance to a microbial pathogen can be built through immunization. Likewise, one can facilitate cognitive resistance to disinformation by warning people they will be targeted, exposing them to a weakened version of a false belief, and equipping them with a counterargument in advance. The most robust immunity is achieved when we can help citizens recognize the propagandistic "vectors" (manipulative techniques) that make it easier for lies to "infect" us.[21]

In the 1960s, US government officials were concerned that soldiers captured by enemy forces could be brainwashed. (There seemed to be little worry about the "patriotic" brainwashing recruits were subject to in their basic military training.) That potential threat led social psychologist William McGuire to embark on a research program to create a cognitive "vaccine" against unwanted persuasion.[22]

In the early years of this research, the focus was on "pre-butting" the content of an anticipated false message. While effective at reducing susceptibility to the specific expected misinformation, that approach was not scalable to the larger world beyond the laboratory because the inoculation did not protect against novel content. How can people be protected against swallowing new lies? To address that problem, social scientists shifted their emphasis to the techniques of manipulation employed to promote a wide range of mis- and disinformation. Researchers trained people to recognize those techniques. As a result, study subjects learned to identify false claims and thus were far less likely to be persuaded by them than were subjects who had not gone through the training.[23]

Different investigators in this field of research have derived slightly different lists of manipulative techniques. Nearly all include some version of the following: fearmongering and other efforts at emotional activation; conspiracy narratives; fake experts; ad hominem attacks on opponents; cherry-picking of data; scapegoating; false dichotomies; logical incoherence: and impossible expectations (e.g., breakthrough cases of an illness among the vaccinated "prove" vaccines don't work). Training to recognize these techniques is achieved by having subjects play a fifteen-minute video game. Like a vaccination that has broad activity against multiple strains of a pathogen, this approach to misinformation can protect against many variants of widely disseminated falsehoods, as most tend to employ the techniques listed.

This approach could easily be used outside the research lab and readily incorporated into critical thinking or media literacy courses, which should be part of every secondary school curriculum. Citizens so educated would stand a much better chance of resisting the propagandistic seductions of a wide variety of cults, political and religious. As multiple episodes of genocide attest, false narratives form the epistemological glue that binds people to destructive groups and animates their hatred for outsiders. Being able to think critically may be one of the most important bulwarks against the dangerous consequences of xenophobic tribalism.

As promising as cognitive immunization trainings are, like anti-microbial vaccines, they rely on people willing to sign up for them. Teaching critical thinking skills, independent of any content, may be viewed as quite threatening to some conservatives. In 2012, Texas Republicans put opposition to courses in "higher order thinking skills" into their party platform.[24] They feared that such training would undermine "parental authority" and threaten students' "fixed beliefs." And that was long before the current post-truth moment in which evidence-free conspiracy mongering has inspired political lynch mobs and many actual murders. So, for that kind of intervention to impact those needing it the most, it would have to be administered in "microdoses" – such as thirty-second ads.

Some Concluding (but Not Conclusive) Thoughts on Evolution: The Conflictual Legacies of Natural Selection

It isn't only those who embrace evolutionary explanations for human social arrangements that can fall prey to reductionism. Even critics who detest it can be ensnared by the seductions of simplistic thinking. Partisans of each camp seem to believe that natural selection has picked a favorite. By nature, humans are predatory or compassionate, autocratic or democratic. Choose your dichotomy. As I've argued throughout this book, the reality is that our nature is a messy and conflictual amalgam of potential. That is an area where most evolutionary psychologists and psychoanalysts agree. Many of our predispositions once promoted genetic fitness, i.e., enabled offspring survival. Some were of little consequence.

But we no longer live under the conditions that shaped our evolutionary adaptions. Some early-acquired predispositions may still serve us, depending on which specific environmental variables exist. Other once-advantageous tendencies may, under current circumstances, hasten our extinction. Among those lethal evolutionary anachronisms, I would include the persistence of xenophobic tribalism and the urge to subjugate others. Fortunately, there is an opposing, more emancipatory set of predispositions that could pull us from the brink.

Another way to put this is that there is a conflict between two fitness-driven tendencies in social groups: the desire among some individuals to exercise power over others and the urge among collectivities of individuals to check the power of anyone seeking to dominate the group. Most of human evolutionary history occurred in societies organized as hunter-gatherer groups. That is not to deny the findings of Graeber and Wengrow indicating that multiple forms of social organization existed simultaneously in the same historical period or changed seasonally within a single culture.[25] Nevertheless, in early, more democratic societies, there were very immediate checks on the autocratic tendencies of any leader who sought to bypass or challenge the predominantly egalitarian norms.

Psychological anthropologist and evolutionary scholar Pascal Boyer points out that leadership was as much of a burden as it was a privilege.[26] While hierarchical and autocratic regimes are now more common than democratic ones, our evolutionary history raises the provocative possibility that there is genetic potential for egalitarian relations to be expressed given the right ecological conditions. We know, for example, that resistance to unjust authority exists in every known society.

Along these lines, anthropologist Christopher Boehm coined the phrase "entrenched egalitarian motivation."[27] It refers to the persistence in modern societies of egalitarian psychology that emerged in very early forms of social organization. He noted that there is minimal concentrated power in small-scale societies. "Egalitarian" does not mean everyone would play the same roles in decision-making. Instead, it refers to the urge to minimize the potential for domination or exploitation. One might have been a leader in one activity—say hunting—but that power did not confer the right to preside over the preparation and dispensing of medicinal herbs. What mattered was circumscribing the power of any individual enough to preempt the possibility of despotism.

Boyer cites the anarchist theoretician Peter Kropotkin and argues that a significant driver of our political psychology is the urge to engage in mutual aid, share the commons, and provide a bulwark against autocratic power.[28]

That predisposition is what I would view as the liberal aspect of our conflictual nature. Of course, that egalitarian potential does not guarantee whether or how it will be realized. It could take the form of radical democracy and compassionate mutuality. And as such, it could express itself in genuine challenges to the wealthy's ability to buy power.

Or it could manifest in the xenophobic anti-democratic pseudo-populism currently spreading across the planet. In that case, it might show up as witch hunts against the vague threats of "cultural elites" and manifest as battles to preserve actual elites' unearned entitlements and regressive tax obligations.

The tension between those who seek unaccountable power and those who insist on holding them to account will always be part of our social "genome." The more we can remain conscious of those potentials, the more we can be deliberate about creating conditions in which our democratic instincts can find expression.

After the 2022 Midterms, Is Optimism Warranted?

This chapter follows the convention of many "social problem" books by concluding with a discussion of possible solutions. But there are constraints on my wish to lift the spirits of readers. I hope this book will not be like others in which the burning urgency of the problems identified requires far more than the tepid solutions offered in the conclusion. The reassurance generated by the potential correctives outlined here may pale next to the anxiety evoked by previous chapters. Nevertheless, I have attempted to leaven this disturbing account of tribal enmity in the United States with evidence-based possibilities for mutual tolerance, if not reconciliation and collaboration. At the same time, that has not eclipsed my awareness that this deeply etched feature of our conflictual human nature may play out in more troubling and less sanguine scenarios. Toxic expressions of political tribalism only seem to be increasing the closer we get to the 2024 election.

After the 2022 midterms, the liberal commentariat sang in near unison about voters saving the United States and pulling the country back from the brink of neofascism. Before election night, it seemed like the evening would be a death watch for American democracy. Instead, our ailing republic rallied—from hospice to long-term care. Indeed, the GOP losses will make it much more challenging for them to engineer a legal coup in 2024. MAGA candidates for secretaries of state, Congress, and governor who would have been in a position to overturn future elections were defeated in swing states. Democratic Party triumphalism aside, GOP losses may only momentarily keep the pro-autocracy party from advancing its ambitions. While the "red wave" did not come to pass, we remain up to our necks in a rapidly rising crimson tide of anti-democracy rhetoric and actions.

Pundits seemed to forget that razor-thin margins often decided the zero-sum election victories for Democrats. That means the massive plurality of voters that Trump has used to threaten Republicans into political and rhetorical compliance remains a readily available tool of coercion should the GOP attempt to discard him.

Before the midterm elections, the MAGA faction vowed that there would be multiple show-trial "investigations" and "impeachment hearings."[29] House Republicans made strenuous efforts to keep that promise. Since 2022, we have seen the mainstreaming of the fringe, resulting in a reprise of some of the most striking past expressions of right-wing projective post-truth. Among the loud but unconvincing performances of MAGA caucus political theater have been fraudulent hearings about "voter fraud," witch hunts related to the FBI "witch hunts," tribunals attacking public health experts featuring "experts" on vaccine microchip implantation, and politicized investigations of "politicized investigations." In addition, there have been nonstop efforts to demonize the work of the January 6 committee, whose evidence of the Trump coup attempt was derived almost entirely from the former president's appointees, aides, and advisers. Last but not least, the GOP's spiritual leader, the ever-vengeful Donald Trump, has insisted that his congressional vassals initiate retaliatory investigations into Joe Biden, his son, and presidential appointees. And they have made valiant, if ultimately unsuccessful, attempts to comply with his wishes. In short, we have seen ruthless tribal warfare under the thin guise of "oversight."

Marjorie Taylor Green, Ron DeSantis, and other right-wing Christian culture war Jihadists have pursued their quixotic crusades against the evils they see in fact-based secular education and multi-racial democracy. It is not clear if their true-believing followers are trembling with fear over the imagined indoctrination of their children by "woke" public school curricula. It is certainly possible that a growing number of parents in the MAGA base have been convinced that kids are being encouraged to identify as cats and accommodated with litter boxes instead of toilets (a myth that was promoted by at least twenty GOP politicians[30]). In 2023, six North Dakota Republicans introduced into their state legislature a bill[31] banning schools from providing facilities and services for students who identify as any species other than humans. Given the apparent gravity of the problem, the bill's authors labeled it an "emergency measure." Needless to say, that moral panic was grounded in nothing but the feverish imagination of Republican demon hunters. So far, there appear to be no bird-identified kindergarteners demanding nests of twigs during nap time.

Florida will continue to be the national testing ground for a wide range of measures designed to ensure that schools become sites of ideological indoctrination. In addition to the growing list of banned books, curricular purges (for example, disallowing the discussion of gender and sexual orientation in AP psychology classes[32]), perhaps the most egregious is the possible installation of cameras and microphones in lecture halls.[33] That will allow the state to monitor "abuse" by teachers and detect any political or religious heresy.

One Trumpian legacy that will likely outlast him is the political utility of biographical fakery. One of the GOP's 2022 House victories was that of now-expelled New York Congressman George Santos. Nearly every element of his life story, as put forward in his campaign narratives, has turned out to be fictional—his upbringing, ethnicity, education, business experience, friendships, marriages, wealth, and funding sources. Then there are the lies of omission, such as his swindling of acquaintances, fraudulent financial schemes, and actual campaign donors. Beyond a handful of embarrassed colleagues, few Republicans seemed to have had a problem with the imposter in their midst, at least in the early phase of his emerging scandals.[34]

Former House Leader Kevin McCarthy had exhausted himself performing outrage over the Democrats who dared to hold the former president accountable for his manifest corruption. As political retaliation, McCarthy banned two of the most prominent Democrats from committees and sought to do the same with a third.[35] Yet, the GOP leader, who claimed to be so concerned about congressional ethics, had been quite happy to overlook the fabrications of his new House member and appointed Santos to two committees.[36] However, calls for disciplinary action from his own constituents became so deafening that McCarthy persuaded Santos in a private meeting to recuse himself from committee assignments until investigations into his fraudulent claims and activities could be completed.[37]

Eventually, a bipartisan House Ethics Committee report exposed details of his profligate corruption that were too mortifying for even Republicans to countenance. Unlike Trump, Santos was a grifter without a base. Bilking campaign donors to fund his Botox and high-end porn habits would have consequences, eventuating in his expulsion from Congress.[38]

While Santos was ultimately held to account, that episode may auger a new era of Trumpian post-truth. The Right's indifference to factuality may be no longer limited to lies about the world but come to encompass the very identities of multiple Republican politicians.[39] For now, Trump still holds his position as the most highly-rated GOP impostor. But the veneer is starting to chip away from his gold-plated throne.

Following the many electoral losses for the GOP, Fox News and other right-wing propaganda outlets showed an eagerness to dump Trump and those he endorsed.[40] Mitch McConnell bemoaned the capacity of the former president and the MAGA message his emulators heralded to repel and frighten independent and swing voters.[41] When it comes to holding power, the Republican elite can quickly become a reality-based community. Votes are math they can easily grasp, even as they make great efforts to fudge the numbers to promote their voter-fraud stories.

For his part, Trump remained undaunted by the loss of many of the candidates he endorsed. On the one hand, he has had multiple resurrections following revelations that would have terminated the career of most other politicians. The former president knows that exposure of his sexual predation, criminality, corruption, admiration of foreign autocrats, murderous efforts to overthrow an election, and thug posturing more generally has elicited loud but short-lived outrage outside his cult of followers. He returned from all that, as well as two impeachments, to dominate his party. So, it is no wonder that, indictments be damned, Trump is not only running for president again but easily vanquished his opponents in the GOP primaries.

On the other hand, the appellation of "loser" may do more damage to his brand than any of his previous scandals. In the tribal universe of the Right, where social dominance is the defining psychological trait of its members and the magnetic north of their moral compass, being a "winner" is everything. Eventually, Trump may be convicted of multiple crimes and end up presiding over his campaign (or even his next administration) in Mar-a-Lockup. Nevertheless, as I've argued elsewhere, Trump*ism* likely will remain central to Republican identity.[42]

For a while, DeSantis seemed like a potential threat to Trump's dominance. Not only was he able to lie in complete sentences, which rendered him a more effective mouthpiece for right-wing post-truth proclamations, but unlike Trump, he had been a *real* winner.[43] In Florida, DeSantis did not need to finesse the Electoral College. He had more than a minority share of the electorate. DeSantis was genuinely popular among conservative Floridians. They apparently relish his successful efforts described earlier to undermine public health, humiliate asylum-seeking immigrants, hobble public education, ban books, and repudiate scientific reasoning. His sweeping regressive and authoritarian "Stop Woke Act" was such a tyrannical infringement on academic freedom and constitutional liberties that the federal judge who blocked its implementation described it as "positively dystopian,"[44] which may end up giving the Floridian führer some welcome costly signaling street cred. Undaunted, he vowed that should he become president, he will "start slitting throats" of federal employees, whom he sees as impediments to his autocratic prerogatives.[45] Fortunately, he will not have that opportunity until at least 2028.

Early in the GOP primary campaign, a survey of Republican voters asked whom they would prefer as their 2024 presidential candidate. The results showed DeSantis besting Trump by 42 percent to 35 percent.[46] Perhaps the Florida governor was easier to idealize then because his name recognition was far less than the former president's.[47] But after his charmless persona became quite familiar, DeSantis's popularity plummeted precipitously.[48] While many pundits read the defeat of so many Trump-endorsed candidates in the 2022 midterms as a rejection of Trumpism, it seemed that for at least a short time some in the GOP base wanted a more stable and reliably successful carrier of the MAGA torch. All but Trump went down in flames.

The Ambiguity of Polls

Speaking of the voter base, when people answer poll questions, especially concerning the motives behind their decisions, we must exercise much caution in interpreting the answers. There are too many uncertainties to take survey responses at face value. Are those being questioned giving interviewers the answers that subjects believe their interrogators want to hear? Are they saying things to outrage or provoke pointy-headed researchers? Are voters even conscious of what motivates their decisions? Respondents' reasons for their political choices are likely driven by multiple determinants—some conscious and reflecting their best effort to weigh the relevant facts, and some unconscious and responsive to inchoate emotional forces.

Then there are the methodological problems. Given the poor response rates to telephone polling, researchers are no longer obtaining random samples. But that has not stopped journalists from extrapolating from such skewed findings and declaring truths about the mind of the electorate, predicting outcomes, and perhaps even impacting turnout. At the end of nearly every election cycle, pundits are shocked that the results, like the failed "red wave," once again defied the polls.[49]

But for the sake of discussion, let's assume voter surveys have at least some validity, at least in terms of issue salience. Before the midterm election, polls suggested that the economy was a top concern of voters and seemed likely to determine voting behavior. Empirically, the economic picture was quite mixed. Wage growth and employment were rising, but inflation was high. While these numbers are objective indicators, they are also projective tests. In other words, they are subject to multiple interpretations concerning how good or bad the numbers are, which statistics are more important, who should be credited for the good news, and who should be blamed for the bad news. We must add that "the economy" is a reification, an abstraction treated as something tangible. It is a mix of different indicators that often conflates the financial well-being of the wealthy with that of everyone else.

In addition, another factor that shaped the public's reading of the economy is our species' tendency to privilege negative or threatening information. As discussed elsewhere in the book, our extraordinary attention to environmental factors that might imperil our survival has enabled humans to endure. Those of our ancestors who took signs of danger more seriously than they did reassuring information enjoyed an obvious evolutionary advantage.

When that negativity bias is coupled with our need for identifiable villains and simplistic narratives, it is no wonder that the complexities of a global economic downturn get reduced to a more comprehensible narrative. However much the Democrats may have "overperformed" in the midterms, that story led to the political punishment of Biden and his party. Only late in the campaign did the Democrats foreground the primary causes of worldwide inflation— Putin's colonial war, the greed of corporations who made record profits from price gauging, and pandemic-induced global supply chain problems

The COVID pandemic began and worsened during the Trump presidency and was a national event far more catastrophic than inflation. And yet, surprisingly, there were no indications that it contributed to the underperformance of MAGA candidates. That was despite the former president's self-serving denial in its early phase and malignant mismanagement in its later phases. The virus and the death and suffering it caused did not disappear. Even on the eve of the midterms, 335 Americans were perishing from the virus daily.[50] And, those conservative politicians whose anti-public health policies added profoundly to the body count—the bulk of which comprised Republican voters[51]—were never held to account at the ballot box.

The reason is that Trump and GOP politicians had at the ready a narrative into which COVID prevention measures like masking, social distancing, and vaccination could be readily folded: The intrusive liberal nanny state is always looking for ways to limit your freedom. We Republicans opposed these measures at every turn and protected your right to do whatever you want, regardless of its impact on others. (The reader will recognize this as the consistent ethos of right-wing "freedom.") So, in the MAGA story, the shutdowns, not the disease that necessitated them, were the real problem. Thus, Trump, who incited armed militias to "liberate" states from public health constraints, emerges as the paradoxical conservative hero of the pandemic, a mantle picked up by Ron DeSantis and other Republican politicians.

The Ghost of MAGA Future and How It Might Be Averted

While the country awaits the outcomes of Trump's many criminal trials, he has announced plans[52] for the ultimate securitarian regime should he find his way back into the White House in 2025: a new and improved Muslim ban, a tariff on imported goods, detention camps for asylum seekers, and mass deportations of immigrants.

In addition, he promised to "totally obliterate the deep state" (government workers whose first loyalty is not to him), fire and prosecute law enforcement officials who have dared hold him to account, end birthright citizenship, stop aid to Ukraine, "fundamentally reevaluate" our commitment to NATO, and militarize the US-Mexico border by withdrawing forces from Europe. Those last three are clearly a big wet kiss aimed at Putin's posterior.

Trump also pledged to accelerate fossil fuel extraction, cut funding to schools that issue mask and vaccine mandates during pandemics, promote the arming of teachers, implement mass incarceration in psychiatric institutions for the "dangerously deranged," and encourage shoot-on-sight policies to address shoplifting. He even promised to indict anyone who dared challenge him politically.[53] We have reached a point at which even pearl-clutching moderates are no longer complaining about the rhetorical imprudence of calling Trump's vision a fascist one.

As the GOP primary drew closer, candidate Trump, the party's presumptive nominee, began to morph even further into his Italian and German role models from the 1930s. He not only referred to his political enemies as "vermin" who must be eliminated,[54] but Steven Cheung, his campaign spokesman, also vowed that the former president's opponents should expect that their "sad, miserable existence will be crushed when President Trump returns to the White House."[55] Trump said that one of his first moves should he become president again will be to imprison his critics.[56]

He also implied that top military officers who challenged his edicts should be executed.[57] Trump's top pick for attorney general, Mike Davis, a former law clerk for Supreme Court Justice Neil Gorsuch, vowed to establish a "DC gulag" for liberal political enemies.[58] Trump seems aligned with that plan. In his view, Democrats comprise "a sick nest of people that needs to be cleaned out and cleaned out immediately."[59] The cleansing must also include immigrants, who are "poisoning the blood."[60] If he does manage to get reelected, it's anybody's guess how quickly the stock price of Zyklon B will surge.

By giving attention to the fluctuating electoral fortunes of Trumpian politicians, I don't want to overlook and underestimate the potential impact of the anti-democracy sentiments and actual terrorism of the MAGA base. A University of Chicago study[61] completed in April 2023 found that 25 percent of Americans still believed Trump's stolen election lie. And by the same percentage, they endorsed the neo-Nazi "Great Replacement" theory. Twelve million said violence was acceptable to restore their leader to the White House. Across the country, election workers are quitting in the face of harassment and death threats. Before the last midterms, 20 percent of them left their jobs out of fear.[62]

In November 2023, MAGA terrorists sent fentanyl-laced letters to voting centers in six states, prompting officials to supply the opioid antagonist naloxone to those offices in the event of exposure. Those acts were clumsily disguised false-flag attacks on voting from the "Left." The envelopes were adorned with Pride, anti-fascist, and satanic symbols. It seems unlikely that those attacks persuaded many Americans that Hitler-hating gay and lesbian activists were aligned with Beelzebub to stop elections. Nevertheless, it was clear that however laughably incoherent the message of those terrorists was, they were deadly serious.[63]

Fascism is not a movement or a mode of governing reliant solely on autocratic leaders. Its success requires the mobilization of large segments of the population and at least the docile complicity of others. That is how elections can ironically be the path to dictatorship. This brings us back to the question of optimism over the future of democracy. The now pro-autocracy GOP can only stay afloat if buoyed up by its voting base. What are the possibilities that Republican voters will question their beliefs and desert their leaders? Early in this chapter, I outlined some ways those on the Left could facilitate that. There are also political developments that could tip the scales.

As I've noted throughout this book, being seen as a loser and, therefore, not a dominator is kryptonite to the political ambitions of Republicans. No one on the Right wants to be one or vote for one. Loser status could be conferred by electoral defeats or the punishments resulting from criminal convictions. Both give the lie to MAGA assertions of omnipotence and impunity. Thus far, election denialism and cries of persecution have prevented those kinds of losses from turning into politically fatal humiliations. However, as the sheer number of those defeats mount up, especially those that involve jail time, they seem likely to take a toll.

Since networks of disinformation are also vital to the success of fascist movements, we can find hope in the end of the long-standing impunity right-wing media have enjoyed for the consequences of their propaganda efforts. The well-known and extraordinary $787 million settlement Fox News had to pay for its election falsehoods showed there could be a substantial cost to promoting slanderous lies, which up until the successful suit had been their business model.[64] Since right-wing libertarian billionaire Elon Musk added Twitter to his toy chest and renamed it X, it has become a largely unmoderated swamp of bigoted rants. After he proclaimed that a neo-Nazi screed accusing Jews of promoting "the Great Replacement" was "the actual truth," advertisers began deserting the platform. Documents leaked to the *New York Times* showed that losses for the company were predicted to reach $75 million by the end of 2023.[65] At this point in 2024, Twitter (now X) limps along in spite of the many subscriber defections.[66] Nevertheless, there may come a point when the promotion of post-truth may become an overhead cost that conservative media outlets will be increasingly unwilling to pay.

Civil War or a Civil Divorce?

In journalist Stephen Marche's *The Next Civil War*, he makes a persuasive case that America has reached a point of no return in the nation's partisan conflicts.[67] Our incommensurate political aims, moral values, and understandings of empirical reality mean that this country has become ungovernable. The GOP routinely opposes any policy, whether concerning economics or public health, that could improve the lives of US citizens if it might redound to the political benefit of Democrats. Fortunately, the pre-midterm promise made by Republican candidates that they would only accept election results that made them winners was mostly not kept. So, for the moment, the American experiment in democratic governance has not come to a formal end.

Nevertheless, as the attempted murder by a MAGA zealot of former Democratic House Speaker Nancy Pelosi and the brutal assault on her husband remind us, the dysfunction and the increasingly violent enmity in America's political culture remains a vivid reality. And it was certainly not reassuring when that act of vicious cruelty was greeted with the now-expectable sadistic snickering by GOP politicians and their online lynch mob.[68] Apparently, few things beyond slaughtering endangered species for "sport" can give Don Jr. the frisson he craves.[69] Learning that a geriatric liberal has had his skull fractured seems to be one of them.[70]

Marche sees only two possibilities for our future: 1) negotiated disunion that allows regional secession from an already disunited United States, or 2) protracted, bloody, and unresolvable civil war. The former scenario would be excruciatingly difficult and complex. While it might be the least violent, it would be logistically impossible. Regions within the United States are not homogenous. Red states have large blue cities. And blue states have significant red rural areas. Nevertheless, as outlined in earlier chapters, multiple secessionist movements are already underway.

As Marche points out, the latter possibility would not look like the country's first civil war, with organized, uniformed opponents facing one another across battlefields.[71] While the American military can bring overwhelming force to bear, some veterans, current members, and police officers are MAGA-identified and anti-democratic.[72] The ubiquitous presence of Fox News on military base televisions has an impact[73] on the mentality of soldiers, just as it does on civilian minds. America's armed forces and police agencies may not be willing to fire upon fellow citizens, especially if they comprise a right-wing militia. Moreover, those self-styled armies have spent many decades accumulating large stockpiles of lethal weaponry. Such a war would more likely resemble the grinding futility of the conflicts in Northern Ireland, Iraq, and Afghanistan. The *United* States is already an oxymoron. In any of these scenarios, it seems likely to fracture into a landscape of hostile territories. Let's hope the sober pessimism of Marche and others turns out to be only grim conjecture.

Can Democracy Be Made More Democratic?

Lastly, I want to mention at least one of the best solutions to malignant political tribalism that has little chance of being implemented: proportional representation.[74] By allocating power based on a party's percentage of the vote, it would allow even small segments of the population to have a voice instead of being silenced by our current winner-take-all system. That process would also enable candidates from more than two parties to run for and hold office.

It would be a profoundly fair means of distributing political agency. But that is precisely why conservatives are unlikely to embrace it. "Fairness" is not one of their moral intuitions. Their strong preference for relations of domination and zero-sum power structures would likely leave them deeply dissatisfied with proportional representation.

Moreover, as noted earlier in this book, they know most of the American electorate rejects their ideas. They must rely on our present system of minority rule to pursue their goals. That more democratic structure would be the antithesis of the extreme partisan gerrymandering that the GOP has worked so hard to achieve in red states nationwide. It will take a political imagination far greater than my own to figure out how proportional representation could be rendered palatable to the Right, who, at least currently, seem allergic to collaborative, cross-party governance, whether or not they hold a majority of seats.

Coda

In the late 1980s, while living in Berkeley, California, I attended a talk by Leo Lowenthal at Black Oak Books. In his nineties and still sharp as a tack, he was the last surviving member of the Frankfurt School, an interdisciplinary group of scholars that sought to understand the fascist potential among ordinary Germans in the pre-Hitler era.

Based on one of their studies, he described how it became apparent that large sections of the population were profoundly bigoted, prone to violence against out-groups, and eager for an authority to sanction their aggressive impulses and whom they could follow without thinking. Their findings alone motivated many of those scholars to quickly emigrate from the Fatherland just before the Nazis took power.

Some came to the United States to found or join academic institutions like the New School for Social Research in New York and the Wright Institute in Berkeley, California (where I obtained my PhD). At the end of his story, Lowenthal wryly commented that that discovery was likely the first and perhaps only time that social research had ever saved the lives of social researchers.

Despite my relief at the 2020 and 2022 election outcomes, I fear we are at the cusp of a similar historical moment. While Trumpism is only the most recent incarnation of American fascism,[75] it is the most "mainstream" expression to date. As the January 6 coup attempt has been justified if not enabled by so many Republican members of Congress, this anti-democracy movement promises to outlast Trump himself. Except for a few party outliers, now the target of death threats for being RINOs (Republicans in name only), the GOP has been completely absorbed by its MAGA faction, even as some repudiate Trump himself. And, at least publicly, it has treated Trump's lies as a catechism that must be uttered at every turn. Before the 2022 midterm elections, more than half of US states had 2020 election deniers on the ballot.[76] Numerous Republican candidates followed Trump's model by refusing to say they would accept an electoral loss.[77] Nineteen red states have already passed voter suppression laws.[78] Moreover, Republican state legislatures are seeking the power to overturn election results, though such laws have not yet been enacted.[79] It seems clear that the Trump coup attempt was not entirely defeated. It has merely moved into a slower mode. The plotters have not been stopped; they have just downshifted to gain more legal torque when the next opportunity arises to overthrow election results that they don't like.

As I complete the writing of this book, the news is replete with almost daily reports of MAGA death threats against perceived enemies, vows to launch a new civil war against liberals, book bans, attempts to abolish the teaching of factual history, and neofascist militia members running for public office. While many election-denying Trump mini-me con artists lost close elections, others won. Like Leo Lowenthal, I, too, wrestle with questions regarding the ease with which a large plurality of the US population has embraced aspiring tyrants and been seduced by xenophobic tribalism. Many have joined the violent national lynch mob of the Trump cult and happily gone through the post-truth looking glass where facts mean nothing. Will I know when it is time to flee as Lowenthal and the other refugee scholars of the Frankfurt School did? The question plagues me.

Only a few years before my father's death at ninety-six, he learned from surviving cousins that his father, Abe, who always moved through the world in a cloud of brooding, agonized silence, had multiple secret siblings. His wife and children knew nothing of them. Abe left Hungary for America at a time when there were only faint foreshadowings of the Holocaust. When he prepared to emigrate, he beseeched numerous brothers and sisters to join him. They stayed behind, insisting things there weren't that bad. Subsequently, my father's uncles, aunts, and many cousins were not only erased by the Nazis but also by Abe's survival guilt. For the duration of his post-emigration life, my grandfather locked the Hungarian branch of his family in the impermeable basement of his banished memories. The psychic cost of that entombment was also borne by his children, who felt his deadening but did not understand the pain that mandated it.

I hope not to join my lost Hungarian relatives in historical oblivion. Nor do I want to replicate, as an American ex-pat, Abe's lifetime of haunted post-emigration existence. Perhaps the research and interpretations presented in this book can further the project that the Frankfurt scholars began, along with the growing genre of insightful academic and popular writing by other pro-democracy public intellectuals. We must align with the legions of committed activists, determined voters, civil liberty organizations, and those remaining political officeholders who have the clarity of mind and bravery to join the fight. On good days, I believe we can preempt the tyranny that threatens us all. As a broad coalition, we could be powerful enough to catalyze a fuller expression of humanity's egalitarian instincts and eclipse what has become a suicidal drive to dominate.

Endnotes

Introduction

1 https://www.statista.com/statistics/1043907/
largest-us-corporate-toxic-air-polluters/
2 https://www.ewg.org/interactive-maps/pfas_contamination/
3 https://wesr.unep.org/landsoilpollution
4 https://www.nytimes.com/2023/04/20/opinion/microplastics-health
-environment.html
5 Warraich, H. J., Kumar, P., Nasir, K., Joynt Maddox, K. E., & Wadhera, R. K.
(2022). Political environment and mortality rates in the United States, 2001–
19: Population-based cross-sectional analysis. *BMJ, 377*: e069308. https://doi
.org/10.1136/bmj-2021-069308.
6 Heron, M. (2019). Deaths: Leading causes for 2017. *National Vital Statistics
Reports, 68*(6): 1–77.
7 Wood, D., & Brumfiel, G. (2022, May 19). Pro-Trump counties continue to
suffer far higher Covid death tolls. *National Public Radio.* https://www.npr
.org/2022/05/19/1098543849/pro-trump-counties-continue-to-suffer-far
-higher-covid-death-tolls (last accessed 14 October 2022).
8 Woodard, C. (2023, September 1) America's Surprising Partisan Divide on Life
Expectancy. *Politico.* https://www.politico.com/news/magazine/2023/09/01
/america-life-expectancy-regions-00113369
9 Woodard, C. (2023, September 1) America's Surprising Partisan Divide on Life
Expectancy. *Politico.* https://www.politico.com/news/magazine/2023/09/01
/america-life-expectancy-regions-00113369
10 Rosenberg, A. (2022, August 12). The horror of people willing to die for
Donald Trump. *The Washington Post.* https://www.washingtonpost.com
/opinions/2022/08/12/fbi-cincinatti-standoff-shiffer-people-willing-to-die-for
-trump (last accessed 14 October 2022).
11 https://www.azquotes.com/quote/303730
12 Chan, M., Lewis, E., Reilly, R. J., & Siemaszko, C. (2022, August 12). Loner
gunman who attacked FBI office was Navy vet who drove fast and was devoted
to Donald Trump. *NBC News.* https://www.nbcnews.com/news/us-news
/loner-gunman-attacked-fbi-office-was-navy-vet-drove-fast-was-devoted-d
-rcna42937 (last accessed 14 October 2022).

[13] Graeber, D., & Wengrow, D. (2021). *The Dawn of Everything: A New History of Humanity*. New York: Farrar, Straus, and Giroux.

[14] Ibid., pp. 276–278.

[15] Egan, T. (2011, December 8). Goodbye to "gays, guns & God." *The New York Times*. https://archive.nytimes.com/opinionator.blogs.nytimes.com/2011/12/08/goodbye-to-gays-guns-god (last accessed 14 October 2022.

[16] Brodwin, E. (2018, February 2). Parts of Oklahoma now have the same earthquake risk as California – and a new study found a scarily direct link to fracking. *Business Insider*. https://www.businessinsider.com/earthquakes-fracking-oklahoma-research-2018-2?r=US&IR=T (last accessed 14 October 2022).

[17] Snyder, T. (2018). *The Road to Unfreedom: Russia, Europe, America*. New York: Crown.

[18] Sebestyen, V. (2017, February 6). Bannon says he's a Leninist: That could explain the White House's new tactics. *The Guardian*. https://www.theguardian.com/commentisfree/2017/feb/06/lenin-white-house-steve-bannon (last accessed 14 October 2022).

[19] Brinton, M. (1970). *The Bolsheviks and Workers' Control, 1917–1921: The State and Counter-revolution* (3rd ed). Montreal: Black Rose Books, 1975.

[20] Avrich, P. (1970). *Kronstadt, 1921*. Princeton, NJ: Princeton University Press, 1991.

[21] Brinton, M., p. 78.

[22] Miller-Idriss, C. (2022). *Hate in the Homeland: The New Global Far Right*. Princeton, NJ: Princeton University Press.

[23] Soufan, A., & Sales, N. (2022, April 5). One of the worst ways Putin is gaslighting the world on Ukraine. *NBC News*. https://www.nbcnews.com/think/opinion/putin-nazi-pretext-russia-war-ukraine-belied-white-supremacy-ties-rcna23043 (last accessed 14 October 2022).

[24] Pew Research Center (2019, March 14). *Political Independents: Who They Are, What They Think*. https://www.pewresearch.org/politics/wp-content/uploads/sites/4/2019/03/Independents-Report.pdf (last accessed 14 October 2022).

[25] Office of the Director of National Intelligence (2021, March 1). *Domestic Violent Extremism Poses Heightened Threat in 2021* (unclassified summary). https://www.dni.gov/files/ODNI/documents/assessments/UnclassSummaryofDVEAssessment-17MAR21.pdf (last accessed 14 October 2022).

[26] Institute for Research and Education on Human Rights (2022). *Breaching the Mainstream: A National Survey of Far-Right Membership in State Legislatures*. https://www.irehr.org/reports/breaching-the-mainstream (last accessed 14 October 2022).

[27] Brown, D. (2017, June 30). Multnomah County Republicans formally allow militia groups to run security. *Portland Mercury*. https://www.portlandmercury

.com/news/2017/06/30/19130461/multnomah-county-republicans-formally -allow-militia-groups-to-run-security? (last accessed 14 October 2022).

28 Beedle, H. (2021, February 1). El Paso County GOP taps militia for security. *Colorado Springs Independent.* https://www.csindy.com/news/el-paso-county -gop-taps-militia-for-security/article_f782d888-64b9-11eb-add3 -f78b7b9191ff.html (last accessed 14 October 2022); Michel, C. (2019, October 10). The Oath Keepers providing volunteer security at Trump's Minneapolis rally are itching for a civil war. *Daily Beast.* https://www .thedailybeast.com/the-oath-keepers-providing-volunteer-security-at-trumps -minneapolis-rally-are-itching-for-a-civil-war? (last accessed 14 October 2022).

29 Harwell, D., & Kornfield, M. (2022). FBI attacker was a prolific contributor to Trump's Truth Social website. *The Washington Post.* https://www .washingtonpost.com/technology/2022/08/12/shiffer-trump-truth-social-fan (last accessed 14 October 2022).

30 Kruse, K., & Zelizer, J. E. (2023) *Myth America: Historians Take On the Biggest Legends and Lies About Our Past.* Basic Books. p.138

31 Kruse, K., & Zelizer, J. E. (2023) *Myth America: Historians Take On the Biggest Legends and Lies About Our Past.* Basic Books. p.140

32 https://nymag.com/intelligencer/2020/08/republican-national-committee -2020-platform-trump.html

33 Otten, T. (2024, February 23). MAGA Republican Pledges "End of Democracy" to Rabid Cheers at CPAC. *New Republic.* https://newrepublic .com/post/179247/jack-posobiec-democracy-cpac-2024 (last accessed 15 March 2024).

34 https://www.bloomberg.com/news/features/2023-08-30 /red-state-governments-are-dominating-democrat-led-blue-cities#xj4y7vzkg

35 Kruse, K., & Zelizer, J. E. (2023) *Myth America: Historians Take On the Biggest Legends and Lies About Our Past.* Basic Books. pp 25–40

36 Kruse, K., & Zelizer, J. E. p 32

37 Caldwell, T. (2021, January 7). Trump's "We love you" to Capitol rioters is more of the same. *CNN.* https://edition.cnn.com/2021/01/07/politics/trump -history-comments-trnd/index.html (last accessed 14 October 2022).

38 https://moralfoundations.org (website of research group).

39 O'Harrow, R. Jr., Ba Tran, A. & Hawkins, D., (2021, April 12). The rise of domestic extremism in America. *The Washington Post.* https://www .washingtonpost.com/investigations/interactive/2021/domestic-terrorism-data / (last accessed 14 October 2021).

40 Gershberg, Z., & Illing, S. (2022). *The Paradox of Democracy: Free Speech, Open Media, and Perilous Persuasion.* Chicago, University of Chicago Press.

41 https://www.bopsecrets.org/

42 Gershberg, Z., & Illing, S. (2022). *The Paradox of Democracy: Free Speech, Open Media, and Perilous Persuasion.* Chicago, University of Chicago Press.

[43] Junger, S. (2016). *Tribe: On Homecoming and Belonging*. New York: Twelve.
[44] https://academicworks.cuny.edu/cgi/viewcontent.cgi?article
=1654&context=wsq

Chapter 1

[1]   Morris, E. (2020, June 16). Threats to protesters preceded the Black Lives
      Matter event. *Wallowa County Chieftain*. https://www.wallowa.com/news
      /local/threats-to-protesters-preceded-the-black-lives-matter-event/article
      _ac0caaba-afff-11ea-a3d2-474654322cc7.html (last accessed 14
      October 2022).
[2]   Stanley-Becker, I. (2020, June 18). As protests spread to small-town America,
      militia groups respond with armed intimidation and online threats. *The
      Washington Post*. https://www.washingtonpost.com/national/as-protests-spread
      -to-small-town-america-militia-groups-respond-with-online-threats-and
      -armed-intimidation/2020/06/18/75c4655e-b0a1-11ea-8f56-63f38c990077
      _story.html (last accessed 14 October 2022).
[3]   Ibid.
[4]   https://www.youtube.com/watch?v=b1_RKu-ESCY
[5]   https://www.azlyrics.com/lyrics/jasonaldean/trythatinasmalltown.html
[6]   https://www.npr.org/2023/08/01/1191405789/
      how-racism-became-a-marketing-tool-for-country-music
[7]   Boyer, P. (2018). *Minds Make Societies: How Cognition Explains the World
      Humans Create*. London: Yale University Press.
[8]   Ryan, W. (2016, November 22). Nazis on retreat: The SS holiday camp near
      Auschwitz – in pictures. *The Guardian*. https://www.theguardian.com/books
      /gallery/2016/nov/22/nazis-retreat-ss-holiday-hut-auschwitz-pictures-mengele
      -photographs (last accessed 14 October 2022).
[9]   Lennon, L. G. (2022). *Lynchings: Postcards from America*. Cincinnati, OH:
      WordTech.
[10] Adams, C., & Bellamy, C. (2022, August 14). From rentals to bathrooms:
      Airbnb listings aren't the first offensive effort to commercialize slave cabins.
      NBC News. https://www.nbcnews.com/news/nbcblk/rentals-bathrooms
      -airbnb-listings-arent-first-offensive-effort-commerc-rcna41774 (last accessed
      14 October 2022).
[11] ktk155 (website user) (2014, September 9). Great historical property: Review
      of Prospect Hill Inn and Restaurant. *Tripadvisor*. https://www.tripadvisor.com
      .ph/ShowUserReviews-g57912-d114564-r227814446-Prospect_Hill_Inn
      _Restaurant-Louisa_Virginia.html (last accessed 14 October 2022).
[12] Luongo, M. T. (2020, October 20). Despite everything, people still have
      weddings at "plantation" sites. *The New York Times*. https://www

.nytimes.com/2020/10/17/style/despite-everything-people
-still-have-weddings-at-plantation-sites.html (last accessed 14 October 2022).

13   https://www.magnoliaplantationweddings.net (website of wedding company).

14   Goldman, A. (2021, March 2). Domestic terrorism threat is "metastasizing"
in US, FBI director says. *The New York Times*. https://www.nytimes.
com/2021/03/02/us/politics/wray-domestic-terrorism-capitol.html (last
accessed 14 October 2022).

15   Miller-Idriss, C. (2022). *Hate in the Homeland: The New Global Far Right*.
Princeton, NJ: Princeton University Press.

16   Wallis, D. (2022, January 30). Trump says he would pardon Jan. 6 rioters if he
runs and wins. *Reuters*. https://www.reuters.com/world/us/trump-says
-he-would-pardon-jan-6-rioters-if-he-runs-wins-2022-01-30 (last accessed 14
October 2022).

17   Fortinsky, S. (2022, January 31). Trump says he wanted Pence to overturn the
2020 election and falsely claims it was vice president's "right." https://www
.cnn.com/2022/01/30/politics/trump-pence-2020-election/index.html (last
accessed 14 October 2022).

18   Rodriguez, S. (2021, January 12). Trump's partially built "big, beautiful wall."
Politico. https://www.politico.com/news/2021/01/12/trump-border-wall
-partially-built-458255 (last accessed 14 October 2022).

19   Weisman, J., & Epstein, R. J. (2022, February 2). GOP declares Jan. 6 attack
"legitimate political discourse." *The New York Times*. https://www.nytimes
.com/2022/02/04/us/politics/republicans-jan-6-cheney-censure.html (last
accessed 14 October 2022).

20   Harris, E. A., & Alter, A. (2022, February 8). Why book ban efforts are
spreading across the US. *The New York Times*. https://www.nytimes
.com/2022/01/30/books/book-ban-us-schools.html (last accessed 14 October
2022); Contreras, R. (2022, February 1). New rules are limiting how teachers
can teach Black History Month. *Axios*. https://www.axios.com/2022/02/01
/black-history-month-critical-race-theory (last accessed 14 October 2022).

21   Scully, R. (2022, January 20). Bill to ban lessons making white students feel
"discomfort" advances in Florida Senate. *The Hill*. https://thehill.com
/homenews/state-watch/590554-bill-to-ban-lessons-making-white-students
-feel-discomfort-advances-in/ (last accessed 14 October 2022).

22   Florida bill would allow cameras in classrooms, teachers to wear microphones
(2022, January 21). *WSVN*. https://wsvn.com/news/politics/florida-bill
-would-allow-cameras-in-classrooms-teachers-to-wear-microphones
/ (last accessed 14 October 2022).

23   Zaleha, B. D. (2015, September 1). Why conservative Christians don't believe
in climate change. *Bulletin of the Atomic Scientists, 71*(5): 19–30. https
://doi.org/10.1177/0096340215599789; Wise use movement (2022).

In: *Wikipedia*. https://en.wikipedia.org/wiki/Wise_use_movement (last accessed 14 October 2022).

[24] Kushner, J. (2016, November 22). Exclusive interview: How Jared Kushner won Trump the White House (interview by S. Bertoni). *Forbes*. https://www.forbes.com/sites/stevenbertoni/2016/11/22/exclusive-interview-how-jared-kushner-won-trump-the-white-house/ (last accessed 14 October 2022).

[25] Hibbing, J. R. (2020). *The Securitarian Personality: What Really Motivates Trump's Base and Why It Matters for the Post-Trump Era*. New York: Oxford University Press. While I have tried to present an accurate account of Hibbing's ideas and research, my aim here is not to summarize it but to integrate his work with those of others and reinterpret his findings in light of more recent developments and my own thinking. As with many of the researchers I draw on for this book, it is possible that he may not be happy with the use I've made of his work and the conclusions drawn from it. And given the fact that the MAGA faction is now essentially indistinguishable from the GOP as a whole, I'm applying Hibbing's findings more broadly than he might, or at least than he did in 2018.

[26] Wade, P. (2021, November 12). Republican lawmakers are now getting death threats over… infrastructure legislation. *Rolling Stone*. https://www.rollingstone.com/politics/politics-news/republicans-death-threats-bipartisan-infrastructure-bill-1257048/ (last accessed 14 October 2022).

[27] Walter, A. (2022, January 21). GOP voters still like Trump, but many ambivalent about 2024 run. *The Cook Political Report with Amy Walter*. https://www.cookpolitical.com/analysis/national/national-politics/gop-voters-still-trump-many-ambivalent-about-2024-run (last accessed 14 October 2022).

[28] Hibbing, J. R.

[29] Kruse, K., & Zelizer, J. E. (2023) *Myth America: Historians Take On the Biggest Legends and Lies About Our Past*. Basic Books. p.57

[30] UMass Amherst Poll (2022, January 14). Toplines and crosstabs December 2021 national poll: CRT and race in America (summary of poll conducted by YouGov PLC for UMass Amherst Poll, University of Massachusetts Amherst). https://polsci.umass.edu/toplines-and-crosstabs-december-2021-national-poll-crt-race-america (last accessed 14 October 2022).

[31] Rose, J. (2022, August 18). A majority of Americans see an "invasion" at the southern border, NPR poll finds. *National Public Radio*. https://www.npr.org/2022/08/18/1117953720/a-majority-of-americans-see-an-invasion-at-the-southern-border-npr-poll-finds (last accessed 14 October 2022).

[32] Ipsos (2022, August 18). *On Immigration, Most Buying into Idea of "Invasion" at Southern Border*. https://www.ipsos.com/sites/default/files/ct/news/documents/2022-08/NPR%20Immigration%20Topline%20%2B%20PR%2008.17.22.pdf (last accessed 14 October 2022).

33 Rhodes, J., La Raja, R., Nteta, T., & Theodoridis, A. (2022, January 17).
    Martin Luther King Jr. was right. Racism and opposition to democracy are
    linked, our research finds. *The Washington Post.* https://www.washingtonpost
    .com/politics/2022/01/17/mlk-racism-democracy-opinion/ (last accessed 14
    October 2022).

34 Hochschild, A. R. (2016). *Strangers in Their Own Land: Anger and Mourning
    on the American Right.* New York: The New Press.

35 Dawsey, J., & Arnsdorf, I. (2022, August 17). Trump rakes in millions off FBI
    search at Mar-a-Lago. *The Washington Post.* https://www.washingtonpost
    .com/politics/2022/08/17/trump-fundraising-fbi-raid/ (last accessed 14
    October 2022).

36 Ibid.

37 Liasson, M. (2001, May 25). Conservative advocate (audio report). *National
    Public Radio.* https://www.npr.org/templates/story/story.php?storyId=1123439
    (last accessed 14 October 2022).

38 Barbaro, M. (2016, September 16). Donald Trump clung to "birther" lie for
    years, and still isn't apologetic. *The New York Times.* https://www.nytimes
    .com/2016/09/17/us/politics/donald-trump-obama-birther.html (last accessed
    6 March 2023).

39 Draper, R. (2022, August 15). The Arizona Republican Party's anti-democracy
    experiment. *The New York Times.* https://www.nytimes.com/2022/08/15
    /magazine/arizona-republicans-democracy.html (last accessed 14
    October 2022).

40 Ibid.

41 McCarthy, J. (1950, February 9). Transcript of speech given at Wheeling, West
    Virginia. History Matters. http://historymatters.gmu.edu/d/6456 (last accessed
    14 October 2022).

42 Hibbing, J. R.

43 Ibid.

44 McFarland, S. (2017). Identification with all humanity: The antithesis of
    prejudice, and more. In: C. G. Sibley & F. K. Barlow (Eds), *The Cambridge
    Handbook of the Psychology of Prejudice* (pp. 632–654). New York: Cambridge
    University Press. https://doi.org/10.1017/9781316161579.028

45 Ibid.

46 Ibid.

47 https://thehill.com/changing-america/opinion/506782-anti-slavery
    -revolutionaries-who-practiced-what-they-preached/

48 https://www.forbes.com/quotes/9313/

49 Hibbing, J. R., p. 206.

50 Ibid.

51 Leonhardt, D. (2022, February 18). Red Covid: An update. *The New York Times*. https://www.nytimes.com/2022/02/18/briefing/red-covid-partisan -deaths-vaccines.html (last accessed 14 October 2022).

52 Feuer, A. (2022). As right-wing rhetoric escalates, so do threats and violence. *The New York Times*. https://www.nytimes.com/2022/08/13/nyregion/right -wing-rhetoric-threats-violence.html (last accessed 17 October 2022).

53 Walter, B. F. (2022). *How Civil Wars Start: And How to Stop Them*. New York: Penguin, p. 141.

54 Hibbing, J. R.

55 Carney, D. R., Jost, J. T., Gosling, S. D., & Potter, J. (2008). The secret lives of liberals and conservatives: Personality profiles, interaction styles, and the things they leave behind. *Political Psychology, 29*(6): 807–840. https://doi .org/10.1111/j.1467-9221.2008.00668.x

56 Pengelly, M., & agencies (2019, July 13). "This is tough stuff": Pence visits caged, unwashed, overcrowded migrants. *The Guardian*. https://www .theguardian.com/us-news/2019/jul/13/pence-visits-caged-unwashed -overcrowded-migrants-tough-stuff (last accessed 17 October 2022).

57 McAuliffe, K. (2019, March). Liberals and conservatives react in wildly different ways to repulsive pictures. *The Atlantic*. https://www.theatlantic .com/magazine/archive/2019/03/the-yuck-factor/580465/ (last accessed 17 October 2022).

58 Whitman, J. Q. (2017). *Hitler's American Model: The United States and the Making of Nazi Race Law*. Princeton, NJ: Princeton University Press, 2018.

59 https://www.snopes.com/fact-check/make-germany-great-again/

60 https://www.nytimes.com/2023/10/05/us/politics/trump-immigration -rhetoric.html

61 https://www.cnn.com/2023/04/29/politics/fact-check-trump-mental- institutions-migrants-doctor/index.html

62 Hibbing, J. R., p. 36.

63 Murray, D. R., & Schaller, M. (2016). The behavioral immune system: Implications for social cognition, social interaction, and social influence. *Advances in Experimental Social Psychology, 53*: 75–129.

64 Watkins, E., & Phillip, A. (2018, January 12). Trump decries immigrants from "shithole countries" coming to US. *CNN*. https://edition.cnn .com/2018/01/11/politics/immigrants-shithole-countries-trump/index.html (last accessed 17 October 2022).

65 Aarøe, L., Peterson, M. B., & Arceneaux, K. (2017). The behavioral immune system shapes political intuitions: Why and how individual differences in disgust sensitivity underlie opposition to immigration. *American Political Science Review, 111*(2): 277–294. https://doi.org/10.1017 /S0003055416000770

66 Brown, M., Keefer, L. A., Sacco, D. F., & Bermond, A. (2019). Is the cure a wall? Behavioral immune system responses to a disease metaphor for

immigration. *Evolutionary Psychological Science, 5*: 343–356. https://doi
.org/10.1007/s40806-019-00191-3

67 McAuliffe, K.

68 Ruisch, B. C., Anderson, R. A., Inbar, Y., & Pizarro, D. A. (2020, September
3). A matter of taste: Gustatory sensitivity predicts political ideology. *Journal of
Personality and Social Psychology.* http://dx.doi.org/10.1037/pspp0000365

69 Weixel, N. (2022, July 25). GOP plots Fauci probe after midterms. *The Hill.*
https://thehill.com/policy/healthcare/3571232-gop-plots-fauci-probe-after
-midterms/ (last accessed 17 October 2022).

70 Bump, P. (2022, November 29). Red America has seen the highest rates of
cases and deaths, and the lowest rate of vaccinations. *The Washington Post.*
https://www.washingtonpost.com/politics/2021/11/29/red-america-has-seen
-highest-rates-cases-deaths-lowest-rate-vaccinations/ (last accessed 17 October).

71 Franck, T. (2022, January 4). Biden disapproval hits new high as voters give
him bad grades on economy, new CNBC/Change poll says. *CNBC.* https
://www.cnbc.com/2022/01/04/biden-disapproval-rating-high-voters-blame
-him-on-economy-cnbc-poll.html (last accessed 17 October 2022).

72 Brennan Center for Justice (2021, December 21). Voting laws roundup:
December 2021. https://www.brennancenter.org/our-work/research-reports/
voting-laws-roundup-december-2021 (last accessed 17 October 2022).

73 Pilkington, E. (2022, January 26). US prosecutors investigate Republicans
who sent fake Trump electors to Congress. *The Guardian.* https://www
.theguardian.com/us-news/2022/jan/26/fake-trump-electors-us-investigation
-doj (last accessed 17 October 2022).

74 So, L. (2021, June 11). Trump-inspired death threats are terrorizing election
workers. *Reuters.* https://www.reuters.com/investigates/special-report
/usa-trump-georgia-threats/ (last accessed 17 October 2022).

75 Johnson, K. (2022, January 20). Mitch McConnell says Black people vote just
as much as "Americans." *USA Today.* https://eu.usatoday.com/story
/news/politics/2022/01/20/mitch-mcconnell-african-americans-vote-much
-americans/6601274001/ (last accessed 17 October 2022).

76 Brennan Center for Justice (2022, January 10). The impact of voter
suppression on communities of color. https://www.brennancenter.org/our
-work/research-reports/impact-voter-suppression-communities-color (last
accessed 17 October 2022).

77 Gest, J. (2021, August 16). The Census shows the GOP base is shrinking fast.
So why does its power seem secure? *CNN.* https://edition.cnn
.com/2021/08/12/opinions/us-census-republican-party-power-gest/index.html
(last accessed 17 October 2022).

78 Hibbing, J. R.

79 Ibid.

[80] Kilgore, E. (2021, December 27). Donald Trump Jr. rejects Christianity's "turn the other cheek" teaching. *New York Magazine*. https://nymag.com /intelligencer/2021/12/donald-trump-jr-rejects-jesuss-turn-the-other-cheek .html (last accessed 17 October 2022).

[81] Hibbing, J. R., p. 61.

[82] Robertson, D. (2021, December 18). How the war on Christmas became America's latest forever war. *Politico Magazine*. https://www.politico.com /news/magazine/2021/12/18/war-on-christmas-525273 (last accessed 17 October 2022).

[83] Hibbing, J. R.

[84] Lewis, G. J., Kandler, C., & Riemann, R. (2014). Distinct heritable influences underpin in-group love and out-group derogation. *Social Psychological and Personality Science, 5*(4): 407–413.

[85] Dawes, C. T., & Weinschenk, A. C. (2020). On the genetic basis of political orientation. *Current Opinion in Behavioral Sciences, 34*: 173–178. https://doi .org/10.1016/j.cobeha.2020.03.012

[86] Hatemi, P. K., Medland, S. E., Klemmensen, R., Oskarsson, S., Littvay, L., Dawes, C. T., Verhulst, B., McDermott, R., Nørgaard, A. S., Klofstad, C. A., Christensen, K., Johannesson, M., Magnusson, P. K. E., Eaves, L. J., & Martin., N. G. (2014). Genetic influences on political ideologies: Twin analyses of 19 measures of political ideologies from five democracies and genome-wide findings from three populations. *Behavior Genetics, 44*: 282–294. https://doi.org/10.1007/s10519-014-9648-8

[87] Europe and right-wing nationalism: A country-by-country guide (2019, November 13). *BBC News*. https://www.bbc.co.uk/news/world -europe-36130006 (last accessed 17 October 2022).

[88] Benjamin, D. J., Cesarini, D., van der Loos, M. J. H. M., Dawes, C. T., Koellinger, P. D., Magnusson, P. K. E., Chabris, C. F., Conley, D., Laibson, D., Johannesson, M., & Visscher, P. M. (2012). The genetic architecture of economic and political preferences. *Proceedings of the National Academy of Sciences of the United States of America, 109*(21): 8026–8031. https://doi .org/10.1073/pnas.1120666109

[89] Nagasawa, M., Mitsui, S., En, S., Ohtani, N., Ohta, M., Sakuma, Y., Onaka, T., Mogi, K., & Kikusui, T. (2015). Oxytocin-gaze positive loop and the coevolution of human-dog bonds. *Science, 348*(6232): 333–336. https://doi .org/10.1126/science.1261022

[90] De Dreu, C. K. W., Greer, L. L., Van Kleef, G. A., Shalvi, S., & Handgraaf, M. J. J. (2011). Oxytocin promotes human ethnocentrism. *Proceedings of the National Academy of Sciences of the United States of America, 108*(4): 1262– 1266. https://doi.org/10.1073/pnas.1015316108

[91] Stallen, M., De Dreu, C. K. W., Shalvi, S., Smidts, A., & Sanfey, A. G. (2012). The herding hormone: Oxytocin stimulates in-group conformity. *Psychological Science, 23*(11): 1–5. https://doi.org/10.1177/0956797612446026

92 Zhang, H., Gross, J., De Dreu, C., & Ma, Y. (2019). Oxytocin promotes coordinated out-group attack during intergroup conflict in humans. *eLife* (8; 2019): e40698. https://doi.org/10.7554/eLife.40698

93 Shamay-Tsoory, S. G., & Abu-Akel, A. (2016). The social salience hypothesis of oxytocin. *Biological Psychiatry, 79*(3): 194–202. https://doi.org/10.1016/j.biopsych.2015.07.020

94 Hibbing, J. R.

95 Shalvi, S., & De Dreu, C. K. W. (2014). Oxytocin promotes group-serving dishonesty. *Proceedings of the National Academy of Sciences of the United States of America, 111*(15): 5503–5507. https://doi.org/10.1073/pnas.1400724111

96 https://www.nbcnews.com/id/wbna32501273

97 Hibbing, J. R., p. 162.

98 Vedantam, S. (Host) (2018, October 8). Nature, nurture and your politics (audio podcast episode). In: *Hidden Brain*. National Public Radio. https://www.npr.org/2018/10/03/654127241/nature-nurture-and-your-politics (last accessed 17 October 2022).

99 Hibbing, J. R., p. 73.

100 Sapolsky, R. M. (2017). *Behave: The Biology of Humans at Our Best and Worst.* New York: Penguin.

101 Nail, P. R., McGregor, I., Drinkwater, A. E., Steele, G. M., & Thompson, A. W. (2009). Threat causes liberals to think like conservatives. *Journal of Experimental Social Psychology, 45*: 901–907.

102 Eidelman, S., Crandall, C. S., Goodman, J. A., & Blanchar, J. C. (2012). Low-effort thought promotes political conservatism. *Personality and Social Psychology Bulletin, 38*(6): 1–13. https://doi.org/10.1177/014616721243921

103 Kanai, R., Feilden, T., Firth, C., & Rees, G. (2011). Political orientations are correlated with brain structure in young adults. *Current Biology, 21*(8): 677–680. https://doi.org/10.1016/j.cub.2011.03.017

104 Bazzle, S. (2022, January 30). Oath Keeper founder's wife says extremist militia is training for civil war. *Hill Reporter*. https://hillreporter.com/watch-oath-keeper-founders-wife-says-extremist-militia-is-training-for-civil-war-123774 (last accessed 17 October 2022).

105 Onraet, E., Van Assche, J., Roets, A., Haesevoets, T., & Van Hiel, A. (2016). The happiness gap between conservatives and liberals depends on country-level threat: A worldwide multilevel study. *Social Psychological and Personality Science, 8*(1): 1–9. https://doi.org/10.1177/1948550616662125

Chapter 2

1 Pratto, F., Sidanius, J., Stallworth, L. M., & Malle, B. F. (1994). Social dominance orientation: A personality variable predicting social and political attitudes. *Journal of Personality and Social Psychology, 67*(4): 741–763. https://doi.org/10.1037/0022-3514.67.4.741

[2] Goudarzi, S., Pliskin, R., Jost, J. T., & Knowles, E. D. (2020). Economic system justification predicts muted emotional responses to inequality. *Nature Communications, 11*(article 383). https://doi.org/10.1038/s41467-019-14193-z

[3] Ho, A. K., Sidanius, J., Kteily, N., Sheehy-Skeffington, J., Pratto, F., Henkel, K. E., Foels, R., & Stewart, A. L. (2015). The nature of social dominance orientation: Theorizing and measuring preferences for intergroup inequality using the new SDO_7 scale. *Journal of Personality and Social Psychology, 109*(6): 1003–1028. https://doi.org/10.1037/pspi0000033

[4] Ibid., p. 104.

[5] https://www.pnas.org/doi/epdf/10.1073/pnas.1818711116

[6] Mason, L. (2018). *Uncivil Agreement: How Politics Became Our Identity*. Chicago: University of Chicago Press.

[7] Ibid., p. 3.

[8] Gonzales, N. (2024, February 26). Vast majority of Republicans still will vote for Trump in November. *Roll Call*. Vast majority of Republicans still will vote for Trump in November (accessed 14 March 2024).

[9] https://www.vox.com/identities/2018/3/5/16796892/trump-cyrus-christian-right-bible-cbn-evangelical-propaganda

[10] Trump sides with Russia against FBI at Helsinki Summit (2018, July 16). *BBC News*. https://www.bbc.co.uk/news/world-europe-44852812 (last accessed 17 October 2022).

[11] Sharlet, J. (2023). The Undertow: Scenes from a Slow Civil War. W. W. Norton & Company. p 148

[12] LaMarre, H. L., Landreville, K. D., & Beam, M. A. (2009). The irony of satire: Political ideology and the motivation to see what you want to see in the Colbert Report. *The International Journal of Press/Politics, 14*(2), 212–231. https://doi.org/10.1177/1940161208330904

[13] Mason, L., pp. 20–21.

[14] Ibid., pp. 50 and 74.

[15] Ibid., p. 140.

[16] Wheeler, T. (2020). The 2020 Republican Party platform: "L'etat, c'est moi." Brookings. https://www.brookings.edu/blog/up-front/2020/08/25/the-2020-republican-party-platform-letat-cest-moi/ (last accessed 17 October 2022).

[17] Mason, L., pp. 114–115.

[18] Ibid., p. 118.

[19] Ibid., p. 121.

[20] Ibid., pp. 33 and 38.

[21] Ibid., p. 76.

[22] Bail, C. (2021). *Breaking the Social Media Prism: How to Make Our Platforms Less Polarizing*. Princeton, NJ: Princeton University Press.

23 Hibbing, J. R. (2020). *The Securitarian Personality: What Really Motivates Trump's Base and Why It Matters for the Post-Trump Era*. New York: Oxford University Press.

24 Mutz, D. C. (2018). Status threat, not economic hardship, explains the 2016 presidential vote. *Proceedings of the National Academy of Sciences of the United States of America, 115*(19): e4330–e4339. https://doi.org/10.1073 /pnas.1718155115

25 Kross, E., Berman, M. G., Mischel, W., Smith, E. E., Wager, T. D. (2011). Social rejection shares somatosensory representations with physical pain. *Proceedings of the National Academy of Sciences of the United States of America, 108*(15): 6270–6275. https://doi.org/10.1073/pnas.1102693108; Woo, C. W., Koban, L., Kross, E., Lindquist, M. A., Banich, M. T., Ruzic, L., Andrews-Hanna, J. R., & Wager, T. D. (2014). Separate neural representations for physical pain and social rejection. *Nature Communications, 5*(article 5380). https://doi.org/10.1038/ncomms6380

26 DeWall, C. N., MacDonald, G., Webster, G. D., Masten, C. L., Baumeister, R. F., Powell, C., Combs, D., Schurtz, D. R., Stillman, T. F., Tice, D. M., & Eisenberger, N. I. (2010). Acetaminophen reduces social pain: Behavioral and neural evidence. *Psychological Science, 21*(7), 931–937. https://doi .org/10.1177/0956797610374741

27 Panksepp, J. (2004). *Affective Neuroscience: The Foundations of Human and Animal Emotions*. New York: Oxford University Press.

28 Elamroussi, A. (2021, July 29). Some people in Missouri are getting vaccinated in secret to avoid backlash from loved ones, doctor says. *CNN*. https://edition .cnn.com/2021/07/29/health/vaccines-in-secret-missouri/index.html (accessed 17 October 2022).

29 https://www.researchgate.net/profile/Diana-Nechita/publication/274071849 _Shame_and_psychopathology_From_research_to_clinical_practice /links/56b1bd7508ae5ec4ed493e4e/Shame-and-psychopathology-From -research-to-clinical-practice.pdf

30 https://theimaginativeconservative.org/2021/02/what-has-happened-our -sense-shame-john-horvat.html

31 Keen, D. (2023). *Shame: The Politics and Power of an Emotion*. Princeton, NJ: Princeton University Press.

32 Planas, A. (2023, July 20). New Florida standards teach students that some Black people benefited from slavery because it taught useful skills. NBC News. https://www.nbcnews.com/news/us-news/new-florida-standards-teach-black -people-benefited-slavery-taught-usef-rcna95418 (accessed 27 February 2024).

33 Keen, D. *Shame: The Politics and Power of an Emotion*. pp. 163–179.

34 Wight, John. (2016, February 8). Who was Cecil Rhodes? *The Herald*. https ://www.herald.co.zw/who-was-cecil-rhodes/ (accessed 27 February 2024).

35 Keen, D. *Shame: The Politics and Power of an Emotion*. pp. 74–91.

[36] Gilligan, J. (2003). Shame, Guilt, and Violence. *Social Research*, 70(4), 1149–1180. https://www.jstor.org/stable/40971965.

[37] Ibid.

[38] Browning, Christopher R. (2017, February 28). *Ordinary Men: Reserve Police Battalion 101 and the Final Solution in Poland*. New York, NY: Harper Perennial.

[39] Keen, D. *Shame: The Politics and Power of an Emotion*. pp. 92–110.

[40] https://slate.com/human-interest/2008/05/in-praise-of-liberal-guilt.html

[41] https://www.ncbi.nlm.nih.gov/pmc/articles/PMC8096906/#:~:text=Evidence%20has%20supported%20the%20idea,et%20al.%2C%202012).

[42] https://spsp.org/news/character-and-context-blog/mallinas-political-ideology-social-errors

[43] Gabbatt, A. (2024, January 13). Trump's novel take on January 6: calling convicted rioters 'hostages.' *The Guardian*. https://www.theguardian.com/us-news/2024/jan/13/trump-january-6-rioters-hostages (last accessed 23 January 2024).

[44] https://www.ncbi.nlm.nih.gov/pmc/articles/PMC8096906/#:~:text=Evidence%20has%20supported%20the%20idea,et%20al.%2C%202012).

[45] https://www.reuters.com/investigates/special-report/usa-politics-violence/

[46] Alonso, M., Yan, H., Alvarado, C., Freeman, D., Boyette, C. and Murphy, P. P. (2024, February 1). Man arrested after video post showed severed head of his father, police say, amid political rant that stayed online for hours. CNN. https://www.cnn.com/2024/01/31/us/justin-mohn-father-beheaded-biden-video/index.html (last accessed 28 February 2024).

[47] Suedfeld, P. (1990). *Psychology and Torture*. Washington, DC: Taylor & Francis.

[48] Eres, R., & Molenberghs, P. (2013). The influence of group membership on the neural correlates involved in empathy. *Frontiers in Human Neuroscience*, 7(article 176). https://doi.org/10.3389/fnhum.2013.00176

[49] Levy, J., Goldstein, A., Influs, M., Masalha, S., Zagoory-Sharon, O., & Feldman, R. (2016). Adolescents growing up amidst intractable conflict attenuate brain response to pain of out-group. *Proceedings of the National Academy of Sciences of the United States of America*, 113(48): 13696–13701. https://doi.org/10.1073/pnas.1612903113

[50] Contreras-Huerta, L. S., Baker, K. S., Reynolds, K. J., Batalha, L., & Cunnington, R. (2013). Racial bias in neural empathic responses to pain. *PLoS ONE*, 8(12): e84001. https://doi.org/10.1371/journal.pone.0084001

[51] Korte, G., & Gomez, A. (2018, May 16). Trump ramps up rhetoric on undocumented immigrants: "These aren't people. These are animals." *USA Today*. https://eu.usatoday.com/story/news/politics/2018/05/16

/trump-immigrants-animals-mexico-democrats-sanctuary-cities/617252002 / (last accessed 17 October 2022).

52 Keen, S. (1986). *Faces of the Enemy: Reflections of the Hostile Imagination.* San Francisco: Harper & Row, 1992.

53 Smith, D. L. (2012). *Less Than Human: Why We Demean, Enslave, and Exterminate Others.* New York: St Martin's Griffin.

54 Friedman, L. J., & De Medeiros, P. (2019). Erik Erikson on negative identity and pseudospeciation – extended and particularized by Ta-Nehisi Coates. *Archaeology & Anthropology: Open Access, 3*(2): 458–463.

55 Marris, E. (2021). *Wild Souls: Freedom and Flourishing in the Non-Human World.* New York: Bloomsbury, pp. 152–167.

56 Slade, J., & Alleyne, E. (2021, July 7). The psychological impact of slaughterhouse employment: A systematic literature review. *Trauma, Violence and Abuse:* 1–12. https://doi.org/10.1177/15248380211030243

57 Dhont, K., Hodson, G., Costello, K., & MacInnis, C. C. (2014). Social dominance orientation connects prejudicial human–human and human–animal relations. *Personality and Individual Differences, 61–62:* 105–108. https://doi.org/10.1016/j.paid.2013.12.020

58 Routledge, C., & Vess, M. (Eds). *Handbook of Terror Management Theory.* Cambridge, MA: Academic Press.

59 Harmon-Jones, E., Greenberg, J., Solomon, S., & Simon, L. (1996). The effects of mortality salience on intergroup bias between minimal groups. *European Journal of Social Psychology, 26*(4): 677–681. https://doi.org/10.1002/(SICI)1099-0992(199607)26:4<677::AID-EJSP777>3.0.CO;2-2. Discussed in: Epstein, M., & Tang, B. (Hosts) (c. 2019, January 29). We are all going to die – someday (audio podcast episode). In: *Mind of State.* https://mindofstate.com/ep-01-we-are-all-going-to-die-someday/ (last accessed 17 October 2022).

60 Cohen, F. (2017). You're hired! Mortality salience increases Americans' support for Donald Trump. *Analyses of Social Issues and Public Policy, 17*(1): 339–357. https://doi.org/10.1111/asap.12143

61 Weise, D. R., Pyszczynski, T., Cox, C. R., Arndt, J., Greenberg, J., Solomon, S., & Kosloff, S. (2008). Interpersonal politics: The role of terror management and attachment processes in shaping political preferences. *Psychological Science, 19*(5): 448–455. https://doi.org/10.1111/j.1467-9280.2008.02108.x

62 Goldenberg, J. L., Pyszczynski, T., Greenberg, J., Solomon, S., Kluck, B., & Cornwell, R. (2001). I am not an animal: Mortality salience, disgust, and the denial of human creatureliness. *Journal of Experimental Psychology: General, 130*(3): 427–435.

63 Leyens, J.-P., Paladino, P. M., Rodriguez-Torres, R., Vaes, J., Demoulin, S., Rodriguez-Perez, A., & Gaunt, R. (2000). The emotional side of prejudice: The attribution of secondary emotions to ingroups and out-groups. *Personality and Social Psychology Review, 4*(2): 182–197.

[64] https://academic.oup.com/book/1358/chapter-abstract/140335107?redirected From=fulltext

[65] Hasson, Y., Tamir, M., Brahms, K. S., Cohrs, J. C., & Halperin, E. (2018). Are liberals and conservatives equally motivated to feel empathy toward others? *Personality and Social Psychology Bulletin, 44*(10): 1449–1459. https://doi .org/10.1177/0146167218769867

[66] Hinze, T., Doster, J. & V. C. Joe. (1997). The relationship of conservatism and cognitive-complexity. *Person. Individ. Diff,* 22(2), 297-298. PII: S0191-8869(96)00171-7 (psu.edu).

[67] Waytz, A., Iyer, R., Young, L., Haidt, J., & Graham, J. (2019). Ideological differences in the expanse of the moral circle. *Nature Communications, 10*(article 4389). https://doi.org/10.1038/s41467-019-12227-0

Chapter 3

[1] Moreno, C. (2017, May 25). Portland burrito cart closes after owners are accused of cultural appropriation. *HuffPost.* https://www.huffingtonpost.co.uk /entry/portland-burrito-cart-closes-after-owners-are-accused-of-cultural-appro priation_n_5926ef7ee4b062f96a348181 (last accessed 18 October 2022).

[2] Chen, T., Lin, C., & Sun, B. (2021). Racial disparities in small business lending. *Nanyang Business School Research Paper* (no. 21–11). http://dx.doi. org/10.2139/ssrn.3821442; Shapiro, T., Meschede, T., & Osoro, S. (2013, February). *The Roots of the Widening Racial Wealth Gap: Explaining the Black-White Economic Divide (Research and Policy Brief).* Institute on Assets and Social Policy. http://hdl.handle.net/1903/24590

[3] Schmidt, S. (2018, May 1). "It's just a dress": Teen's Chinese prom attire stirs cultural appropriation debate. *The Washington Post.* https://www .washingtonpost.com/news/morning-mix/wp/2018/05/01/its-just-a-dress -teens-chinese-prom-attire-stirs-cultural-appropriation-debate/ (last accessed 18 October 2022).

[4] Graeber, D., & Wengrow, D. (2021). *The Dawn of Everything: A New History of Humanity.* New York: Farrar, Straus and Giroux.

[5] Serwer, A. (2021). *The Cruelty Is the Point: The Past, Present, and Future of Trump's America.* New York: One World.

[6] https://www.hrw.org/news/2016/11/26/cuba-fidel-castros-record-repression

[7] Amnesty International (2022). *Israel's Apartheid Against Palestinians: Cruel System of Domination and Crime Against Humanity.* https://www.amnestyusa .org/wp-content/uploads/2022/01/Full-Report.pdf (last accessed 17 October 2022).

[8] Beinart, P. (2023, February 19). You can't save democracy in a Jewish State. *The New York Times.* https://www.nytimes.com/2023/02/19/opinion/israel -democracy-protests.html (last accessed 6 March 2023).

9   Monbiot, G. (2022, March 2). We must confront Russian propaganda – even when it comes from those we respect. *The Guardian.* https://www.theguardian.com/commentisfree/2022/mar/02/russian-propaganda-anti-imperialist-left-vladimir-putin (last accessed 17 October 2022).

10 https://www.nytimes.com/2023/10/10/world/middleeast/peace-activists-killed-israel.html

11 https://news.yahoo.com/socialist-rally-in-times-square-praising-hamas-terror-attack-draws-widespread-condemnation-204123785.html

12 https://www.theatlantic.com/international/archive/2023/10/hamas-covenant-israel-attack-war-genocide/675602/

13 https://www.telegraph.co.uk/world-news/2023/10/10/black-lives-matter-palestine-twitter-hamas-chicago-israel/

14 https://www.nytimes.com/2023/12/07/opinion/social-work-columbia-ideology.html

15 https://www.amnesty.org/en/latest/news/2015/05/gaza-palestinians-tortured-summarily-killed-by-hamas-forces-during-2014-conflict/

16 https://www.hrw.org/news/2023/02/02/israel-collective-punishment-against-palestinians

17 https://www.telegraph.co.uk/world-news/2023/10/10/black-lives-matter-palestine-twitter-hamas-chicago-israel/

18 https://www.theatlantic.com/international/archive/2023/10/israel-hamas-war-iran-trap/675628/

19 https://www.savethechildren.net/news/least-2000-children-killed-gaza-airstrikes-continue-unabated#:~:text=Ramallah%2C%2023%20October%20%E2%80%93%20At%20least,to%20piles%20of%20smoking%20rubble.

20 https://www.nytimes.com/live/2023/10/23/world/israel-hamas-war-gaza-news

21 https://www.pbs.org/newshour/world/live-updates-whats-happening-on-day-15-of-the-israel-hamas-war

22 https://thehill.com/policy/defense/4310635-us-support-for-israel-is-declining-survey/#:~:text=About%2032%20percent%20of%20respondents,27%20percent%20a%20month%20ago.

23 https://www.nytimes.com/2023/11/25/world/middleeast/israel-gaza-death-toll.html?smid=nytcore-ios-share&referringSource=articleShare

24 https://www.theguardian.com/world/2023/dec/09/civilian-toll-israeli-airstrikes-gaza-unprecedented-killing-study

25 https://news.yahoo.com/israeli-president-says-no-innocent-154330724.html#:~:text=As%20Israel%20engages%20in%20a,left%20over%201%2C200%20people%20dead.

26 https://www.cnbc.com/2023/06/01/russia-targets-food-water-to-starve-ukrainians-international-report-says.html

27 https://www.nytimes.com/2023/11/03/podcasts/transcript-ezra-klein-interviews-amaney-jamal.html

[28] https://www.pbs.org/newshour/world/no-such-thing-as
-palestinian-people-top-israeli-minister-says

[29] https://foreignpolicy.com/2022/07/04/us-politics-ukraine
-russia-far-right-left-progressive-horseshoe-theory/

[30] https://news.yahoo.com/why-some-american-leftists-are-critical-of-us
-assistance-to-ukraine-185013163.html

[31] https://www.newsweek.com/lefts-peculiar-alignment-russia-opinion-1808768

[32] https://www.nytimes.com/2022/11/01/opinion/ukraine-war-national-identity.
html

[33] https://www.washingtonpost.com/history/2023/11/03/israel-nakba
-history-1948/

[34] Lerman, A. (2009, October 15). A strike against silence. *The Guardian*. https
://www.theguardian.com/commentisfree/2009/oct/15/israel-palestine
-psychoactive-conference (last accessed 15 March 2024).

[35] https://www.tandfonline.com/doi/full/10.1080/10481885.2023.2220764

[36] Baptist, E. E. (2016). *The Half Has Never Been Told: Slavery and the Making of
American Capitalism*. New York: Basic Books.

[37] Bar-On, T. (2022). The metapolitics of the alt-right: A "cultural war" for the
United States, European identity, and the "white race." In: T. Bar-On (Ed.),
*The Right and Radical Right in the Americas: Ideological Currents from Interwar
Canada to Contemporary Chile* (pp. 185–214). Lanham, MD: Lexington.

[38] Dreisinger, B. (2008). *Near Black: White-to-Black Passing in American Culture*.
Amherst, MA: University of Massachusetts Press.

[39] American Psychological Association, Task Force on Gender Identity and
Gender Variance (2009). *Report of the Task Force on Gender Identity and Gender
Variance*. https://www.apa.org/pubs/reports/gender-identity; De Cuypere,
G., Van Hemelrijck, M., Michel, A., Carael, B., Heylens, G., Rubens,
R., Hoebeke, P., & Monstrey, S. (2007). Prevalence and demography of
transsexualism in Belgium. *European Psychiatry, 22*(3), 137–141. https://doi
.org/10.1016/j.eurpsy.2006.10.002

[40] Ghorayshi, A. (2022, September 26). More trans teens are choosing "top
surgery." *The New York Times*. https://www.nytimes.com/2022/09/26/health
/top-surgery-transgender-teenagers.html (last accessed 17 October 2022).

[41] Goldberg, M. (2015, December 9). The trans women who say that trans
women aren't women. *Slate*. https://slate.com/human-interest/2015/12
/gender-critical-trans-women-the-apostates-of-the-trans-rights-movement.html
(last accessed 17 October 2022).

[42] Srinivasan, A. (2021, September 6). Who lost the sex wars? *The New Yorker*.
https://www.newyorker.com/magazine/2021/09/13/who-lost-the-sex-wars (last
accessed 17 October 2022).

[43] Sax, L. (2002, February 5). How common is intersex? A response to Anne
Fausto-Sterling. *The Journal of Sex Research, 39*(3): 174–178. https://doi
.org/10.1080/00224490209552139

44 Digitale, E. (2008, November 12). Stanford author explores the struggles of intersex individuals, their families, and doctors. Stanford Medicine. https ://med.stanford.edu/news/all-news/2008/11/stanford-author-explores -struggles-of-intersex-individuals-their-families-and-doctors.html (last accessed 6 March 2023).

45 Dahlen, S. (2021). Rapid response to Alpert, A. B, Ruddick, R., & Manzano, C. (2021). Rethinking sex-assigned-at-birth questions. *British Medical Journal, 373*(n1261). https://doi.org/10.1136/bmj.n1261

46 Powell, M. (2022). How gender-neutral language is shaping the fight for abortion rights. *The New York Times*. https://www.nytimes.com/2022/06/08 /us/women-gender-aclu-abortion.html (last accessed 17 October 2022).

47 Dahlen, S. (2021). Do we need the word "woman" in healthcare? *Postgraduate Medical Journal, 97*: 483–484. https://doi.org/10.1136 /postgradmedj-2021-140193

48 Stock, K. (2021). *Material Girls: Why Reality Matters for Feminism*. London: Fleet, pp. 240–276.

49 Van Arsdale, A. P. (2019). Population demography, ancestry, and the biological concept of race. *Annual Review of Anthropology, 48*: 227–241. https://doi .org/10.1146/annurev-anthro-102218-011154

50 Butler, J. (1990). *Gender Trouble: Feminism and the Subversion of Identity*. New York: Routledge.

51 Ducat, S. (2005). *The Wimp Factor: Gender Gaps, Holy Wars, and the Politics of Anxious Masculinity*. Boston, MA: Beacon, pp. 32–47.

52 Browder, L., (2000). *Slippery Characters: Ethnic Impersonators and American Identities*. Chapel Hill, NC: University of North Carolina Press.

53 Conaboy, C. (2022, August 26). Maternal instinct is a myth that men created. *The New York Times*. https://www.nytimes.com/2022/08/26/opinion/sunday /maternal-instinct-myth.html? (last accessed 17 October 2022).

54 Joyce, H. (2021). *Trans: When Ideology Meets Reality*. London: One World, pp. 149–173.

55 MurrayBlackburnMackenzie (2021). "Long-term follow-up of transsexual persons undergoing sex reassignment surgery: Cohort study in Sweden": A review of Dhejne et al.'s findings on criminal convictions (article on research collective's website). https://mbmpolicy.files.wordpress.com/2021/04/mbm -briefing-on-dhjene-et-al.-april-2021-1.pdf (last accessed 17 October 2022).

56 Roscoe, W. (1993). How to become a *berdache*: Toward a unified analysis of gender diversity. In: G. Herdt (Ed.), *Third Sex, Third Gender: Beyond Sexual Dimorphism in Culture and History* (pp. 329–372). New York: Zone Books.

57 https://moralfoundations.org (website of research group).

58 Joyce, H.

59 Kyriacou, S. (2020, February 22). Thousands of gay people are being forced to undergo gender reassignment surgery in Iran for a vile reason. *PinkNews*.

https://www.pinknews.co.uk/2020/02/22/iran-gay-forced-gender
-reassignment-surgery-the-sun/ (last accessed 17 October 2022); Human
Dignity Trust (2022). Pakistan. https://www.humandignitytrust.org/country
-profile/pakistan/ (last accessed 17 October 2022).

60 Shappley, K., as told to Randall, B. (2017, April 13). I had 4 boys – until one
of them told me she was really a girl. *Good Housekeeping*. https://www
.goodhousekeeping.com/life/parenting/a43702/transgender-child-kimberly
-shappley/ (last accessed 18 October 2022).

61 Palmer, E. (2023, February 27). Ron DeSantis "will destroy our democracy,"
says fascism expert. *Newsweek*. https://www.newsweek.com/ron-desantis
-fascist-ruth-ben-ghiat-1784017 (last accessed 6 March 2023).

62 Skolnik, J. (2022, January 26). Book-banning fever heats up in red states.
Salon. https://www.salon.com/2022/01/26/book-banning-heats-up-in-red
-states/ (last accessed 6 March 2023).

63 Applebaum, A. (2021, August 31). The new Puritans. *The Atlantic*. https://
www.theatlantic.com/magazine/archive/2021/10/new-puritans-mob-justice
-canceled/619818/ (last accessed 6 March 2023).

64 Wright, C. (2021, February 1). Sex is not a spectrum. *Reality's Last Stand*.
https://www.realityslaststand.com/p/sex-is-not-a-spectrum (last accessed 6
March 2023).

65 Wright, C. (2021, January 12). Think cancel culture doesn't exist? My own
"lived experience" says otherwise. *Reality's Last Stand*. https://www
.realityslaststand.com/p/think-cancel-culture-doesnt-exist (last accessed 6
March 2023).

66 Joyce, H.

67 Gender self-identification (2022). In: *Wikipedia*. https://en.wikipedia.org
/wiki/Gender_self-identification (last accessed 18 October 2022).

68 Hilton, E. N. (2021). Transgender women in the female category of sport:
Perspectives on testosterone suppression and performance advantage. *Sports
Medicine, 51*: 199–214. https://doi.org/10.1007/s40279-020-01389-3

69 Joyce, H., pp. 175–199.

70 Paul, P. (2023, February 16). In defense of J. K. Rowling. *The New York Times*.
https://www.nytimes.com/2023/02/16/opinion/jk-rowling-transphobia.html
(last accessed 6 March 2023).

71 https://music.amazon.com/podcasts/66896636-
8562-466b-a50d-81b85b14b8f2/
the-witch-trials-of-j-k-rowling

72 Smith, R. (2024, March 7). JK Rowling Declares War on Her Nemesis.
Newsweek. https://www.newsweek.com/jk-rowling-india-willoughby
-transgender-women-police-twitter-x-1876787 (last accessed 15 March, 2024).

73 https://www.chronicle.com/article/the-real-free-speech-crisis-is-professors
-being-disciplined-for-liberal-views-a-scholar-finds/

74 https://www.newyorker.com/news/news-desk/a-conservative-nonprofit-that
   -seeks-to-transform-college-campuses-faces-allegations-of-racial-bias-and
   -illegal-campaign-activity
75 https://www.thefire.org/research-learn/scholars-under-fire
   -attempts-sanction-scholars-2000-2022
76 https://www.thefire.org/research-learn/scholars-under-fire
   -attempts-sanction-scholars-2000-2022

Chapter 4

1   Nossiter, A. (2008, October 15). For some, uncertainty starts at racial identity.
    The New York Times. https://www.nytimes.com/2008/10/15/world
    /americas/15iht-15biracial.16962018.html (last accessed 18 October 2022).
2   Plecker, W. A. (1925). Virginia's attempt to adjust the color problem. *American
    Journal of Public Health, 15*(2): 111–115. https://doi.org/10.2105
    /ajph.15.2.111
3   Brandt, M. J., & Reyna, C. (2014). To love or hate thy neighbor: The
    role of authoritarianism and traditionalism in explaining the link between
    fundamentalism and racial prejudice. *Political Psychology, 35*(2): 207–223.
    https://doi.org/10.1111/pops.12077
4   Johnson, M. K., Rowatt, W. C., Barnard-Brak, L. M., Patock-Peckham, J. A.,
    LaBouff, J. P., & Carlisle, R. D. (2011). A mediational analysis of the role of
    right-wing authoritarianism and religious fundamentalism in the religiosity–
    prejudice link. *Personality and Individual Differences, 50*(6): 851–856. https
    ://doi.org/10.1016/j.paid.2011.01.010.
5   Rowatt, W., & Franklin, L. M. (2004). Christian orthodoxy, religious
    fundamentalism, and right-wing authoritarianism as predictors of implicit
    racial prejudice. *International Journal for the Psychology of Religion, 14*(2):
    125–138. https://doi.org/10.1207/s15327582ijpr1402_4
6   Brandt, M. J., & Reyna, C. (2010). The role of prejudice and the need for
    closure in religious fundamentalism. *Personality and Social Psychology Bulletin,
    36*(5), 715–725. https://doi.org/10.1177/0146167210366306
7   Orbán, V. (2022, July 23). Transcript of speech given at the 31st Bálványos
    Summer Free University and Student Camp. About Hungary. https
    ://abouthungary.hu/speeches-and-remarks/speech-by-prime-minister-viktor
    -orban-at-the-31-st-balvanyos-summer-free-university-and-student-camp (last
    accessed 18 October 2022).
8   Noack, R. (2022, July 27). Hungary's Viktor Orban faces outrage after saying
    Europeans shouldn't become "mixed race." *The Washington Post.* https://www
    .washingtonpost.com/world/2022/07/27/viktor-orban-mixed-race-cpac/ (last
    accessed 18 October 2022).
9   Allison, N., & Johnson, L. (2022, August 4). Orbán gets warm CPAC
    reception after "mixed race" speech blowback. *Politico.* https://www.politico

.com/news/2022/08/04/viktor-orban-cpac-00049935 (last accessed 18 October 2022).

10 Óry, M. (2022, August 1). Viktor Orbán's advisor Zsuzsa Hegedüs "unresigns." *Hungary Today.* https://hungarytoday.hu/viktor-orbans-advisor-zsuzsa-hegedus -unresigns/ (last accessed 18 October 2022).

11 Westen, D. (2007). *The Political Brain: The Role of Emotion in Deciding the Fate of the Nation.* New York: Public Affairs.

12 Serwer, A. (2021). *The Cruelty Is the Point: The Past, Present, and Future of Trump's America.* New York: One World.

13 Mason, L., Wronski, J., & Kane, J. V. (2021). Activating animus: The uniquely social roots of Trump support. *American Political Science Review, 115*(4): 1508–1516. https://doi.org/10.1017/S0003055421000563

14 Ibid.

15 Banaji, M. R., Fiske, S. T., & Massey, D. S. (2021). Systemic racism: Individuals and interactions, institutions and society. *Cognitive Research: Principles and Implications, 6*(82). https://doi.org/10.1186 /s41235-021-00349-3

16 Enns, P. K., & Jardina, A. (2021). Complicating the role of white racial attitudes and anti-immigrant sentiment in the 2016 US presidential election. *Public Opinion Quarterly, 85*(2): 539–570. https://doi.org/10.1093/poq /nfab040

17 Edsall, T. B. (2022, August 10). How we think about politics changes what we think about politics. *The New York Times.* https://www.nytimes .com/2022/08/10/opinion/republicans-democrats-polarization-inequality.html (last accessed 18 October 2022).

18 Zhirkov, K., & Valentino, N. A. (2022, April 6). The origins and consequences of racialized schemas about US parties. *Journal of Race, Ethnicity, and Politics.* https://doi.org/10.1017/rep.2022.4

19 https://www.thedailybeast.com/candace-owens-white-supremacy-is-nothing -more-than-an-election-strategy

20 https://www.splcenter.org/fighting-hate/extremist-files/group/proud-boys

21 https://www.nytimes.com/2022/11/25/us/politics/trump-nick-fuentes-dinner .html

22 Tankersley, J., & Cochrane, E. (2019, August 21). Budget deficit on path to surpass. trillion under Trump. *The New York Times.* https://www.nytimes .com/2019/08/21/us/politics/deficit-will-reach-1-trillion-next-year-budget -office-predicts.html (last accessed 18 October 2022).

23 Tankersley, J., & Cochrane, E. (2019, August 21). Budget deficit on path to surpass. trillion under Trump. *The New York Times.* https://www.nytimes .com/2019/08/21/us/politics/deficit-will-reach-1-trillion-next-year-budget -office-predicts.html (last accessed 18 October 2022).

24 https://thehill.com/homenews/house/4018798-gaetz-says-most-in-gop-dont
    -feel-like-we-should-negotiate-with-our-hostage/#:~:text=Rep.%20Matt%20
    Gaetz%20(R%2D,on%20a%20debt%2Dlimit%20compromise.

25 Select Committee on Intelligence, United States Senate (2020, November
    10). *Report of the Select Committee on Intelligence, United States Senate, on the
    Russian Active Measures Campaigns and Interference in the 2016 US Election,
    Volume 1: Russian Efforts Against Election Infrastructure, with Additional Views*
    https://www.intelligence.senate.gov/sites/default/files/documents/Report
    _Volume1.pdf (last accessed 18 October 2022).

26 United States House Committee on the Judiciary (2019–2020). *The
    Impeachment of Donald John Trump Evidentiary Record from the House of
    Representatives (116th)*. https://judiciary.house.gov/the-impeachment-of
    -donald-john-trump/ (last accessed 18 October 2022).

27 Bump, P. (2022, August 31). The photo of classified documents at Trump's
    Mar-a-Lago resort, annotated. *The Washington Post*. https://www
    .washingtonpost.com/politics/2022/08/31/trump-mar-a-lago-fbi-search
    -classified-documents/ (last accessed 18 October 2022).

28 Sheth, S. (2019, September 10). The US extracted a top spy from Russia
    after Trump revealed classified information to the Russians in an Oval Office
    meeting. *Business Insider*. https://www.businessinsider.com/us-extracted-russia
    -spy-trump-classified-info-oval-office-2019-9?r=US&IR=T (last accessed 18
    October 2022).

29 Folley, A. (2018, August 28). Trump supporters whose Russia shirts went viral:
    "We're not traitors." *The Hill*. https://thehill.com/blogs/blog-briefing-room
    /news/404017-trump-supporters-whose-pro-russia-shirts-went-viral-were-not
    / (last accessed 18 October 2022).

30 Cummings, W. (2019, November 25). "God's used imperfect people
    throughout history": Perry shares why he thinks Trump is the "chosen one."
    USA Today. https://eu.usatoday.com/story/news/politics/2019/11/25/rick-
    perry-trump-gods-chosen-one/4295185002/ (last accessed 18 October 2022).

31 Iadarola, J., Uygur, C., et al. (Producers) (2019, March 19). Raging Trump
    supporter wants Trump to be dictator (online political news video episode). In:
    The Damage Report. https://www.youtube.com/watch?v=fLdHCyz8uXg (last
    accessed 18 October 2022).

32 Haberman, M., Berzon, A., & Schmidt, M. S. (2022, April 18). Trump allies
    are still feeding the false 2020 election narrative. *The New York Times*. https
    ://www.nytimes.com/2022/04/18/us/politics/trump-allies-election-decertify
    .html (last accessed 18 October 2022).

33 Klein, R., Harper, A., & Wiersema, A. (2022, April 26). "Big lie" animates
    GOP primaries ahead of voting season: The note. *ABC News*. https://abcnews
    .go.com/Politics/big-lie-animates-gop-primaries-ahead-voting-season
    /story?id=84301867 (last accessed 18 October 2022).

34 Hayes, C. (2018). What "law and order" means to Trump. *The New York Times*. https://www.nytimes.com/2018/03/17/opinion/sunday/chris-hayes -trump-law-order.html? (last accessed 18 October 2022).

35 Fraser, S. (2015). *The Age of Acquiescence: The Life and Death of American Resistance to Organized Wealth and Power*. New York: Little, Brown and Company.

36 Lau, T. (2019, December 12). *Citizens United* explained. Brennan Center for Justice. https://www.brennancenter.org/our-work/research-reports/citizens -united-explained (last accessed 18 October 2022).

37 Totenberg, N. (2014, July 28). When did companies become people? Excavating the legal evolution. *National Public Radio*. https://www.npr .org/2014/07/28/335288388/when-did-companies-become-people-excavating -the-legal-evolution (last accessed 18 October 2022).

38 Scola, N. (2012, April 14). Exposing ALEC: How Conservative-backed state laws are all connected. *The Atlantic*. https://www.theatlantic.com/politics /archive/2012/04/exposing-alec-how-conservative-backed-state-laws-are-all -connected/255869/ (last accessed 18 October 2022).

39 Graeber, D., & Wengrow, D. (2021). *The Dawn of Everything: A New History of Humanity*. New York: Farrar, Straus and Giroux.

40 Riffkin, R. (2014, August 12). In US, 55% of workers get sense of identity from their job. *Gallup*. https://news.gallup.com/poll/175400/workers-sense -identity-job.aspx (last accessed 18 October 2022).

41 Chancer, L. S. (1992). *Sadomasochism in Everyday Life: The Dynamics of Power and Powerlessness*. New Brunswick, NJ: Rutgers University Press.

42 Anderson, E. (2017). *Private Government: How Employers Rule Our Lives (and Why We Don't Talk about It)*. Princeton, NJ: Princeton University Press.

43 Durkin, E. (2019, January 24). Trump commerce chief wonders why federal workers are using food banks. *The Guardian*. https://www.theguardian.com /us-news/2019/jan/24/wilbur-ross-government-shutdown-federal-workers -food-banks (last accessed 18 October 2022).

44 Cowie, J. (2022). *Freedom's Dominion: A Saga of White Resistance to Federal Power*. New York: Basic Books, pp. 268–269.

45 Ibid., pp. 216–225.

46 Ibid., p. 5.

47 Williams, J. C. (2017). *White Working Class: Overcoming Class Cluelessness in America*. Boston, MA: Harvard Business Review Press.

48 Cobb, J., & Sennett, R. (1972). *The Hidden Injuries of Class*. New York: W. W. Norton and Company, 1993.

49 Vance, J. D. (2016). *Hillbilly Elegy: A Memoir of a Family and Culture in Crisis*. New York: Harper.

50 Ibid., p. 226.

51 Marche, S. (2022, January 5). How Ivy League elites turned against democracy. *The Atlantic*. https://www.theatlantic.com/ideas/archive/2022/01

/ivy-league-apologists-january-6-gop-elitism-populsim/621153/ (last accessed 18 October 2022).

52 Hartline-Grafton, H., & Vollinger, E. (2019). New USDA report provides picture of who participates in SNAP (blog post). Food Research & Action Center. https://frac.org/blog/new-usda-report-provides-picture-of-who -participates-in-snap (last accessed 18 October 2022).

53 Sit, R. (2018, January 12). Trump thinks only black people are on welfare, but really, white Americans receive most benefits. *Newsweek*. https://www .newsweek.com/donald-trump-welfare-black-white-780252 (last accessed 18 October 2022).

54 Metzl, J. M. (2020). *Dying of Whiteness: How the Politics of Racial Resentment Is Killing America's Heartland*. New York: Basic Books.

55 Hochschild, A. R. (2016). *Strangers in Their Own Land: Anger and Mourning on the American Right*. New York: New Press.

56 Lincoln, A. (1864, April 18). Speech given at Baltimore, MD. Quoted in Cowie, J. (2022), p. 112.

57 Cheney, K., & Wu, N. (2023, January 6). Enablers, line-straddlers and quiet resisters: How GOP lawmakers contributed to Jan. 6. *Politico*. https ://www.politico.com/news/2023/01/06/enablers-line-straddlers-and-quiet -resistors-how-gop-lawmakers-contributed-to-jan-6-00076581 (last accessed 1 February 2023)

58 Venkataramanan, M. (2023, January 16). Two states still observe King-Lee Day, honoring Robert E. Lee with MLK. *The Washington Post*. https://www .washingtonpost.com/history/2023/01/16/king-lee-day/ (last accessed 1 February 2023).

59 Indigenous Peoples' Day (2023) In: *Wikipedia*. https://en.wikipedia.org/wiki /Indigenous_Peoples'_Day (last accessed 1 February 2023).

60 Cineas, F. (2021). Whiteness is at the core of the insurrection. *Vox*. https ://www.vox.com/2021/1/8/22221078/us-capitol-trump-riot-insurrection (last accessed 19 October 2022).

61 Ibid.

62 Drill, baby, drill (2020). In: *Wikipedia*. https://en.wikipedia.org/wiki/Drill ,_baby,_drill (last accessed 18 October 2022).

63 Censky, A. (2020). Heavily armed protesters gather again at Michigan Capitol to decry stay-at-home order. *National Public Radio*. https://www.npr .org/2020/05/14/855918852/heavily-armed-protesters-gather-again-at -michigans-capitol-denouncing-home-order (last accessed 18 October 2022).

64 O'Connell, O. (2023, January 14). Tucker Carlson mocked for wondering "why is tobacco so dangerous?" *Independent*. https://www.independent .co.uk/news/world/americas/us-politics/tucker-carlson-smoking-congress -freedom-b2262331.html (last accessed 1 February 2023).

65 Piketty, T. (2022). *A Brief History of Equality*. Cambridge, MA: Belknap Press, p. 101.

66 Leonhardt, D. (2022, May 17). The right's violence problem: Most extremist violence in the US comes from the political right. *The New York Times*. https ://www.nytimes.com/2022/05/17/briefing/right-wing-mass-shootings.html (last accessed 1 February 2023).

67 Continetti, M. (2022). *The Right: The Hundred-Year War for American Conservatism*. New York: Basic Books.

68 Klein, E. (2023, January 15). Three reasons the Republican Party keeps coming apart at the seams. *The New York Times*. https://www.nytimes .com/2023/01/15/opinion/mccarthy-republicans-coming-apart.html (last accessed 1 February 2023).

69 Shephard, A. (2021, July 7). If you want to get ahead in the GOP, you'd better support Trump's Big Lie. *The New Republic*. https://newrepublic. com/article/162911/jd-vance-big-lie-pledge-2022-election (last accessed 18 October 2022).

70 Zuckerman, J. (2022, May 5). Ohio man who painted Trump's face in front yard wins GOP primary. *Ohio Capital Journal*. https://ohiocapitaljournal .com/2022/05/05/ohio-man-who-painted-trumps-face-in-front-yard-wins -gop-primary/ (last accessed 18 October 2022).

71 Gedeon, J. (2022, February 23). Trump calls Putin "genius" and "savvy" for Ukraine invasion. *Politico*. https://www.politico.com/news/2022/02/23/ trump-putin-ukraine-invasion-00010923 (last accessed 18 October 2022).

72 Cillizza, C., & Williams, B. (2019, July 2). 15 times Donald Trump praised authoritarian rulers. *CNN*. https://www.cnn.com/2019/07/02/politics/donald -trump-dictators-kim-jong-un-vladimir-putin/index.html (last accessed 18 October 2022).

73 Berman, M. (2017, July 28). Trump tells police not to worry about injuring suspects during arrests. *The Washington Post*. https://www.washingtonpost.com /news/post-nation/wp/2017/07/28/trump-tells-police-not-to-worry-about -injuring-suspects-during-arrests/ (last accessed 18 October 2022).

74 Jacobs, B., Siddiqui, S., & Bixby, S. (2016, October 8). "You can do anything": Trump brags on tape about using fame to get women. *The Guardian*. https://www.theguardian.com/us-news/2016/oct/07/donald-trump -leaked-recording-women (last accessed 18 October 2022).

75 Richardson, H. C. (2021, January 16). Untitled blog post. https ://heathercoxrichardson.substack.com/p/january-16-2021? (last accessed 18 October 2022).

76 Daniels, C. M. (2022, August 13). GOP lawmakers adopt "defund" rallying cry for FBI, not police. *The Hill*. https://thehill.com/homenews /house/3599029-gop-lawmakers-adopt-defund-rallying-cry-for-fbi-not-police / (last accessed 1 February 2023).

77 Who's against the jab (2021, July 31). *The Economist*. https://www.economist .com/united-states/2021/07/31/whos-against-the-jab (last accessed 18 October 2022).

78 Ellwood, B. (2022, May 5). Longitudinal study finds that prosociality is consistently associated with greater willingness to receive a Covid-19 vaccine. *PsyPost*. https://www.psypost.org/2022/05/longitudinal-study-finds-that-prosociality-is-consistently-associated-with-greater-willingness-to-receive-a-covid-19-vaccine-63080? (last accessed 18 October 2022).

79 Rodriguez, A. (2022, June 7). The "mortality gap" between Republican and Democratic counties is widening, study says. Here's why. *USA Today*. https://eu.usatoday.com/story/news/health/2022/06/07/republican-democratic-counties-study-shows-widening-death-rate-gap/7530296001/ (last accessed 18 October 2022).

80 Levitan, D. (2015, May 18). Does a fetus feel pain at 20 weeks? *FactCheck.org*. https://www.factcheck.org/2015/05/does-a-fetus-feel-pain-at-20-weeks/ (last accessed 18 October 2022).

81 Casas, X. (2019). They are girls, not mothers: The violence of forcing motherhood on young girls in Latin America. *Health and Human Rights, 21*(2): 157–167.

82 American Psychological Association (2022). Abortion. https://www.apa.org/topics/abortion (last accessed 18 October 2022).

83 Herd, P., Higgins, J., Sicinski, K., & Merkurieva, I. (2016). The implications of unintended pregnancies for mental health in later life. *American Journal of Public Health, 106*(3): 421–429. https://doi.org/10.2105/AJPH.2015.302973

84 Amnesty International (2020). *Forced Pregnancy: A Commentary on the Crime in International Criminal Law*. https://www.amnesty.org/en/documents/ior53/2711/2020/en/ (last accessed 18 October 2022).

85 Foster, D. G., Raifman, S. E., Gipson, J. D., Rocca, C. H., & Biggs, M. A. (2018). Effects of carrying an unwanted pregnancy to term on women's existing children. *Journal of Pediatrics, 205*: 183–189. https://doi.org/10.1016/j.jpeds.2018.09.026

86 Su, J. H. (2017). Unintended birth and children's long-term mental health. *Journal of Health and Social Behavior, 58*(3): 357–370. https://doi.org/10.1177/0022146517717037

87 Calmes, J. (2022, May 13). Republican "pro-life" advocacy ends with a child's birth. *Los Angeles Times*. https://www.latimes.com/opinion/story/2022-05-13/republicans-pro-life-mothers-children-abortion-birth-pregnancy-roe (last accessed 18 October 2022).

88 Cathey, L. (2022, May 11). Senate Republicans block bill that would codify Roe v. Wade abortion rights. *ABC News*. https://abcnews.go.com/Politics/senate-republicans-block-bill-codify-roe-wade/story?id=84627147 (last accessed 18 October 2022).

89 Scott, E., & Sonmez, F. (2022, May 19). Nearly 200 Republicans vote against bill to ease baby formula shortage. *The Washington Post*. https://www.washingtonpost.com/politics/2022/05/19/republicans-baby-formula/ (last accessed 18 October 2022).

90 Badger, E., Sanger-Katz, M., Miller, C. C., & Washington, E. (2022, July 28). States with abortion bans are among least supportive for mothers and children. *The New York Times*. https://www.nytimes.com/2022/07/28/upshot/abortion -bans-states-social-services.html (last accessed 18 October 2022).

91 Aguilera, J. (2022, May 12). Overturning Roe could lead to restrictions on birth control. *Time*. https://time.com/6175213/birth-control-after-roe-v -wade/ (last accessed 18 October 2022).

92 https://www.bloomberg.com/news/features/2023-08-30/ red-state-governments-are-dominating-democrat-led-blue-cities#xj4y7vzkg

93 Filkins, D. (2022, June 20). Can Ron DeSantis displace Donald Trump as the GOP's combatant-in-chief? *The New Yorker*. https://www.newyorker.com /magazine/2022/06/27/can-ron-desantis-displace-donald-trump-as-the-gops -combatant-in-chief (last accessed 18 October 2022).

94 Ceballos, A. (2022, April 15). Florida targets school math textbooks over critical race theory objections. *Miami Herald*. https://www.miamiherald.com /news/local/education/article260469692.html (last accessed 18 October 2022).

95 CNN Editorial Research. (2023, December 14). Flint Water Crisis Fast Facts. CNN. https://www.cnn.com/2016/03/04/us/flint-water-crisis-fast-facts/index .html.

96 https://www.prwatch.org/news/2016/03/13064/ flint-casualty-right-wing-government-experiment.

97 US Census Bureau (2021). *Quick Facts: Jackson City, Mississippi*. https ://www.census.gov/quickfacts/jacksoncitymississippi (last accessed 18 October 2022); Shah, A. (2022, September 2). "There are no white people there": Jackson's water crisis, explained. *Salon*. https://www.salon.com/2022/09/02 /there-are-no-people-there-jacksons-water-crisis-explained/ (last accessed 18 October 2022).

98 Gov. Reeves vetoes bill to help Jackson collect delinquent water accounts (2020, June 30). *WJTV*. https://www.wjtv.com/news/gov-reeves-vetoes -bill-to-help-jackson-collect-delinquent-water-accounts/ (last accessed 18 October 2022).

99 Ganucheau, A., Pender, G., & Harrison, B. (2021, March 24). Legislative leaders kill key proposal to address Jackson water crisis. *Mississippi Today*. https://mississippitoday.org/2021/03/24/legislative-leaders-kill-key-proposal -to-address-jackson-water-crisis/ (last accessed 18 October 2022).

100 Reeves, T. (2020, June 30). For the last week or so, I've spent countless hours reviewing hundreds of bills from the legislature. It's the last… (Facebook user status update). Facebook. https://www.facebook.com/tatereeves /posts/3639545496062884 (last accessed 18 October 2022).

101 Shah, A.

102 Iyer, R., Koleva, S., Graham, J., Ditto, J., & Haidt, J. (2012). Understanding libertarian morality: The psychological dispositions of self-identified

libertarians. *PLoS ONE, 7*(8): e42366. https://doi.org/10.1371/journal
.pone.0042366

[103] Graham, J., Nosek, B. A., Haidt, J., Iyer, R., Koleva, S., & Ditto, P. H. (2011).
Mapping the moral domain. *Journal of Personality and Social Psychology,*
101(2), 366–385. https://doi.org/10.1037/a0021847

[104] https://academic.oup.com/joc/advance-article-abstract/doi/10.1093/joc
/jqad029/7275800?redirectedFrom=fulltext&login=false

[105] https://journals.plos.org/plosone/article?id=10.1371/journal.pone.0042366

[106] Saunders, J. (2022, June 22). Businesses: Florida's "Stop WOKE" law violates
speech rights. *ClickOrlando*. https://www.clickorlando.com/news/2022/06/22
/businesses-floridas-stop-woke-law-violates-speech-rights/ (last accessed 1
February 2023).

[107] Rakshit, D. (2021). Why "Asperger's syndrome" is no longer an official
diagnosis. *The Swaddle*. https://theswaddle.com/why-aspergers-syndrome-is
-no-longer-an-official-diagnosis/ (last accessed 18 October 2022).

[108] Elon Musk reveals he has Asperger's on Saturday Night Live (2021, May 1).
BBC News. https://www.bbc.co.uk/news/world-us-canada-57045770 (last
accessed 1 February 2023).

[109] Iyer, R., Koleva, S., Graham, J., Ditto, J., & Haidt, J.

[110] MacLean, N. (2017). *Democracy in Chains: The Deep History of the Radical*
Right's Stealth Plan for America. New York: Penguin, 2018.

[111] Baptist, E. E. (2016). *The Half Has Never Been Told: Slavery and the Making of*
American Capitalism. New York: Basic Books

[112] Schermerhorn, C. (2019, June 19). Why the racial wealth gap persists, more
than 150 years after emancipation. *The Washington Post*. https://www
.washingtonpost.com/outlook/2019/06/19/why-racial-wealth-gap-persists
-more-than-years-after-emancipation/ (last accessed 18 October 2022).

Chapter 5

[1] Cowie, J. (2022). *Freedom's Dominion: A Saga of White Resistance to Federal*
Power. New York: Basic Books, p. 391.

[2] Acharya, A., Blackwell, M., & Sen, M. (2016). The political legacy of
American slavery. *Journal of Politics, 78*(3): 621–641. http://dx.doi
.org/10.1086/686631

[3] Bright Line Watch (2021, June). Still miles apart: Americans and the state of
US democracy half a year into the Biden presidency: Bright Line Watch June
2021 surveys. http://brightlinewatch.org/still-miles-apart-americans-and-the
-state-of-u-s-democracy-half-a-year-into-the-biden-presidency/ (last accessed
18 October 2022).

[4] https://www.nbcnews.com/news/us-news/new-florida-standards-teach-black
-people-benefited-slavery-taught-usef-rcna95418

5   Hagen, L. (2018). GOP candidate: Civil War wasn't about slavery. *The Hill.*
    https://thehill.com/hilltv/rising/393927-gop-candidate-civil-war-wasnt-about
    -slavery/ (last accessed 18 October 2022).

6   Flanagin, J. (2015, April 8). For the last time, the American Civil War was not
    about states' rights. *Quartz.* https://qz.com/378533/for-the-last
    -time-the-american-civil-war-was-not-about-states-rights/ (last accessed 19
    October 2022).

7   Finkelman, P. (2015, July 17). Secession, the Confederate flag, and slavery
    (blog post). National Constitution Center. https://constitutioncenter.org/blog
    /secession-the-confederate-flag-and-slavery (last accessed 19 October 2022).

8   Blake, A. (2021, May 4). GOP state lawmakers: The Three-Fifths Compromise
    was actually good. *The Washington Post.* https://www.washingtonpost.com
    /politics/2021/05/04/gop-state-lawmakers-three-fifths-compromise-was
    -actually-good/ (last accessed 19 October 2022).

9   Kruse, K., & Zelizer, J. E. (2023) Myth America: Historians Take On the
    Biggest Legends and Lies About Our Past. Basic Books. p 318

10 Saric, I. (2022, May 2). The times Trump has advocated for violence.
    Axios. https://www.axios.com/2022/05/02/trump-call-violence-presidency (last
    accessed 19 October 2022).

11 Cineas, F. (2021, January 9). Donald Trump is the accelerant:
    A comprehensive timeline of Trump encouraging hate groups and political
    violence. *Vox.* https://www.vox.com/21506029/trump-violence-tweets-racist
    -hate-speech (last accessed 19 October 2022).

12 Mangan, D. (2020, December 22). Trump pardons 15, including people
    convicted in Mueller probe. *CNBC.* https://www.cnbc.com/2020/12/22/
    -trump-pardons-15-including-people-convicted-in-mueller-probe-.html (last
    accessed 19 October 2022); Finnegan, M., & Bierman, N. (2016, March 13).
    Trump's endorsement of violence reaches new level: He may pay legal fees for
    assault suspect. *Los Angeles Times.* https://www.latimes.com/politics
    /la-na-trump-campaign-protests-20160313-story.html (last accessed 19
    October 2022).

13 Freeman, J. B. (2019). *The Field of Blood: Violence in Congress and the Road to
    Civil War.* New York: Picador.

14 Paybarah, A., Sotomayor M., and L. Goodwin. (2023, November 14).
    McCarthy accused of elbowing lawmaker, while fight nearly breaks out in
    Senate. *Washington Post.* https://www.washingtonpost.com
    /politics/2023/11/14/kevin-mccarthy-elbow-senate-fight/ (last accessed 11
    January 2024).

15 Hibbing, J. R. (2020). *The Securitarian Personality: What Really Motivates
    Trump's Base and Why It Matters for the Post-Trump Era.* New York: Oxford
    University Press.

16 Kirkpatrick, D. D., Astor, M., & Edmondson, C. (2022, February 24). Trump
    praises Putin, leaving Republicans in a bind. *The New York Times.* https://www

.nytimes.com/2022/02/24/world/europe/trump-putin-russia-ukraine.html
(last accessed 19 October 2022).

17 Richards, L. L. (2000). *The Slave Power: The Free North and Southern
Domination 1780–1860.* Baton Rouge, LA: Louisiana State University Press, p.
86.

18 Brands, H. W. (2017, April 5). The real story of Reagan's 11th commandment.
Politico. https://www.politico.com/magazine/story/2017/04/11th
-commandment-gop-republican-reagan-trump-214982/ (last accessed 19
October 2022).

19 Sommer, W. (2021, July 27). Republicans recast Jan. 6 riot defendants as
"political prisoners." *Daily Beast.* https://www.thedailybeast.com
/republicans-recast-jan-6-riot-defendants-as-political-prisoners (last accessed
19 October 2022).

20 *Campaign of fear: The Trump world's assault on US election workers* (series of
reports, 2021–2022). Reuters. https://www.reuters.com/investigates/section
/campaign-of-fear/ (last accessed 19 October 2022).

21 Marche, S. (2022). *The Next Civil War: Dispatches from the American Future.*
New York: Avid Reader.

22 Sinha, M. (2003). The caning of Charles Sumner: Slavery, race, and ideology
in the age of the Civil War. *Journal of the Early Republic, 23*(2): 233–262.
https://doi.org/10.2307/3125037

23 Fischer, A. (2022, November 8). Oregon measure 112 election results 2022:
Remove constitutional language allowing slavery as punishment. *The New York
Times.* https://www.nytimes.com/interactive/2022/11/08/us/elections/results
-oregon-measure-112-remove-constitutional-language-allowing-slavery
-as-punishment.html (last accessed 1 February 2023).

24 Cowie, pp. 148–151.

25 Kruse, K., & Zelizer, J. E. (2023) *Myth America: Historians Take On the Biggest
Legends and Lies About Our Past.* Basic Books. pp 169–196

26 Ibid, 173.

27 Ibid, 183.

28 Ibid, 182.

29 https://www.nbclosangeles.com/news/local/city-of-glendale-apologizes
-for-its-history-as-a-sundown-town/2443011/

30 Kruse, K., & Zelizer, J. E. (2023) *Myth America.* 185–186.

31 Ibid, 193.

32 Ducat, S. (2005). *The Wimp Factor: Gender Gaps, Holy Wars, and the Politics of
Anxious Masculinity.* Boston, MA: Beacon, pp 91–96

33 Kruse, K., & Zelizer, J. E. (2023) *Myth America: Historians Take On the Biggest
Legends and Lies About Our Past.* Basic Books. p 196

34 Kruse, K., & Zelizer, J. E. (2023) *Myth America: Historians Take On the Biggest
Legends and Lies About Our Past.* Basic Books. p 196

Chapter 6

[1] https://www.politico.com/blogs/2016-gop-primary-live-updates
     -and-results/2016/03/trump-defends-protest-violence-220638

[2] https://www.youtube.com/watch?v=1agLQmZ4qVI

[3] Vyse, G. (2018, March 30). "Compassionate conservatism" won't be back
     anytime soon. *The New Republic.* https://newrepublic.com/article/147694
     /compassionate-conservatism-wont-back-anytime-soon (last accessed 19
     October 2022).

[4] Sharlet, J. (2023) The Undertow: Scenes from a Slow Civil War. W. W. Norton
     & Company. p 132

[5] Serwer, A. (2021). *The Cruelty Is the Point: The Past, Present, and Future of
     Trump's America.* New York: One World.

[6] Zirin, D. (2016, March 7). "Trump" has become a racial taunt at high school
     sporting events. *The Nation.* https://www.thenation.com/article/archive
     /trump-has-become-a-racial-taunt-at-high-school-sporting-events/ (last
     accessed 19 October 2022).

[7] Associated Press (2021, September 21). Migrants met with force at Texas
     Border (video). *The New York Times.* https://www.nytimes.com
     /video/us/100000007986229/haitians-texas-border.html (last accessed 19
     October 2022).

[8] Levine, M. (2020, May 30). "No blame?" *ABC News* finds 54 cases invoking
     "Trump" in connection with violence, threats, alleged assaults. *ABC News.*
     https://abcnews.go.com/Politics/blame-abc-news-finds-17-cases-invoking-
     trump/story?id=58912889 (last accessed 19 October 2022).

[9] Burke, M. (2018, October 26). Van connected to pipe bomb suspect Cesar
     Sayoc Jr. was covered in pro-Trump images and stickers. *NBC News.* https
     ://www.nbcnews.com/news/us-news/van-connected-pipe-bomb-suspect
     -covered-pro-trump-images-stickers-n924906 (last accessed 19 October 2022).

[10] Gross, J. (2020, October 24). Far-right groups are behind most US terrorist
     attacks, report finds. *The New York Times.* https://www.nytimes
     .com/2020/10/24/us/domestic-terrorist-groups.html (last accessed 19
     October 2022).

[11] Mazzei, P. (2019, January 7). "It's just too much": A Florida town grapples
     with a shutdown after a hurricane. *The New York Times.* https://www.nytimes
     .com/2019/01/07/us/florida-government-shutdown-marianna.html (last
     accessed 19 October 2022).

[12] Rubin, J. (2020, October 8). New report on Trump's child separation policy
     makes it clear: Cruelty was always the point. *The Washington Post.* https
     ://www.washingtonpost.com/opinions/2020/10/08/cruelty-was-always
     -point-lies-standard-procedure/ (last accessed 19 October 2022).

[13] Dickerson, D. (2020, October 21). Parents of 545 children separated at the
     border cannot be found. *The New York Times.* https://www.nytimes

.com/2020/10/21/us/migrant-children-separated.html (last accessed 19
October 2022).

14 Gamboa, S. (2020, August 22). "White supremacy" was behind child
separations – and Trump officials went along, critics say. *NBC News.*
https://www.nbcnews.com/news/latino/white-supremacy-was-behind
-child-separations-trump-officials-went-along-n1237746 (last accessed 19
October 2022).

15 https://historymatters.gmu.edu/d/4929/

16 https://www.nytimes.com/2022/09/27/magazine/spain-stolen-babies.html

17 https://www.dw.com/en/forgotten-victims-polish-children-abducted-during
-world-war-ii-still-seeking-truth/a-41981284

18 https://daily.jstor.org/stolen-children-of-argentina/

19 https://www.bbc.com/news/world-latin-america-48929112

20 https://www.washingtonpost.com/opinions/2022/12/27/russia-genocide
-ukraine-children/

21 Shear, M. D., & Davis, J. H. (2019, October 1). Shoot migrants' legs, build
alligator moat: Behind Trump's ideas for border. *The New York Times.* https
://www.nytimes.com/2019/10/01/us/politics/trump-border-wars.html (last
accessed 19 October 2022).

22 Suebsaeng, A., & Rawnsley, A., (2022, September 18). Trump fumes: DeSantis
stole my plan for shipping migrants. *Rolling Stone.* https://www.rollingstone
.com/politics/politics-news/marthas-vineyard-migrants-trump-desantis
-mad-1234595332/ (last accessed 19 October 2022).

23 Ngowi, R., Salomon, G., & Torrens, C. (2022, September 17). Surprise is key
part of migrant travel from Florida, Texas. *AP News.* https://apnews.com
/article/florida-immigration-ron-desantis-charlie-baker-massachusetts-7e97720
aceae5d70f137ece06851f3fc (last accessed 19 October 2022).

24 Bierman, N. (2022, September 15). GOP governors bused migrants to liberal
cities. Texas sent them to the vice president's home. *Los Angeles Times.* https
://www.latimes.com/politics/story/2022-09-15/migrants-vice-president-harris
-residence (last accessed 19 October 2022).

25 Lombardo, C. (2019, January 9). Virginia study finds increased school
bullying in areas that voted for Trump. *National Public Radio.* https://www
.npr.org/2019/01/09/683177489/virginia-study-finds-increased-school
-bullying-in-areas-that-voted-for-trump (last accessed 19 October 2022).

26 Blad, E. (2016, April 13). Donald Trump's rhetoric has made some students
feel unsafe, report says. *Education Week.* https://www.edweek.org/leadership
/donald-trumps-rhetoric-has-made-some-students-feel-unsafe-report
-says/2016/04 (last accessed 19 October 2022).

27 Huang, F. L., & Cornell, D. G. (2019). School teasing and bullying after the
presidential election. *Educational Researcher, 48*(2): 69–83. https://doi
.org/10.3102/0013189X18820291

28 Natanson, H., Cox, J. W., & Stein, P. (2020, February 13). Trump's words used by kids to bully classmates at school. *The Washington Post*. https://www.washingtonpost.com/graphics/2020/local/school-bullying-trump-words/ (last accessed 19 October 2022).

29 Moser, L. (2015, October 21). Students in the South still get paddled in schools. A lot. In 2015. *Slate*. https://slate.com/human-interest/2015/10/corporal-punishment-deep-south-students-still-paddled-in-schools.html (last accessed 19 October 2022).

30 Human Rights Watch (2008, August 19). *A Violent Education: Corporal Punishment of Children in US Public Schools*. https://www.hrw.org/report/2008/08/19/violent-education/corporal-punishment-children-us-public-schools (last accessed 19 October 2022); Human Rights Watch & American Civil Liberties Union (2009, August). *Impairing Education: Corporal Punishment of Students with Disabilities in US Public Schools*. https://www.aclu.org/report/impairing-education-corporal-punishment-students-disabilities-us-public-schools (last accessed 19 October 2022).

31 Clark, J. (2017, April 12). Where corporal punishment is still used in schools, its roots run deep. *National Public Radio*. https://www.npr.org/sections/ed/2017/04/12/521944429/where-corporal-punishment-is-still-used-its-roots-go-deep (last accessed 19 October 2022).

32 Gershoff, E., Larzelere, R., et al. (2002). Is corporal punishment an effective means of discipline? American Psychological Association. https://www.apa.org/news/press/releases/2002/06/spanking (last accessed 19 October 2022).

33 Milburn, M. A., & Conrad, S. D. (1996). *The Politics of Denial*. Cambridge, MA: Massachusetts Institute of Technology.

34 Savage, M. (2002). *The Savage Nation: Saving America from the Liberal Assault on Our Borders, Language and Culture*. Nashville: WND Books.

35 Fritz, B. (2003, February 19). Savage with the truth. *Salon*. https://www.salon.com/2003/02/19/savage_9/ (last accessed 19 October 2022).

36 Sullivan, M. (2022, March 6). Putin's full-scale information war got a key assist from Donald Trump and right-wing media. *The Washington Post*. https://www.washingtonpost.com/media/2022/03/06/putin-information-war-trump/ (last accessed 19 October 2022).

37 Costa, R., & Demirjian, K. (2019, December 3). GOP embraces a debunked Ukraine conspiracy to defend Trump from impeachment. *The Washington Post*. https://www.washingtonpost.com/politics/gop-embraces-a-debunked-ukraine-conspiracy-to-defend-trump-from-impeachment/2019/12/03/af3aa372-15ea-11ea-8406-df3c54b3253e_story.html (last accessed 19 October 2022).

38 Cohen, M. (2022, March 30). Trump brazenly asks Putin to release dirt about Biden's family. *CNN*. https://edition.cnn.com/2022/03/29/politics/trump-putin-hunter-biden/index.html (last accessed 19 October 2022).

[39] Weinger, M. (2012, April 26). 7 pols who praised Ayn Rand. *Politico*. https ://www.politico.com/story/2012/04/7-pols-who-praised-ayn-rand-075667 (last accessed 19 October 2022).

[40] Crosbie, J. (2022, April 26). Rand Paul brings Putin's core argument against Ukraine to Congress. *Rolling Stone*. https://www.rollingstone.com/politics /politics-news/rand-paul-anthony-blinken-russia-ukraine-1343073/ (last accessed 19 October 2022).

[41] Sparkman, D. J., Eidelman, S., & Till, D. F. (2019). Ingroup and outgroup interconnectedness predict and promote political ideology through empathy. *Group Processes and Intergroup Relations, 22*(8), 1161–1180 (p. 1164). https ://doi.org/10.1177/1368430218819794

[42] Hudson, S. T. J., Cikara, M., & Sidanius, J. (2019). Preference for hierarchy is associated with reduced empathy and increased counter-empathy towards others, especially outgroup targets. *Journal of Experimental Social Psychology, 85*: 103871. https://doi.org/10.1016/j.jesp.2019.103871.

[43] Ibid.

[44] Fiske, S. T., Cuddy, A. J. C., Glick, P., & Xu, J. (2002). A model of (often mixed) stereotype content: Competence and warmth respectively follow from perceived status and competition. *Journal of Personality and Social Psychology, 82*(6): 878–902. https://doi.org/10.1037//0022-3514.82.6.878

[45] irwinmcraw (2009, March 17). Enron traders talking about Grandma Millie (audio). YouTube. https://www.youtube.com/watch?v=DOLNWF5QMxY (last accessed 19 October 2022).

[46] Oppel, R. A., Jr. (2004, June 13). Word for word/energy hogs; Enron traders on Grandma Millie and making out like bandits. *The New York Times*. https ://www.nytimes.com/2004/06/13/weekinreview/word-for-word-energy-hogs -enron-traders-grandma-millie-making-like-bandits.html (last accessed 19 October 2022).

[47] van de Ven, N., Hoogland, C. E., Smith, R. H., van Dijk, W. W., Breugelmans, S. M., & Zeelenberg, M. (2015). When envy leads to schadenfreude. *Cognition and Emotion, 29*(6), 1007–1025. https://doi.org /10.1080/02699931.2014.961903

[48] Hudson, S. T. J., Cikara, M., & Sidanius, J., p. 8.

Chapter 7

[1] Wolfson, S. (2022, April 18). Tucker Carlson's answer to masculinity's supposed crisis? "Testicle tanning." *The Guardian*. https://www.theguardian .com/world/2022/apr/18/tucker-carlson-masculinity-crisis-testicle-tanning (last accessed 19 October 2022).

[2] Miller-Idriss, C. (2022). *Hate in the Homeland: The New Global Far Right*. Princeton, NJ: Princeton University Press, p. 95.

[3] Mazza, E. (2022, August 5). Tucker Carlson's attempt at revenge on Jon Stewart backfires spectacularly. *HuffPost*. Viewed at: https://www.yahoo.com /news/tucker-carlsons-attempt-revenge-jon-091727058.html? (last accessed 19 October 2022).

[4] Elgenaidi, D. (2022, August 5). Tucker Carlson re-ignites decades-long feud with Jon Stewart. *Primetimer*. https://www.primetimer.com/news/tucker -carlson-jon-stewart-feud (last accessed 19 October 2022).

[5] Miller-Idriss, C.

[6] Yuhas, A. (2015, August 13). "Cuckservative": The internet's latest Republican insult hits where it hurts. *The Guardian*. https://www.theguardian.com /us-news/2015/aug/13/cuckservative-republicans-conservatives-jeb-bush (last accessed 19 October 2022).

[7] Sharlet, J. (2023) The Undertow: Scenes from a Slow Civil War. W. W. Norton & Company. pp 85–106

[8] Ducat, S. (2005). *The Wimp Factor: Gender Gaps, Holy Wars, and the Politics of Anxious Masculinity*. Boston, MA: Beacon.

[9] Winkler, J. J. (1990). *The Constraints of Desire: The Anthropology of Sex and Gender in Ancient Greece*. New York: Routledge, pp. 45–70.

[10] Sidanius, J., Sinclair, S., & Pratto, F. (2006). Social dominance orientation, gender, and increasing educational exposure. *Journal of Applied Social Psychology, 36*(7): 1640–1653. https://doi.org/10.1111 /j.0021-9029.2006.00074.x

[11] Wilson, M. S., & Liu, J. H. (2003). Social dominance orientation and gender: The moderating role of gender identity. *British Journal of Social Psychology, 42*(2):187–198. https://doi.org/10.1348/014466603322127175

[12] Mason, L. (2018). *Uncivil Agreement: How Politics Became Our Identity*. Chicago: University of Chicago Press.

[13] Snyder, T. (2018). *The Road to Unfreedom: Russia, Europe, America*. New York: Crown.

[14] Ibid., p. 52.

[15] Ibid., p. 92.

[16] Jones, S. (2018, February 25). How social conservatism fueled Russia's HIV epidemic. *Politico Magazine*. https://www.politico.com/magazine /story/2018/02/25/russia-hiv-aids-epidemic-social-conservatism-orthodox -church-217011/ (last accessed 19 October 2022).

[17] Snyder, T., p. 132.

[18] Ibid., p. 140.

[19] Associated Press (2014, January 19). Vladimir Putin equates homosexuals to pedophiles. *Business Insider*. https://www.businessinsider.com/putin -equates-homosexuals-to-pedophiles-2014-1?r=US&IR=T (last accessed 19 October 2022).

[20] Itkowitz, C. (2022, April 20). GOP turns to false insinuations of LGBTQ grooming against Democrats. *The Washington Post*. https://www

.washingtonpost.com/politics/2022/04/20/republicans-grooming-democrats/ (last accessed 19 October 2022).

[21] https://www.politico.com/news/magazine/2023/07/14/masculinity-polling-00105414

[22] Jacobs, S., Alemany, J., & Dawsey, J. (2022, September 6). Steve Bannon faces state indictment in NY, will surrender Thursday. *The Washington Post*. https://www.washingtonpost.com/national-security/2022/09/06/bannon-border-wall-indictment/ (last accessed 19 October 2022).

[23] Here's every word of the second Jan. 6 committee hearing on its investigation (2022, June 13). *National Public Radio*. https://www.npr.org/2022/06/13/1104690690/heres-every-word-of-the-second-jan-6-committee-hearing-on-its-investigation (last accessed 25 October 2022).

[24] Shivaram, D. (2022). The Jan. 6 committee says the Trump campaign ripped off donors. But was it illegal? *National Public Radio*. https://www.npr.org/2022/06/16/1105279623/jan-6-committee-trump-campaign-legal-defense-fund (last accessed 19 October 2022).

[25] Goffman, E. (1952). On cooling the mark out: Some aspects of adaptation to failure. *Psychiatry: Interpersonal and Biological Processes, 15*(4): 451–463. https://doi.org/10.1080/00332747.1952.11022896

[26] Graham, D. A. (2017, January 23). The many scandals of Donald Trump: A cheat sheet. *The Atlantic*. https://www.theatlantic.com/politics/archive/2017/01/donald-trump-scandals/474726/ (last accessed 19 October 2022).

[27] DiMuccio, S. H., & Knowles, E. D. (2020). The political significance of fragile masculinity. *Current Opinion in Behavioral Sciences, 34*: 25–28. https://doi.org/10.1016/j.cobeha.2019.11.010

[28] Knowles, E. D., & DiMuccio, S. H. (2018, November 29). How Donald Trump appeals to men secretly insecure about their manhood. *The Washington Post*. https://www.washingtonpost.com/news/monkey-cage/wp/2018/11/29/how-donald-trump-appeals-to-men-secretly-insecure-about-their-manhood/? (last accessed 19 October 2022).

[29] Higher Education Research Institute, University of California, Los Angeles (2017, May 5). Survey reveals stark gender gap in political views among college freshmen. https://www.universityofcalifornia.edu/news/survey-reveals-stark-gender-gap-political-views-among-college-freshmen (last accessed 19 October 2022).

[30] Igielnik, R. (2020, August 18). Men and women in the US continue to differ in voter turnout rate, party identification. Pew Research Center. https://www.pewresearch.org/fact-tank/2020/08/18/men-and-women-in-the-u-s-continue-to-differ-in-voter-turnout-rate-party-identification/ (last accessed 19 October 2022).

[31] Edsall, T. B. (2022, March 30). What we know about the women who vote for republicans and the men who do not. *The New York Times*. https://www.nytimes.com/2022/03/30/opinion/gender-gap-republicans-democrats.html (last accessed 19 October 2022).

[32] Brough, A. R., & Wilkie, J. E. B. (2017, December 26). Men resist green behavior as unmanly. *Scientific American*. https://www.scientificamerican.com/article/men-resist-green-behavior-as-unmanly/ (last accessed 19 October 2022).

[33] Thomson, P. (Producer) (1992, October 30). *Living on Earth* (radio broadcast). Cambridge, MA: World Media Foundation.

[34] Gelin, M. (2019, August 28). The misogyny of climate deniers. *The New Republic*. https://newrepublic.com/article/154879/misogyny-climate-deniers (last accessed 19 October 2022).

[35] McCright, A. M., & Dunlap, R. E. (2011). Cool dudes: The denial of climate change among conservative white males in the United States. *Global Environmental Change, 21*(4): 1163–1172. https://doi.org/10.1016/j.gloenvcha.2011.06.003.

[36] Krange, O., Kaltenborn, B. P., & Hultman, M. (2019). Cool dudes in Norway: Climate-change denial among conservative Norwegian men. *Environmental Sociology, 5*(1): 1–11. https://doi.org/10.1080/23251042.2018.1488516

[37] Pederby, T. (2019). Cool dudes in Europe: Climate-change denial amongst conservative "white" men (unpublished bachelor's thesis). Lund University. https://doi.org/10.13140/RG.2.2.22416.15366

[38] Gun Violence Archive (2013–2022). *Gun Violence Archive*. https://www.gunviolencearchive.org/ (last accessed 20 October 2022).

[39] Arain, M., Haque, M., Johal, L., Mathur, P., Nel, W., Rais, A., Sandhu, R., & Sharma, S. (2013). Maturation of the adolescent brain. *Neuropsychiatric Disease and Treatment, 9*: 449–461. https://doi.org/10.2147/NDT.S39776.

[40] Sonmez, F. (2020, March 24). Texas Lt Gov. Dan Patrick comes under fire for saying seniors should "take a chance" on their own lives for the sake of grandchildren during the coronavirus crisis. *The Washington Post*. https://www.washingtonpost.com/politics/texas-lt-gov-dan-patrick-comes-under-fire-for-saying-seniors-should-take-a-chance-on-their-own-lives-for-sake-of-grandchildren-during-coronavirus-crisis/2020/03/24/e6f64858-6de6-11ea-b148-e4ce3fbd85b5_story.html (last accessed 20 October 2022).

[41] Mikkelson, D. (2014). Did Republicans actually say these things about rape? *Snopes*. https://www.snopes.com/fact-check/personal-foul/ (last accessed 20 October 2022).

[42] Kornfield, M., & Alfaro, M. (2022, January 1). 1 in 3 Americans say violence against government can be justified, citing fears of political schism, pandemic. *The Washington Post*. https://www.washingtonpost

.com/politics/2022/01/01/1-3-americans-say-violence-against-government -can-be-justified-citing-fears-political-schism-pandemic/ (last accessed 20 October 2022).

43 Mebane, M. E., Aiello, A., & Francescato, D. (2020). Political gender gap and social dominance orientation. In: D. S. Sheriff (Ed.), *Psycho-Social Aspects of Human Sexuality and Ethics*. London: IntechOpen, 2021. https://doi .org/10.5772/intechopen.73465

44 Edsall, T. B. (2022, January 12). The gender gap is taking us to unexpected places. *The New York Times*. https://www.nytimes.com/2022/01/12/opinion /gender-gap-politics.html (last accessed 20 October 2022).

45 Pinker, S. (2011). *The Better Angels of our Nature*. New York: Viking.

46 Faludi, S. (1991). *Backlash: The Undeclared War Against American Women*. New York: Three Rivers Press, 2006.

47 Center for American Women and Politics (2022). *Gender Gap* (collection of fact sheets). https://cawp.rutgers.edu/facts/voters/gender-gap (last accessed 20 October 2022).

48 Edsall, T. B. (2022, January 12).

49 Black, S. (2019, June 21).

50 Crockett, E. (2016, September 7). Phyllis Schlafly started the war on women. But it will outlive her. *Vox*. https://www.vox.com/2016/9/7/12817756/phyllis -schlafly-dies-started-war-on-women (last accessed 20 October 2022); Johnson, E. S. (2018). God, country, and Anita Bryant: Women's leadership and the politics of the new Christian right. *Religion and American Culture: A Journal of Interpretation, 28*(2): 238–268. https://doi.org/10.1525 /rac.2018.28.2.238; Johnson, E. (2019, April 16). How prominent women built and sustained the religious right. *Religion & Politics*. https ://religionandpolitics.org/2019/04/16/how-prominent-women- built-and-sustained-the-religious-right/ (last accessed 20 October 2022); Beverly LaHaye Institute (n.d.). Webpage showing latest articles published by the Beverly LaHaye Institute. Concerned Women for America. https://concernedwomen.org/beverly-lahaye-institute/ (last accessed 7 November 2022).

51 Ladies Against Women (2015?). Our ladyfesto. https://ladiesagainstwomen .com/ (last accessed 20 October 2022); https://ladiesagainstwomen.com.

52 Sharlet, J. (2023) The Undertow: Scenes from a Slow Civil War. W. W. Norton & Company. pp 94–106

53 Dickinson, T. (2022, June 9). "Coordinated and planned": Proud Boys ran recon at Capitol hours before Jan. 6 attack. *Rolling Stone*. https://www .rollingstone.com/politics/politics-news/proud-boys-recon-capitol-jan-6 -hearing-1365850/ (last accessed 20 October 2022).

54 Poniewozik, J. (2022, June 10). The Jan. 6 hearing put a true-crime drama on prime-time TV. *The New York Times*. https://www.nytimes.com/2022/06/10

/arts/television/january-6-broadcast-prime-time.html (last accessed 20
October 2022).

[55] Bump, P. (2022, June 16). Trump put Pence in more danger than we knew.
The Washington Post. https://www.washingtonpost.com/politics/2022/06/16
/trump-put-pence-more-danger-than-we-knew/ (last accessed 20
October 2022).

[56] Goba, K. (2022, June 17). Donald Trump called Mike Pence "the P-word" for
not illegally overturning the election, according to Jan. 6 committee testimony.
BuzzFeed News. https://www.buzzfeednews.com/article/buzzfeednews/about
-buzzfeed-news (last accessed 20 October 2022).

[57] Southern Poverty Law Center (n.d.). Proud boys. https://www.splcenter
.org/fighting-hate/extremist-files/group/proud-boys (last accessed 20
October 2022).

[58] Hatewatch. (2018, August 4). At the #Portland rally today, Proud Boy and
close associate of Joey Gibson Tusitala "Tiny" Toese is wearing a T-shirt...
(quote tweet of tweet and photo posted by user michaelbivins44, 4 August
2018). Twitter. https://twitter.com/Hatewatch/status/1025850638691917830
(last accessed 20 October 2022).

[59] Southern Poverty Law Center (n.d.). Proud boys.

[60] Rebel News (2017, April 24). Gavin McInnes: Feminism is a war on
masculinity (video). YouTube. https://www.youtube.com/watch?v
=vaVs4Ey5x8E (last accessed 20 October 2022).

[61] Williams, J. C. (2017). *White Working Class: Overcoming Class Cluelessness in
America.* Boston, MA: Harvard Business Review Press.

[62] Ducat, S., pp. 60–83.

[63] Ducat, S. (2005). *The Wimp Factor: Gender Gaps, Holy Wars, and the Politics of
Anxious Masculinity.* Boston, MA: Beacon, pp 71–72

[64] Hantover, J. P. (1978). The Boy Scouts and the validation of masculinity.
Journal of social issues, 34(1), p 186.

[65] Theweleit, K. (1987) Male Fantasies, Vol. 1: Women, Floods, Bodies, History
(Theory and History of Literature, Vol. 22). University of Minnesota Press.

[66] Citizens for Responsibility and Ethics in Washington (2021, January 15).
President Trump's legacy of corruption, four years and 3,700 conflicts of
interest later. https://www.citizensforethics.org/reports-investigations/crew
-reports/president-trump-legacy-corruption-3700-conflicts-interest/ (last
accessed 20 October 2022).

[67] Shaw, C. (2022, March 1). President Trump's staggering record of uncharged
criminal misconduct. Citizens for Responsibility and Ethics in Washington.
https://www.citizensforethics.org/reports-investigations/crew-reports
/president-trump-staggering-record-of-uncharged-criminal-misconduct/ (last
accessed 20 October 2022).

[68] Heil, E. (2018, October 23). "Be kind to each other": Melania Trump continues anti-bullying campaign. *The Washington Post*. https://www .washingtonpost.com/arts-entertainment/2018/10/23/be-kind-each -other-melania-trump-continues-anti-bullying-campaign/ (last accessed 20 October 2022).

[69] Mazzei, P., & Feuer, A. (2022, June 2). How the Proud Boys gripped the Miami-Dade Republican Party. *The New York Times*. https://www.nytimes .com/2022/06/02/us/miami-republicans-proud-boys.html (last accessed 20 October 2022).

[70] Mesa, B. (2021, March 12). Joel Campbell used to be a Proud Boy member. Now, he's running for Topeka City Council. *The Topeka Capital-Journal*. https://eu.cjonline.com/story/news/politics/elections/local/2021/03/12 /former-proud-boy-joel-campbell-running-topeka-city-council-capitol -riots/4632855001/ (last accessed 20 October 2022).

[71] Daniel Tooze Sr (n.d.). In: *Ballotpedia*. https://ballotpedia.org/Daniel_Tooze _Sr (last accessed 20 October 2022).

[72] Mazzei, P., & Feuer, A.

[73] Wilson, J. (2023, August 22). US businessman is wannabe 'warlord' of secretive far-right men's network. *The Guardian*. https://www.theguardian .com/world/2023/aug/22/charles-haywood-claremont-institute-sacr-far-right (last accessed 11 January 2024).

Chapter 8

[1] Franz, J. (2021, November 24). For sale: God, guns and separatism in the American Redoubt. *Montana Free Press*. https://montanafreepress.org/about -mtfp/ (last accessed 20 October 2022).

[2] https://www.survivalrealty.com/

[3] Black Rifle Real Estate (n.d.). Home (Facebook page). Facebook. https://www .facebook.com/blackriflerealestate (last accessed 25 October 2022).

[4] Geranios, N. K. (2022, March 7). Realtors to conservatives living in liberal areas: Try Idaho. *Los Angeles Times*. https://www.latimes.com/business /story/2022-03-07/realtors-to-conservatives-living-in-liberal-areas-try -idaho (last accessed 20 October 2022).

[5] Pew Research Center (2014, June). Section 2: Growing partisan antipathy. In: *Political Polarization in the American Public*. https://www.pewresearch.org /politics/2014/06/12/section-2-growing-partisan-antipathy/ (last accessed 20 October 2022).

[6] Pew Research Center (2014, June). Section 3: Political polarization and personal life. In: *Political Polarization in the American Public*. https ://www.pewresearch.org/politics/2014/06/12/section-3-political -polarization-and-personal-life/ (last accessed 20 October 2022).

[7] Gimpel, J. G., & Iris, H. (2015). Seeking politically compatible neighbors? The role of neighborhood partisan composition in residential sorting. *Political Geography, 48*: 130–142. https://doi.org/10.1016/j.polgeo.2014.11.003

[8] https://pocket-neighborhoods.net/

[9] Hibbing, J. R. (2020). *The Securitarian Personality: What Really Motivates Trump's Base and Why It Matters for the Post-Trump Era*. New York: Oxford University Press.

[10] Mockaitis, T. (2021, November 11). "Legacy American" is the latest catchphrase in the racist lexicon. *The Hill*. https://thehill.com/opinion/civil-rights/580980-legacy-american-is-the-latest-catchphrase-in-the-racist-lexicon/ (last accessed 20 October 2022).

[11] Thakker, P. (2023, February 20). Marjorie Taylor Greene Commits Borderline Sedition. *New Republic*. https://newrepublic.com/post/170674/marjorie-taylor-greene-national-divorce-tweet (last accessed 11 January 2024).

[12] Thakker, P. (2023, February 21). Marjorie Taylor Greene Says She Wants to Manipulate People's Votes. *New Republic*. https://newrepublic.com/post/170711/marjorie-taylor-greene-says-wants-manipulate-peoples-votes (last accessed 11 January 2024).

[13] America's urban–rural partisan gap is widening (2020, November 10). *The Economist*. https://www.economist.com/graphic-detail/2020/11/10/americas-urban-rural-partisan-gap-is-widening (last accessed 20 October 2022).

[14] Bacon, P., Jr. (2022, June 20). How the GOP is making national policy one state at a time. *The Washington Post*. https://www.washingtonpost.com/opinions/2022/06/20/gop-making-national-policy-one-state-time/ (last accessed 20 October 2022).

[15] Levin, B. (2022, June 1). The GOP's new election rule: Voter fraud is only real when we lose to Democrats. *Vanity Fair*. https://www.vanityfair.com/news/2022/06/republicans-election-fraud-rules (last accessed 20 October 2022); Herenstein, E., & Wolf, T. (2022, June 6). The "independent state legislature theory," explained. Brennan Center for Justice. https://www.brennancenter.org/our-work/research-reports/independent-state-legislature-theory-explained (last accessed 20 October 2022).

[16] Hertel-Fernandez, A. (2019). *State Capture: How Conservative Activists, Big Businesses, and Wealthy Donors Reshaped the American States – and the Nation*. New York: Oxford University Press.

[17] Hixenbaugh, M. (2022, May 27). Protesters' anguished shouts fail to dampen gun enthusiasm at NRA convention in Houston. *NBC News*. https://www.nbcnews.com/news/us-news/nra-houston-gun-protesters-uvalde-rcna30917 (last accessed 20 October 2022).

[18] Natanson, H. (2022, May 10). The next book ban: States aim to limit titles students can search for. *The Washington Post*. https://www.washingtonpost.com/education/2022/05/10/school-library-database-book-ban/ (last accessed

20 October 2022); Contreras, R. (2022, February 1). New rules are limiting how teachers can teach Black History Month. *Axios*. https://www.axios.com/2022/02/01/black-history-month-critical-race-theory (last accessed 14 October 2022); Sainato, M. (2022, May 28). Vast majority of educators reject Republican proposals for arming teachers. *The Guardian*. https://www.theguardian.com/education/2022/may/28/arming-teachers-reject-republican-proposals (last accessed 20 October 2022); Bella, T. (2022, May 27). Police slow to engage with gunman because "they could've been shot," official says. *The Washington Post*. https://www.washingtonpost.com/nation/2022/05/27/uvalde-shooting-police-gunman-shot-olivarez/ (last accessed 20 October 2022).

19 Bishop, B. (2008). *The Big Sort: Why the Clustering of Like-Minded America Is Tearing Us Apart*. New York: Houghton Mifflin.

20 Kruse, M. (2022, May 30). Why Trump isn't to blame for the nation's toxic political tribalism. *Politico*. https://www.politico.com/news/magazine/2022/05/30/bill-bishop-tribalism-worse-polarization-trump-00035785 (last accessed 20 October 2022).

21 Bishop, B., p. 44.

22 Sunstein, C. R., Hastie, R., & Schkade, D. (2007). What happened on deliberation day? *California Law Review, 95*: 915–940.

23 Martin, G. J., & Webster, S. W. (2018). Does residential sorting explain geographic polarization? *Political Science Research and Methods, 8*(2): 215–231. https://doi.org/10.1017/psrm.2018.44

24 Sharlet, J. (2023) The Undertow: Scenes from a Slow Civil War. W. W. Norton & Company. pp 63–81

25 Ruderer, S. (2015). Between religion and politics. The military clergy during the dictatorships of the late twentieth century in Argentina and Chile. *Journal of Latin American Studies, 47*(3): 463–489. Summary accessed 20 October 2022 at: https://www.panoramas.pitt.edu/politics/military-clergy-during-late-twentieth-century-dictatorships-argentina-and-chile

26 Morales-Franceschini, E. (2018, May 9). Latin American liberation theology. *Global South Studies: A Collective Publication with the Global South*. https://globalsouthstudies.as.virginia.edu/key-thinkers/latin-american-liberation-theology (last accessed 20 October 2022).

27 Sebastian, S. (2022, March 10). New effort focused on financial issues facing rural communities. Consumer Financial Protection Bureau. https://www.consumerfinance.gov/about-us/blog/new-effort-focused-on-financial-issues-facing-rural-communities/ (last accessed 20 October 2022).

28 Rupar, A. (2021, March 15). Republicans shamelessly take credit for Covid relief they voted against. *Vox*. https://www.vox.com/2021/3/15/22331722/american-rescue-plan-salazar-wicker (last accessed 20 October 2022).

29 Pickert, K. (2010, October 21). "Keep your gov't hands off my Medicare"
    cont… *Time*. https://swampland.time.com/2010/10/21/keep-your-govt
    -hands-off-my-medicare-cont/ (last accessed 20 October 2022).

30 Valladares, M. R. (2019, August 12). Trump's trade wars are hurting Midwest
    farmers, banks, and state coffers. *Forbes*. https://www.forbes.com
    /sites/mayrarodriguezvalladares/2019/08/12/trumps-trade-wars-are-hurting
    -midwest-farmers-banks-and-state-coffers/?sh=6f0bedfd5140 (last accessed 20
    October 2022).

31 1960 United States presidential election in Oregon (2022). In: *Wikipedia*.
    https://en.wikipedia.org/wiki/1960_United_States_presidential_election_in
    _Oregon (last accessed 20 October 2022).

32 Politics and voting in Wallowa County, Oregon (n.d.). In: *Best Places*.
    https://www.bestplaces.net/voting/county/oregon/wallowa (last accessed 20
    October 2022).

33 https://www.greateridaho.org/

34 Mathias, C. (2022, May 19). Living with the far-right insurgency in Idaho.
    HuffPost. https://www.huffingtonpost.co.uk/entry/far-right-idaho_n_628277e
    2e4b0c84db7282bd6 (last accessed 20 October 2022).

35 Woodward, A. (2022, March 18). Rapists and their families could sue victims
    who have abortions under the new Idaho bill. *Independent*. https://www
    .independent.co.uk/news/world/americas/us-politics/idaho-abortion-planned
    -parenthood-texas-b2039330.html (last accessed 20 October 2022).

36 Miller-Idriss, C. (2022). *Hate in the Homeland: The New Global Far Right*.
    Princeton, NJ: Princeton University Press.

37 Miller-Idriss, C. (2020). Hate in the homeland: The new global far right.
    Princeton University Press. pp 35–36

38 https://www.daterightstuff.com/optin-581071101675109977541

39 https://www.economist.com/united-states/2023/06/01/conservative
    -americans-are-building-a-parallel-economy

40 https://www.economist.com/united-states/2023/06/01/conservative
    -americans-are-building-a-parallel-economy

41 https://www.redballoon.work/

42 https://www.economist.com/united-states/2023/06/01/conservative-americans
    -are-building-a-parallel-economy

43 https://www.economist.com/united-states/2023/06/01/conservative-americans
    -are-building-a-parallel-economy

44 https://www.economist.com/united-states/2023/06/01/conservative-americans
    -are-building-a-parallel-economy

45 https://www.businessinsider.com/you-can-buy-christian-assault-rifle-2015-9

46 https://washingtonmonthly.com/2010/06/19/angles-second
    -amendment-remedies/

47 https://en.wikipedia.org/wiki/BuyBlue.org

48 https://www.washingtonpost.com/politics/2023/02/01/oil-giant-shell-accused
    -greenwashing-misleading-investors/

49 Simpson, A. (2019, October 21). As local news outlets shutter, rural America
    suffers the most. The Pew Charitable Trusts. https://www.pewtrusts.org/en
    /research-and-analysis/blogs/stateline/2019/10/21/as-local-news-outlets
    -shutter-rural-america-suffers-most (last accessed 20 October 2022).

50 Russell, A. (2017). Food deserts, news deserts and how they affect a
    community's health (unpublished master's thesis). University of North
    Carolina. https://doi.org/10.17615/h9wd-9423

51 Domonoske, C. (2018, April 2). Video reveals power of Sinclair, as local news
    anchors recite script in unison. *National Public Radio*. https://www.npr.org
    /sections/thetwo-way/2018/04/02/598794433/video-reveals-power-of-sinclair
    -as-local-news-anchors-recite-script-in-unison (last accessed 20 October 2022).

52 https://www.newsweek.com/
    tucker-carlson-fox-news-texts-about-election-five-bombshells-1782130

53 Firozi, P. (2016, October 14). CNN president: Airing so many full Trump
    rallies was a "mistake." *The Hill*. https://thehill.com/blogs/ballot-box
    /presidential-races/301147-cnn-president-airing-so-many-full-trump-rallies
    -was-a/ (last accessed 20 October 2022); Fearnow, B. (2019, June 19). CNN,
    MSNBC cut away from Orlando Trump rally as networks shy away from
    "free" coverage offered in 2016. *Newsweek*. https://www.newsweek.com/trump
    -rally-cnn-msnbc-fox-news-2020-1444780 (last accessed 10 October 2022).

54 Johnson, T. (2020, March 21). CNN, MSNBC hosts speak out against airing
    Donald Trump's press briefings live. *Deadline*. https://deadline.com/2020/03
    /coronavirus-chris-hayes-don-lemon-1202896531/ (last accessed 20
    October 2022).

55 https://www.nytimes.com/2023/05/10/us/politics/trump-cnn-town
    -hall-fact-check.html?smid=fb-share&fbclid=IwAR34i6GmZ_EIUv
    K1CEBtN8cNnQhc_WdAwBdH8u0Cuc5KQcslAGHMqF4C9ck

Chapter 9

1   Gilbert, D. (2022, May 25). The far right is falsely blaming a trans woman for
    the Texas school shooting. *Vice*. https://www.vice.com/en/article/5dgnbq
    /texas-school-shooting-far-right-trans-woman (last accessed 20 October 2022).

2   Voltaire (1767). *Collection des Lettres sur les Miracles: Écrites a Geneve, et a
    Neufchatel*. Neufchatel, p. 150.

3   Cineas, F. (2021, January 9). Donald Trump is the accelerant:
    A comprehensive timeline of Trump encouraging hate groups and political
    violence. *Vox*. https://www.vox.com/21506029/trump-violence-tweets-racist
    -hate-speech (last accessed 19 October 2022).

4   Hauck, G., Hughes, T., Abdel-Baqui, O., Torres, R., & Gardner, H. (2020,
    October 24). "A fanciful reality": Trump claims Black Lives Matter protests are

violent, but the majority are peaceful. *USA Today*. https://eu.usatoday.com
/in-depth/news/nation/2020/10/24/trump-claims-blm-protests-violent-but
-majority-peaceful/3640564001/ (last accessed 20 October 2022); Maxouris,
C. (2021, November 19). Kyle Rittenhouse was acquitted on all charges.
Here's what we know about the three men he shot. *CNN*. https://edition.cnn
.com/2021/11/01/us/kyle-rittenhouse-shooting-victims-trial/index.html (last
accessed 20 October 2022).

5 Popli, N. (2022, May 16). How the "great replacement theory" has fueled
   racist violence. *Time*. https://time.com/6177282/great-replacement-theory
   -buffalo-racist-attacks/ (last accessed 20 October 2022); Montanaro, C. (2022,
   May 17). How the "replacement" theory went mainstream on the political
   right. *National Public Radio*. https://www.npr.org/2022/05/17/1099223012
   /how-the-replacement-theory-went-mainstream-on-the-political-right (last
   accessed 20 October 2022).

6 Snyder, T. (2017). *On Tyranny: Twenty Lessons from the Twentieth Century*.
   New York: Crown.

7 Malka, A., & Lelkes, Y. (2017, August 10). In a new poll, half of Republicans
   say they would support postponing the 2020 election if Trump proposed it.
   The Washington Post. https://www.washingtonpost.com/news/monkey-cage
   /wp/2017/08/10/in-a-new-poll-half-of-republicans-say-they-would-support
   -postponing-the-2020-election-if-trump-proposed-it/ (last accessed 20
   October 2022).

8 Brennan Center for Justice (n.d.). *The Myth of Voter Fraud* (project
   encompassing various reports and resources). https://www.brennancenter.org
   /issues/ensure-every-american-can-vote/vote-suppression/myth-voter-fraud (last
   accessed 25 October 2022).

9 Alemany, J., Dawsey, J., & Hamburger, T. (2022, April 27). Talk of martial
   law, Insurrection Act draws notice of Jan. 6 committee. *The Washington Post*.
   https://www.washingtonpost.com/politics/2022/04/27/talk-martial
   -law-insurrection-act-draws-notice-jan-6-committee/ (last accessed 20
   October 2022).

10 Pomerantsev, P. (2014). *Nothing is True and Everything is Possible: The Surreal
   Heart of the New Russia*. New York: PublicAffairs, 2015.

11 Lakoff, G. (2004, September 12). Framing the debate: It's all GOP. *Boston
   Globe*. http://archive.boston.com/news/globe/editorial_opinion/oped
   /articles/2004/09/12/framing_the_debate_its_all_gop?pg=full (last accessed 20
   October 2022).

12 Tavernise, S., & Gardiner, A. (2019, November 18). "No one believes
   anything": Voters worn out by a fog of political news. https://www
   .nytimes.com/2019/11/18/us/polls-media-fake-news.html (last accessed 20
   October 2022).

13 Pomerantsev, P.

14 Kruse, K., & Zelizer, J. E. (2023) *Myth America: Historians Take On the Biggest Legends and Lies About Our Past.* Basic Books. pp 299–311

15 Miller-Idriss, C. (2020). *Hate in the homeland: The new global far right.* Princeton University Press. p 300

16 Miller-Idriss, p 302

17 Miller-Idriss, p 304

18 Miller-Idriss, p 304

19 Miller-Idriss, p 305

20 Rabin-Havt, A., & Media Matters (2016). *Lies, Incorporated: The World of Post-Truth Politics.* New York: Anchor Books, p. 134.

21 https://www.brennancenter.org/our-work/research-reports/voting-laws-roundup-may-2022

22 https://www.brennancenter.org/our-work/research-reports/voting-laws-roundup-may-2022

23 https://www.brennancenter.org/our-work/research-reports/impact-voter-suppression-communities-color

24 Kessler, G. (2021, January 23). Trump made 30,573 false or misleading claims as president. Nearly half came in his final year. *The Washington Post.* https://www.washingtonpost.com/politics/how-fact-checker-tracked-trump-claims/2021/01/23/ad04b69a-5c1d-11eb-a976-bad6431e03e2_story.html (last accessed 20 October 2022).

25 Donald Trump's inheritance (2018, October 6). *The Economist.* https://www.economist.com/united-states/2018/10/06/donald-trumps-inheritance (last accessed 20 October 2022).

26 Unger, C. (2019, March 29). Trump's businesses are full of dirty Russian money. The scandal is that it's legal. *The Washington Post.* https://www.washingtonpost.com/outlook/trumps-businesses-are-full-of-dirty-russian-money-the-scandal-is-thats-legal/2019/03/29/11b812da-5171-11e9-88a1-ed346f0ec94f_story.html (last accessed 20 October 2022).

27 Cassidy, J. (2020, December 3). Donald Trump's latest grift may be his most cynical yet. *The New Yorker.* https://www.newyorker.com/news/our-columnists/donald-trumps-latest-grift-may-be-his-most-cynical-yet (last accessed 20 October 2022); Enrich, D., Buettner, R., McIntire, M., & Craig, S. (2020, October 27). How Trump maneuvered his way out of trouble in Chicago. *The New York Times.* https://www.nytimes.com/2020/10/27/business/trump-chicago-taxes.html (last accessed 20 October 2022); Cortellessa, E. (2017, June 5). How Trump made wage theft routine. *The American Prospect.* https://prospect.org/power/trump-made-wage-theft-routine/ (last accessed 20 October 2022); Protess, B., Rashbaum, W. K., & Bromwich, J. E. (2021, July 1). Trump organization is charged with running 15-year employee tax scheme. *The New York Times.* https://www.nytimes

.com/2021/07/01/nyregion/allen-weisselberg-charged-trump-organization.
html (last accessed 20 October 2022).

28   Chait, J. (2018, July 9). Will Trump be meeting with his counterpart – or his
     handler? *New York Magazine*. https://nymag.com/intelligencer/2018/07
     /trump-putin-russia-collusion.html (last accessed 20 October 2022); Harding,
     L., Borger, J., & Sabbagh, D. (2021, July 15). Kremlin papers appear to show
     Putin's plot to put Trump in White House. *The Guardian*. https://www
     .theguardian.com/world/2021/jul/15/kremlin-papers-appear-to-show-putins
     -plot-to-put-trump-in-white-house (last accessed 20 October 2022).

29   Schwartz, T. (2020, October 4). "Emperor has no clothes": Man who helped
     make Trump myth says facade has fallen (interview by D. Smith). *The
     Guardian*. https://www.theguardian.com/us-news/2020/oct/04/donald-trump
     -tony-schwartz-interview-art-of-the-deal (last accessed 20 October 2022).

30   Blake, A. (2020, June 9). The frequent overlap between Trump's conspiracy
     theories and Russian propaganda. *The Washington Post*. https://www
     .washingtonpost.com/politics/2020/06/09/frequent-overlap-between-trumps
     -conspiracy-theories-russian-propaganda/ (last accessed 20 October 2022).

31   Menn, J. (2020, August 24). Russian-backed organizations amplifying QAnon
     conspiracy theories, researchers say. *Reuters*. https://www.reuters.com/article
     /us-usa-election-qanon-russia/russian-backed-organizations-amplifying-qanon
     -conspiracy-theories-researchers-say-idUSKBN25K13T (last accessed 20
     October 2022).

32   Wendling, M. (2016, December 2). The saga of "Pizzagate": The fake story
     that shows how conspiracy theories spread. *BBC News*. https://www.bbc.co.uk
     /news/blogs-trending-38156985 (last accessed 6 March 2023).

33   Pengelly, M. (2020, August 21). Fox host blames "deep state" for Bannon
     arrest – Bannon says that's for "nut cases." *The Guardian*. https://www
     .theguardian.com/us-news/2020/aug/21/steve-bannon-lou-dobbs-deep-stat
     e-conspiracy-theory (last accessed 20 October 2022).

34   United States House Committee on the Judiciary (2019–2020). *The
     Impeachment of Donald John Trump Evidentiary Record from the House of
     Representatives (116th)*. https://judiciary.house.gov/the-impeachment-of
     -donald-john-trump/ (last accessed 18 October 2022).

35   Graham-Harrison, E. (2018, August 3). "Enemy of the people": Trump's
     phrase and its echoes of totalitarianism. *The Guardian*. https://www.
     theguardian.com/us-news/2018/aug/03/trump-enemy-of-the-people-meaning
     -history (last accessed 20 October 2022).

36   https://www.washingtonpost.com/lifestyle/style/the-press-always-got-booed
     -at-trump-rallies-but-now-the-aggression-is-menacing/2016/10/14/6092ea34
     -922d-11e6-9c52-0b10449e33c4_story.html

37   Hill, F. (2021). *There Is Nothing for You Here: Finding Opportunity in the
     Twenty-First Century*. New York: Mariner Books.

38 Dunning, D. (2011). The Dunning–Kruger effect: On being ignorant of one's own ignorance. *Advances in Experimental Social Psychology, 44*: 247–296. https://doi.org/10.1016/B978-0-12-385522-0.00005-6.

39 Yang, M. (2022, March 9). Trump "admired" Putin's ability to "kill whoever," says Stephanie Grisham. *The Guardian.* https://www.theguardian.com /us-news/2022/mar/09/donald-trump-vladimir-putin-stephanie-grisham (last accessed 20 October 2022).

40 Jurkowitz, M., Mitchell, A., Shearer, E., & Walker, M. (2020, January 24). US media polarization and the 2020 election: A nation divided. Pew Research Center. https://www.pewresearch.org/journalism/2020/01/24/u-s -media-polarization-and-the-2020-election-a-nation-divided/ (last accessed 20 October 2022).

41 Bartlett, B. (2015, June 3). How Fox News changed American media and political dynamics (unpublished research paper). http://dx.doi.org/10.2139 /ssrn.2604679

42 Drucker, J. (2020, June 13). Fox News removes a digitally altered image of Seattle protests. *The New York Times.* https://www.nytimes.com/2020/06/13 /business/media/fox-news-george-floyd-protests-seattle.html (last accessed 20 October 2022).

43 Mayer, J. (2019, March 4). The making of the Fox News White House. *The New Yorker.* https://www.newyorker.com/magazine/2019/03/11/the-making -of-the-fox-news-white-house (last accessed 20 October 2022).

44 Confessore, N. (2022, April 30). How Tucker Carlson stoked white fear to conquer cable. *The New York Times.* https://www.nytimes.com/2022/04/30/us /tucker-carlson-gop-republican-party.html (last accessed 20 October 2022).

45 Folkenflik, D. (2020, September 29). You literally can't believe the facts Tucker Carlson tells you. So say Fox's lawyers. *National Public Radio.* https://www .npr.org/2020/09/29/917747123/you-literally-cant-believe-the-facts-tucker -carlson-tells-you-so-say-fox-s-lawye (last accessed 20 October 2022).

46 Bowles, N. (2019, March 18). "Replacement theory," a racist, sexist doctrine, spreads in far-right circles. *The New York Times.* https://www.nytimes .com/2019/03/18/technology/replacement-theory.html (last accessed 20 October 2022).

47 Mockaitis, T. (2021, November 11). "Legacy American" is the latest catchphrase in the racist lexicon. *The Hill.* https://thehill.com/opinion/civil -rights/580980-legacy-american-is-the-latest-catchphrase-in-the-racist-lexicon / (last accessed 20 October 2022).

48 Bowles, N.

49 McKinley, J., Traub, A., & Closson, T. (2022, May 14). 10 people killed and 3 wounded in shooting at a Buffalo supermarket. *The New York Times.* https ://www.nytimes.com/live/2022/05/14/nyregion/buffalo-shooting (last accessed 20 October 2022).

50 Rosenwald, B. (2021, November 7). Why Fox News won't cut Tucker Carlson loose – even after "Patriot Purge." *NBC News*. https://www.nbcnews .com/think/opinion/why-fox-news-won-t-cut-tucker-carlson-loose-even -ncna1283380 (last accessed 20 October 2022).

51 Associated Press (2022, May 12). Poll finds one-third of adults say they think an effort is afoot to replace native-born Americans with new immigrants for electoral purposes. *MarketWatch*. https://www.marketwatch.com/story /poll-finds-one-third-of-adults-say-they-think-an-effort-is-afoot-to-replace -native-born-americans-with-new-immigrants-for-electoral- purposes-01652314775 (last accessed 20 October 2022); Bump, P. (2022, May 9). Nearly half of Republicans agree with "great replacement theory." *The Washington Post*. https://www.washingtonpost.com/politics/2022/05/09 /nearly-half-republicans-agree-with-great-replacement-theory/ (last accessed 20 October 2022).

52 Pecorin, A. (2022, May 18). McConnell, when asked, fails to denounce racist "replacement theory." *ABC News*. https://abcnews.go.com/Politics/mcconnell -asked-fails-denounce-racist-replacement-theory/story?id=84788037 (last accessed 21 October 2022).

53 Hassig, R., & Oh, K. (2009). *The Hidden People of North Korea: Everyday Life in the Hermit Kingdom*. Lanham, MD: Rowman & Littlefield, 2015, p. 111.

54 Grynbaum, M. M., & Koblin, J. (2020, November 22). Newsmax, once a right-wing also-ran, is rising, and Trump approves. *The New York Times* . https://www.nytimes.com/2020/11/22/business/media/newsmax-trump-fox -news.html (last accessed 21 October 2022).

55 Smith, B. (2020, November 29). The king of Trump TV thinks you're dumb enough to buy it. *The New York Times*. https://www.nytimes.com/2020/11/29 /business/media/newsmax-chris-ruddy-trump.html (last accessed 21 October 2022).

56 Hsu, T. (2020, February 24). Tracking viral misinformation: Latest updates. *The New York Times*. https://www.nytimes.com/live/2020/2020-election -misinformation-distortions#qanon-believers-us-survey (last accessed 21 October 2022).

57 Beer, T. (2020, September 2). Majority of Republicans believe the QAnon conspiracy theory is partly or mostly true, survey finds. *Forbes*. https ://www.forbes.com/sites/tommybeer/2020/09/02/majority-of-republicans -believe-the-qanon-conspiracy-theory-is-partly-or-mostly-true-survey -finds/?sh=76f0b0495231 (last accessed 21 October 2022).

58 Kornfield, M. (2021, November 2). Why hundreds of QAnon supporters showed up in Dallas, expecting JFK Jr's return. *The Washington Post*. https ://www.washingtonpost.com/nation/2021/11/02/qanon-jfk-jr-dallas/ (last accessed 21 October 2022).

59 Steck, E., McDermott, N., & Hickey, C. (2020, October 30). The congressional candidates who have engaged with the QAnon conspiracy theory. *CNN*. https://edition.cnn.com/interactive/2020/10/politics/qanon -cong-candidates/ (last accessed 20 October 2022).

60 Zitser, J., & Ankel, S. (2021, June 27). A Trump-loving insurrectionist and a convicted stalker are among 36 QAnon supporters running for Congress in 2022. *Business Insider*. https://www.businessinsider.com/the-36-qanon -supporters-running-congress-in-the-2022-midterms-2021-6?r=US&IR=T (last accessed 21 October 2022).

61 Hsu, T. (2022, August 29). On Truth Social, QAnon accounts found a home and Trump's support. *The New York Times*. https://www.nytimes .com/2022/08/29/technology/qanon-truth-social-trump.html (last accessed 21 October 2022).

62 Kahan, D. M. (2017). Misconceptions, misinformation, and the logic of identity-protective cognition. *Cultural Cognition Project Working Paper Series, no. 164*. http://dx.doi.org/10.2139/ssrn.2973067

63 Kerr, J. R., & Wilson, M. S. (2021). Right-wing authoritarianism and social dominance orientation predict rejection of science and scientists. *Group Processes & Intergroup Relations, 24*(4): 550–567. https://doi .org/10.1177/1368430221992126

64 McCright, A. M., & Dunlap, R. E. (2011). Cool dudes: The denial of climate change among conservative white males in the United States. *Global Environmental Change, 21*(4): 1163–1172. https://doi.org/10.1016/j .gloenvcha.2011.06.003

65 Lobato, E. J. C., Powell, M., Padilla, L. M. K., & Holbrook, C. (2020). Factors predicting willingness to share Covid-19 misinformation. *Frontiers in Psychology, 11*(article 566108). https://doi.org/10.3389/fpsyg.2020.566108

66 Orth, T. (2022, March 30). Which groups of Americans are most likely to believe conspiracy theories? YouGov. https://today.yougov.com/topics/politics /articles-reports/2022/03/30/which-groups-americans-believe-conspiracies (last accessed 21 October 2022).

67 Arendt, H. (1951). *The Origins of Totalitarianism*. London: Folio Society, 2022, pp. 588–590.

68 Hochschild, A. R. (1983). *The Managed Heart: Commercialization of Human Feeling*. Berkeley and Los Angeles, CA: University of California Press, 2012.

69 Vaneigem, R. (2012). *Revolution of Everyday Life*. PM Press. pp 23–28.

70 Hamm, M., & Spaaj, R. (2015). Lone wolf terrorism in America: Using knowledge of radicalization pathways to forge prevention strategies (grant report funded but not published by US Department of Justice). https ://www.ojp.gov/pdffiles1/nij/grants/248691.pdf

71 Kayyem, J. (2022, May 15). A "lone-wolf" shooter has an online pack. *The Atlantic*. https://www.theatlantic.com/ideas/archive/2022/05/lone-wolf -shooters-ideology/629871/? (last accessed 21 October 2022).

72 Dolan, E. W. (2021, July 3). New study indicates conspiracy theory believers have less developed critical thinking abilities. *PsyPost*. https://www.psypost .org/2021/07/new-study-indicates-conspiracy-theory-believers-have-less-developed-critical-thinking-ability-61347 (last accessed 21 October 2022).

73 Bergamaschi Ganapini, M. (2021). The signaling function of sharing fake stories. *Mind & Language*, early online view. https://doi.org/10.1111 /mila.12373

74 McAndrew, F. T. (2019). Costly signaling theory. In: T. Shackelford & V. Weekes-Shackelford (Eds), *Encyclopedia of Evolutionary Psychological Science*. Cham: Springer, n.d. https://doi.org/10.1007/978-3-319-16999-6_3483-1

75 Bergamaschi Ganapini, M.

76 Spence, D. P., & Wallerstein, R. S. (1982). *Narrative Truth and Historical Truth: Meaning and Interpretation in Psychoanalysis*. New York: W. W. Norton & Company, 1984.

77 Owen, Q., & Gutman, M. (2019). Fact Check: No evidence for Trump's tales of duct-taped women, prayer rugs at border. *ABC News*. https ://abcnews.go.com/Politics/fact-check-trumps-tales-duct-taped-women-prayer /story?id=60723806 (last accessed 21 October 2022).

78 Levin, B. (2020, September 18). Trump warns 2020 election will be "the scam of all time" (unless he wins). *Vanity Fair*. https://www.vanityfair.com /news/2020/09/donald-trump-election-scam (last accessed 21 October 2022).

79 Todd, C., Murray, M., & Dann, C. (2018, February 28). Trump slammed Clinton over handling of classified info. That looks like hypocrisy now. *NBC News*. https://www.nbcnews.com/politics/first-read/trump-slammed-clinton -over-handling-classified-info-looks-hypocrisy-now-n851891 (last accessed 21 October 2022).

80 Mazza, E. (2022, August 10). Eric Trump's accidental confession about his father has Twitter users howling. *HuffPost*. https://www.huffingtonpost.co.uk/ entry/eric-trump-confession_n_62f31f70e4b001e175d89c19 (last accessed 21 October 2022).

81 Graham, D. A. (2018, June 19). Trump says Democrats want immigrants to "infest" the US. *The Atlantic*. https://www.theatlantic.com/politics /archive/2018/06/trump-immigrants-infest/563159/ (last accessed 21 October 2022); Associated Press (2017, April 13). Rust, mold, parasites: Trump's Mar-a-Lago cited for 78 health violations in the last three years. *Los Angeles Times*. https://www.latimes.com/nation/nationnow/la-na-trump-mar-a-lago-health -violations-20170413-story.html (last accessed 21 October 2022).

82 Rosenthal, A. (2017, January 20). What we saw as Trump took office. *The New York Times*. https://www.nytimes.com/interactive/projects/cp/opinion /presidential-inauguration-2017/trump-gives-us-american-carnage (last accessed 21 October 2022).

83 COVID Data Tracker. CDC. https://covid.cdc.gov/covid-data -tracker/#datatracker-home (accessed 14 March 2024).

84 Wood, D., & Brumfiel, G. (2022, May 19). Pro-Trump counties continue to suffer far higher Covid death tolls. *National Public Radio.* https://www.npr.org/2022/05/19/1098543849/pro-trump-counties-continue-to-suffer-far-higher-covid-death-tolls (last accessed 14 October 2022).

85 Ulmer, A., & Layne, N. (2022, April 28). Trump allies breach US voting systems in search of 2020 fraud "evidence." *Reuters.* https://www.reuters.com/investigates/special-report/usa-election-breaches/ (last accessed 21 October 2022).

86 Ibid.

87 van Prooijen, J.-W., & van Vugt, M. (2018). Conspiracy theories: Evolved functions and psychological mechanisms. *Perspectives on Psychological Science, 13*(6), 770–788. https://doi.org/10.1177/1745691618774270

88 Barras, C. (2014, May 7). Only known chimp war reveals how societies splinter. *New Scientist.* https://www.newscientist.com/article/mg22229682-600-only-known-chimp-war-reveals-how-societies-splinter/ (last accessed 21 October 2022).

89 https://blog.ucsusa.org/elliott-negin/how-the-american-legislative-exchange-council-turns-disinformation-into-law/

90 Hayakawa, S., Kawai, N., & Masataka, N. (2011). The influence of color on snake detection in visual search in human children. *Scientific Reports, 1*(article 80). https://doi.org/10.1038/srep00080

91 van Prooijen, J.-W., & van Vugt, M.

92 Boyer, P. (2018). *Minds Make Societies: How Cognition Explains the World Humans Create.* London: Yale University Press, p. 78–81.

93 Taylor, J. (2006, July 13). Killer kangaroo was ultimate fighting marsupial. *Independent.* https://www.independent.co.uk/news/world/australasia/killer-kangaroo-was-ultimate-fighting-marsupial-407739.html (last accessed 21 October 2022).

94 Dunn, R. (2012, October 15). What are you so scared of? Saber-toothed cats, snakes, and carnivorous kangaroos. *Slate.* https://slate.com/technology/2012/10/evolution-of-anxiety-humans-were-prey-for-predators-such-as-hyenas-snakes-sharks-kangaroos.html (last accessed 21 October 2022).

95 Orth, T.

96 https://www.splcenter.org/fighting-hate/intelligence-report/2010/fear-fema

97 Klein, N (2023) Doppelganger: A Trip into the Mirror World, Farrar, Straus and Giroux, pp 100–113

98 https://www.vox.com/recode/22238755/telegram-messaging-social-media-extremists

99 Seaver, J. D (2020, December 14). If you're a conservative, "Be afraid. Be very afraid" (reader letter). *Clark County Today.* https://www.clarkcountytoday.com/opinion/letter-if-youre-a-conservative-be-afraid-be-very-afraid/ (last accessed 21 October 2022).

100 Klein, N. (2023) *Doppelganger: A Trip into the Mirror World*, Farrar, Straus and Giroux

101 Chang, B. (2020, May 23). More than 40% of Republicans in a new poll say they think Bill Gates wants to use Covid-19 vaccines to implant location-tracking microchips in recipients. *Business Insider*. https://www.businessinsider.com/republicans-bill-gates-covid-19-vaccine-tracking-microchip-study-2020-5? (last accessed 21 October 2022).

102 Loeffler, M. (2022, October 28). 4 victories for churches standing up to government discrimination during Covid-19. Alliance Defending Freedom. https://adflegal.org/ (last accessed 7 November 2022).

103 Fact check: Covid-19 is not a hoax to eliminate Trump (2021, June 29). *Reuters*. https://www.reuters.com/article/uk-factcheck-covid-hoax-eliminate-trump/fact-check-covid-19-is-not-a-hoax-to-eliminate-trump-idUSKBN27S31E (last accessed 21 October 2022); Uscinski, J. E., & Enders, A. M. (2020, April 30). The coronavirus conspiracy boom. *The Atlantic*. https://www.theatlantic.com/health/archive/2020/04/what-can-coronavirus-tell-us-about-conspiracy-theories/610894/ (last accessed 21 October 2022).

104 https://time.com/6311911/impeachment-biden-marjorie-greene-hunter/

105 Aratani, L. (2020, June 29). How did face masks become a political issue in America? *The Guardian*. https://www.theguardian.com/world/2020/jun/29/face-masks-us-politics-coronavirus (last accessed 21 October 2022); Lizza, R., & Lippman, D. (2020, January 5). Wearing a mask is for smug liberals. Refusing to is for reckless Republicans. *Politico*. https://www.politico.com/news/2020/05/01/masks-politics-coronavirus-227765 (last accessed 21 October 2022).

106 Hollingsworth, H., & Schulte, G. (2021, September 30). Health workers once saluted as heroes now get threats. *AP News*. https://apnews.com/article/coronavirus-pandemic-business-health-missouri-omaha-b73e167eba4987cab9e58fdc92ce0b72 (last accessed 21 October 2022); America's far right is energized by covid-19 lockdowns (2020, May 17). *The Economist*. https://www.economist.com/united-states/2020/05/17/americas-far-right-is-energised-by-covid-19-lockdowns (last accessed 21 October 2022).

107 Beres, D., Remski, M., & Walker, J. (Hosts) (2020–present). *Conspirituality* (audio podcast). https://www.conspirituality.net/

108 Wood, D., & Brumfiel, G.

109 Levin, B. (2020, March 4). Texas Lt Governor: Old people should volunteer to die to save the economy. *Vanity Fair*. https://www.vanityfair.com/news/2020/03/dan-patrick-coronavirus-grandparents (last accessed 21 October 2022).

110 Harrington, B. (2021, August 1). The anti-vaccine con job is becoming untenable. *The Atlantic*. https://www.theatlantic.com/ideas/archive/2021/08/vaccine-refusers-dont-want-blue-americas-respect/619627/ (last accessed 21 October 2022).

111 Wood, D., & Brumfiel, G. (2021, December 5); Stein, R. (2022, May 14).

112 Garett, R. and S. D. Young (2021, December). Online misinformation and vaccine hesitancy. *Translational Behavioral Medicine*, 11(12): 2194–2199. https://doi.org/10.1093/tbm/ibab128.

113 Motta, M., Motta, G., and D. Stecula (2023, September 22). Sick as a dog? The prevalence, politicization, and health policy consequences of canine vaccine hesitancy (CVH). *Vaccine*, 41(41): 5946-5950. https://doi .org/10.1016/j.vaccine.2023.08.059.

114 Branson-Potts, H. (2023, October 19). Shasta County appoints public health officer who fought COVID-19 vaccine mandates. *Los Angeles Times*. https ://www.latimes.com/california/story/2023-10-19/la-me-covid-vaccine-public-health-officer-shasta-county-california#:~:text=The%20hiring%20of%20 Redding%20family,and%20vaccinations%20during%20the%20pandemic (last accessed 11 January 2024).

115 Anguiano, D. (2023, September 28). California county abuzz after far-right figure appointed for mosquito control. *The Guardian*. https://www .theguardian.com/us-news/2023/sep/28/california-shasta-county-far-right -mosquito-vaccine (last accessed 11 January 2024).

116 Shepard, S. (2023, September 23). Our new poll shows just how much GOP voters have diverged from everyone else on vaccines. *Politico*. https://www. politico.com/news/2023/09/23/gop-voters-vaccines-poll -00117125#:~:text=Our%20new%20poll%20shows%20just,be%20 encouraged%20to%20get%20them.&text=This%20is%20the%20fourth%20 story,the%20anti%2Dvaccine%20political%20movement (last accessed 11 January 2024

117 Hanlon, A. (2018, August 31). Postmodernism didn't cause Trump. It explains him. *The Washington Post*. https://www.washingtonpost.com/outlook /postmodernism-didnt-cause-trump-it-explains-him/2018/08/30/0939f7c4-9b12-11e8-843b-36e177f3081c_story.html (21 October 2022).

118 Lyotard, J.-F. (1984). *The Postmodern Condition: A Report on Knowledge* (G. Bennington & B. Massumi, Trans.). Manchester: Manchester University Press. (Original work published 1979.)

119 Illing, S. (2019, November 16). The post-truth prophets. *Vox*. https://www .vox.com/features/2019/11/11/18273141/postmodernism-donald-trump -lyotard-baudrillard (last accessed 21 October 2022).

120 Fausto-Sterling, A. (1993). The five sexes: Why male and female are not enough. *The Sciences, 33*(2): 20–24. https://doi .org/10.1002/j.2326-1951.1993.tb03081.x

121 Stock, K. (2021). *Material Girls: Why Reality Matters for Feminism*. London: Fleet, p. 57.

122 Walia, R., Singla, M., Vaiphei, K., Kumar, S., & Bhansali, A. (2018). Disorders of sex development: A study of 194 cases. *Endocrine Connections, 7*(2): 364–371. https://doi.org/10.1530/EC-18-0022

123 Délot, E. C., Papp, J. C., DSD-TRN Genetics Workgroup, Sandberg, D. E., & Vilain, E. (2017). Genetics of disorders of sex development: The DSD-TRN experience. *Endocrinology and Metabolism Clinics of North America, 46*(2): 519–537. https://doi.org/10.1016/j.ecl.2017.01.015

124 Martin, E. (1991). The egg and the sperm: How science has constructed a romance based on stereotypical male–female roles. *Signs: Journal of Women in Culture and Society, 16*(3) 485–501. http://www.jstor.org/stable/3174586.

125 Rabin-Havt, A., & Media Matters, p. 7.

126 Peters, J. W., & Robertson, K. (2023, February 16). Fox stars privately expressed disbelief about Trump's election fraud claims. *The New York Times.* https://www.nytimes.com/2023/02/16/business/media/fox-dominion-lawsuit.html (last accessed 6 March 2023).

127 Robertson, K. (2023, March 9). Tucker Carlson's private contempt for Trump: "I hate him passionately." *The New York Times.* https://www.nytimes.com/2023/03/08/business/media/tucker-carlson-trump.html (last accessed 9 March 2023).

128 Kapur, S. (2023, March 7). *NBC News.* https://www.nbcnews.com/politics/justice-department/tucker-carlson-new-video-provided-speaker-mccarthy-falsely-depicts-jan-rcna73673 (last accessed 9 March 2023).

129 https://www.cnn.com/2023/05/09/media/tucker-carlson-twitter/index.html#:~:text=Tucker%20Carlson%20announces%20plans%20to%20relaunch%20his%20show%20on%20Twitter

130 https://www.nbcnews.com/politics/justice-department/proud-boy-sentenced-rcna102857

131 Ibid.

132 Rosen, J. (2021, November 21). Transcript: Nicole Hemmer interviews Jay Rosen for *The Ezra Klein Show. The New York Times.* https://www.nytimes.com/2021/11/12/podcasts/transcript-ezra-klein-show-jay-rosen.html (last accessed 24 October 2022).

133 Harwood, J. (2022, May 1). Telling lies has become the norm for today's Republicans. *CNN.* https://edition.cnn.com/2022/05/01/politics/republican-party-kevin-mccarthy/index.html (last accessed 24 October 2022).

134 Rosen, J.

135 Cillizza, C. (2018, July 25). Donald Trump just said something truly terrifying. *CNN.* https://edition.cnn.com/2018/07/25/politics/donald-trump-vfw-unreality/index.html (last accessed 24 October 2022).

Chapter 10

1 Thompson, F. J. (2020, October 9). Six ways Trump has sabotaged the Affordable Care Act. Brookings. https://www.brookings.edu/project/brookings-initiative-on-climate-research-and-action/ (last accessed 24 October 2022).

2   Stolberg, S. G. (2020, October 31). Stanford study seeks to quantify infections stemming from Trump rallies. *The New York Times*. https://www.nytimes .com/2020/10/31/us/politics/stanford-study-infections-trump-rallies.html (last accessed 24 October 2022).

3   Reimann, N. (2020, October 30). Trump supporters pass out from extreme heat at rallies days after he held event in freezing cold. *Forbes*. https://www .forbes.com/sites/nicholasreimann/2020/10/29/weather-be-damned-trump -keeps-holding-rallies-in-extreme-conditions/? (last accessed 24 October 2022); Elfrink, T., Shammas, B., & Griffiths, B. D. (2020, October 28). Hundreds of Trump supporters stuck in the cold for hours when buses can't reach Omaha rally. *The Washington Post*. https://www.washingtonpost.com /nation/2020/10/28/trump-omaha-supporters-stuck-cold/ (last accessed 24 October 2022).

4   Goldberg, J. (2020, September 3). Trump: Americans who died in war are "losers" and "suckers." *The Atlantic*. https://www.theatlantic.com /politics/archive/2020/09/trump-americans-who-died-at-war-are-losers -and-suckers/615997/ (last accessed 24 October 2022); Dorman, J. L (2020, September 29). "They're all hustlers": President Trump privately ridicules Christian leaders, according to new report. *Insider*. https://www .businessinsider.com/donald-trump-religion-faith-evangelical-christians -republicans-2020-9? (last accessed 24 October 2022).

5   Reisner, S. (2017, March 15). Stop saying Donald Trump is mentally ill. *Slate*. https://slate.com/technology/2017/03/donald-trump-isnt-mentally-ill-hes-evil .html (last accessed 24 October 2022).

6   Rucker, P. (2017, October 30). John Kelly refuses to apologize for false attacks on Florida congresswoman. *The Washington Post*. https://www.washingtonpost .com/news/post-politics/wp/2017/10/30/john-kelly-refuses-to-apologize-for -false-attacks-on-florida-congresswoman/ (last accessed 24 October 2022).

7   https://www.theguardian.com/us-news/2023/oct/03/ trump-john-kelly-chief-of-staff

8   Graham, D. A. (2020, June 11). Trump corrupts everyone around him. *The Atlantic*. https://www.theatlantic.com/ideas/archive/2020/06/how-trump -corrupts-his-lieutenants/612928/ (last accessed 24 October 2022).

9   Trump, M. L. (2020). *Too Much and Never Enough: How My Family Created the World's Most Dangerous Man*. New York: Simon and Schuster.

10   Frances, A. (2017, February). An eminent psychiatrist demurs on Trump's mental state (reader letter). *The New York Times*. https://www.nytimes .com/2017/02/14/opinion/an-eminent-psychiatrist-demurs-on-trumps -mental-state.html (last accessed 24 October 2022).

11   Din, B. (2021, January 1). Poll: Majority of Americans support Trump impeachment and conviction. *Politico*. https://www.politico.com /news/2021/01/25/majority-supports-trump-impeachment-462264 (last accessed 24 October 2022).

12 Haberman, M., Thrush, G., & Baker, P. (2017, December 9). Inside Trump's hour-by-hour battle for self-preservation. *The New York Times*. https://www .nytimes.com/2017/12/09/us/politics/donald-trump-president.html (last accessed 24 October 2022).

13 Klein, N. (2017). *No Is Not Enough: Resisting Trump's Shock Politics and Winning the World We Need*. Chicago: Haymarket Books.

14 Walsh, J. (2021, November 9). "Presidents are not kings": Judge rejects Trump's bid to block records from Jan. 6 committee. *Forbes*. https://www .forbes.com/sites/joewalsh/2021/11/09/presidents-are-not-kings-judge -rejects-trumps-bid-to-block-records-from-jan-6-committee/ (last accessed 24 October 2022).

15 Reuters (2016, January 24). Donald Trump: "I could shoot somebody, and I wouldn't lose any voters." *The Guardian*. https://www.theguardian.com /us-news/2016/jan/24/donald-trump-says-he-could-shoot-somebody-and-still -not-lose-voters (last accessed 24 October 2022).

16 Stolberg, S. G.

17 https://www.forbes.com/sites/nicholasreimann/2021/12/09/ christie-says-its-undeniable-trump-gave-him-covid/?sh=2dc010f654e7

18 Gollwitzer, A., Martel, C., Brady, W. J., Pärnamets, P., Freedman, I. G., Knowles, E. D., & Van Bavel, J. J. (2020). Partisan differences in physical distancing are linked to health outcomes during the Covid-19 pandemic. *Nature Human Behaviour, 4*: 1186–1197. https://doi.org/10.1038 /s41562-020-00977-7

19 Kommenda, N., Voce, A., Hulley-Jones, F., Leach, A., & Clarke, S. (2020, December 8). US election results 2020: Joe Biden's defeat of Donald Trump. *The Guardian*. https://www.theguardian.com/us-news/ng-interactive/2020 /dec/08/us-election-results-2020-joe-biden-defeats-donald-trump-to-win -presidency (last accessed 24 October 2022); 2015 presidential election results (2017, August 9). *The New York Times*. https://www.nytimes.com /elections/2016/results/president (last accessed 24 October 2022).

20 https://www.cnn.com/2016/05/26/politics/trump-clothing-foreign-made /index.html

21 Illing, S. (2018 October 24). Why Christian conservatives supported Trump – and why they might regret it. *Vox*. https://www.vox.com/2017 /10/4/16346800/donald-trump-christian-right-conservative-clinton (last accessed 24 October 2022).

22 Relman, E. (2020, September 17). The 26 women who have accused Trump of sexual misconduct. *Insider*. https://www.businessinsider.com/women -accused-trump-sexual-misconduct-list-2017-12? (last accessed 24 October 2022); Stern, M. J. (2016). Let's be clear: Donald Trump bragged about sexual assault. *Slate*. https://www.slate.com/blogs/the_slatest/2016/10/07 /donald_trump_brags_about_committing_criminal_sexual_assault.html (last

accessed 24 October 2022); Kelly, M. (2020, January 21). Some in South
Jersey have a message for Trump: Pay your old Atlantic City casino bills. *North
Jersey Media Group*. https://eu.northjersey.com/story/news/columnists/mike
-kelly/2020/01/24/donald-trump-still-owes-money-to
-contractors-who-built-taj-mahal-atlantic-city/4547037002/ (last accessed 24
October 2022); Cortellessa, E. (2017, June 5). How Trump made wage theft
routine. *The American Prospect*. https://prospect.org/power/trump-made-wage-
theft-routine/ (last accessed 20 October 2022); Unger, C. (2019, March 29).
Trump's businesses are full of dirty Russian money. The scandal is that it's legal.
The Washington Post. https://www.washingtonpost.com
/outlook/trumps-businesses-are-full-of-dirty-russian-money-the-scandal-is
-thats-legal/2019/03/29/11b812da-5171-11e9-88a1-ed346f0ec94f_story.html
(last accessed 20 October 2022); Liptak, K. (2019, June 29). Trump embraces
dictators and despots in deal-making G20 summit. *CNN*. https
://edition.cnn.com/2019/06/29/politics/g20-donald-trump-bin-salman-putin-
xi-dictators (last accessed 24 October 2022); Rawnsley, A. (2020, February 6).
How Trump really invited Russia's election attack. *Daily Beast*. https
://www.thedailybeast.com/how-trump-really-invited-russias-election-attack
(last accessed 24 October 2022); Bowden, J. (2019, January 6). Trump's
evolving remarks on Russian election interference. *The Hill*. https://thehill
.com/homenews/administration/446392-trumps-evolving-remarks-on-russian
-election-interference/ (last accessed 24 October 2022); Bor, J., Himmelstein,
D. U., & Woolhandler, S. (2021, March 5). Trump's policy failures have
exacted a heavy toll on public health. *Scientific American*. https://www
.scientificamerican.com/article/trumps-policy-failures-have-exacted-a-heavy
-toll-on-public-health1/ (last accessed 24 October 2022).

23 Lynch, S. N. (2022, September 6). US judge agrees to special master in Trump
search case, delaying probe. *Reuters*. https://www.reuters.com
/world/us/trumps-request-special-master-raid-case-granted-part-by-us-court
-filing-2022-09-05/ (last accessed 24 October 2022).

24 Gray, R. (2017, August 15). Trump defends white-nationalist protesters:
"Some very fine people on both sides." *The Atlantic*. https://www.theatlantic
.com/politics/archive/2017/08/trump-defends-white-nationalist-protesters
-some-very-fine-people-on-both-sides/537012/ (last accessed 24 October
2022); Reuters (2017, September 30). Donald Trump blames Puerto Ricans
for not being able "to get their workers to help" after Hurricane Maria.
Fortune. https://fortune.com/2017/09/30/donald-trump-blames-puerto-rico
-hurricane-maria/ (last accessed 24 October 2022).

25 Liptak, Adam. (2024, January 1). Trump's Most Ambitious Argument in His
Bid for 'Absolute Immunity.' *New York Times*. https://www.nytimes
.com/2024/01/01/us/trump-immunity-impeachment.html (last accessed 23
January 2024).

26 Bailey, Jeremy D., ed. Transcript of David Frost's Interview with Richard
    Nixon. Teaching American History. https://teachingamericanhistory.org
    /document/transcript-of-david-frosts-interview-with-richard-nixon/ (last
    accessed 23 January 2024).

27 Tebault, R. (2023, December 23). DeSantis, Haley pledge to pardon Trump if
    he's convicted. *Washington Post*. https://www.washingtonpost.com
    /politics/2023/12/31/desantis-haley-pledge-pardon-trump-if-hes-convicted
    / (last accessed 23 January 2024).

28 Becker, J., Goldman, A., & Apuzzo, M. (2017, July 11). Russian dirt on
    Clinton? "I love It," Donald Trump Jr. Said. *The New York Times*. https://www
    .nytimes.com/2017/07/11/us/politics/trump-russia-email-clinton.html (last
    accessed 24 October 2022).

29 Haberman, M., & Martin, J. (2017, November 28). Trump once said the
    "Access Hollywood" tape was real. Now he's not sure. *The New York Times*.
    https://www.nytimes.com/2017/11/28/us/politics/trump-access-hollywood
    -tape.html (last accessed 24 October 2022).

30 Stracqualursi, V. (2019, September 6). *Washington Post*: Trump was the one
    who altered Dorian trajectory map with Sharpie. *CNN*. https://edition.cnn
    .com/2019/09/06/politics/trump-sharpie-hurricane-dorian-alabama/index
    .html (last accessed 24 October 2022).

31 Crowley, M., & Baker, P. (2019, September 24). Trump says he will release the
    transcript of call with Ukraine's president. *The New York Times*. https
    ://www.nytimes.com/2019/09/24/us/politics/trump-ukraine-transcript.html
    (last accessed 24 October 2022).

32 Gessen, M. (2020). *Surviving Autocracy*. New York: Riverhead Books.

33 https://www.nytimes.com/2023/08/29/style/trump-mug-shot-marketing
    -merch.html

34 https://abcnews.go.com/Politics/
    trump-told-supporters-retribution-now-im-indicted/story?id=100386551

35 https://www.bbc.com/news/world-us-canada-66274979

36 https://truthout.org/articles/1-in-5-republicans-who-think-trump-committed
    -crimes-say-theyll-vote-for-him/

37 Greene, J. (2020, September 15). In this election, "costly signal deployment."
    The Harvard Gazette. https://news.harvard.edu/gazette/story/2020/09/a-look
    -at-how-trumps-pointed-rhetoric-binds-him-to-his-tribe-and-it-to-him/ (last
    accessed 24 October 2022).

38 Reality-based community (2022). In: *Wikipedia*. https://en.wikipedia.org
    /wiki/Reality-based_community (last accessed 24 October 2022).

39 https://www.latimes.com/politics/story/2023-04-04/
    donald-trump-alleged-hush-money-investigation-indictment-arraignment

40 Monmouth University Polling Institute (2020, November 18). More
    Americans happy about Trump loss than Biden win (poll report). https://www

.monmouth.edu/polling-institute/reports/monmouthpoll_us_111820/ (last accessed 24 October 2022).

41 Levine, S. (2020, December 11). Nearly two-thirds of House Republicans join baseless effort to overturn election. *The Guardian*. https://www.theguardian .com/us-news/2020/dec/11/house-republicans-texas-election-lawsuit-supreme -court (last accessed 24 October 2022).

42 Friedman, L., & Plumer, B. (2020, April 28). Trump's response to virus reflects a long disregard for science. *The New York Times*. https://www.nytimes. com/2020/04/28/climate/trump-coronavirus-climate-science.html (last accessed 24 October 2022).

43 Bond, S. (2020, November 14). Conservatives flock to Mercer-funded Parler, claim censorship on Facebook and Twitter. *National Public Radio*. https ://www.npr.org/2020/11/14/934833214/conservatives-flock-to-mercer -funded-parler-claim-censorship-on-facebook-and-twi (last accessed 24 October 2022).

44 https://www.nbcdfw.com/news/local/group-says-textbook-publishers -pressured-to-adjust-evolution-climate-change-lessons/2090345/

45 Sharlet, J. (2023) The Undertow: Scenes from a Slow Civil War. W. W. Norton & Company. p 119

46 https://www.politico.com/news/2022/09/21/ trump-i-could-declassify-documents-by-thinking-about-it-00058212

47 Hamblin, J. (2020, November 10). How Trump sold failure to 70 million people. *The Atlantic*. https://www.theatlantic.com/health/archive/2020/11 /trump-voters-pandemic-failures/617051/ (last accessed 24 October 2022).

48 Eidelman, S., Crandall, C. S., Goodman, J. A., & Blanchar, J. C. (2012). Low-effort thought promotes political conservatism. *Personality and Social Psychology Bulletin, 38*(6), 808–820. https://doi.org/10.1177/0146167212439213

49 Zhong, W., Cristofori, I., Bulbulia, J., Krueger, F., & Grafman, J. (2017). Biological and cognitive underpinnings of religious fundamentalism. *Neuropsychologia, 100*: 18–25. https://doi.org/10.1016/j. neuropsychologia.2017.04.009.

50 https://www.rawstory.com/raw-investigates/donald-trump-supporters/

51 Bennett, D., & Satija, N. (2020, December 8). Giuliani witness whose testimony went viral says she isn't self-quarantining despite his Covid-19 diagnosis. *The Washington Post*. https://www.washingtonpost.com/ investigations/mellissa-carone-covid-rudy-giuliani/2020/12/08/f9d40afc-3981 -11eb-bc68-96af0daae728_story.html (last accessed 24 October 2022).

52 Stein, A. *Terror, Love and Brainwashing*, 2nd Edition. New York, Routledge, 2021.

53 Dutton, Donald G. and Susan Painter. (1993). Emotional Attachments in Abusive Relationships: A Test of Traumatic Bonding Theory. *Violence and Victims*, 8(2).

54 Reisz, S. (2017, September). Disorganized attachment and defense: exploring John Bowlby's unpublished reflections. *Attachment & Human Development*, 20(2). https://doi.org/10.1080/14616734.2017.1380055.

55 Pilkington, E. (2017, January 21). 'American carnage': Donald Trump's vision casts shadow over day of pageantry. *The Guardian*. https://www.theguardian .com/world/2017/jan/20/donald-trump-transition-of-power-president-first -speech (last accessed 11 January 2024).

56 Cillizza, C. (2018, July 25). Donald Trump just said something truly terrifying. CNN Politics. https://www.cnn.com/2018/07/25/politics/donald -trump-vfw-unreality/index.html (last accessed 11 January 2024).

57 McCann Ramirez, N. (2024, January 9). Trump Lawyer Claims Presidential Immunity Covers Having Rivals Assassinated. *Rolling Stone*. https://www. rollingstone.com/politics/politics-news/trump-lawyer-argues-president-order -assassinations-immunity-1234942963/ (last accessed 23 January 2024).

58 Ibid.

59 Pengelly, M. (2024, January 9). Roger Stone reportedly said leading Democratic congressman 'has to die.' *The Guardian*. https://www.theguardian .com/us-news/2024/jan/09/roger-stone-eric-swalwell-jerry-nadler-die-mediate (last accessed 23 January 2024).

60 Frazier, K. (2024, January 12). The violent political threats public officials are facing amid Trump's legal woes. *Politico*. https://www.politico.com /news/2024/01/12/trump-legal-public-official-threats-00135084 (last accessed 23 January 2024).

61 Campaign of Fear: The Trump world's assault on U.S. election workers. *Reuters*. https://www.reuters.com/investigates/section/campaign-of-fear/ (last accessed 24 January 2024).

62 Bump, P. (2023, February 8). Underrecognized: Extremist murders are usually from right-wing actors. *Washington Post*. https://www.washingtonpost. com/politics/2023/02/28/extremism-right-wing-deaths/ (last accessed 24 January 2024).

63 Beauchamp, Z. (2024, January 2). How death threats get Republicans to fall in line behind Trump. *Vox*. https://www.vox.com/23899688/2024-election -republican-primary-death-threats-trump (last accessed 23 January 2024).

64 Kleinfeld, R. (2023, December). Political Violence and the 2022 Elections. Carnegie Endowment for International Peace. https://ceipfiles.s3.amazonaws .com/pdf/Political+Violence+the+2022+Midterm+Elections.pdf?v=2 (last accessed 23 January 2024).

65 Pierce, C. P. (2021, January 29). Kevin McCarthy Made a Pilgrimage to the Holy Shrine of the Golden Commode. *Esquire*. https://www.esquire.com /news-politics/politics/a35364290/kevin-mccarthy-visit-trump-mar-a-lago -republican-party/ (last accessed 23 January 2024).

[66] Axelrod, T. (2019, February 3). Trump hugs American flag after walking onstage at CPAC. *The Hill*. https://thehill.com/blogs/blog-briefing-room /news/432323-trump-hugs-american-flag-after-walking-on-stage-at-cpac/ (last accessed 24 October 2022).

[67] Wise, J. (2018, June 19). Trump hugs flag at end of speech to business group. *The Hill*. https://thehill.com/latino/393040-trump-hugs-flag-at-end-of-speech -to-business-group/ (last accessed 24 October 2022).

[68] Shill, G. H. (2020, November 3). How vehicular intimidation became the norm. *The Atlantic*. https://www.theatlantic.com/ideas/archive/2020/11 /how-trump-train-trucks-became-a-political-weapon/616979/ (last accessed 24 October 2022).

[69] https://www.amazon.com/DGFhk-Outdoor-Donald-Trump -Decoration-Resistant/dp/B09CZCZC57/

[70] https://www.nbcnews.com/politics/donald-trump/trump-deliver -fiery-post-indictment-speech-georgia-rcna88561

[71] Barry, D., & Eligon, J. (2017, December 16). "Trump, Trump, Trump!" How a president's name became a racial jeer. *The New York Times*. https ://www.nytimes.com/2017/12/16/us/trump-racial-jeers.html? (last accessed 24 October 2022).

[72] Southern Poverty Law Center (2016). *The Trump Effect: The Impact of the 2016 Presidential Election on Our Nation's Schools*. https://www.splcenter. org/20161128/trump-effect-impact-2016-presidential-election-our-nations -schools (last accessed 24 October 2022).

[73] Hitler hints at further Nazi expansion (1940, February 24). *The St Louis Star and Times*. Viewed at: https://www.newspapers.com/newspage/204365993 / (last accessed 24 October 2022).

[74] Skelley, G. (2017, June 1). Just how many Obama 2012–Trump 2016 voters were there? *Sabato's Crystal Ball*. https://centerforpolitics.org/crystalball /articles/just-how-many-obama-2012-trump-2016-voters-were-there/ (last accessed 24 October 2022).

[75] Beauchamp, Z. (2018, October 16). A new study reveals the real reason Obama voters switched to Trump. *Vox*. https://www.vox.com/policy-and -politics/2018/10/16/17980820/trump-obama-2016-race-racism-class -economy-2018-midterm (last accessed 24 October 2022).

[76] Major, B., Blodorn, A., & Major Blascovich, G. (2018). The threat of increasing diversity: Why many white Americans support Trump in the 2016 presidential election. *Group Processes & Intergroup Relations, 21*(6), 931–940. https://doi.org/10.1177/1368430216677304

[77] https://www.ipsos.com/en-us/news-polls/hispanic-americans-us-politics

[78] https://www.ipsos.com/en-us/news-polls/hispanic-americans-us-politics

[79] https://www.theatlantic.com/politics/archive/2020/10/trump-latinos -biden-2020/616901/

[80] https://www.ipsos.com/en-us/news-polls/hispanic-americans-us-politics

[81] https://www.nytimes.com/2019/08/03/us/patrick-crusius-el-paso-shooter
-manifesto.html

[82] https://www.cambridge.org/core/journals/du-bois-review-social-science
-research-on-race/article/abs/hispanics-para-trump/
BF09A48E9470FDFEDBF0C7EA0DBA2696

[83] https://www.latimes.com/california/story/2020-02-24/presidential
-campaigns-ethnic-food-photo-ops

[84] https://www.latimes.com/california/story/2020-02-24/presidential
-campaigns-ethnic-food-photo-ops

[85] https://www.theguardian.com/us-news/2022/oct/17/democrats-republicans
-campaign-latinos-hispanics-midterms#:~:text=Republicans%20see%20
that%20as%20an,margins%20to%20win%20statewide%20contests.

[86] https://www.washingtonpost.com/politics/2022/10/14/
hispanic-voters-democrats/

[87] https://www.washingtonpost.com/politics/2023/09/19/
trump-poll-support-black-hispanic/

[88] https://www.theguardian.com/us-news/2022/oct/17/democrats-republicans
-campaign-latinos-hispanics-midterms#:~:text=Republicans%20see%20
that%20as%20an,margins%20to%20win%20statewide%20contests.

[89] Epstein, M., & Tang, B. (Hosts) (*c*. 2019, January 29). The symbolic power of Trump's wall (audio podcast episode). In: *Mind of State*. https://mindofstate. com/ep-03-no-lindsay-the-wall-is-not-a-metaphor/ (last accessed 24 October 2022).

[90] Milgram, S. (1974). *Obedience to Authority: An Experimental View*. New York: Harper Perennial, 2009.

[91] https://apnews.com/article/wrong-place-shootings-3c6e5061adb30d889ac3d0 71893ef129

[92] https://www.vice.com/en/article/5d9b45/ralph-yarl-shot-andrew-lester-foxnews

[93] Tajfel, H., Billig, M. G., Bundy, R. P., & Flament, C. (1971). Social categorization and intergroup behaviour. *European Journal of Social Psychology, 1*(2): 149–178. https://doi.org/10.1002/ejsp.2420010202

[94] Pratto, F., Sidanius, J., Stallworth, L. M., & Malle, B. F. (1994). Social dominance orientation: A personality variable predicting social and political attitudes. *Journal of Personality and Social Psychology, 67*(4): 741–763. https ://doi.org/10.1037/0022-3514.67.4.741; Womick, J., Rothmund, T., Azevedo, F., King, L. A., & Jost, J. T. (2019). Group-based dominance and authoritarian aggression predict support for Donald Trump in the 2016 US presidential election. *Social Psychological and Personality Science, 10*(5), 643–652. https ://doi.org/10.1177/1948550618778290

[95] Mason, L. (2018). *Uncivil Agreement: How Politics Became Our Identity*. Chicago: University of Chicago Press.

[96] https://www.vanityfair.com/news/2022/03/
donald-trump-vladimir-putin-murder

[97] Sharlet, J. (2020, June 18). "He's the chosen one to run America": Inside the
cult of Trump, his rallies are church and he is the gospel. *Vanity Fair*. https
://www.vanityfair.com/news/2020/06/inside-the-cult-of-trump-his-rallies-are
-church-and-he-is-the-gospel (last accessed 24 October 2022).

[98] Stewart, K. (2018, December 2018). Why Trump reigns as King Cyrus. *The
New York Times*. https://www.nytimes.com/2018/12/31/opinion/trump
-evangelicals-cyrus-king.html (last accessed 24 October 2022).

[99] Bump, P. (2019, February 14). Nearly half of Republicans think God wanted
Trump to be president. *The Washington Post*. https://www.washingtonpost
.com/politics/2019/02/14/nearly-half-republicans-think-god-wanted-trump
-be-president/ (last accessed 24 October 2022).

[100] https://www.theguardian.com/law/2023/apr/26/
democrats-condemn-roberts-refusal-testify-supreme-court-ethics

[101] https://www.blumenthal.senate.gov/newsroom/press/release/blumenthal-at
-hearing-on-supreme-court-ethics-reform-the-nations-highest-court-is
-seeming-to-put-itself-higher-than-the-law

[102] https://www.rcreader.com/news-releases/
iowa-auditor-state-rob-sand-responds-governors-claims-about-sf-478-worst-pro

[103] https://www.theguardian.com/books/2023/mar/30/jeff-sharlet
-undertow-fascism-far-right-religion-trump

[104] https://www.npr.org/2022/02/08/1079112803/fla-bill-bans
-businesses-and-schools-from-making-anyone-feel-guilt-about-race

[105] Gallagher, G. W., & Nolan, A. T. (Eds.). (2000). *The myth of the lost cause and
Civil War history*. Indiana University Press.

[106] https://www.holidaysmart.com/articles/
many-states-still-celebrate-confederate-holidays

[107] https://www.rollingstone.com/politics/politics-news/marjorie-taylor
-greene-states-consider-seceding-from-the-union-1234822567/

[108] https://www.rollingstone.com/politics/politics-news/texas-republican
-bill-secession-referendum-1234691622/

[109] https://www.libraryofsocialscience.com/ideologies/resources/griffin
-the-palingenetic-core/

[110] https://www.theatlantic.com/national/archive/2014/08/the-evangelical
-persecution-complex/375506/

[111] https://www.theguardian.com/us-news/2023/mar/05/i-am-your-retribution
-trump-rules-supreme-at-cpac-as-he-relaunches-bid-for-white-house

[112] https://www.rollingstone.com/politics/politics-features/donald-trump
-indictment-surrender-alvin-bragg-1234708673/

[113] https://www.rollingstone.com/politics/politics-features/donald-trump
-indictment-surrender-alvin-bragg-1234708673/

[114] Beresford, J. (2020, November 2). Donald Trump recites controversial poem "The snake" during rally. *Irish Post*. https://www.irishpost.com/news/donald-trump-recites-controversial-poem-the-snake-during-rally-196725 (last accessed 24 October 2022).

[115] Dolan, E. W. (2019, September 3). People with lower emotional intelligence are more likely to hold right-wing views, study finds. *PsyPost*. https://www.psypost.org/2019/09/people-with-lower-emotional-intelligence-are-more-likely-to-hold-right-wing-views-study-finds-54369 (last accessed 24 October 2022).

[116] Horsey, D. (2014, March 7). Conservatives harbor an odd admiration for Vladimir Putin. *Los Angeles Times*. https://www.latimes.com/opinion/topoftheticket/la-xpm-2014-mar-07-la-na-tt-conservatives-admiration-for-putin-20140306-story.html (last accessed 24 October 2022).

[117] Swift, A. (2017, February 21). Putin's image rises in US, mostly among Republicans. *Gallup*. https://www.latimes.com/opinion/topoftheticket/la-xpm-2014-mar-07-la-na-tt-conservatives-admiration-for-putin-20140306-story.html (last accessed 24 October).

[118] Hale, H. E., & Kamenchuk, O. (2020, February 4). Why are Republicans using Putin's talking points? This study helps explain. *The Washington Post*. https://www.washingtonpost.com/politics/2020/02/04/why-are-republicans-using-putins-talking-points-this-study-helps-explain/ (last accessed 24 October 2022).

[119] Sommerlad, J. (2019, January 18). Donald Trump's gushing praise of Vladimir Putin under fresh scrutiny after Michael Cohen allegations. *Independent*. https://www.independent.co.uk/news/world/americas/us-politics/trump-cohen-putin-russia-investigation-mueller-congress-fbi-a8734231.html (last accessed 24 October 2022).

[120] Ibid.

[121] Truscott IV, L. K. (2019, November 16). Donald Trump's body count: He's not just a narcissist and a liar. He's a killer. *Salon*. https://www.salon.com/2019/11/16/donald-trumps-body-count-hes-not-just-a-narcissist-and-a-liar-hes-a-killer/ (last accessed 24 October 2022).

[122] Robertson, C., & Smith, M. (2017, January 7). "What's the big deal?" Ask Trump voters on Russia hacking report. *The New York Times*. https://www.nytimes.com/2017/01/07/us/russia-hacking-election-trump-voters.html (last accessed 24 October 2022).

[123] Blake, A. (2017, December 4). Trump's lawyer says a president can't technically obstruct justice. Experts say that's fanciful. *The Washington Post*. https://www.washingtonpost.com/news/the-fix/wp/2017/12/04/trumps-lawyer-says-a-president-cant-technically-obstruct-justice-experts-say-thats-fanciful/ (last accessed 24 October 2022).

[124] https://www.nytimes.com/2023/09/13/us/politics/trump-gop-biden-impeachment.html

[125] Levine, M. (2020, May 30). "No Blame?" *ABC News* finds 54 cases invoking "Trump" in connection with violence, threats, alleged assaults. *ABC News.* https://abcnews.go.com/Politics/blame-abc-news-finds-17-cases-invoking -trump/story?id=58912889 (last accessed 24 October 2022).

[126] Milbank, D. (2017, December 8). The GOP's all-out assault on justice. *The Washington Post.* https://www.washingtonpost.com/opinions/the -gops-all-out-assault-on-justice/2017/12/08/2e1ce9ba-dc28-11e7-b1a8 -62589434a581_story.html (last accessed 24 October 2022).

[127] jonathanalter (Alter, J.) (2017, July 24). That's what you get from Banana Republicans… (quote tweet of tweet posted by ChrisMurphyCT, 24 July 2017). Twitter. https://twitter.com/jonathanalter/status /889613617427095556.

[128] https://www.washingtonpost.com/politics/2023/03/31/how-gop -went-fretting-about-trumps-witch-hunt-mantra-embracing-it/

[129] https://psycnet.apa.org/doiLanding?doi=10.1037%2Fa0015141

[130] https://www.theguardian.com/us-news/2023/jun/11/trump-indictment -republicans-rhetoric-violence

[131] https://www.cbsnews.com/news/cbs-news-poll-most-see -security-risk-after-trump-indictment/

[132] Luntz, F. (2007). *Words That Work: It's Not What You Say, It's What People Hear.* New York: Hyperion.

[133] https://www.washingtonpost.com/lifestyle/style/how-should-we-talk-about -whats-happening-to-our-planet/2019/08/26/d28c4bcc-b213-11e9-8f6c -7828e68cb15f_story.html

[134] PRRI. (2023, October 25). Threats to American Democracy Ahead of an Unprecedented Presidential Election. https://www.prri.org/research/threats -to-american-democracy-ahead-of-an-unprecedented-presidential-election / (accessed 14 March 2024).

[135] Giridharadas, A. (2022). *The Persuaders: At the Front Lines of the Fight for Hearts, Minds, and Democracy.* New York: Alfred A. Knopf, pp. 203–253.

[136] Berman, G. (2022). *Holding the Line: Inside the Nation's Preeminent US Attorney's Office and Its Battle with the Trump Justice Department.* New York: Penguin.

[137] Weiser, B., & Rashbaum, W. K. (2020, September 21). Trump could be investigated for tax fraud, DA says for first time. *The New York Times.* https ://www.nytimes.com/2020/09/21/nyregion/donald-trump-taxes-cyrus-vance. html (last accessed 24 October 2022).

[138] Weissmann, A. (2020, November 24). Should Trump be prosecuted? *The New York Times.* https://www.nytimes.com/2020/11/24/opinion/trump -prosecution.html (last accessed 24 October 2022).

[139] https://www.pbs.org/newshour/politics/read-the-full-trump-indictment- on-mishandling-of-classified-documents#:~:text=Special%20Counsel%20 Jack%20Smith%20on,and%20scope%20of%20the%20charges.

[140] McQuade, B., & Vance, J. W. (2020, October 16). A rap sheet for a former president. *The Washington Post.* https://www.washingtonpost.com/outlook/rap -sheet-trump-crimes/2020/10/16/c6a539da-0e61-11eb-8a35-237ef1eb2ef7 _story.html (last accessed 24 October 2022).

[141] Walker, J. (2021, January 7). 45 percent of Republican voters support storming of Capitol building: Poll. *Newsweek.* https://www.newsweek.com/45- percent-republican-voters-support-storming-capitol-1559662 (last accessed 24 October 2022).

[142] Gerstein, J. (2021, January 14). Lawmakers who conspired with Capitol attackers in legal peril. *Politico.* https://www.politico.com/news/2021/01/14 /lawmakers-capitol-attackers-legal-459519 (last accessed 24 October 2022); Dreisbach, T., & Anderson, M. (2021, January 21). Nearly 1 in 5 defendants in Capitol riot cases served in the military. *National Public Radio.* https://www .npr.org/2021/01/21/958915267/nearly-one-in-five-defendants-in-capitol -riot-cases-served-in-the-military (last accessed 24 October 2022); McLaughlin, J. (2021, January 14). Large bitcoin payments to right-wing activists a month before Capitol riot linked to foreign account. *Yahoo! News.* https://www.yahoo.com/entertainment/exclusive-large-bitcoin-payments -to-rightwing-activists-a-month-before-capitol-riot-linked-to-foreign- account-181954668.html (last accessed 24 October 2022); Kirchgaessner, S. (2021, January 15). Billionaires backed Republicans who sought to reverse US election results. *The Guardian.* https://www.theguardian.com/us-news/2021 /jan/15/trump-republicans-election-defeat-club-for-growth (last accessed 24 October 2022).

[143] Swan, B. W. (2020, September 4). DHS draft document: White supremacists are greatest terror threat. *Politico.* https://www.politico.com/news/2020/09/04 /white-supremacists-terror-threat-dhs-409236 (last accessed 24 October 2022).

[144] Ben-Ghiat, R. (2022, April 8). Webcast discussion hosted by R. Ben-Ghiat. *Lucid* (host's online subscription publication). https://lucid.substack.com / (direct link unavailable).

[145] Kirchgaessner, S. (2024, January 18). 'Different rules': special policies keep US supplying weapons to Israel despite alleged abuses. *The Guardian.* https://www .theguardian.com/world/2024/jan/18/us-supply-weapons-israel-alleged-abuses -human-rights (last accessed 15 March 2024).

[146] https://www.politico.com/news/2023/08/01/biden-trump -2024-poll-00109161

[147] FiveThirtyEight. Latest Polls. https://projects.fivethirtyeight.com/polls /president-general/2024/national/ (last accessed 15 March 2024).

[148] Rucker, P., Parker, A., & Dawsey, J. (2020, November 21). Trump privately plots his next act – including a potential 2024 run. *The Washington Post.* https://www.washingtonpost.com/politics/trump-2024 -rematch/2020/11/21/58ce87ac-2a8d-11eb-8fa2-06e7cbb145c0_story.html (last accessed 24 October 2022).

[149] Dawsey, J., & Arnsdorf, I. (2022, August 17). Trump rakes in millions off FBI search at Mar-a-Lago. *The Washington Post.* https://www.washingtonpost.com/politics/2022/08/17/trump-fundraising-fbi-raid/ (last accessed 24 October 2022).

[150] Stevens, S. (2020). *It Was All a Lie: How the Republican Party Became Donald Trump.* New York: Alfred A. Knopf.

[151] Corn, D. (2022). *American Psychosis: A Historical Investigation of How the Republican Party Went Crazy.* New York: Twelve.

[152] Neukirch, R. (2020, October 19). "There will be unrest, dead civilians." *Der Spiegel.* https://www.spiegel.de/international/america-s-trump-supporting-militias-there-will-be-unrest-dead-civilians-a-72a3d3f0-ebbd-4036-a71f-987dffcb215c (last accessed 25 October 2022).

[153] Tully-McManus, K. (2020, November 5). QAnon goes to Washington: Two supporters win seats in Congress. *Roll Call.* https://rollcall.com/2020/11/05/qanon-goes-to-washington-two-supporters-win-seats-in-congress/ (last accessed 25 October 2022).

[154] Ghitis, F. (2021, September 14). The Trump brand of politics is spreading around the world. *CNN.* https://edition.cnn.com/2021/09/14/opinions/trumpism-politics-global-impact-ghitis/index.html (last accessed 25 October 2022).

[155] https://www.amazon.com/Donald-Trump-Success-Deodorant-Fragrance/dp/B00A8XHA6G/

[156] Unger, C. (2019, March 29); Hirsh, M. (2018, December 21). How Russian Money Helped Save Trump's Business. *Foreign Policy.* https://foreignpolicy.com/2018/12/21/how-russian-money-helped-save-trumps-business/ (last accessed 25 October 2022).

[157] https://newrepublic.com/article/177318/stop-trump-boycott-businesses?mc_cid=27a0cd94d5&mc_eid=4feb6e80fb

[158] https://newrepublic.com/article/177363/trump-dictator-day-one-second-term-hannity?mc_cid=87530465f8&mc_eid=4feb6e80fb

Chapter 11

[1] Halleran, M. A. (2010). *The Better Angels of Our Nature: Freemasonry in the American Civil War.* Tuscaloosa, AL: University of Alabama Press.

[2] Sapolsky, R. M. (2017). *Behave: The Biology of Humans at Our Best and Worst.* New York: Penguin.

[3] Cowie, J. (2022). *Freedom's Dominion: A Saga of White Resistance to Federal Power.* New York: Basic Books, pp. 404–416.

[4] Voelkel, J. G., & Feinberg, M. (2018). Morally reframed arguments can affect support for political candidates. *Social Psychological and Personality Science, 9*(8), 917–924. https://doi.org/10.1177/1948550617729408

[5] To the newcomers from Syria: Welcome to Canada (2015, December 10). *Toronto Star*. https://www.thestar.com/opinion/editorials/2015/12/10/to-the-newcomers-from-syria-welcome-to-canada-editorial.html (last accessed October 25 2022).

[6] Gaucher, D., Friesen, J. P., Neufeld, K. H. S., & Esses, V. M. (2018). Changes in the positivity of migrant stereotype content: How system-sanctioned pro-migrant ideology can affect public opinions of migrants. *Social Psychological and Personality Science, 9*(2), 223–233. https://doi.org/10.1177/1948550617746463

[7] Kay, A. C., & Jost, J. T. (2003). System justification scale (database record). In: APA PsycTests (database). https://doi.org/10.1037/t22834-000

[8] Kantor, J., & Einhorn, C. (2017, March 25). Canadians adopted refugee families for a year. Then came "month 13." *The New York Times*. https://www.nytimes.com/2017/03/25/world/canada/syrian-refugees.html (last accessed October 25 2022).

[9] Sparkman, D. J., Eidelman, S., & Till, D. F. (2019). Ingroup and outgroup interconnectedness predict and promote political ideology through empathy. *Group Processes and Intergroup Relations, 22*(8), 1161–1180. https://doi.org/10.1177/1368430218819794

[10] Ibid., p. 844.

[11] Binder, J., Zagefka, H., Brown, R., Funke, F., Kessler, T., Mummendey, A., Maquil, A., Demoulin, S., & Leyens, J.-P. (2009). Does contact reduce prejudice, or does prejudice reduce contact? A longitudinal test of the contact hypothesis among majority and minority groups in three European countries. *Journal of Personality and Social Psychology, 96*(4): 843–856. https://doi.org/10.1037/a0013470

[12] Gerodimos, R., ed. (2022, August 24). *Interdisciplinary Applications of Shame/Violence Theory: Breaking the Cycle*. New York: Palgrave Macmillan, 77–94.

[13] Fetterman, A. K., Boyd, R. L., & Robinson, M. D. (2015). Power versus affiliation in political ideology: Robust linguistic evidence for distinct motivation-related signatures. *Personality and Social Psychology Bulletin, 41*(9): 1195–1206. https//doi.org/10.1177/0146167215591960

[14] Van der Toorn, J., Napier, J., & Dovidio, J. F. (2013). We the people. *Social Psychological and Personality Science, 5*(5): 616–622. https://doi.org/10.1177/1948550613512511

[15] Ibid., p. 617.

[16] Ibid.

[17] McFarland, S. (2017). Identification with all humanity: The antithesis of prejudice, and more. In: C. G. Sibley & F. K. Barlow (Eds), *The Cambridge Handbook of the Psychology of Prejudice* (pp. 632–654). New York: Cambridge University Press. https://doi.org/10.1017/9781316161579.028

[18] Todd, A. R., & Galinsky, A. D. (2014). Perspective-taking as a strategy for improving intergroup relations: Evidence, mechanisms, and qualifications.

Social and Personality Psychology Compass, 8(7): 374–387. https://doi
.org/10.1111/spc3.12116

[19] De Pinto, J. (2022, April 22). Fewer Americans see climate change as a priority
than they did a year ago – *CBS News* poll. *CBS News.* https://www
.cbsnews.com/news/fewer-americans-see-climate-change-as-priority-opinion
-poll-2022-04-22/ (last accessed October 25 2022).

[20] Polasky, S., & Dampha, N. K. (2021). Discounting and global environmental
change. *Annual Review of Environment and Resources, 46*: 691–717. https
://doi.org/10.1146/annurev-environ-020420-042100

[21] Compton, J., van der Linden, S., Cook, J., & Basol, M. (2021). Inoculation
theory in the post-truth era: Extant findings and new frontiers for contested
science, misinformation, and conspiracy theories. *Social and Personality
Psychology Compass, 15*(6): article e12602. https://doi.org/10.1111/spc3.12602

[22] McGuire, W. J. (1964). Some contemporary approaches. *Advances in
Experimental Social Psychology, 1*: 191–229. https://doi.org/10.1016/S0065
-2601(08)60052-0; McGuire, W. J. (1970). A vaccine for brainwash.
Psychology Today, 3(9): 37–64.

[23] Roozenbeek, J., Traberg, C. S., & van der Linden, S. (2022). Technique-based
inoculation against real-world misinformation. *Royal Society Open Science,
9*(211719). https://doi.org/10.1098/rsos.211719

[24] https://www.washingtonpost.com/blogs/answer-sheet/post/texas-gop-rejects
-critical-thinking-skills-really/2012/07/08/gJQAHNpFXW_blog.html

[25] Graeber, D., & Wengrow, D. (2021). *The Dawn of Everything: A New History
of Humanity.* New York: Farrar, Straus and Giroux.

[26] Boyer, P. (2018). *Minds Make Societies: How Cognition Explains the World
Humans Create.* London: Yale University Press.

[27] Boehm, C. (1999). *Hierarchy in the Forest: The Evolution of Egalitarian
Behavior.* Cambridge, MA: Harvard University Press.

[28] Boyer, P., p. 216.

[29] Zanona, M., & Raju, M. (2022, January 13). GOP plots onslaught of Biden
probes in the run-up to 2024. *CNN.* https://edition.cnn.com/2022/01/13
/politics/republican-majority-investigation-plans-midterms/index.html (last
accessed October 25 2022).

[30] Kingkade, T., Goggin, B., Collins, B., & Zadrozny, B. (2022, October 14).
How an urban myth about litter boxes in schools became a GOP talking
point. *NBC News.* https://www.nbcnews.com/tech/misinformation/urban
-myth-litter-boxes-schools-became-gop-talking-point-rcna51439 (last accessed
December 1 2022).

[31] https://www.nbcnews.com/nbc-out/out-politics-and-policy
/north-dakota-bill-fuels-myth-students-are-identifying-animals-rcna67304

[32] https://www.washingtonpost.com/education/2023/06/15
/florida-ap-psychology-college-board/

33 https://www.cbsnews.com/news/florida-bill-would-allow-cameras
    -in-classrooms-and-microphones-on-teachers/

34 Stieb, M. (2023). Here's every single lie told by George Santos. *New York
    Magazine*. https://nymag.com/intelligencer/2023/01/the-everything-guide-to
    -george-santoss-lies.html (last accessed February 1 2023).

35 Saric, I. (2023, January 23). Schiff, Swalwell and Omar condemn GOP bid to
    remove them from committees. *Axios*. https://www.axios.com/2023/01/29
    /schiff-swalwell-omar-republican-committee-assignment (last accessed
    February 1 2023).

36 Raju, M., Zanona, M., & Foran, C. (2023, January 18). Santos named to two
    House committees even as he faces growing calls to resign. *CNN*. https
    ://edition.cnn.com/2023/01/17/politics/george-santos-committee-
    assignments/index.html (last accessed February 1 2023).

37 Karni, A., & Demirjian, K. (2023, January 31). George Santos will
    temporarily step aside from House committees. *The New York Times*. https
    ://www.nytimes.com/2023/01/31/us/politics/santos-house-committees.html
    (last accessed February 1 2023).

38 https://www.nytimes.com/2023/11/16/nyregion/santos-botox-ferragamo
    -expenses.html

39 https://www.msnbc.com/opinion/msnbc-opinion/
    third-gop-freshman-accused-fake-resume-blame-trump-rcna71801

40 Barr, J. (2022, November 9). After midterms, Ron DeSantis eclipses Trump on
    Fox News. *Washington Post*. https://www.washingtonpost.com
    /media/2022/11/09/trump-desantis-fox-news-midterms/ (last accessed
    December 1 2022).

41 Peterson, K. (2022, November 15). Mitch McConnell says Republican
    messaging "frightened" some swing voters. *The Wall Street Journal*. https
    ://www.wsj.com/livecoverage/midterm-elections-congress-house-results/card
    /mitch-mcconnell-says-republican-messaging-frightened-some-swing-voters
    -P0YKnPfB8UeYPcwxyWBd (last accessed December 1 2022).

42 Scocca, T. (2022, November 14). Don't be fooled, Trump's hold on the
    GOP is stronger than ever. *The New York Times*. https://www.nytimes.
    com/2022/11/14/opinion/trump-republican-gop-midterms.html (last accessed
    December 1 2022).

43 Ron DeSantis (n.d.). *PolitiFact*. https://www.politifact.com/personalities/ron
    -desantis/ (last accessed 1 December 2022).

44 Aratani, L. (2022, November 18). "Positively dystopian": Judge blocks key
    parts of Florida's "Stop-Woke" law. *The Guardian*. https://www.theguardian
    .com/us-news/2022/nov/18/judge-florida-ron-desantis-stop-woke-law (last
    accessed December 1 2022).

45 https://www.theguardian.com/us-news/2023/aug/04/
    ron-desantis-slitting-throats-federal-jobs-president-campaign

46 Orth, T. (2022). How Americans feel about the prospect of a divided Congress. *YouGov*. https://today.yougov.com/topics/politics/articles-reports /2022/11/11/how-americans-feel-about-prospect-divided-congress (last accessed December 1 2022).

47 Silver, N. (2022, November 16). Why DeSantis is a major threat to Trump's reelection. *FiveThirtyEight*. https://fivethirtyeight.com/features/why-desantis -is-a-major-threat-to-trumps-reelection/ (last accessed December 1 2022).

48 https://www.newsweek.com/ron-desantis-popularity-plunges-lowest-polls -history-1815896#:~:text=The%20Civiqs%20poll%20concluded%20 that,10%20percent%20who%20were%20unsure.

49 https://www.nytimes.com/2023/11/15/podcasts/transcript-ezra-klein -interviews-michael-podhorzer.html?searchResultPosition=1

50 Centers for Disease Control and Prevention (n.d.). Trends in number of COVID-19 cases and deaths in the US reported to CDC, by state/territory. https://covid.cdc.gov/covid-data-tracker/#trends_weeklydeaths_select_00 (last accessed December 1 2022).

51 Wallace, J., Goldsmith-Pinkham, P., & Schwartz, J. L. (2022). Excess death rates for Republicans and Democrats during the COVID-19 Pandemic (working paper 30512). National Bureau of Economic Research. http ://www.nber.org/papers/w30512

52 https://apnews.com/article/trump-policies-agenda-election-2024-second -term-d656d8f08629a8da14a65c4075545e0f

53 https://www.nytimes.com/article/trump-2025-second-term.html

54 https://www.nytimes.com/2023/11/20/us/politics/trump-rhetoric-fascism .html

55 https://www.nytimes.com/2023/11/20/us/politics/trump-rhetoric-fascism .html

56 https://www.theguardian.com/us-news/2023/aug/30/trump-interview -jail-political-opponents-glenn-beck

57 https://www.theatlantic.com/ideas/archive/2023/09/trump-milley -execution-incitement-violence/675435/

58 https://news.yahoo.com/mehdi-hasan-sarcastically-torches-potential -095905439.html#:~:text=Hasan%20sarcastically%20responded%3A%20

59 https://www.nytimes.com/2023/11/20/us/politics/trump-rhetoric-fascism .html

60 https://www.nytimes.com/2023/10/05/us/politics/trump-immigration -rhetoric.html

61 https://www.theguardian.com/us-news/2023/jun/09/january-6-trump -political-violence-survey

62 https://www.reuters.com/world/us/one-five-us-election-workers-may-quit -amid-threats-politics-survey-2022-03-10/

63 https://www.theguardian.com/us-news/2023/nov/18/voting-centers-naloxone -letters-fentanyl#:~:text=Voting%20centers%20stock%20naloxone%20

amid%20recent%20fentanyl%2Dlaced%20letter%20attacks,-Election%20
workers%20continue&text=The%20suspicious%20letters%20sent%20
to,threats%20and%20dubious%20political%20symbols.

64 https://www.nbcnews.com/media/
fox-news-settles-dominion-defamation-lawsuit-rcna80285

65 https://www.nytimes.com/2023/11/24/business/x-elon-musk-advertisers
.html?smid=nytcore-ios-share&referringSource=articleShare

66 Kantrowitz, A. (2023, October 23). The Elon Effect. *Slate.* https://slate.com
/technology/2023/10/twitter-users-decline-apptopia-elon-musk-x-rebrand
.html (last accessed March 15 2024).

67 Marche, S. (2022). *The Next Civil War: Dispatches from the American Future.*
New York: Avid Reader.

68 Wang, A. B. (2022, November 2). Attack on Paul Pelosi becomes punchline
for some Republicans. *The Washington Post.* https://www.washingtonpost.com
/politics/2022/11/01/paul-pelosi-attack-youngkin-lake/ (last accessed March
6 2023).

69 https://www.propublica.org/article/trump-inc-podcast-donald-trump-jr-went
-to-mongolia-got-special-treatment-from-the-government-and-killed-an
-endangered-sheep

70 Pearson, J., ProPublica, & Tumurtogoo, A. (2019, December 11). Donald
Trump Jr. went to Mongolia, got special treatment from the government and
killed an endangered sheep. *ProPublica.* https://www.propublica.org/article
/trump-inc-podcast-donald-trump-jr-went-to-mongolia-got-special-treatment
-from-the-government-and-killed-an-endangered-sheep (last accessed
March 6 2023).

71 Marche, S., pp. 153–174.

72 Steinhauer, J. (2020, September 11). Veterans fortify the ranks of militias
aligned with Trump's views. *The New York Times.* https://www.nytimes.
com/2020/09/11/us/politics/veterans-trump-protests-militias.html (last
accessed October 25 2022); Richer, A. D., & Kunzelman, M. (2022,
September 7). Elected officials, police officers and members of military on
Oath Keepers membership list, report says. *PBS NewsHour.* https://www.pbs.
org/newshour/politics/elected-officials-police-officers-and-members-
of-military-on-oath-keepers-membership-list-report-says (last accessed
October 25 2022).

73 https://www.commondreams.org/views/2022/02/10/its-time
-pentagon-pulled-plug-fox-news

74 https://www.theatlantic.com/politics/archive/2023/07/proportional
-representation-house-congress/674627/

75 Rosenfeld, G. D., & Ward, J. (Eds.) (2023), *Fascism in America.*
https://www.amazon.com/Fascism-America-Gavriel-D-Rosenfeld/dp
/1009337432/ref=sr_1_1?crid=2DBR1KJ3O4FXB&keywords=fascism

+in+america&qid=1700427316&s=books&sprefix=fascism+in+america
%2Cstripbooks%2C170&sr=1-1

76 60 percent of Americans will have an election denier on the ballot this fall
    (2022). *Five ThirtyEight*. https://projects.fivethirtyeight.com/republicans-
    trump-election-fraud/ (last accessed October 25 2022).

77 Gardner, A., Knowles, H., Itkowitz, C., & Linskey, A. (2022, September 18).
    Republicans in key battleground races refuse to say they will accept results.
    The Washington Post. https://www.washingtonpost.com/politics/2022/09/18
    /republicans-refuse-accept-results/ (last accessed October 25 2022).

78 Sullivan, C. (2022, April 12). Checking in with the major voter suppression
    laws. *Democracy Docket*. https://www.democracydocket.com/analysis/checking
    -in-with-the-major-voter-suppression-laws/ (last accessed October 25 2022).

79 Jacobson, L., & Sherman, A. (2021, July 14). Are state legislators really seeking
    power to overrule the voters? *PolitiFact*. https://www.politifact.com
    /article/2021/jul/14/are-state-legislators-really-seeking-power-overrul/ (last
    accessed October 25 2022).

Index